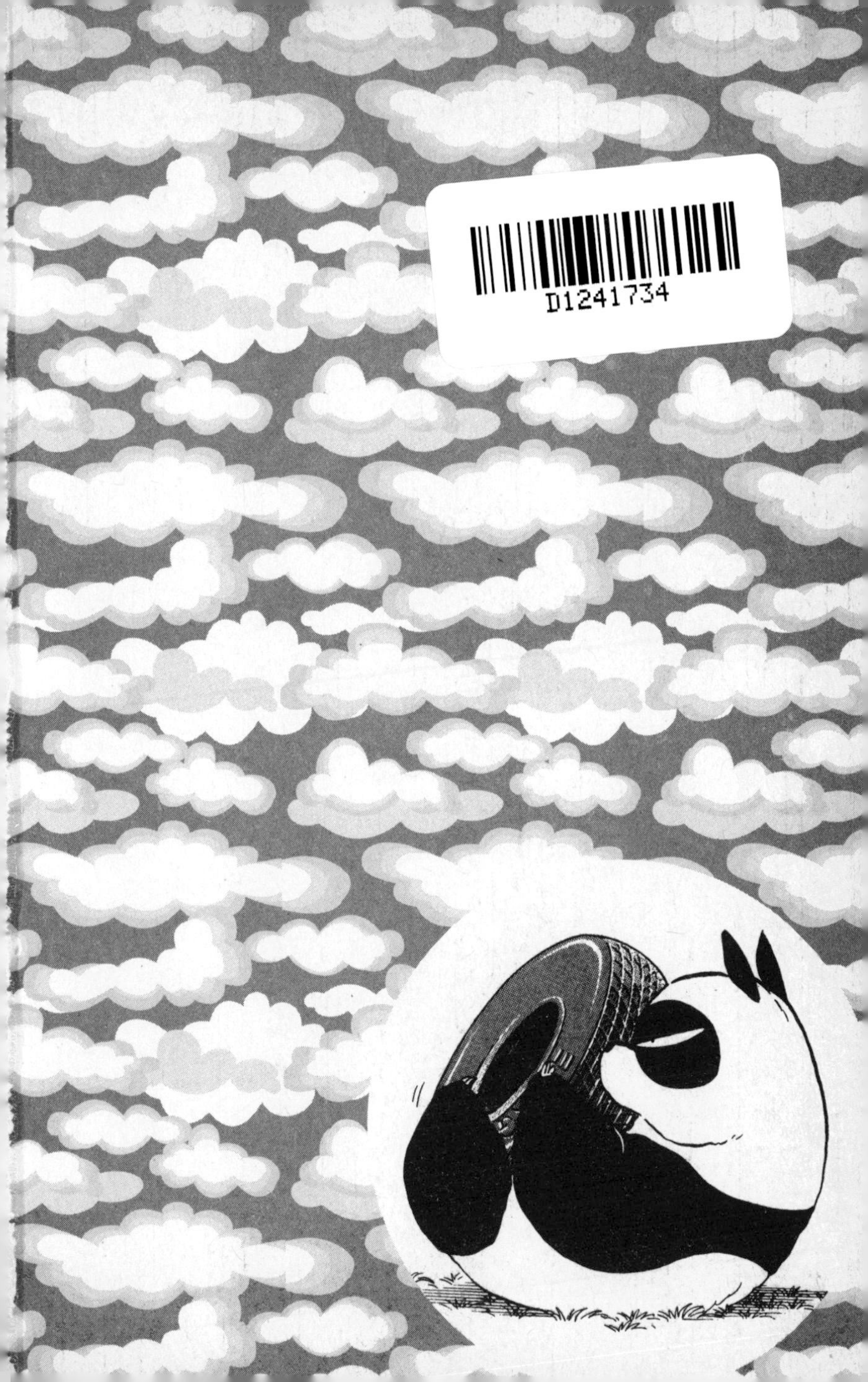

VOL. 17
Action Edition

Story and Art by
RUMIKO TAKAHASHI

English Adaptation/Gerard Jones and Toshifumi Yoshida
Touch-Up Art & Lettering/Wayne Truman
Cover and Interior Design /Yuki Ameda
Editor (1st Edition)/Julie Davis
Editor (Action Edition)/Avery Gotoh
Supervising Editor (Action Edition)/Michelle Pangilinan

Managing Editor/Annette Roman
Director of Production/Noboru Watanabe
Editorial Director/Alvin Lu
Sr. Director of Acquisitions/Rika Inouye
Vice President of Sales & Marketing/Liza Coppola
Executive Vice President/Hyoe Narita
Publisher/Seiji Horibuchi

Printed in Canada.

Published by VIZ, LLC
P.O. Box 77010
San Francisco, CA 94107

1st Edition Published 2001

Action Edition
10 9 8 7 6 5 4 3 2 1
First Printing, April 2005

www.viz.com

RATED T+ FOR OLDER TEENS

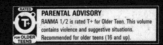

PARENTAL ADVISORY
RANMA 1/2 is rated T+ for Older Teen. This volume contains violence and suggestive situations. Recommended for older teens (16 and up).

store.viz.com

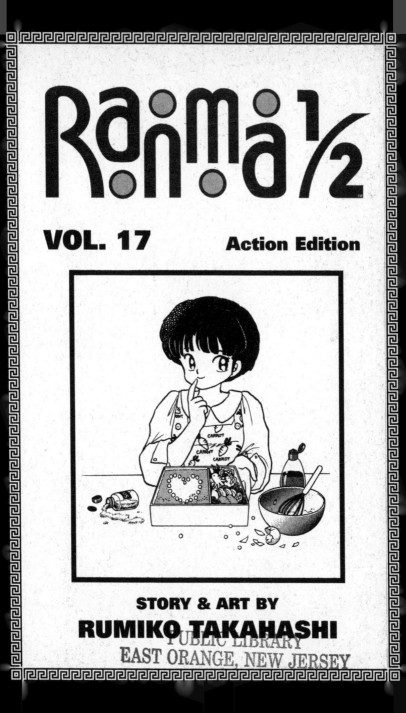

Ranma 1/2

VOL. 17 — Action Edition

STORY & ART BY

RUMIKO TAKAHASHI

STORY THUS FAR

The Tendos are an average, run-of-the-mill Japanese family—on the surface, that is. Soun Tendo is the owner and proprietor of the Tendo Dojo, where "Anything Goes Martial Arts" is practiced. Like the name says, anything goes, and usually does.

When Soun's old friend Genma Saotome comes to visit, Soun's three lovely young daughters—Akane, Nabiki and Kasumi—are told that it's time for one of them to become the fiancée of Genma's teenage son, as per an agreement made between the two fathers years ago. Youngest daughter Akane—who says she hates boys—is quickly nominated for bridal duty by her sisters.

Unfortunately, Ranma and his father have suffered a strange accident. While training in China, both plunged into one of many "cursed" springs at the legendary martial arts training ground of Jusenkyo. These springs transform the unlucky dunkee into whoever—or whatever—drowned there hundreds of years ago.

From then on, a splash of cold water turns Ranma's father into a giant panda, and Ranma becomes a beautiful, busty young woman. Hot water reverses the effect...but only until next time. As it turns out, Ranma and Genma aren't the only ones who have taken the Jusenkyo plunge—and it isn't long before they meet several other members of the Jusenkyo "cursed."

Although their parents are still determined to see Ranma and Akane marry and assume ownership of the training hall, Ranma seems to have a strange talent for accumulating surplus fiancées...and Akane has a few stubbornly determined suitors of her own. Will the two ever work out their differences and get rid of all these "extra" people, or will they just call the whole thing off? What's a half-boy, half-girl (not to mention all-girl, *angry* girl) to do...?

CAST OF CHARACTERS

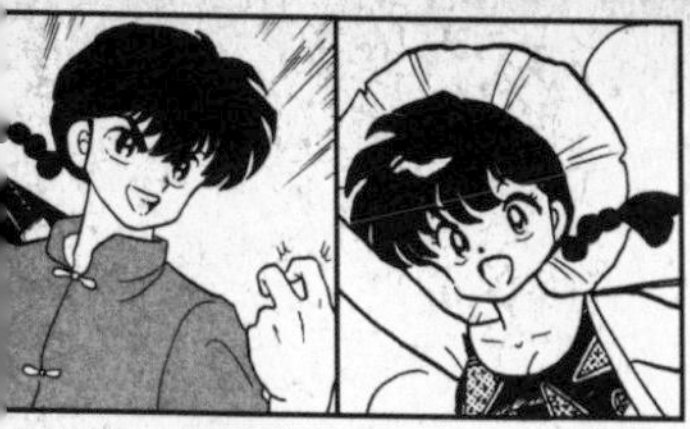

RANMA SAOTOME
Martial artist with far too many fiancées and an ego that won't let him take defeat. Changes into a girl when splashed with cold water.

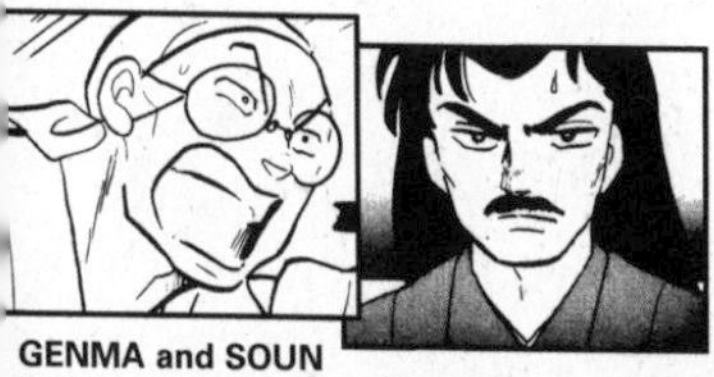

GENMA and SOUN
Buffoonish (to clown a phrase) former disciples of the panty-raiding Happosai. Also fathers to Ranma and Akane, respectively. (Genma turns into a roly-poly panda).

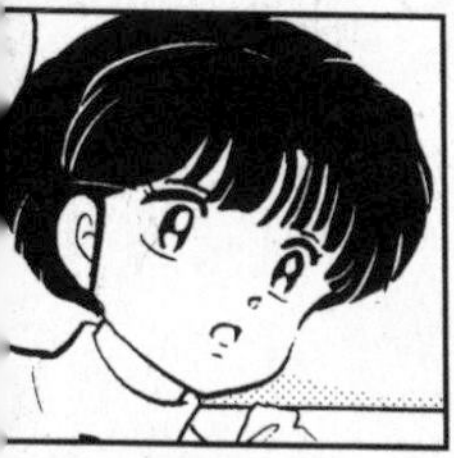

AKANE TENDO
Martial artist, tomboy and Ranma's reluctant fiancée. Has no clue how much Ryoga likes her, or what relation he might have to her pet black pig, P-chan.

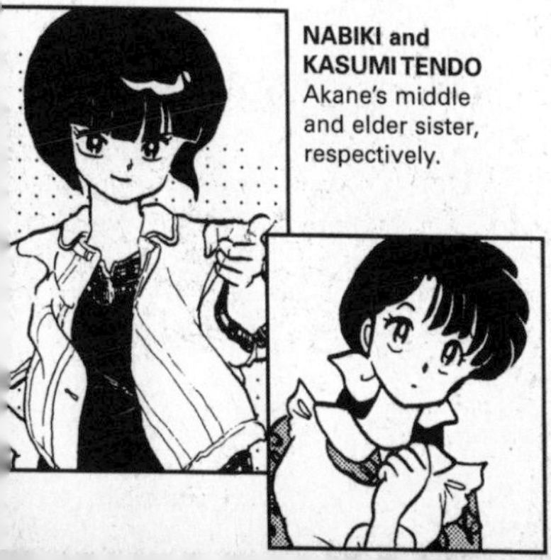

NABIKI and KASUMI TENDO
Akane's middle and elder sister, respectively.

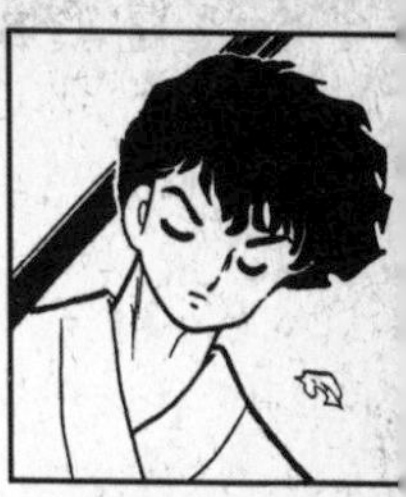

TATEWAKI KUNO
Age 17. Patron of the traditional Japanese arts and swinger of a bamboo sword, this BMOC ([B]ig [M]oron [o]n [C]ampus) loves both Akane Tendo and the mysterious pig-tailed girl.

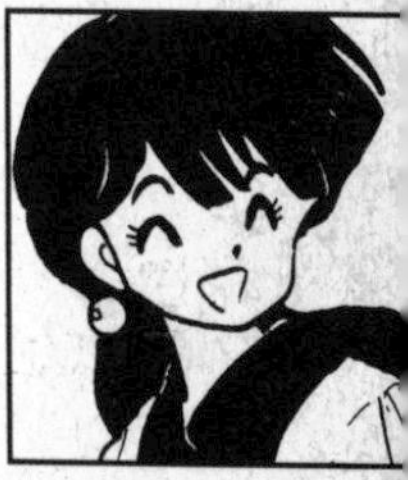

UKYO KUONJI
Ranma's childhood friend. Wields a mean spatula, as she is the owner of a one-woman *okonomiyaki* business.

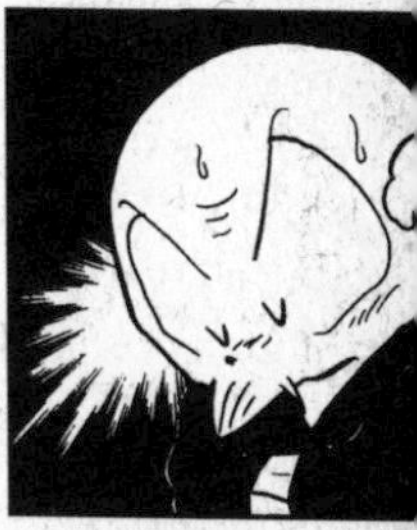

HAPPOSAI
Meddling martial arts master who trained both Genma and Soun. Also a world-class pervert.

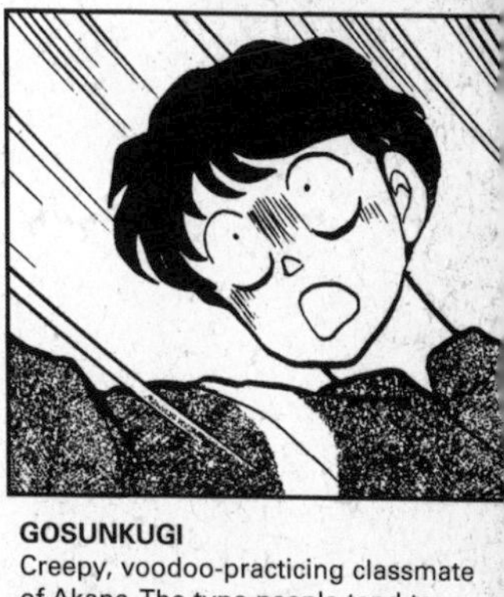

GOSUNKUGI
Creepy, voodoo-practicing classmate of Akane. The type people tend to ignore, he's constantly coming up with kee-razy schemes to get Akane's attention (and love!).

CONTENTS

PART 1 Melonhead 7

PART 2 The Horror of Party Beach 23

PART 3 Catcher in the Rind 39

PART 4 The Sauce of Ten Years 56

PART 5 For the Love of Sauce .73

PART 6 The Truth About the Truth 89

PART 7 The Honeymoon Period 105

PART 8 Please Hate Me 121

PART 9 Nightmare on Hot Springs Street 137

PART 10 Paper Dolls of Love .153

PART 11 The Pill of Obedience 169

Part 1
MELONHEAD

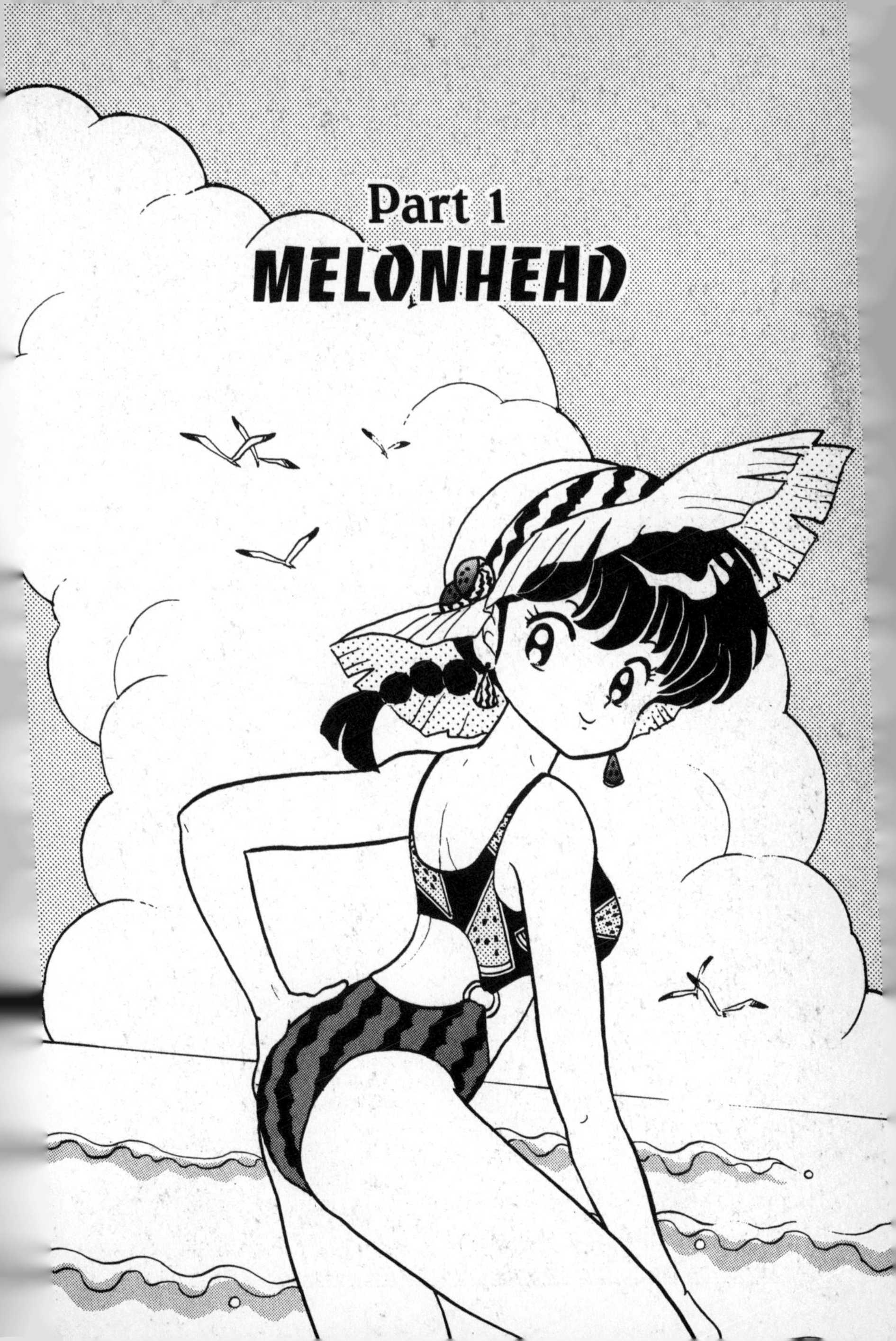

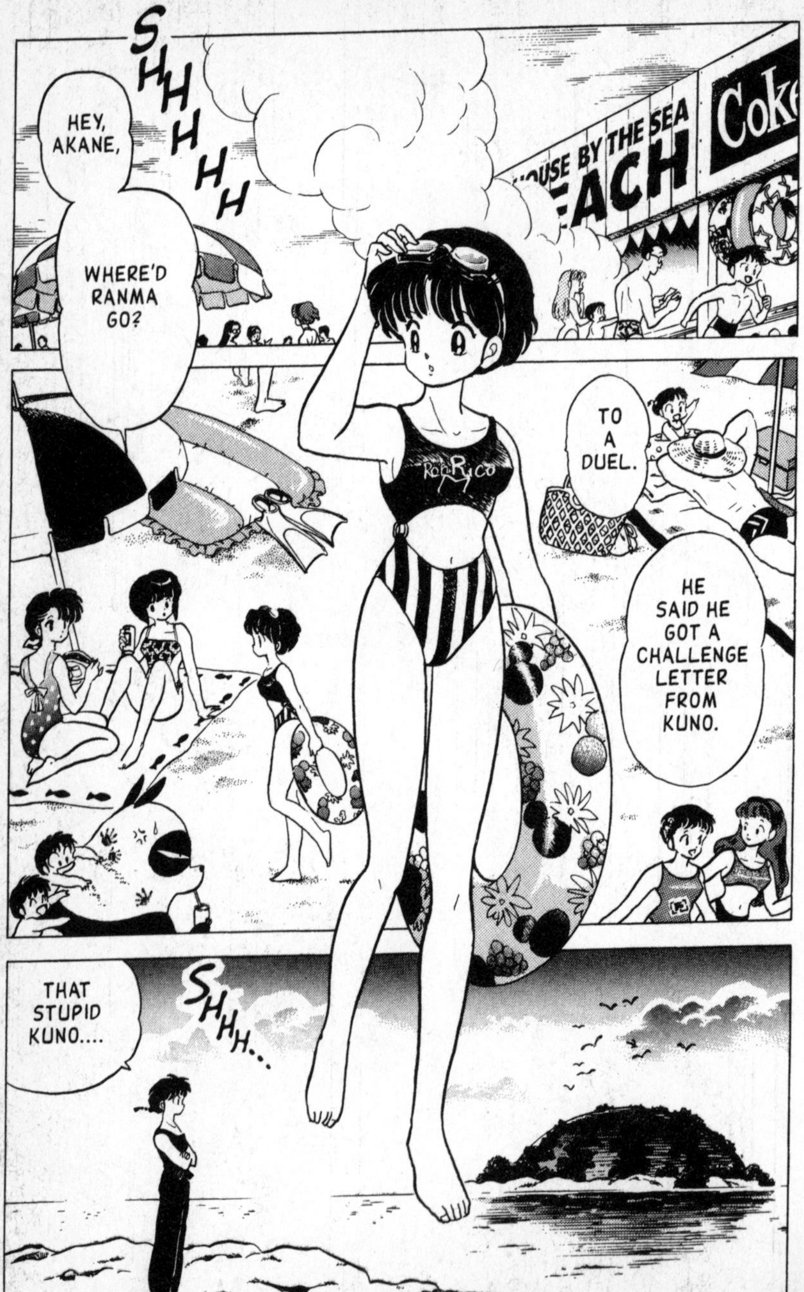
SHHHHH
HEY, AKANE,
WHERE'D RANMA GO?
TO A DUEL.
HE SAID HE GOT A CHALLENGE LETTER FROM KUNO.
THAT STUPID KUNO....
SHHH...

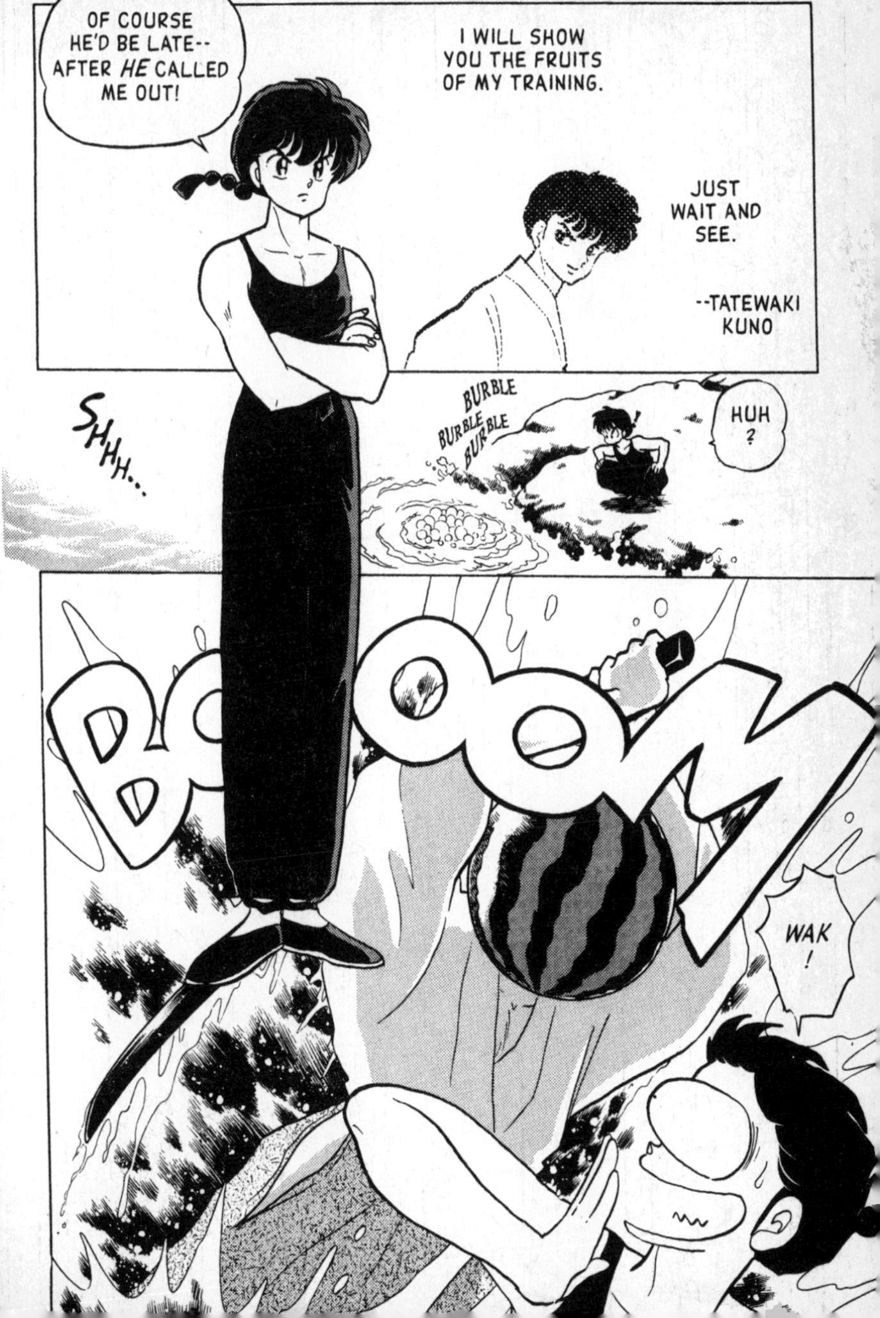
OF COURSE HE'D BE LATE-- AFTER *HE* CALLED ME OUT!
I WILL SHOW YOU THE FRUITS OF MY TRAINING.
JUST WAIT AND SEE.
--TATEWAKI KUNO
SHHH...
BURBLE BURBLE BURBLE BURBLE
HUH?
BOOOM
WAK!

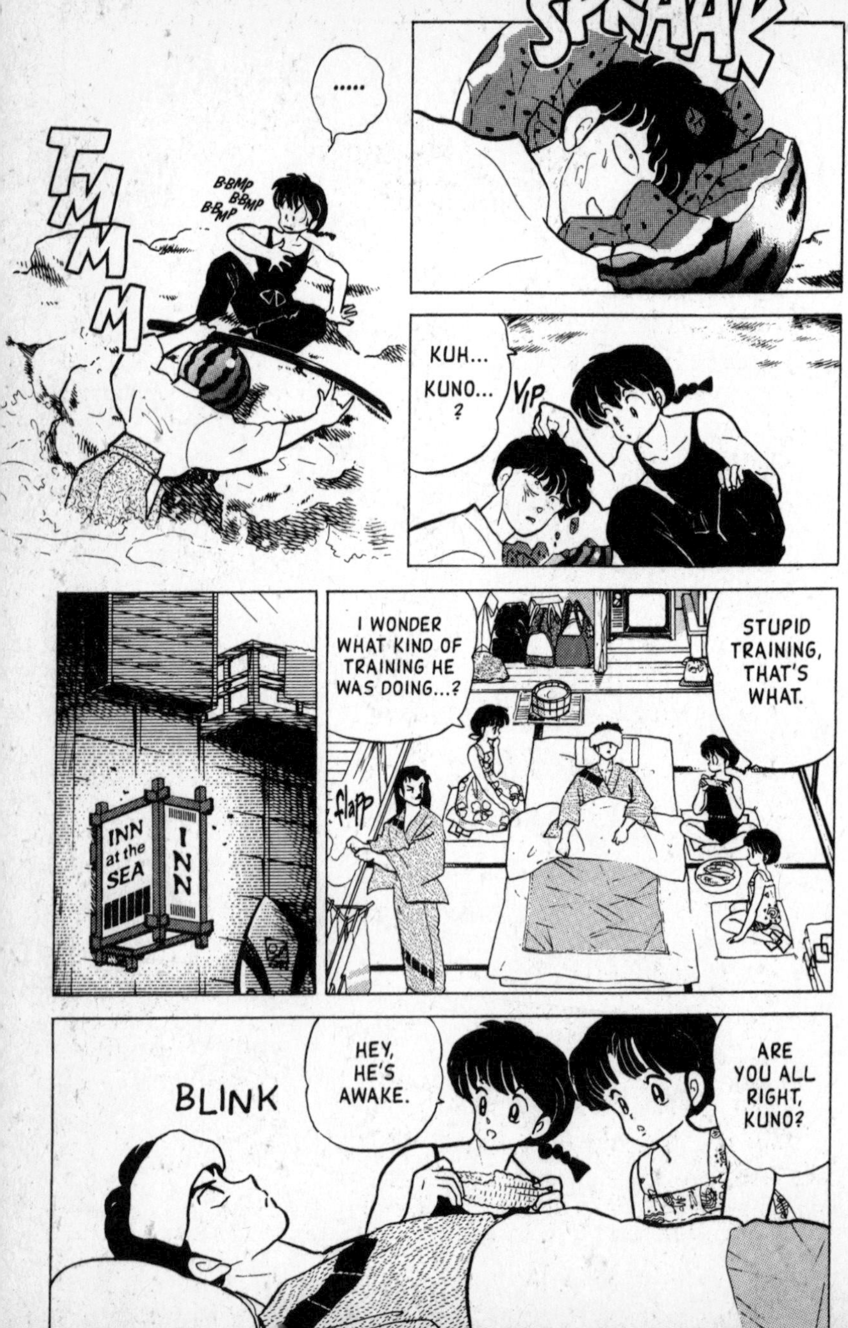

.....
TMMM
B-BMP B-BMP B-BMP
SPRAAK
KUH... KUNO...?
VIP
INN at the SEA
INN
I WONDER WHAT KIND OF TRAINING HE WAS DOING...?
flapp
STUPID TRAINING, THAT'S WHAT.
BLINK
HEY, HE'S AWAKE.
ARE YOU ALL RIGHT, KUNO?

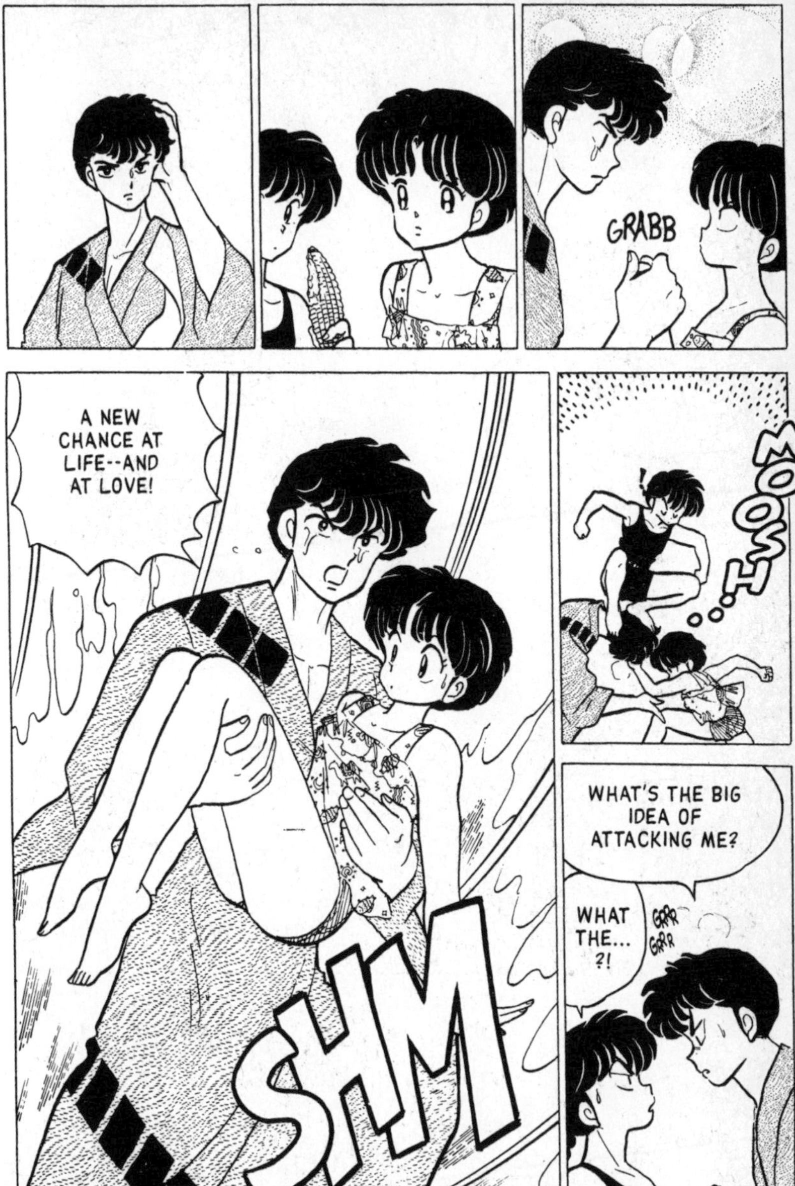
GRABB
A NEW CHANCE AT LIFE--AND AT LOVE!
SHM
MOOSH...
WHAT'S THE BIG IDEA OF ATTACKING ME?
WHAT THE... ?!
GRRR GRRR

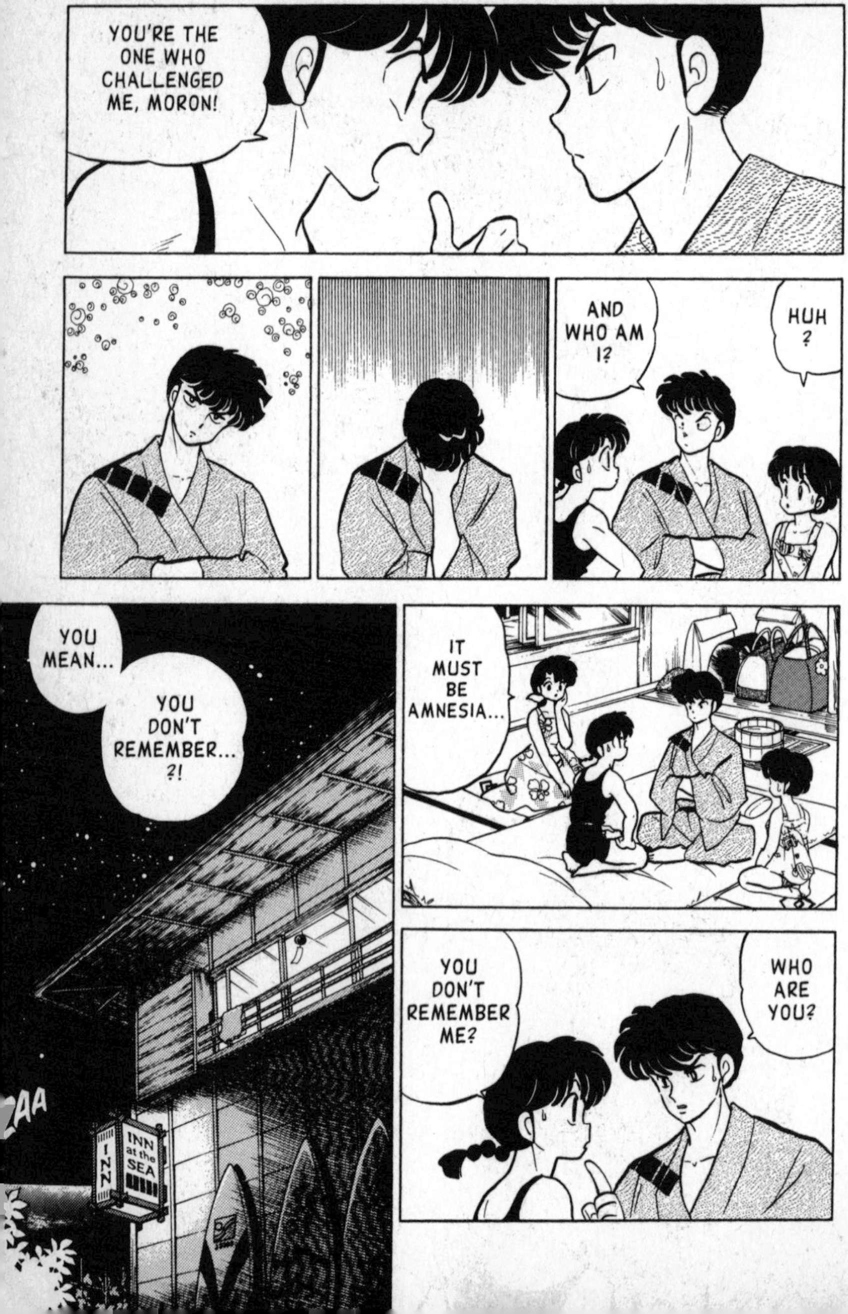
YOU'RE THE ONE WHO CHALLENGED ME, MORON!
AND WHO AM I?
HUH?
YOU MEAN...
YOU DON'T REMEMBER...?!
ZAA
INN
INN at the SEA
IT MUST BE AMNESIA...
YOU DON'T REMEMBER ME?
WHO ARE YOU?

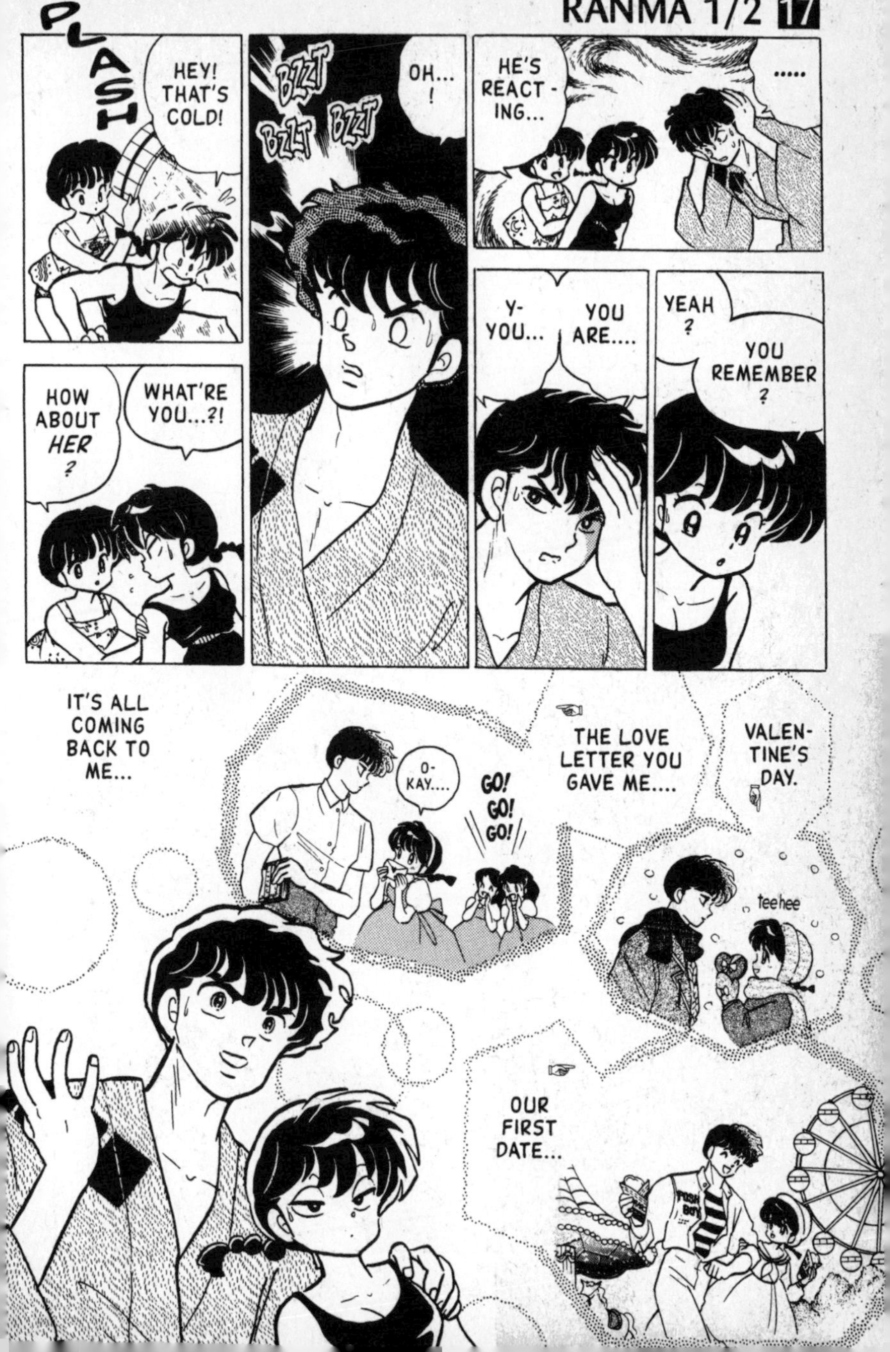
PLASH
HEY! THAT'S COLD!
HOW ABOUT HER?
WHAT'RE YOU...?!
BZZT BZZT BZZT
OH...!
HE'S REACTING...
.....
Y-YOU...
YOU ARE....
YEAH? YOU REMEMBER?
IT'S ALL COMING BACK TO ME...
O-KAY....
GO! GO! GO!
THE LOVE LETTER YOU GAVE ME....
VALENTINE'S DAY.
teehee
OUR FIRST DATE...

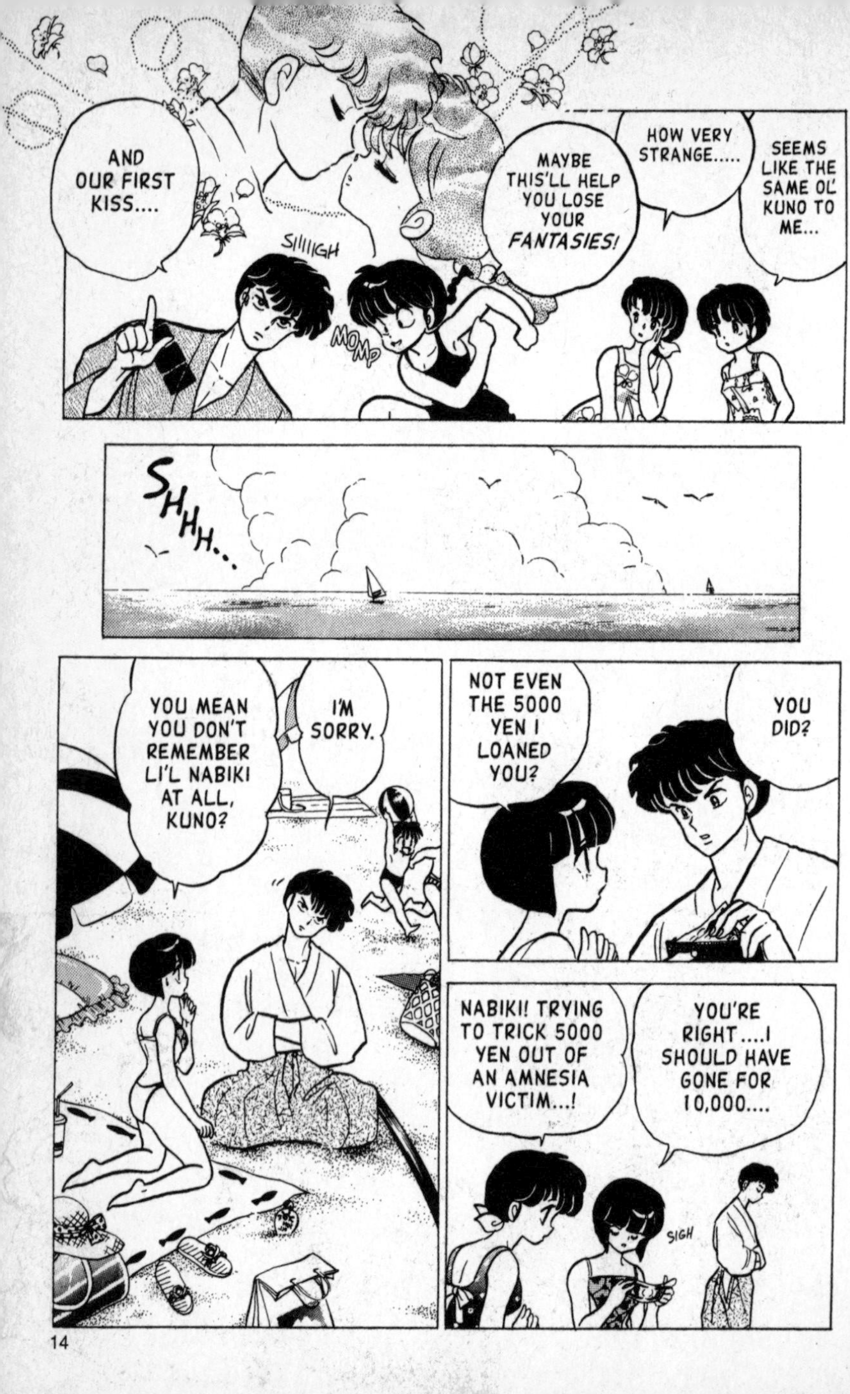
AND OUR FIRST KISS....
SIIIIGH
MOMP
MAYBE THIS'LL HELP YOU LOSE YOUR FANTASIES!
HOW VERY STRANGE.....
SEEMS LIKE THE SAME OL' KUNO TO ME...
SHHH...
YOU MEAN YOU DON'T REMEMBER LI'L NABIKI AT ALL, KUNO?
I'M SORRY.
NOT EVEN THE 5000 YEN I LOANED YOU?
YOU DID?
NABIKI! TRYING TO TRICK 5000 YEN OUT OF AN AMNESIA VICTIM...!
YOU'RE RIGHT....I SHOULD HAVE GONE FOR 10,000....
SIGH

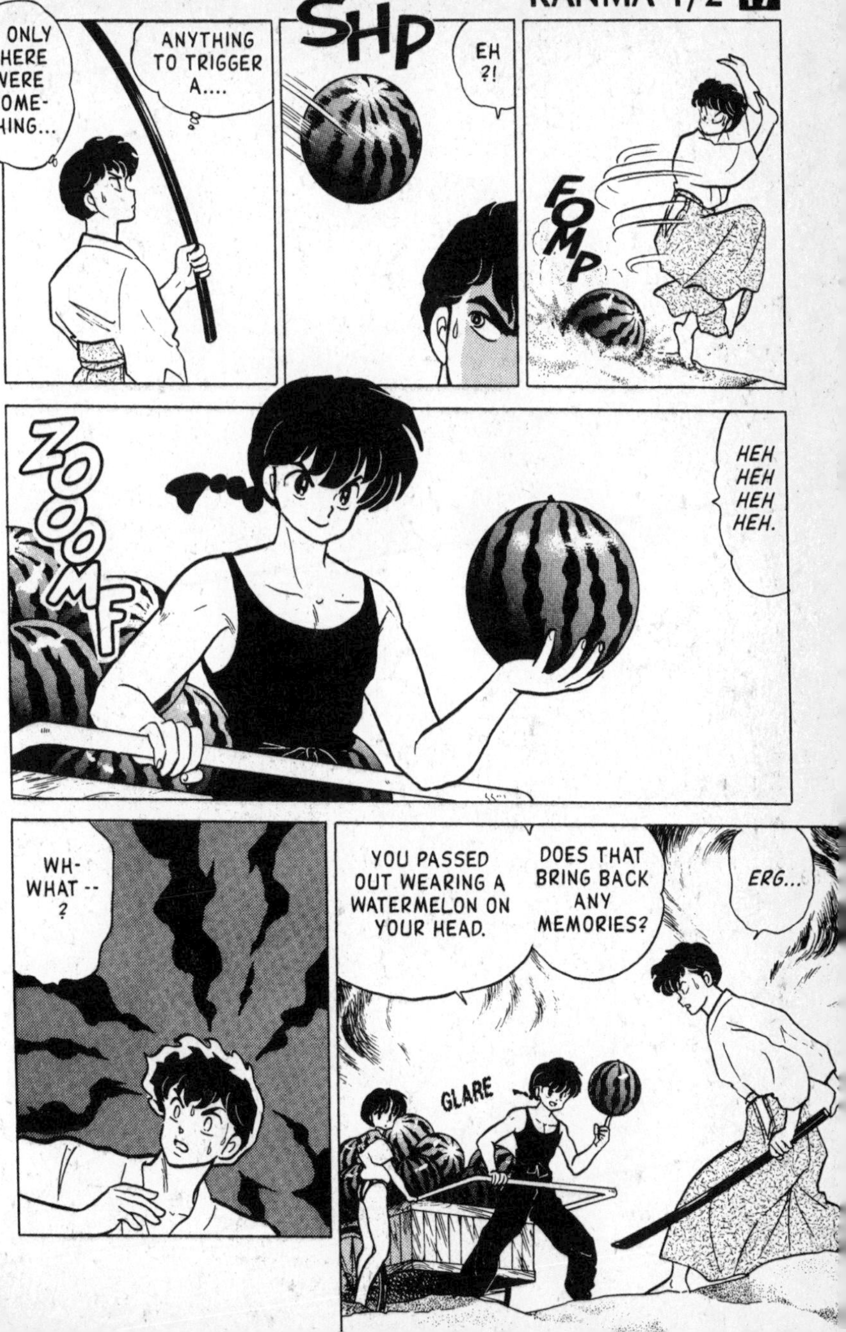
IF ONLY THERE WERE SOME-THING...
ANYTHING TO TRIGGER A....
SHP
EH ?!
FOMP
ZOOOOMF
HEH HEH HEH HEH.
WH-WHAT -- ?
YOU PASSED OUT WEARING A WATERMELON ON YOUR HEAD.
DOES THAT BRING BACK ANY MEMORIES?
ERG...
GLARE

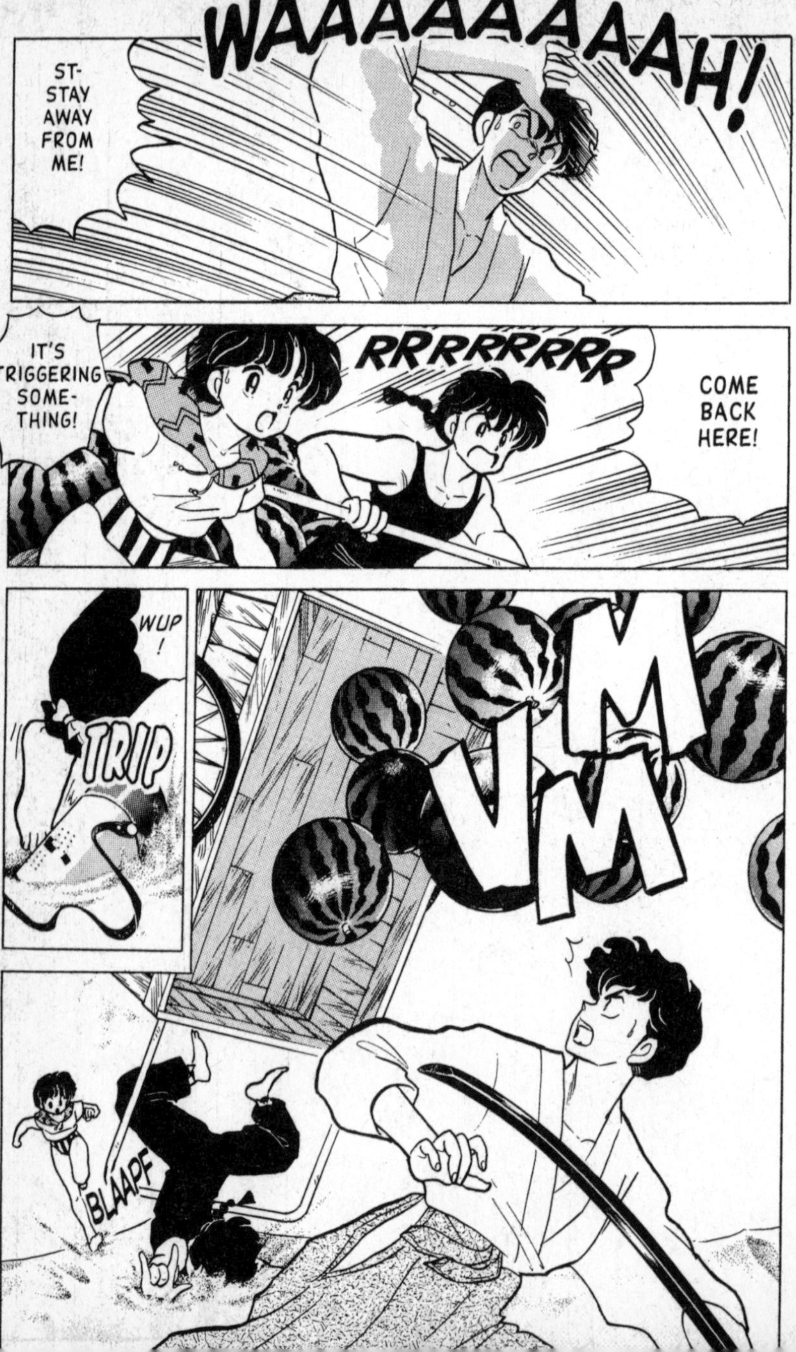

WAAAAAAAAAH!
ST- STAY AWAY FROM ME!
IT'S TRIGGERING SOME-THING!
RRRRRRRR
COME BACK HERE!
WUP!
TRIP
MM
BLAAPF

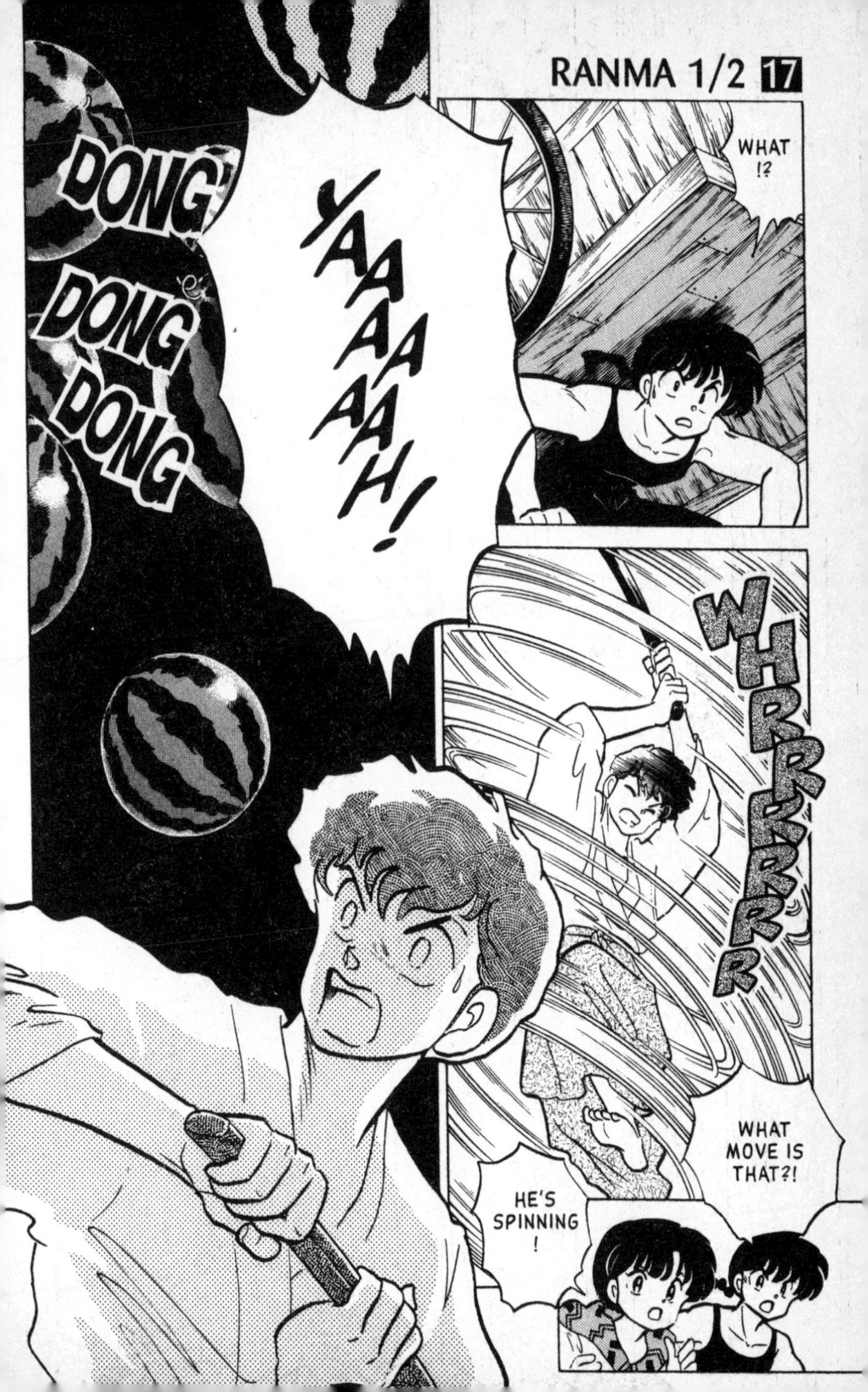
DONG
DONG
DONG
DONG
YAAAAAAAH!
WHAT !?
WHRRRRRRRR
WHAT MOVE IS THAT?!
HE'S SPINNING !

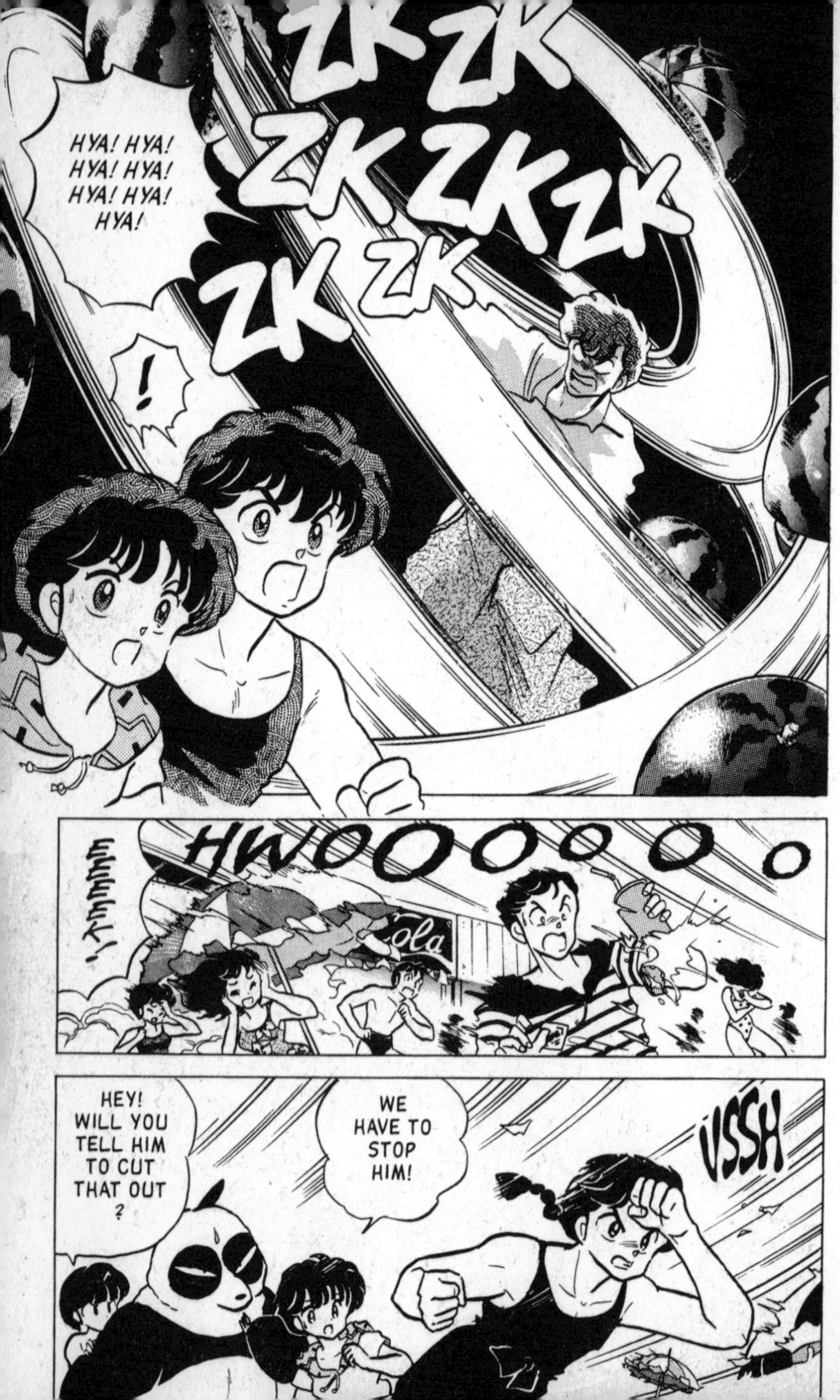
HYA! HYA! HYA! HYA! HYA! HYA! HYA!
ZK ZK ZK ZK ZK ZK ZK ZK
!
EEEEEEK!!
HWOOOOOOO
HEY! WILL YOU TELL HIM TO CUT THAT OUT?
WE HAVE TO STOP HIM!
VSSH

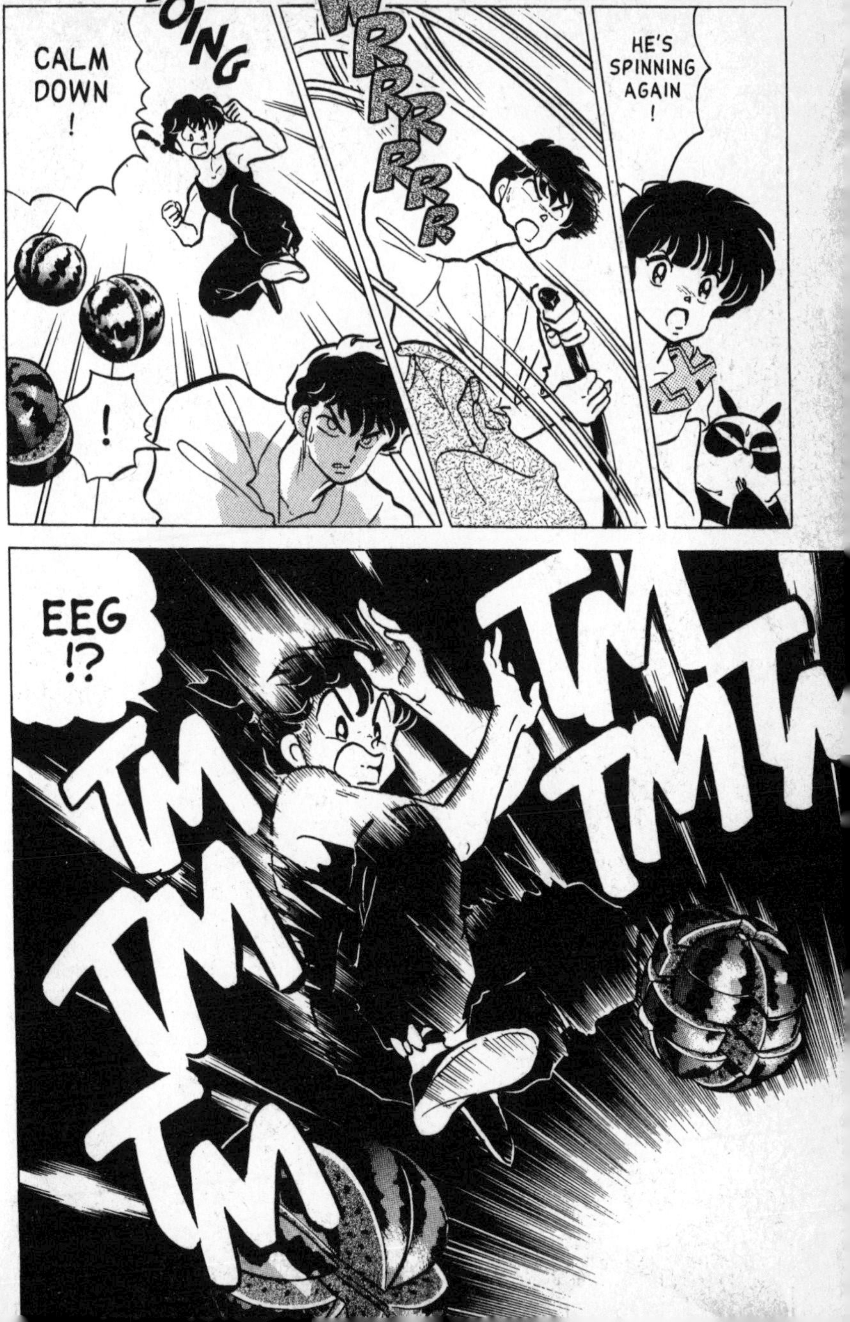
BOING
CALM DOWN!
!
WRRRRRRR
HE'S SPINNING AGAIN!
EEG!?
TM TM TM TM
TM TM TM TM

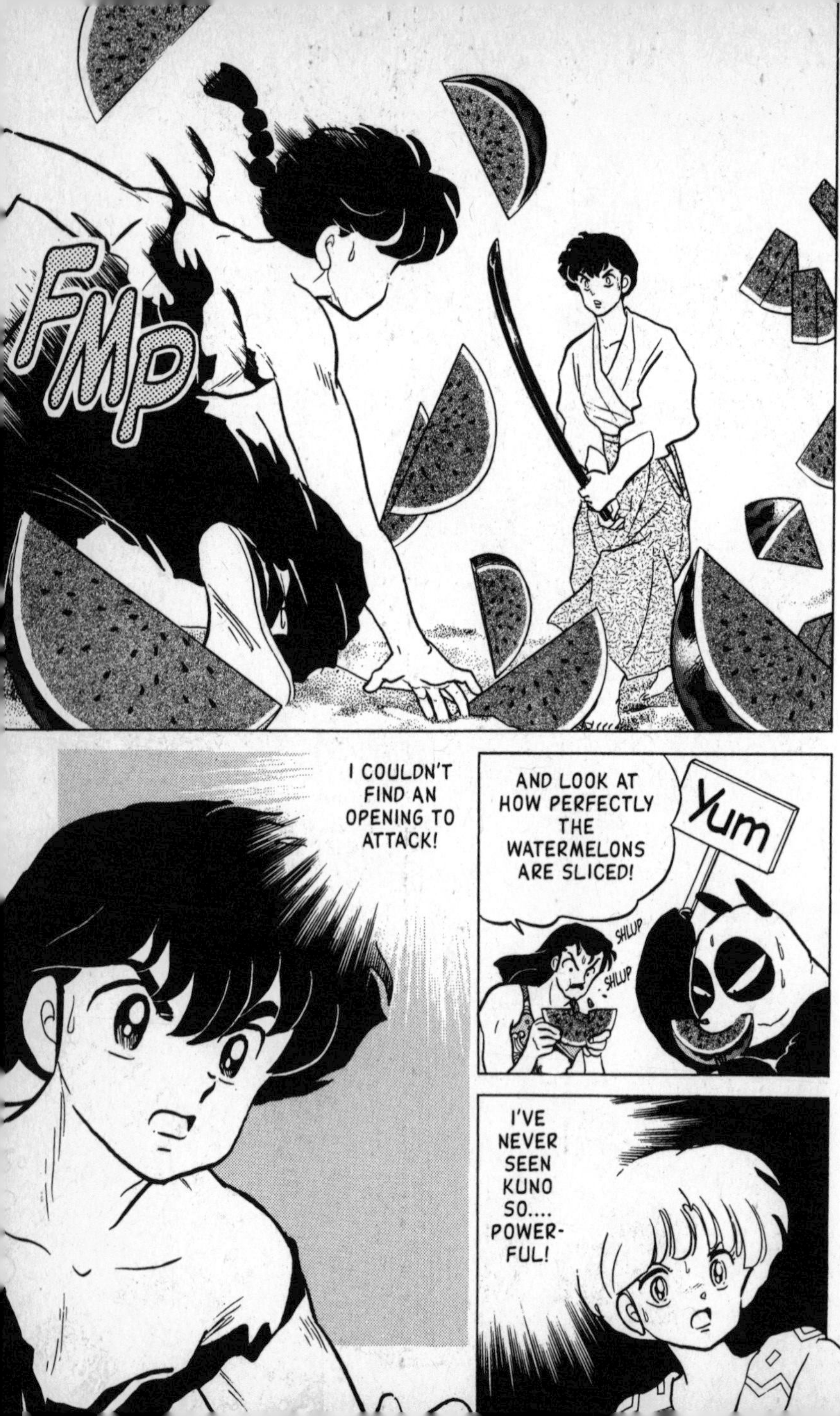
FMP
I COULDN'T FIND AN OPENING TO ATTACK!
AND LOOK AT HOW PERFECTLY THE WATERMELONS ARE SLICED!
Yum
SHLUP
SHLUP
I'VE NEVER SEEN KUNO SO.... POWER-FUL!

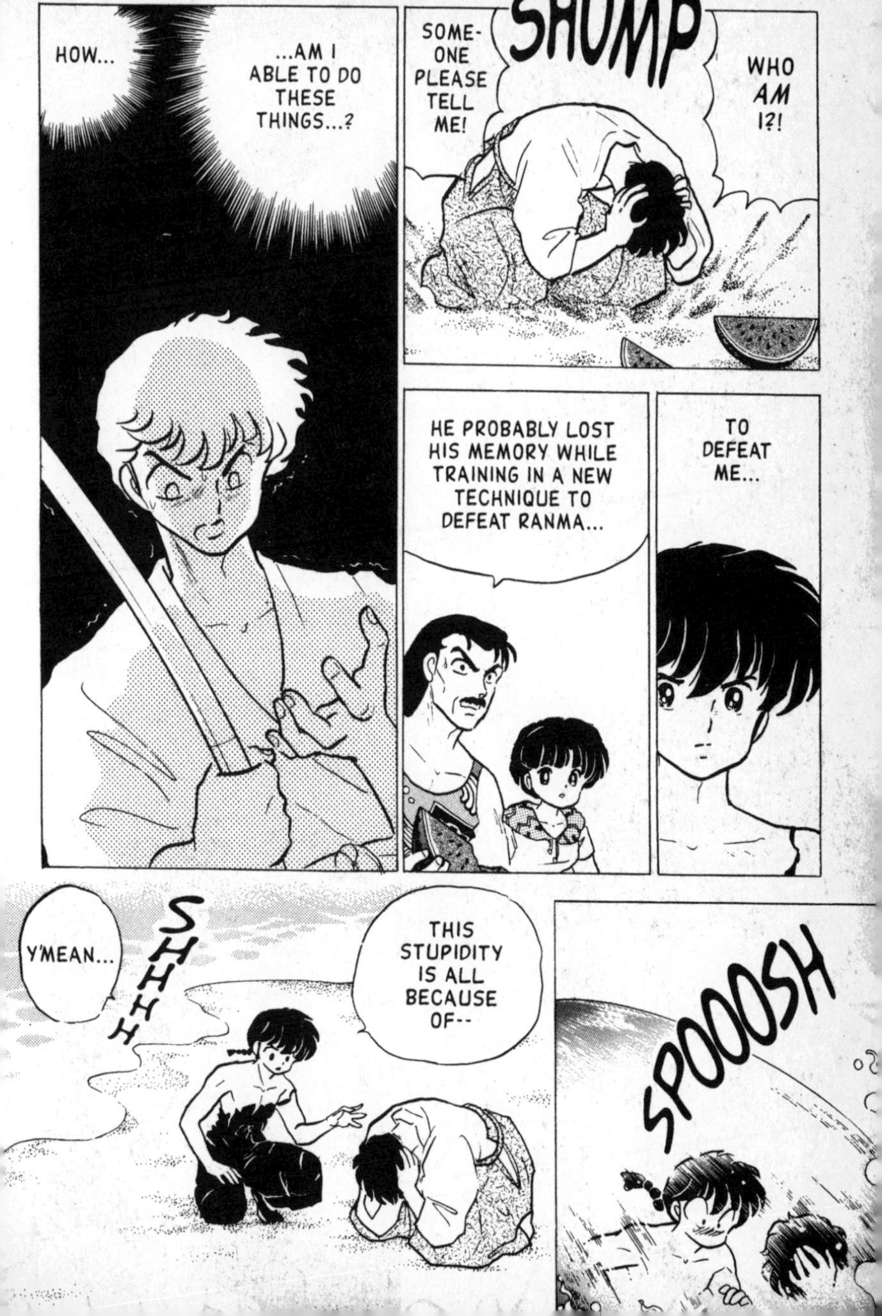
HOW...
...AM I ABLE TO DO THESE THINGS...?
SOME-ONE PLEASE TELL ME!
SHUMP
WHO AM I?!
HE PROBABLY LOST HIS MEMORY WHILE TRAINING IN A NEW TECHNIQUE TO DEFEAT RANMA...
TO DEFEAT ME...
Y'MEAN...
SHHHH
THIS STUPIDITY IS ALL BECAUSE OF--
SPOOOSH

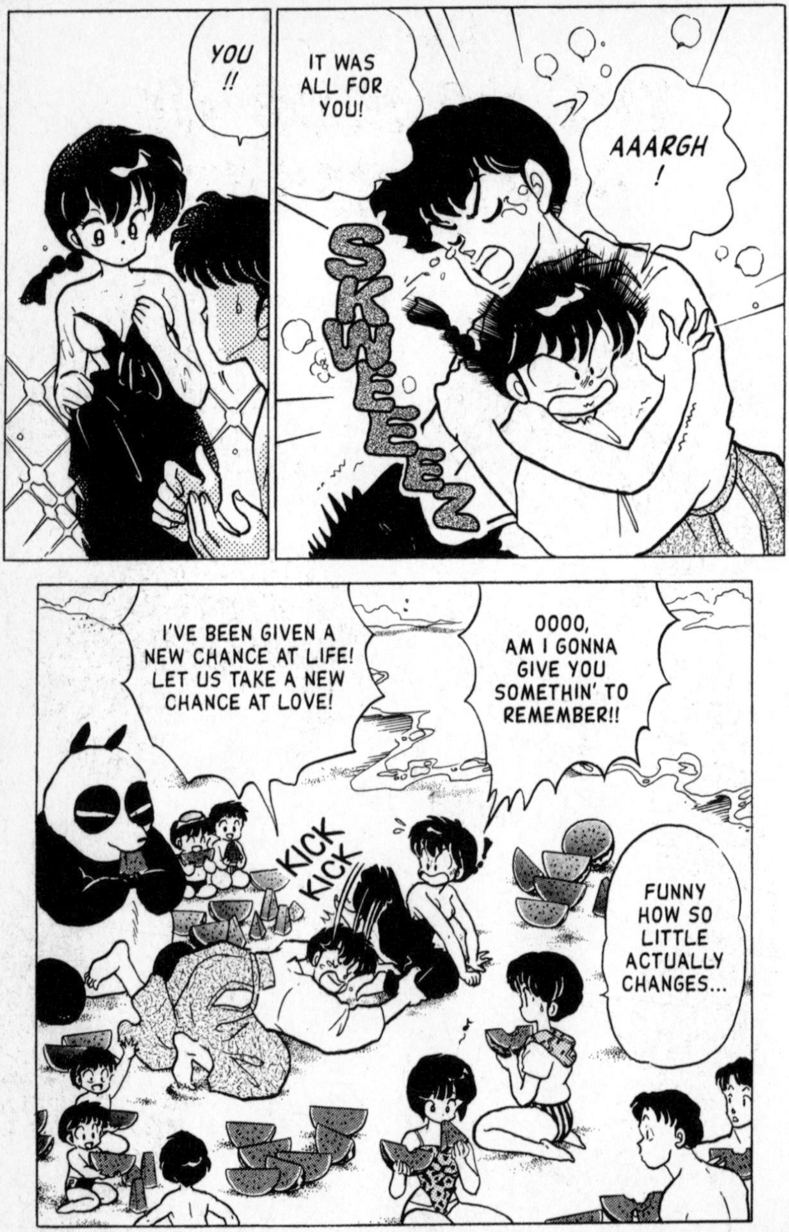
YOU !!
IT WAS ALL FOR YOU!
AAARGH !
SKWEEEZ
I'VE BEEN GIVEN A NEW CHANCE AT LIFE! LET US TAKE A NEW CHANCE AT LOVE!
OOOO, AM I GONNA GIVE YOU SOMETHIN' TO REMEMBER!!
KICK KICK
FUNNY HOW SO LITTLE ACTUALLY CHANGES...

Part 2
THE HORROR OF PARTY BEACH

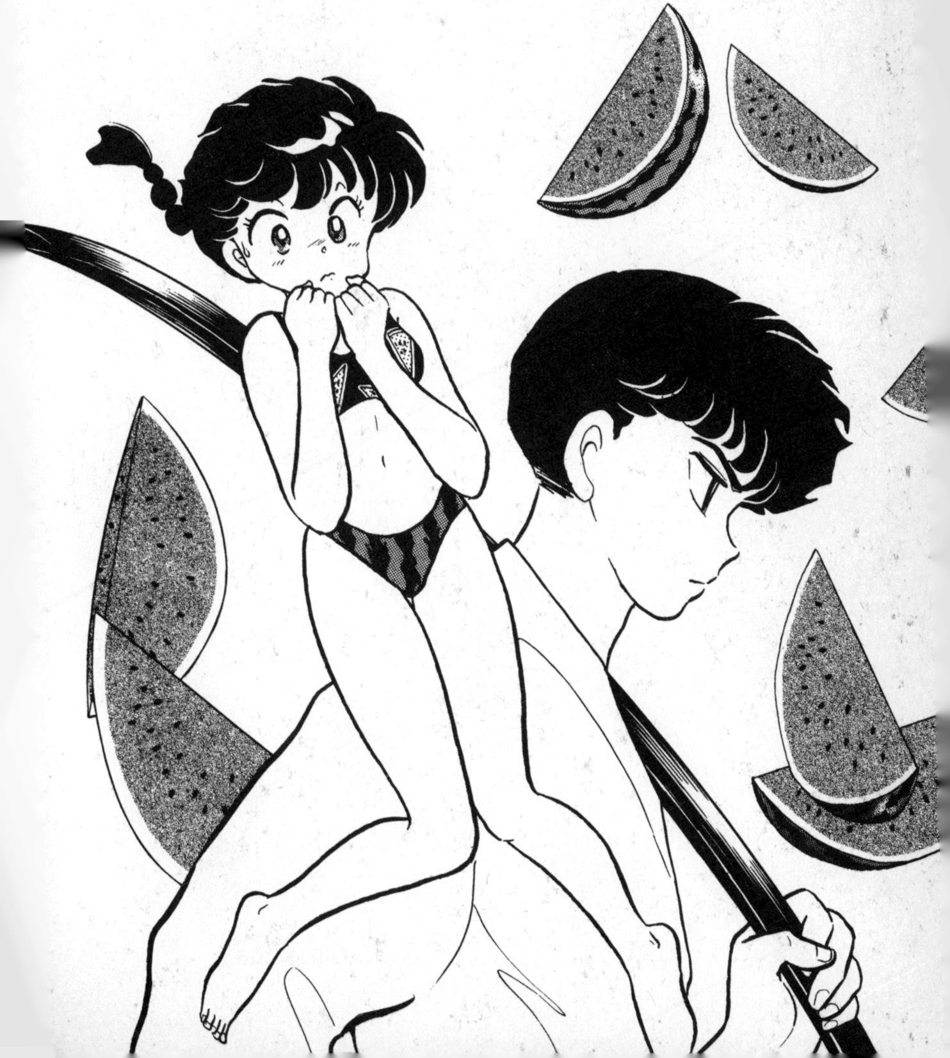

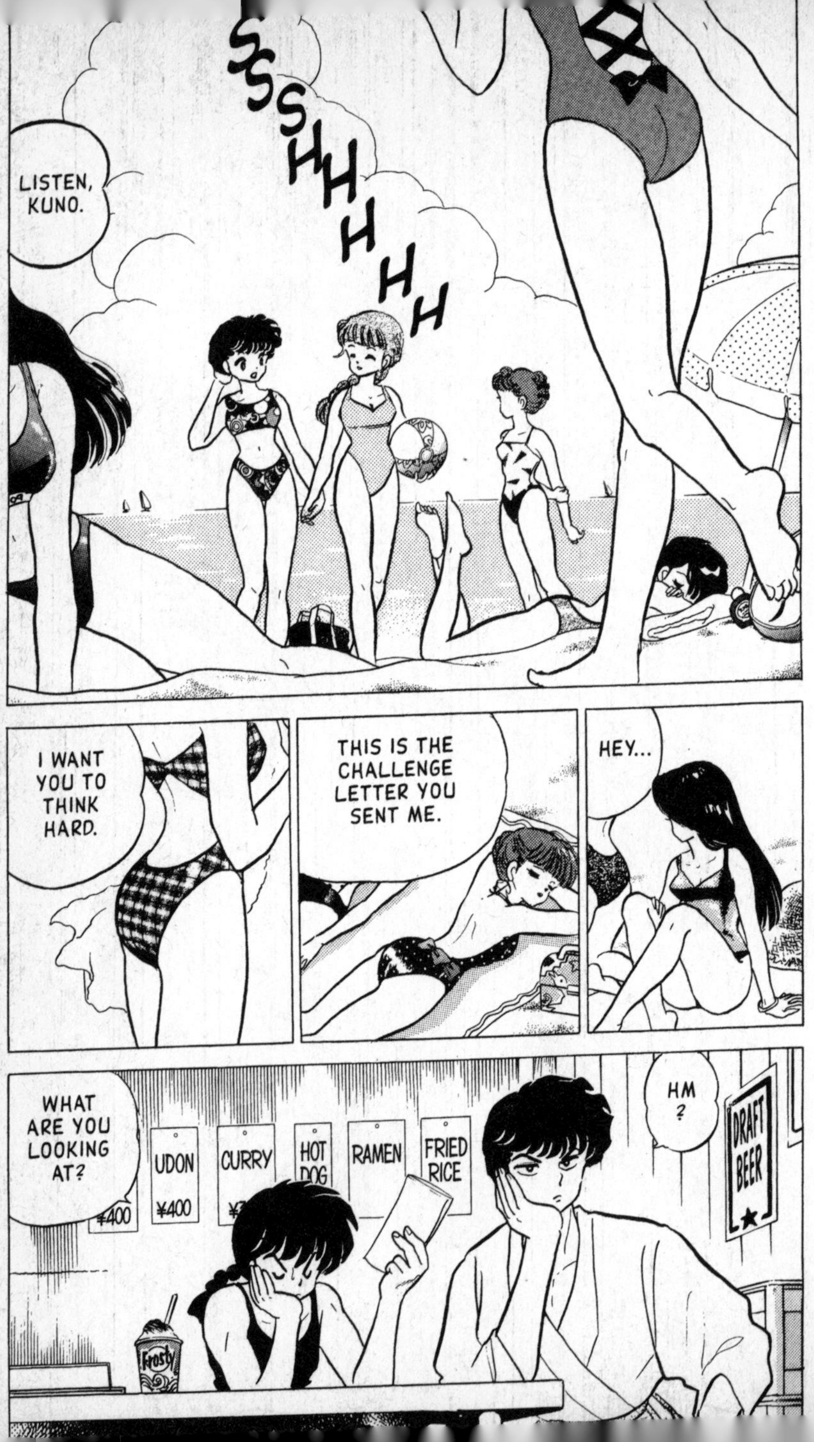
LISTEN, KUNO.
SSSHHHHHH
I WANT YOU TO THINK HARD.
THIS IS THE CHALLENGE LETTER YOU SENT ME.
HEY...
WHAT ARE YOU LOOKING AT?
UDON
¥400
CURRY
HOT DOG
RAMEN
FRIED RICE
¥400
HM?
DRAFT BEER
Frosty

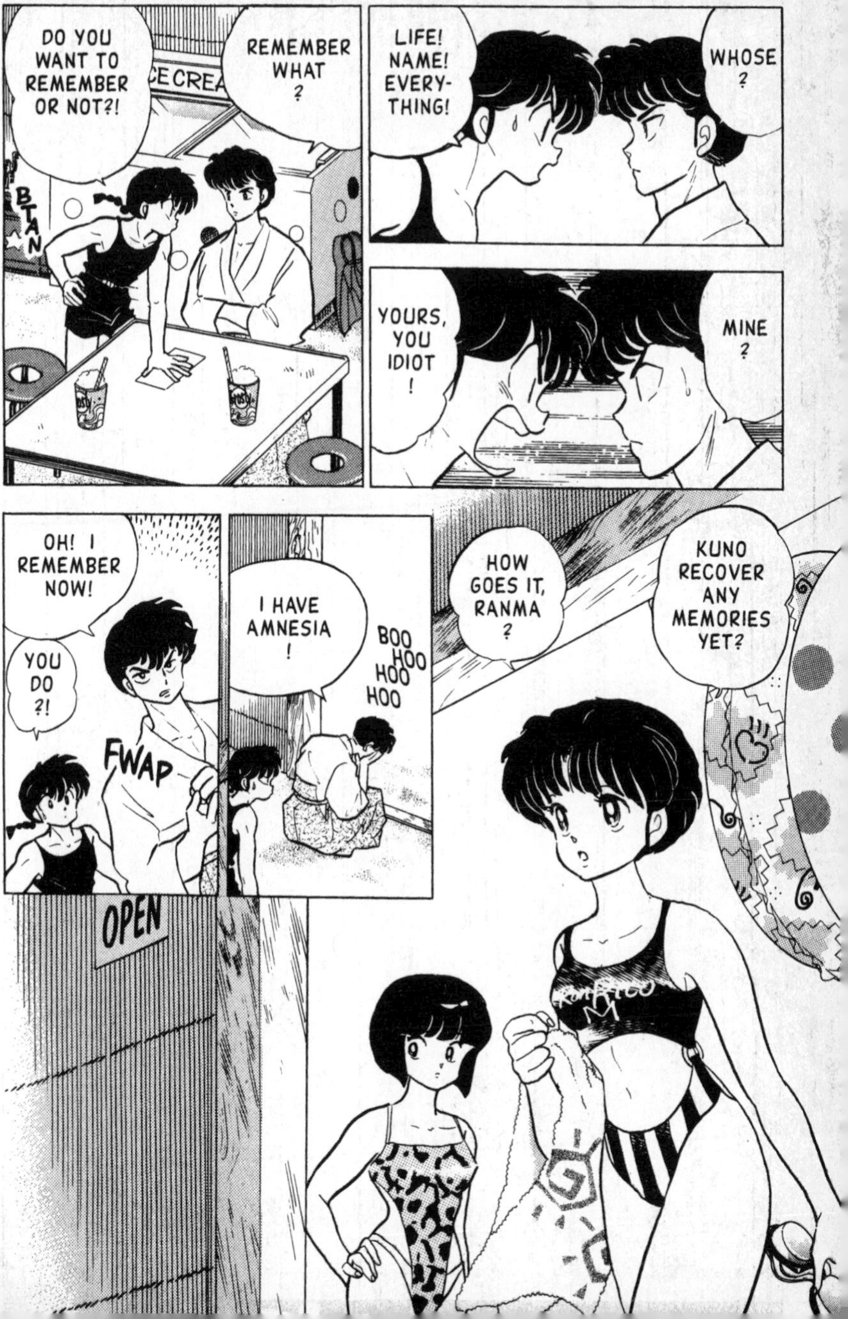
DO YOU WANT TO REMEMBER OR NOT?!
REMEMBER WHAT?
CE CREA
BTAN
LIFE! NAME! EVERY-THING!
WHOSE?
YOURS, YOU IDIOT!
MINE?
OH! I REMEMBER NOW!
YOU DO?!
FWAP
I HAVE AMNESIA!
BOO HOO HOO HOO
HOW GOES IT, RANMA?
KUNO RECOVER ANY MEMORIES YET?
OPEN

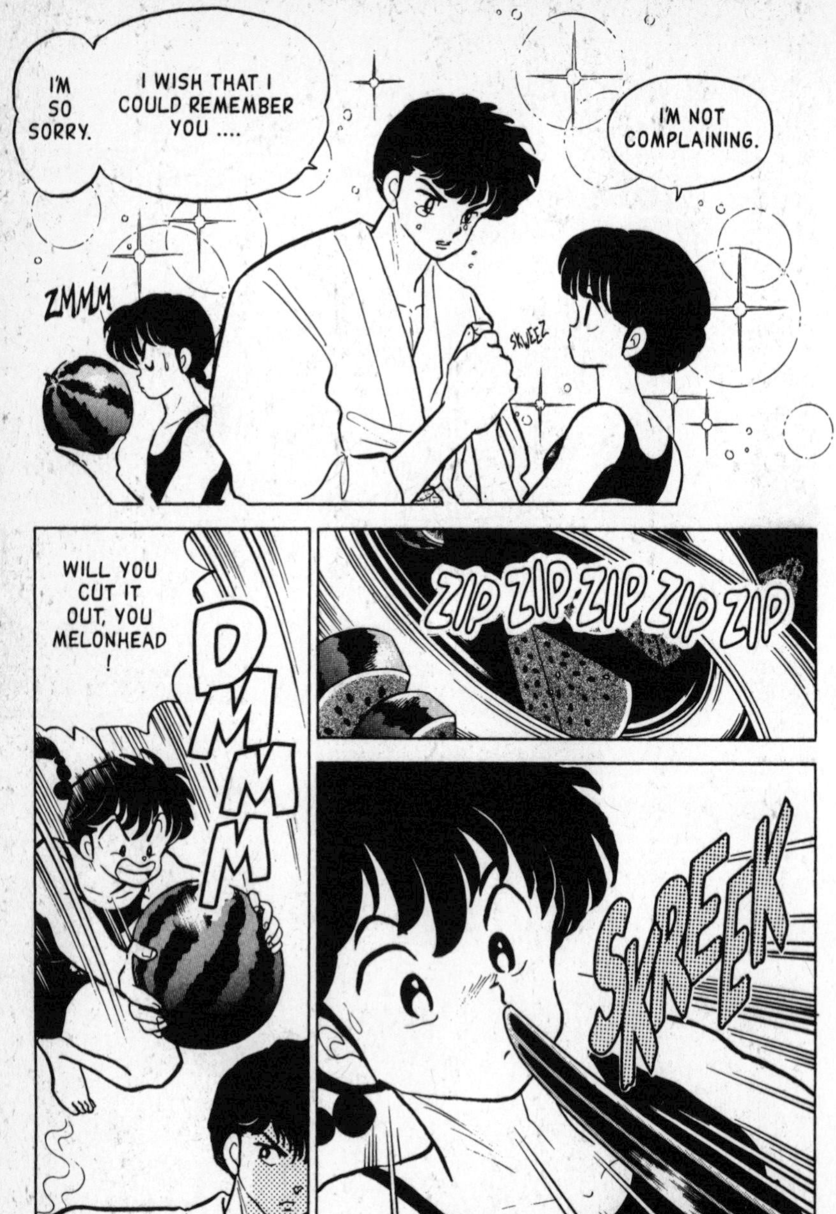
I'M SO SORRY.
I WISH THAT I COULD REMEMBER YOU ....
I'M NOT COMPLAINING.
ZMMM
SKWEEZ
WILL YOU CUT IT OUT, YOU MELONHEAD !
DMMMM
ZIP ZIP ZIP ZIP ZIP
SKREEK

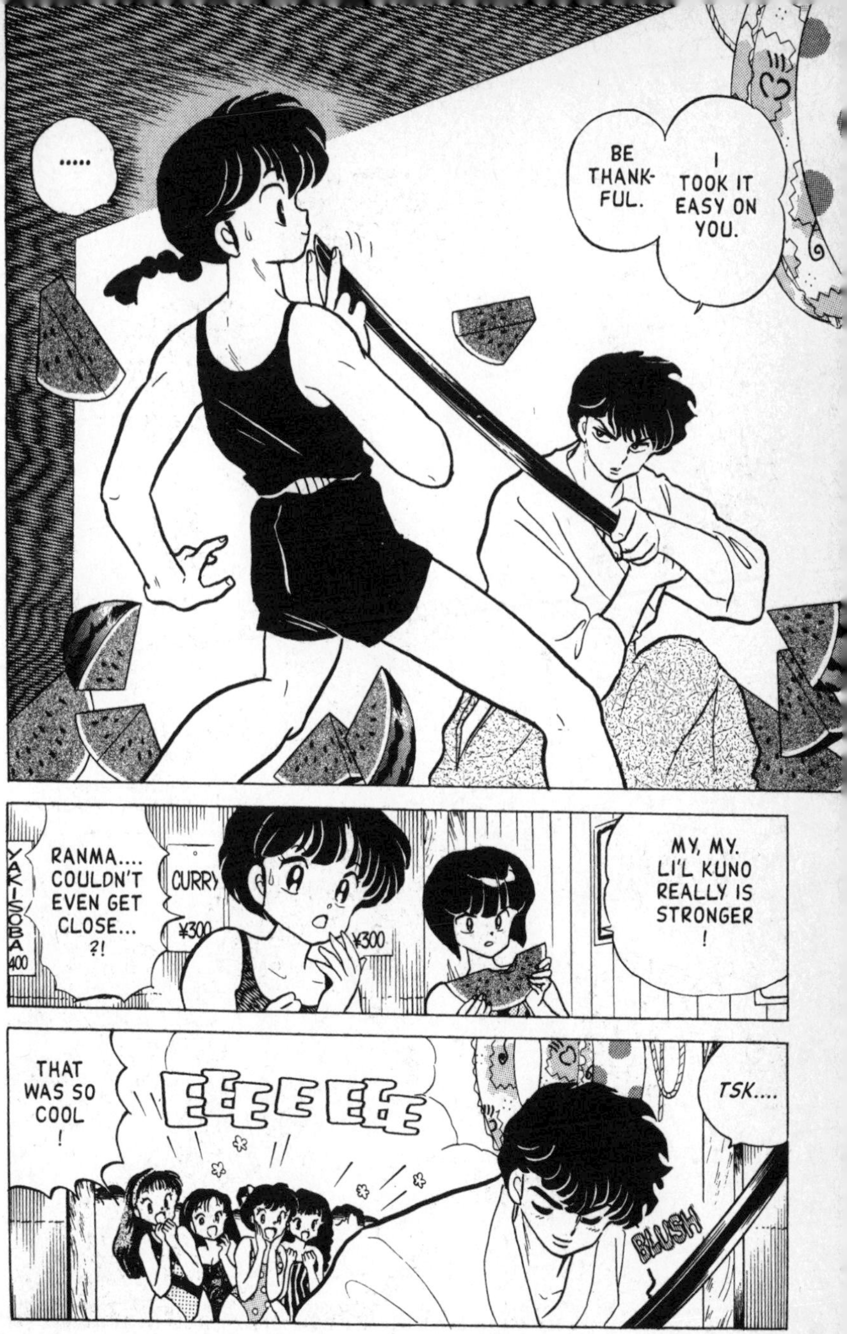
......
BE THANKFUL.
I TOOK IT EASY ON YOU.
YAKISOBA 400
RANMA.... COULDN'T EVEN GET CLOSE... ?!
CURRY
¥300
¥300
MY, MY. LI'L KUNO REALLY IS STRONGER!
THAT WAS SO COOL!
EEEEEEE
TSK....
BLUSH

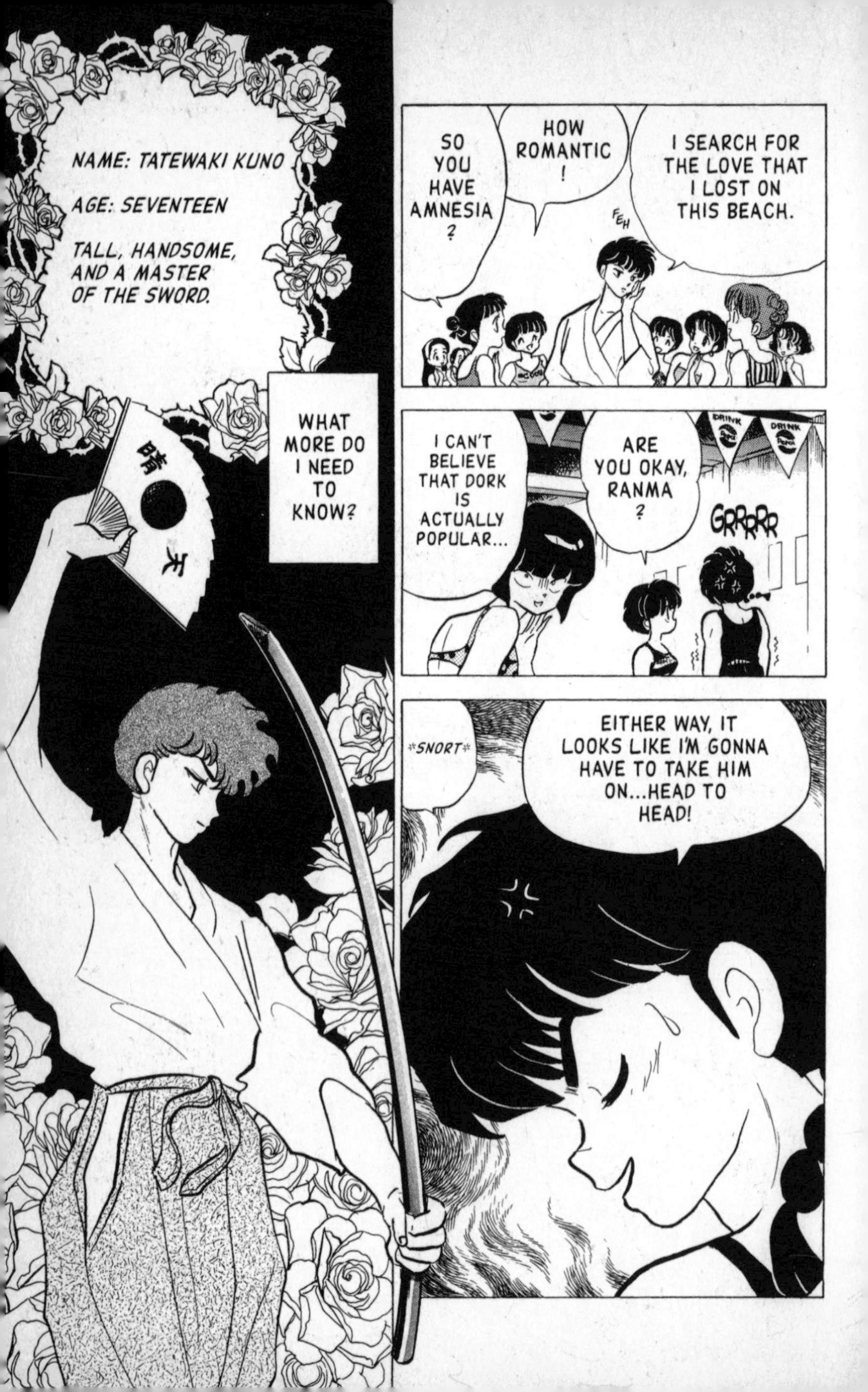
NAME: TATEWAKI KUNO
AGE: SEVENTEEN
TALL, HANDSOME, AND A MASTER OF THE SWORD.
WHAT MORE DO I NEED TO KNOW?
SO YOU HAVE AMNESIA?
HOW ROMANTIC!
I SEARCH FOR THE LOVE THAT I LOST ON THIS BEACH.
FEH
I CAN'T BELIEVE THAT DORK IS ACTUALLY POPULAR...
ARE YOU OKAY, RANMA?
DRINK
DRINK
GRRRRR
SNORT
EITHER WAY, IT LOOKS LIKE I'M GONNA HAVE TO TAKE HIM ON...HEAD TO HEAD!

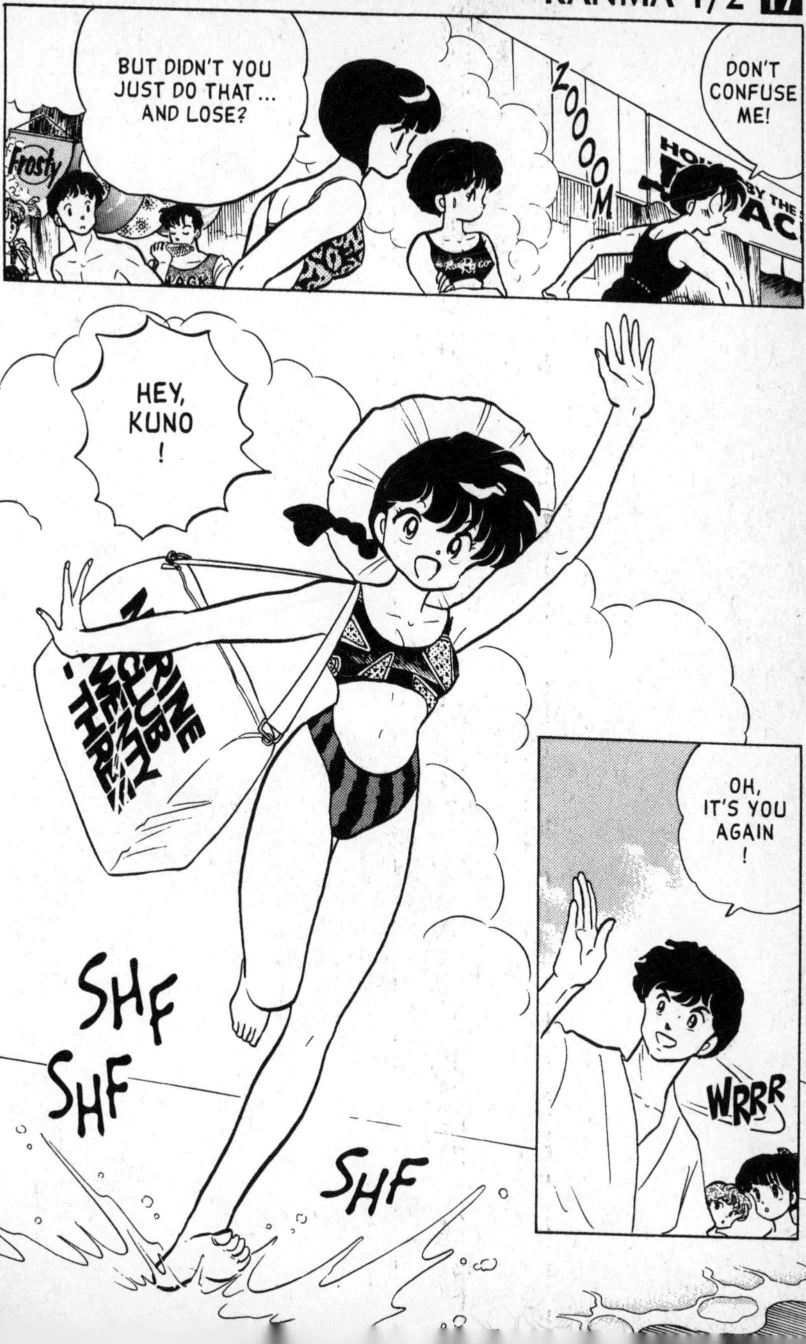
Frosty
BUT DIDN'T YOU JUST DO THAT... AND LOSE?
ZOOOOOM
DON'T CONFUSE ME!
HEY, KUNO!
SHF
SHF
SHF
OH, IT'S YOU AGAIN!
WRRR

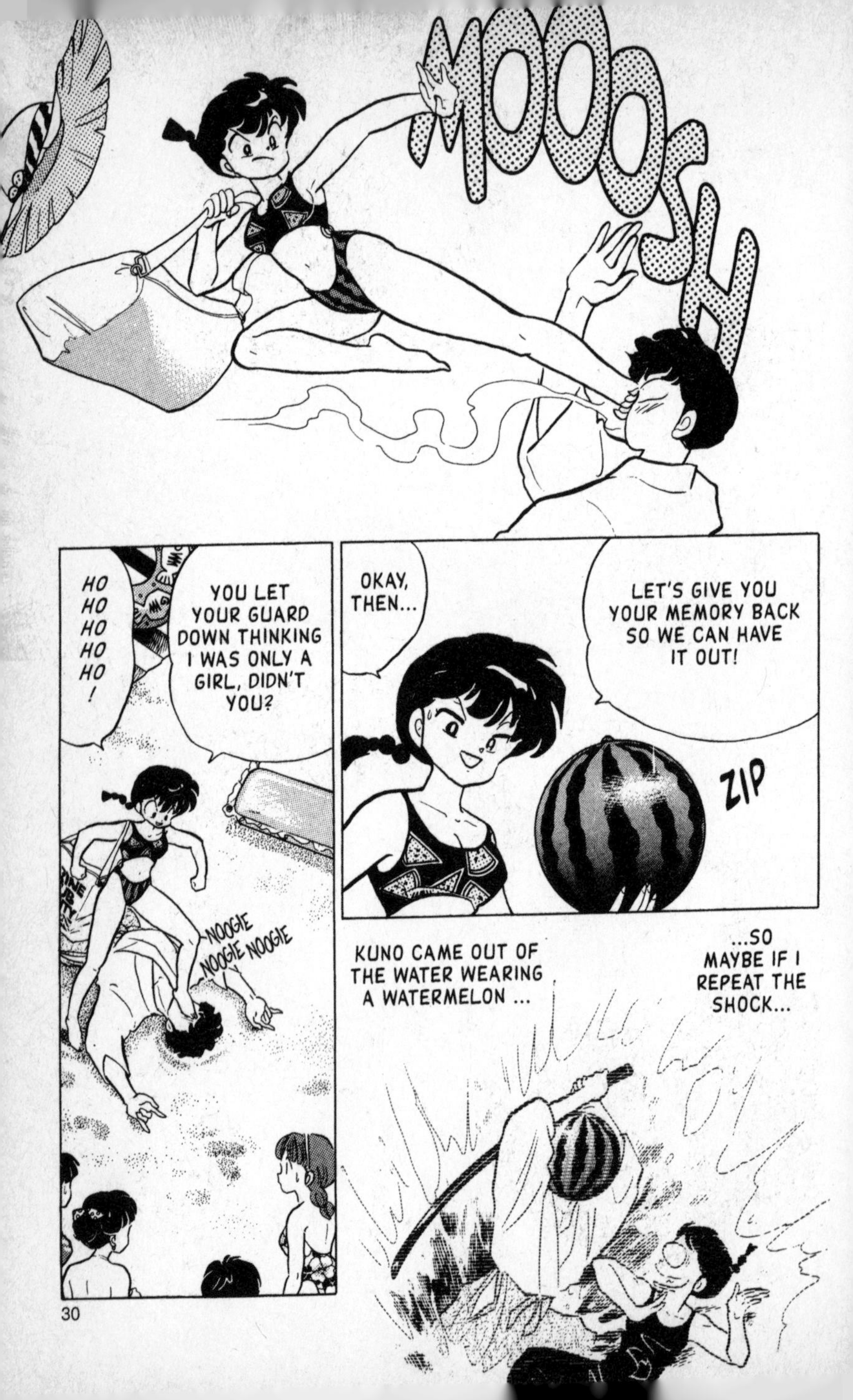
MOOOOSH
HO HO HO HO HO !
YOU LET YOUR GUARD DOWN THINKING I WAS ONLY A GIRL, DIDN'T YOU?
NOOGIE NOOGIE NOOGIE
OKAY, THEN...
LET'S GIVE YOU YOUR MEMORY BACK SO WE CAN HAVE IT OUT!
ZIP
KUNO CAME OUT OF THE WATER WEARING A WATERMELON ...
...SO MAYBE IF I REPEAT THE SHOCK...

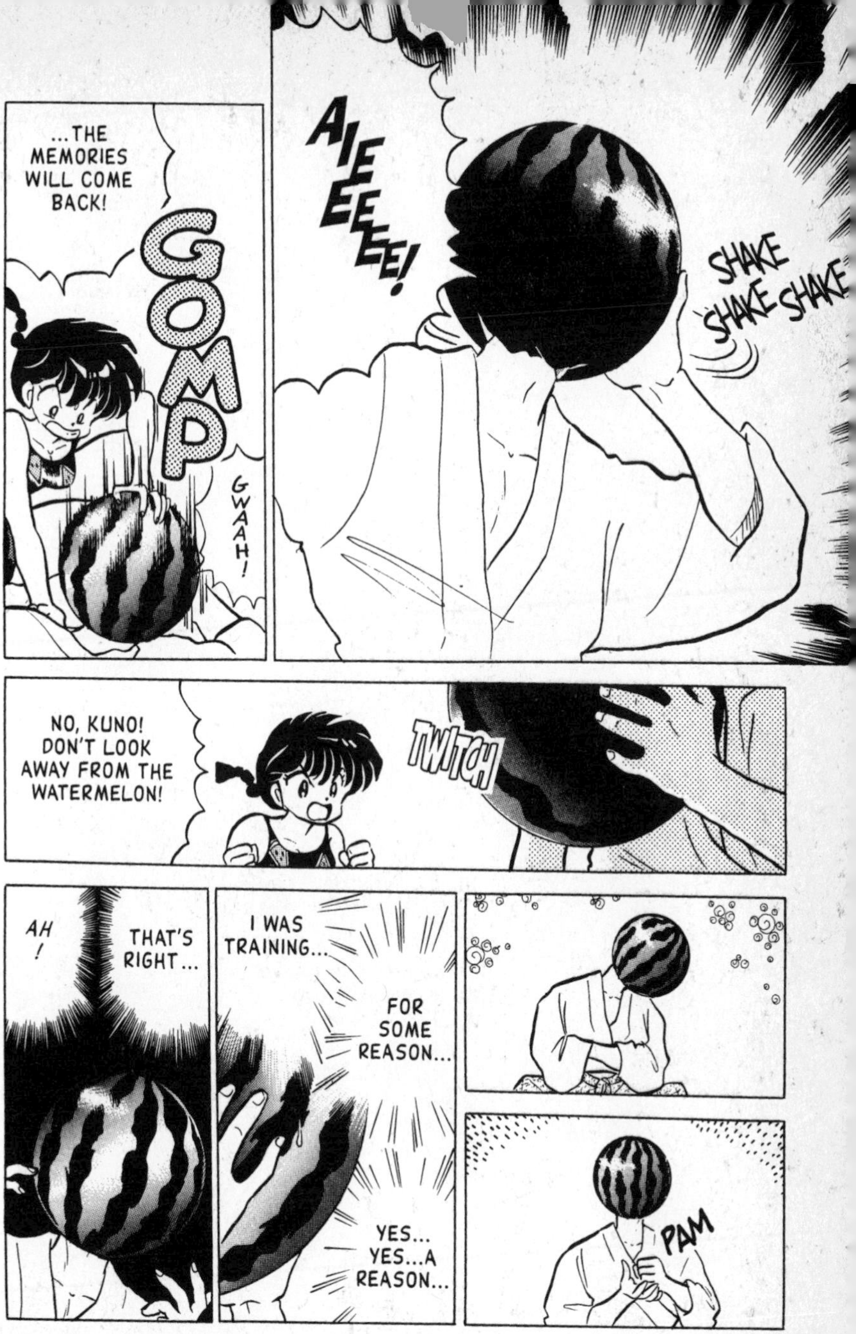

...THE MEMORIES WILL COME BACK!
GOMP
GWAAH!
AIEEEEEE!
SHAKE SHAKE SHAKE
NO, KUNO! DON'T LOOK AWAY FROM THE WATERMELON!
TWITCH
AH!
THAT'S RIGHT...
I WAS TRAINING...
FOR SOME REASON...
YES... YES...A REASON...
PAM

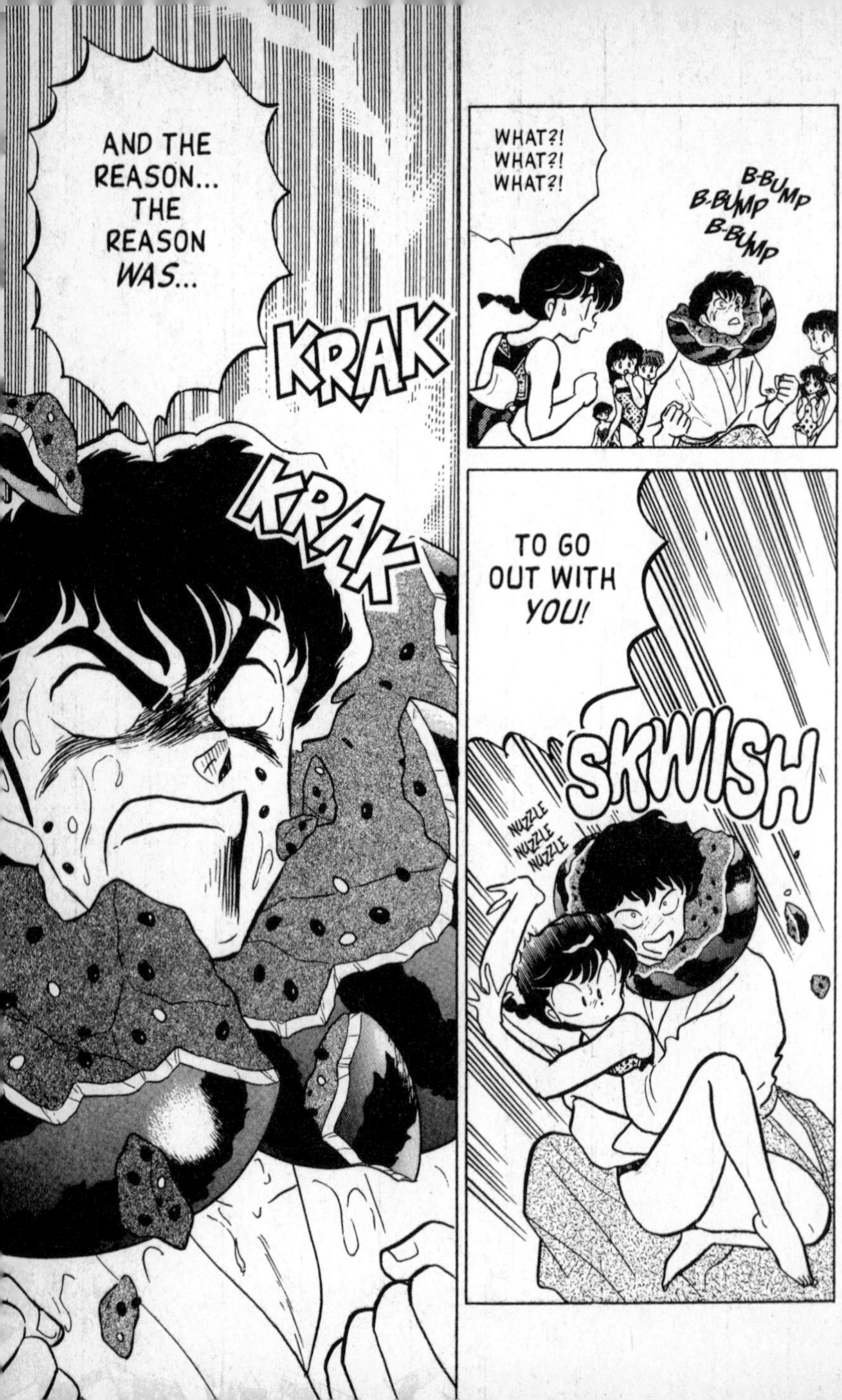
AND THE REASON... THE REASON WAS...
KRAK
KRAK
WHAT?! WHAT?! WHAT?!
B-BUMP
B-BUMP
B-BUMP
TO GO OUT WITH YOU!
SKWISH
NUZZLE NUZZLE NUZZLE

NO, IDIOT!

LOOK AT THIS!

EH?

I will show you the fruits of my training. Just wait and see.
Tatewaki Kuno

I WILL SHOW YOU THE FRUITS OF MY TRAINING.

JUST WAIT AND SEE.

-- TATEWAKI KUNO

TH-THIS IS A LOVE LETTER.

IT'S A CHALLENGE LETTER!

LISTEN, YOU WERE IN TRAINING TO HAVE A BATTLE WITH--

RANMA, QUICK!

YOU HAVE TO CHANGE BACK BEFORE YOU FIGHT!

RIGHT!

FSSH

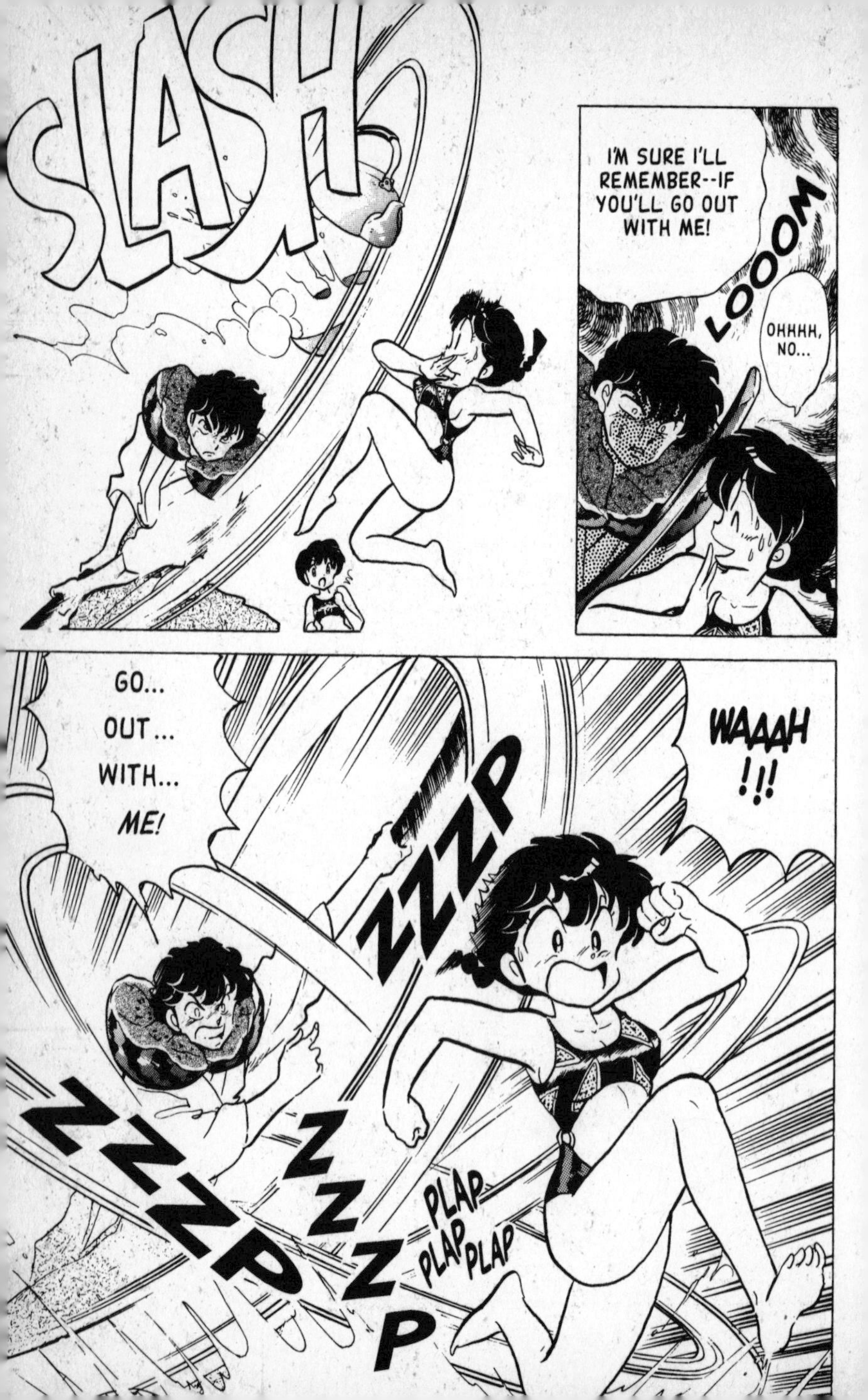
SLASH
I'M SURE I'LL REMEMBER--IF YOU'LL GO OUT WITH ME!
LOOOM
OHHHH, NO...
GO... OUT... WITH... ME!
ZZZP
WAAAH !!!
ZZZP
ZZZP
PLAP PLAP PLAP PLAP

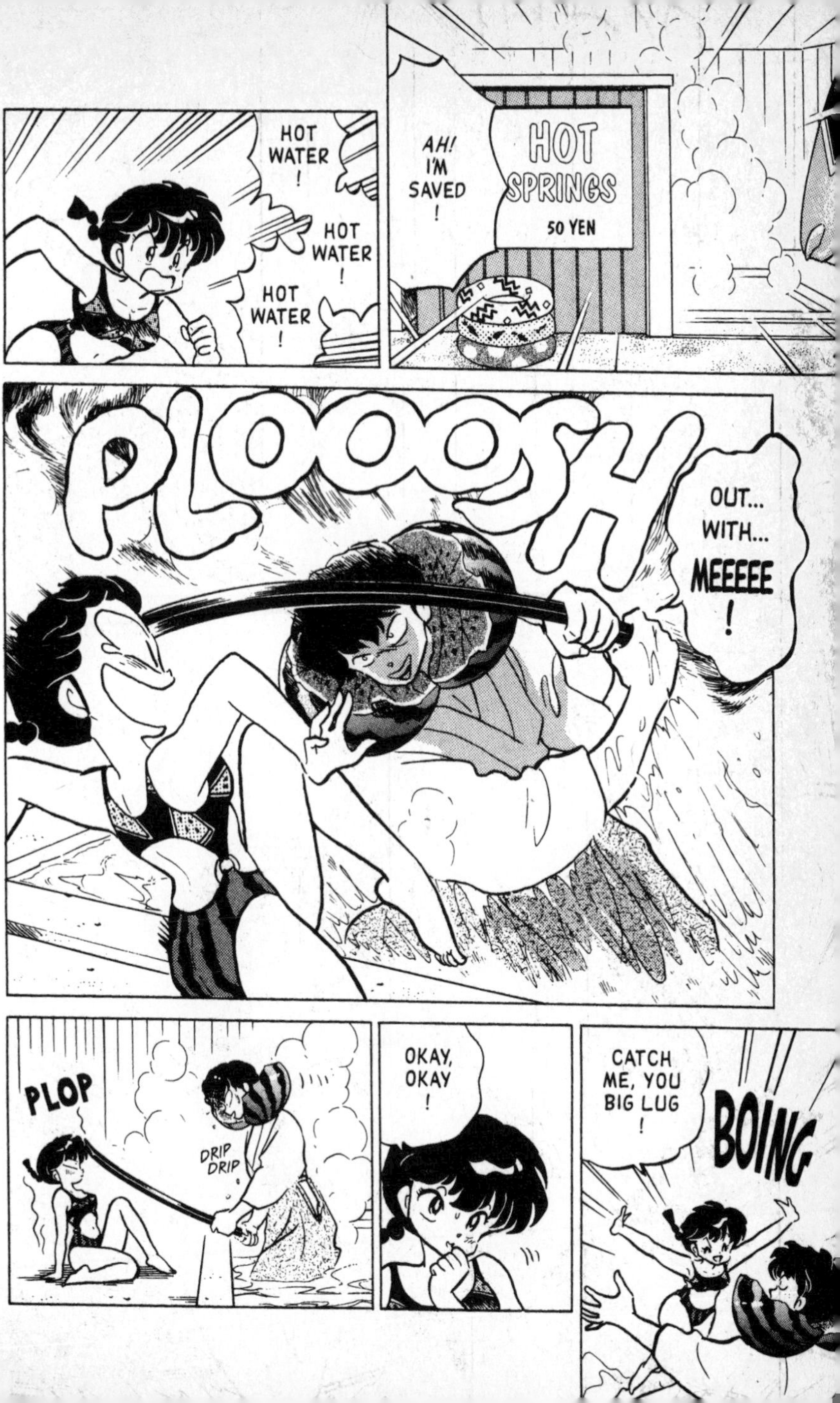
HOT WATER !
HOT WATER !
HOT WATER !
AH! I'M SAVED !
HOT SPRINGS
50 YEN
PLOOOSH
OUT... WITH... MEEEEE !
PLOP
DRIP DRIP
OKAY, OKAY !
CATCH ME, YOU BIG LUG !
BOING

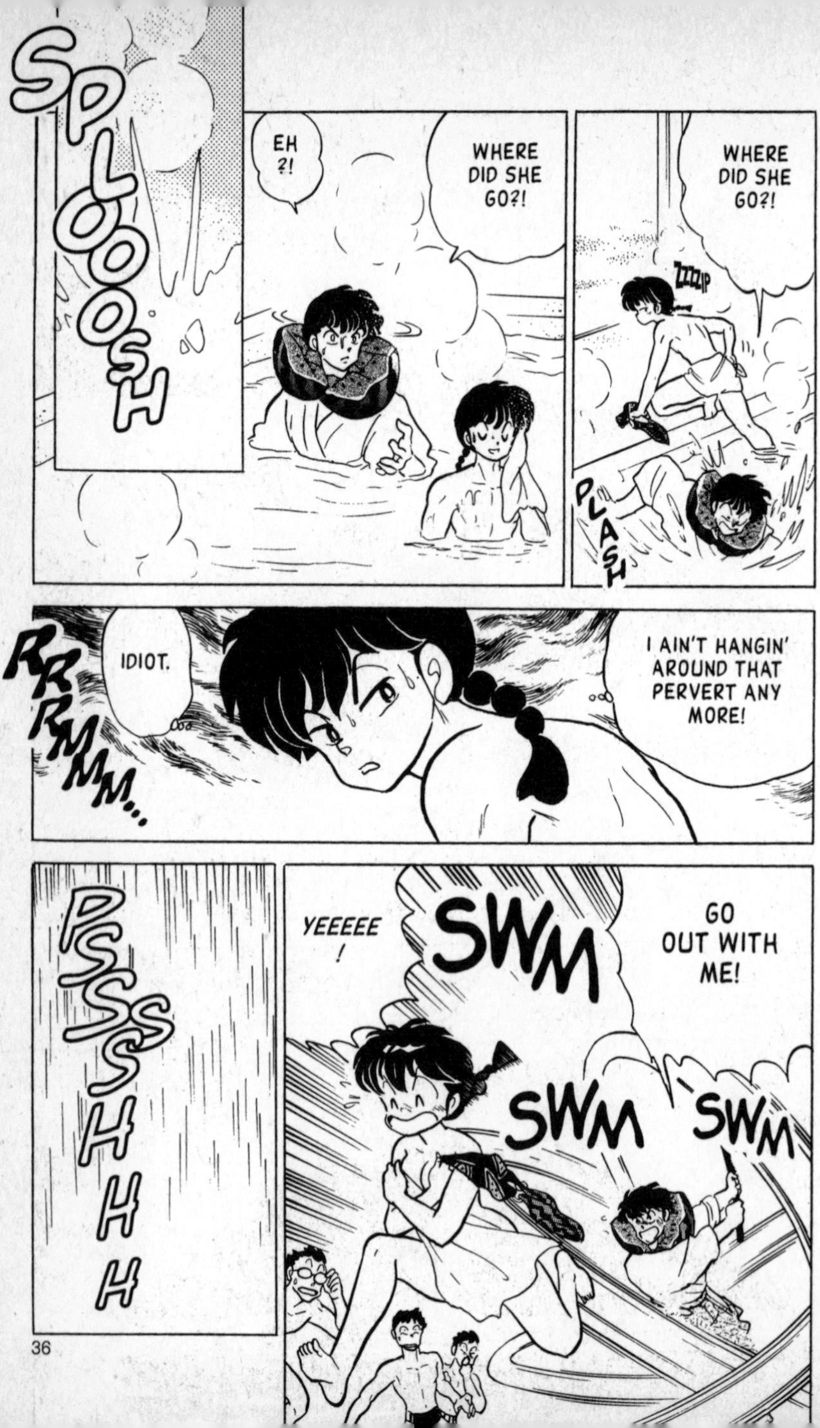
SPLOOOOSH
EH ?!
WHERE DID SHE GO?!
WHERE DID SHE GO?!
ZZZZIP
PLASH
RRRMMM...
IDIOT.
I AIN'T HANGIN' AROUND THAT PERVERT ANY MORE!
PSSSSHHHH
YEEEEE !
SWM
GO OUT WITH ME!
SWM SWM

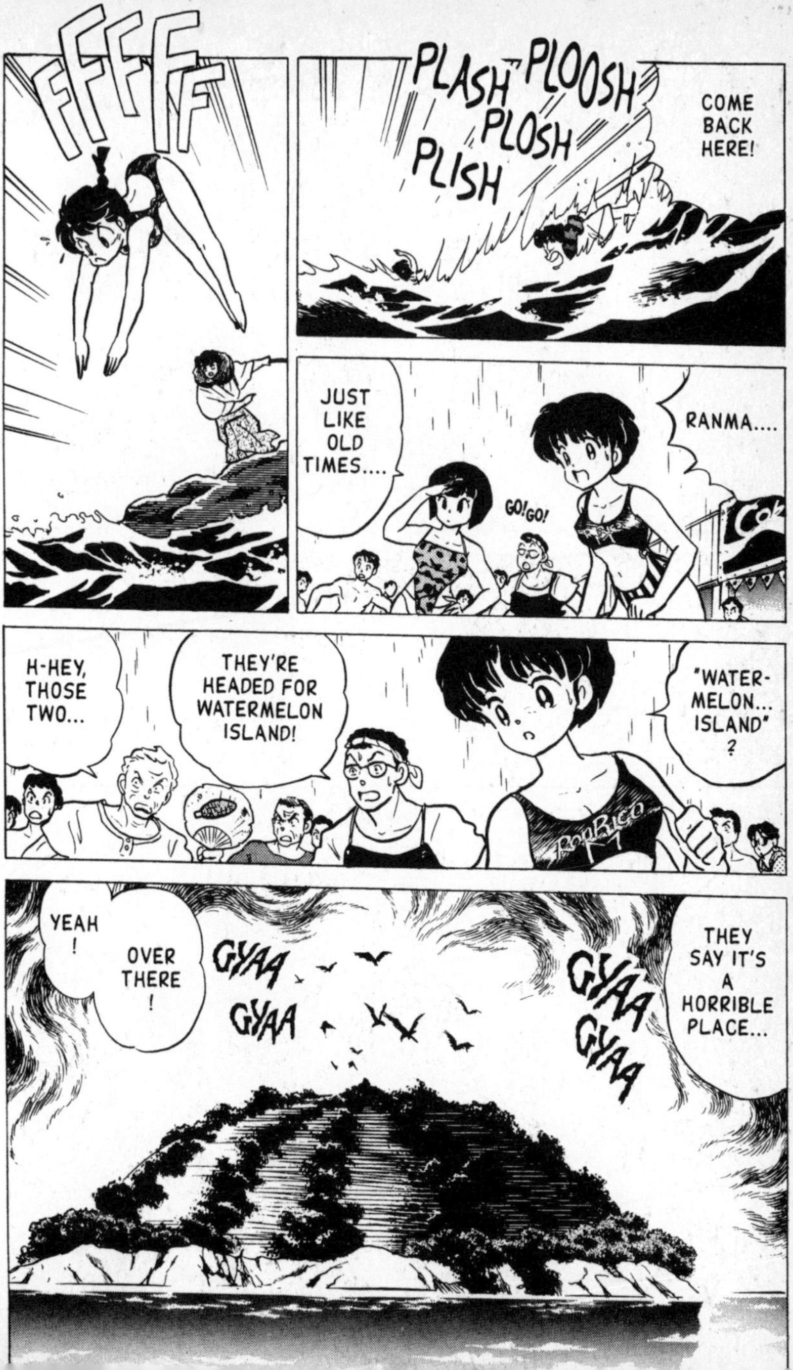
FFFFFF
PLASH PLOOSH PLOSH PLISH
COME BACK HERE!
JUST LIKE OLD TIMES....
GO! GO!
RANMA....
H-HEY, THOSE TWO...
THEY'RE HEADED FOR WATERMELON ISLAND!
"WATER-MELON... ISLAND" ?
YEAH !
OVER THERE !
GYAA GYAA
GYAA GYAA GYAA
THEY SAY IT'S A HORRIBLE PLACE...

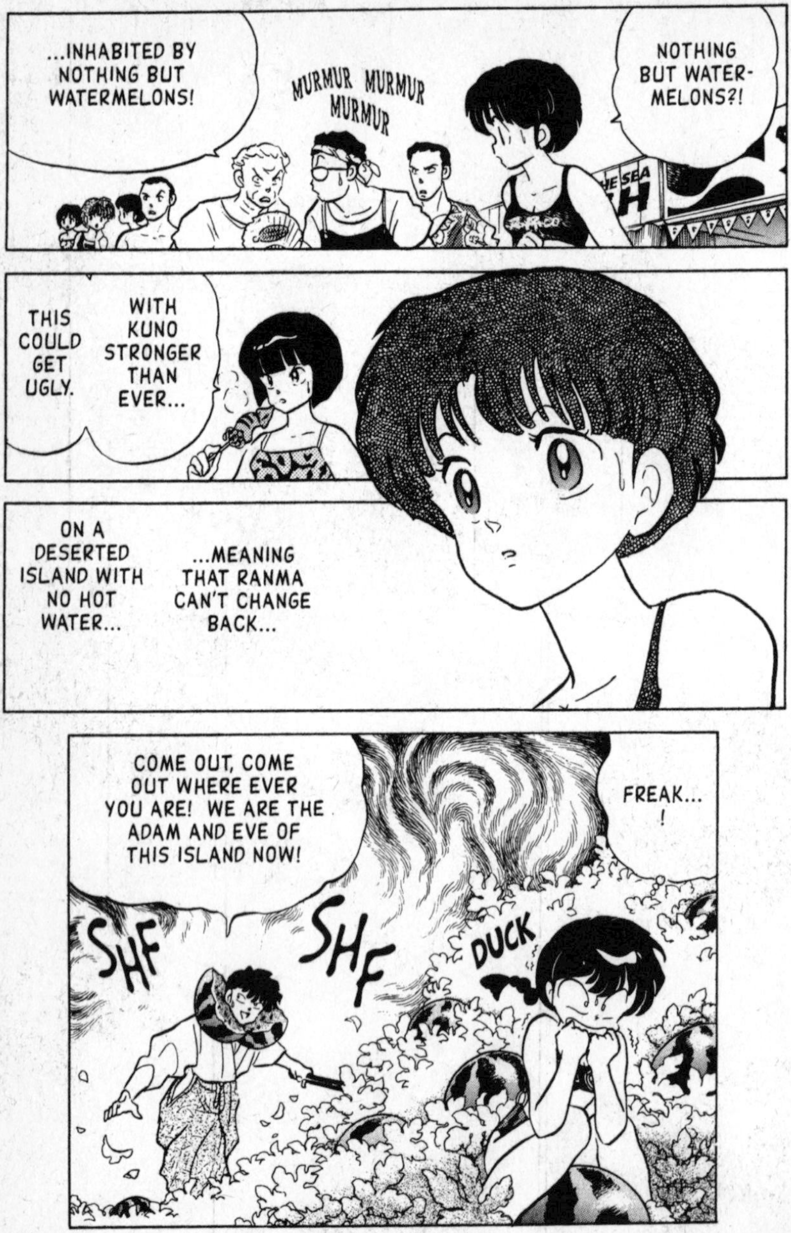
...INHABITED BY NOTHING BUT WATERMELONS!
MURMUR MURMUR MURMUR
NOTHING BUT WATER-MELONS?!
THIS COULD GET UGLY.
WITH KUNO STRONGER THAN EVER...
ON A DESERTED ISLAND WITH NO HOT WATER...
...MEANING THAT RANMA CAN'T CHANGE BACK...
COME OUT, COME OUT WHERE EVER YOU ARE! WE ARE THE ADAM AND EVE OF THIS ISLAND NOW!
SHF
SHF
DUCK
FREAK... !

Part 3
CATCHER IN THE RIND

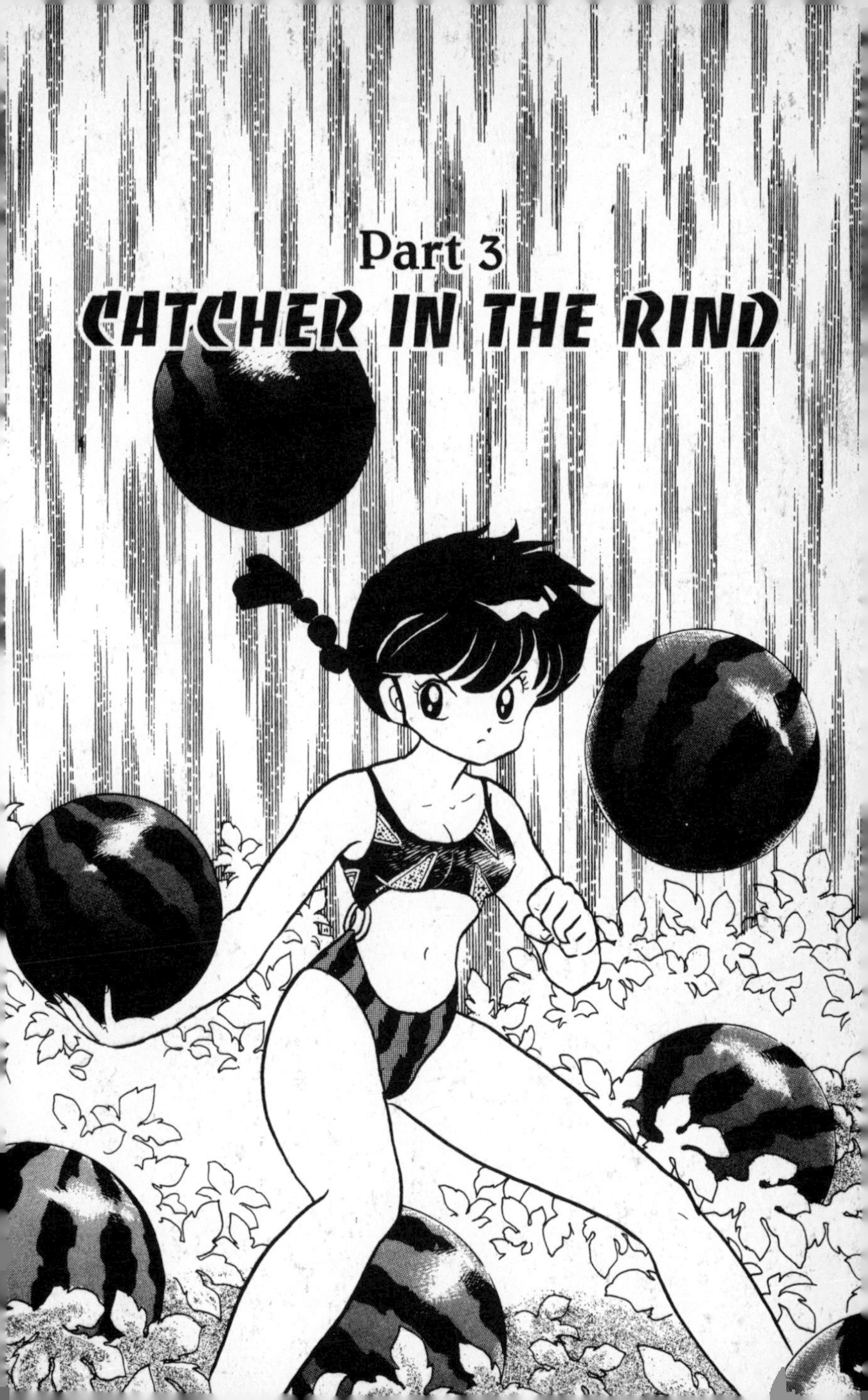

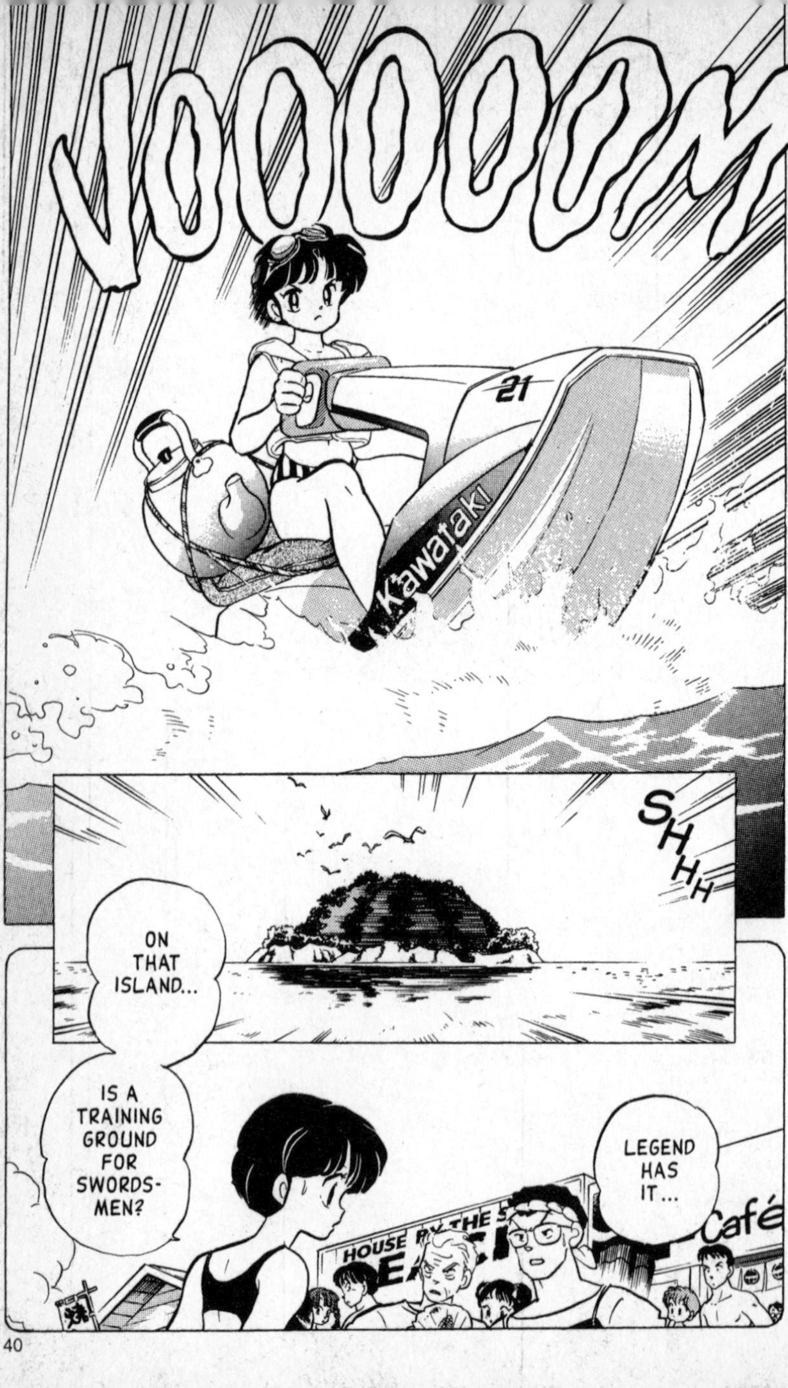
VOOOOOM
21
Kawataki
SHHH
ON THAT ISLAND...
IS A TRAINING GROUND FOR SWORDS-MEN?
LEGEND HAS IT...
Café

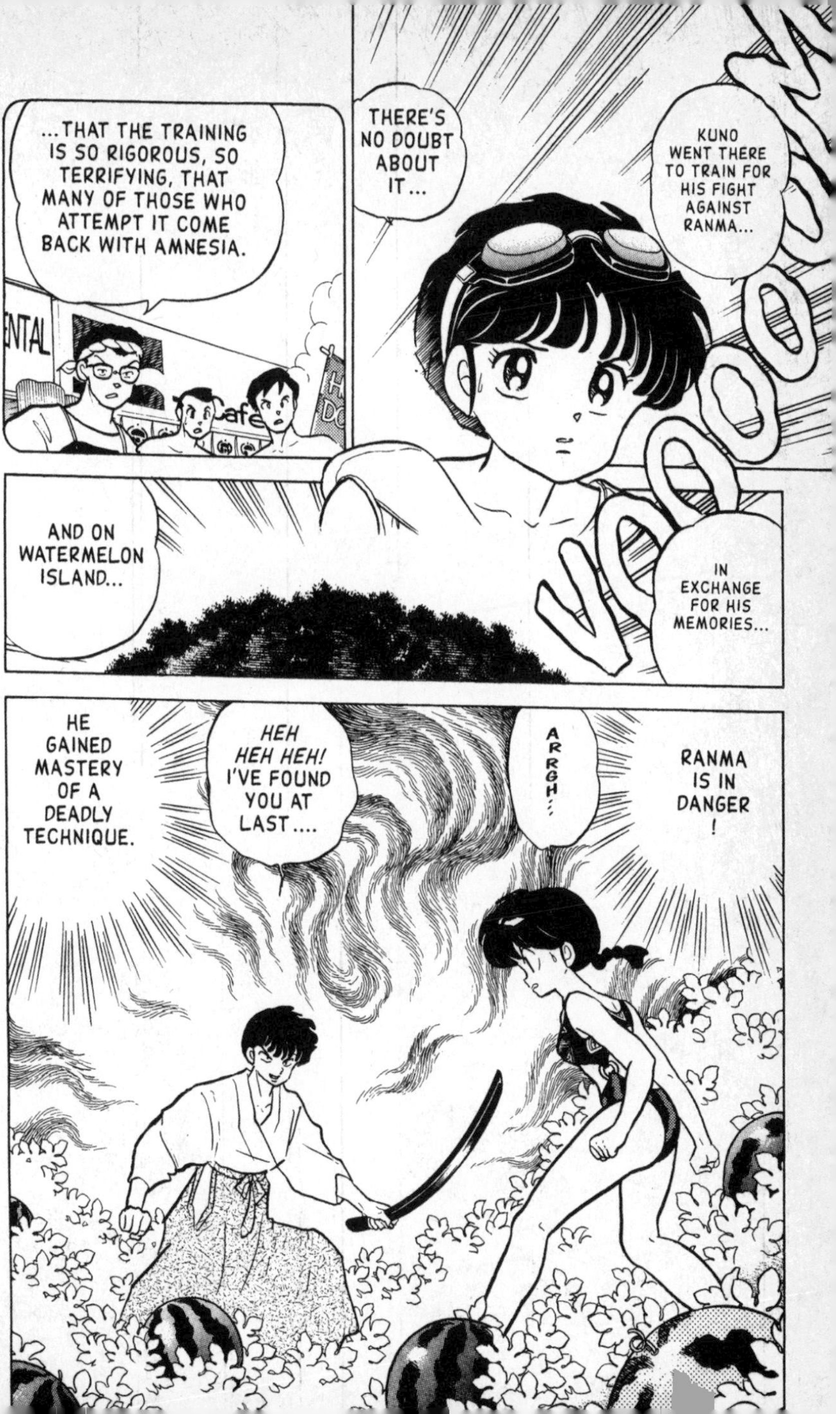
...THAT THE TRAINING IS SO RIGOROUS, SO TERRIFYING, THAT MANY OF THOSE WHO ATTEMPT IT COME BACK WITH AMNESIA.
ENTAL
Cafe
THERE'S NO DOUBT ABOUT IT...
KUNO WENT THERE TO TRAIN FOR HIS FIGHT AGAINST RANMA...
AND ON WATERMELON ISLAND...
IN EXCHANGE FOR HIS MEMORIES...
HE GAINED MASTERY OF A DEADLY TECHNIQUE.
HEH HEH HEH! I'VE FOUND YOU AT LAST....
ARRGH...
RANMA IS IN DANGER !

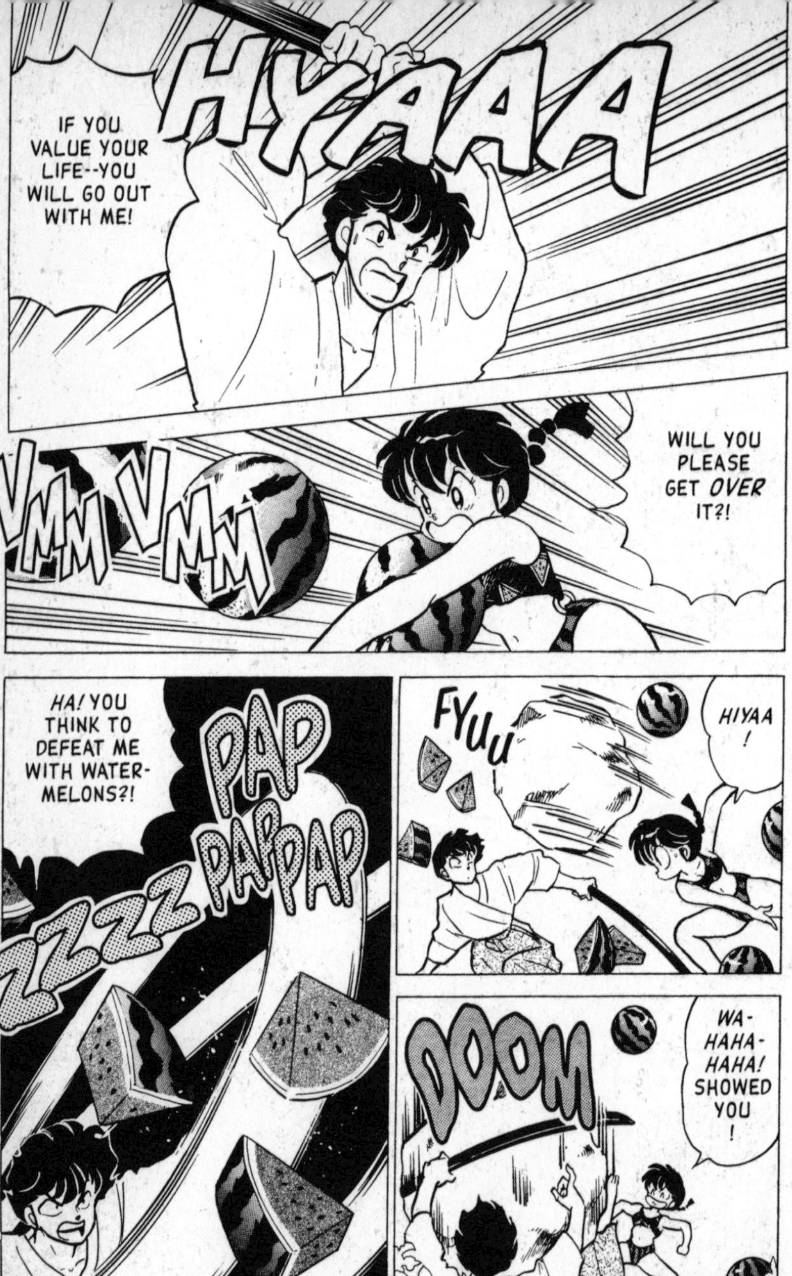
HYAAA
IF YOU VALUE YOUR LIFE--YOU WILL GO OUT WITH ME!
VMM VMM
WILL YOU PLEASE GET *OVER* IT?!
HA! YOU THINK TO DEFEAT ME WITH WATER-MELONS?!
PAP PAPPAP
ZZZZ
FYUU
HIYAA!
DOOM
WA-HAHA-HAHA! SHOWED YOU!

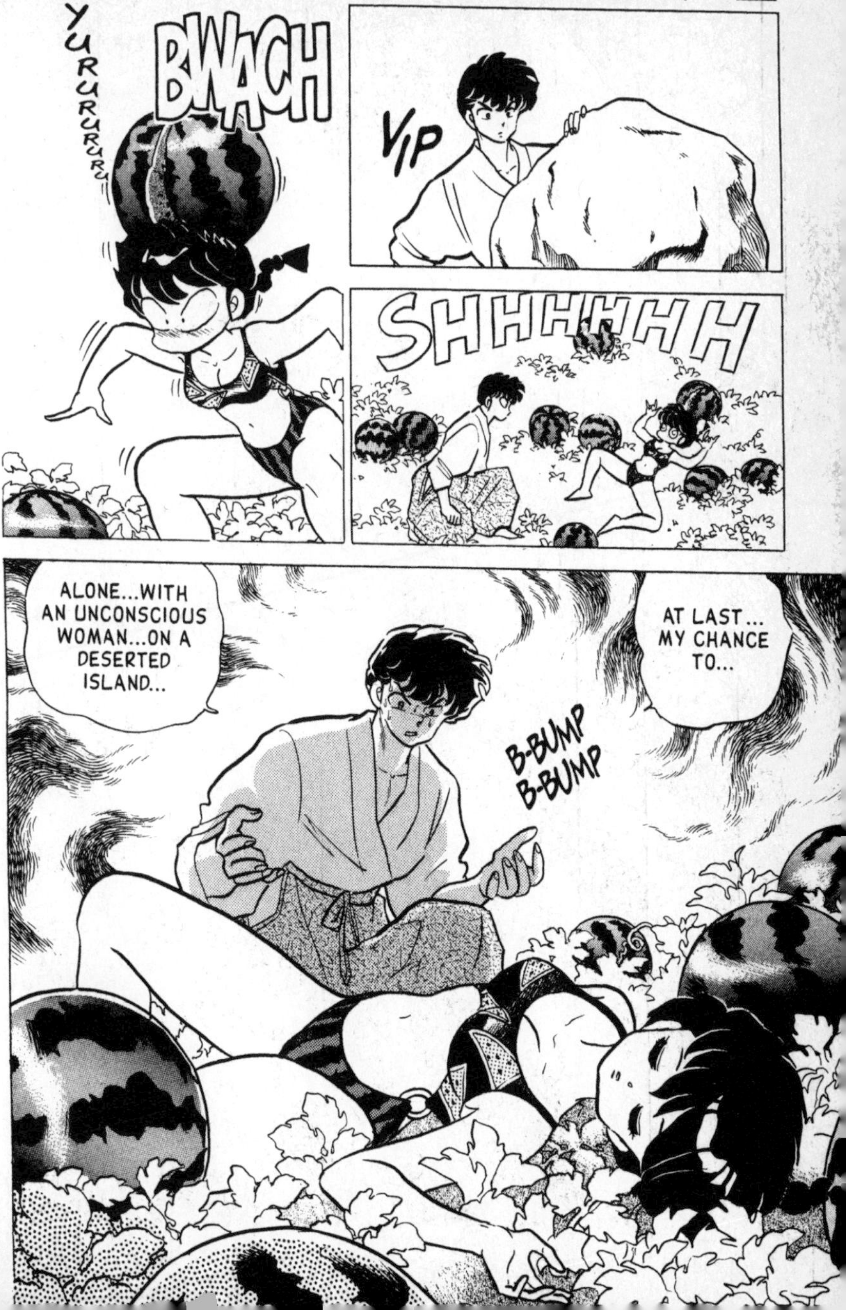
HYURURURURU
BWACH
VIP
SHHHHHH
ALONE...WITH AN UNCONSCIOUS WOMAN...ON A DESERTED ISLAND...
AT LAST... MY CHANCE TO...
B-BUMP B-BUMP

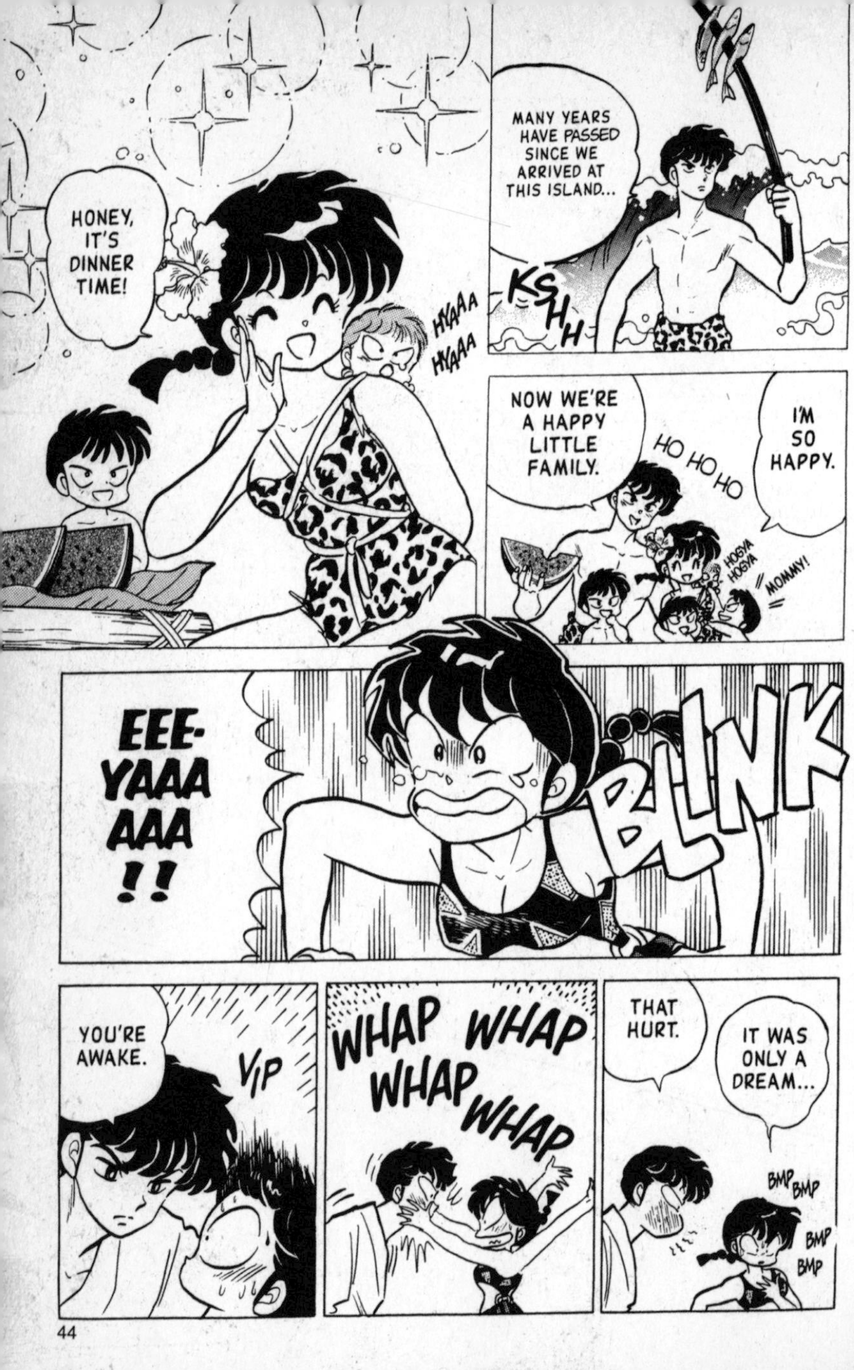
HONEY, IT'S DINNER TIME!
HYAAA HYAAA
MANY YEARS HAVE PASSED SINCE WE ARRIVED AT THIS ISLAND...
KSHH
NOW WE'RE A HAPPY LITTLE FAMILY.
HO HO HO
I'M SO HAPPY.
HOGYA HOGYA
MOMMY!
EEE-YAAAAAA!!
BLINK
YOU'RE AWAKE.
VIP
WHAP WHAP WHAP WHAP
THAT HURT.
IT WAS ONLY A DREAM...
BMP BMP BMP BMP

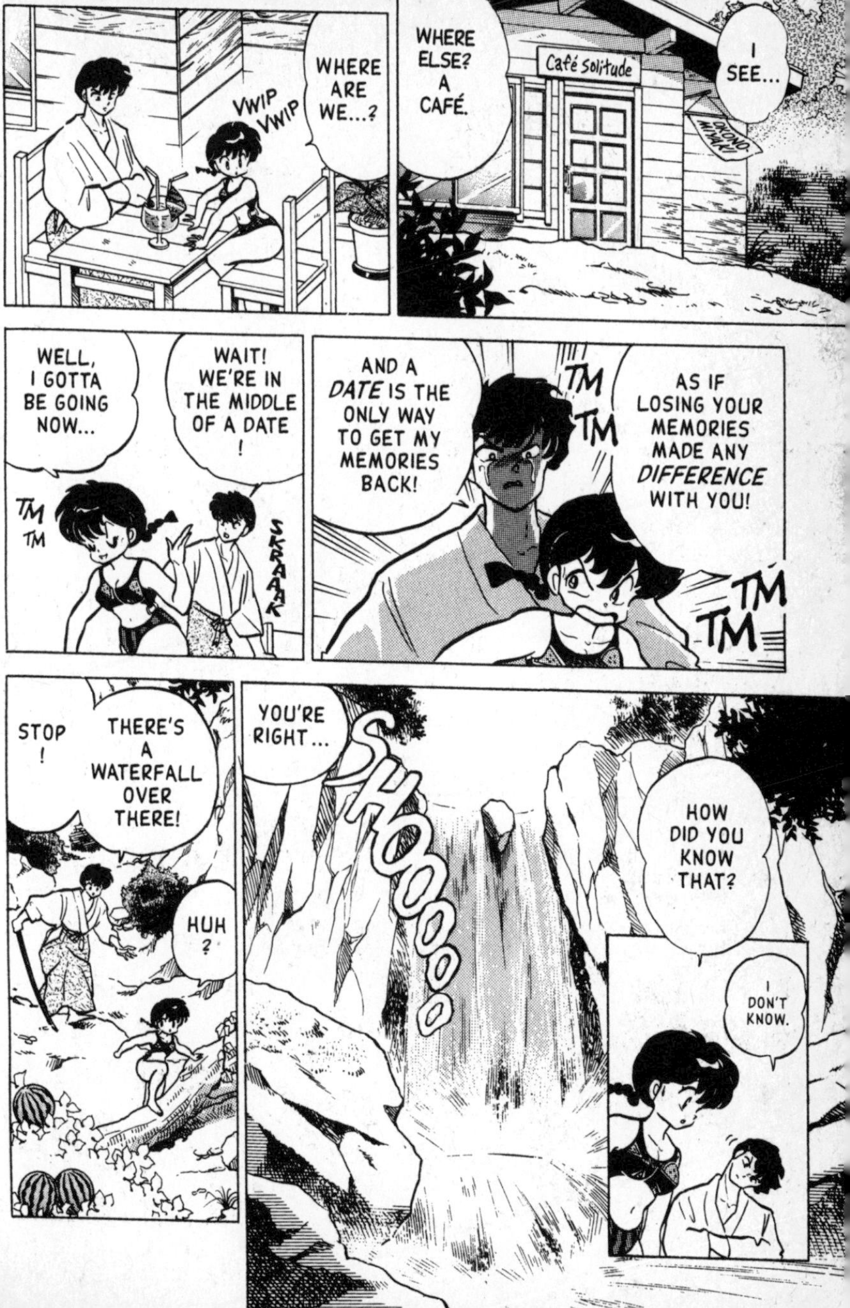
VWIP VWIP
WHERE ARE WE...?
WHERE ELSE? A CAFÉ.
Café Solitude
OKONOMIYAKI!
I SEE...
WELL, I GOTTA BE GOING NOW...
WAIT! WE'RE IN THE MIDDLE OF A DATE!
TM TM
SKRAAAK
AND A *DATE* IS THE ONLY WAY TO GET MY MEMORIES BACK!
TM TM
AS IF LOSING YOUR MEMORIES MADE ANY *DIFFERENCE* WITH YOU!
TM TM
STOP!
THERE'S A WATERFALL OVER THERE!
HUH?
YOU'RE RIGHT...
SHOOOOOO
HOW DID YOU KNOW THAT?
I DON'T KNOW.

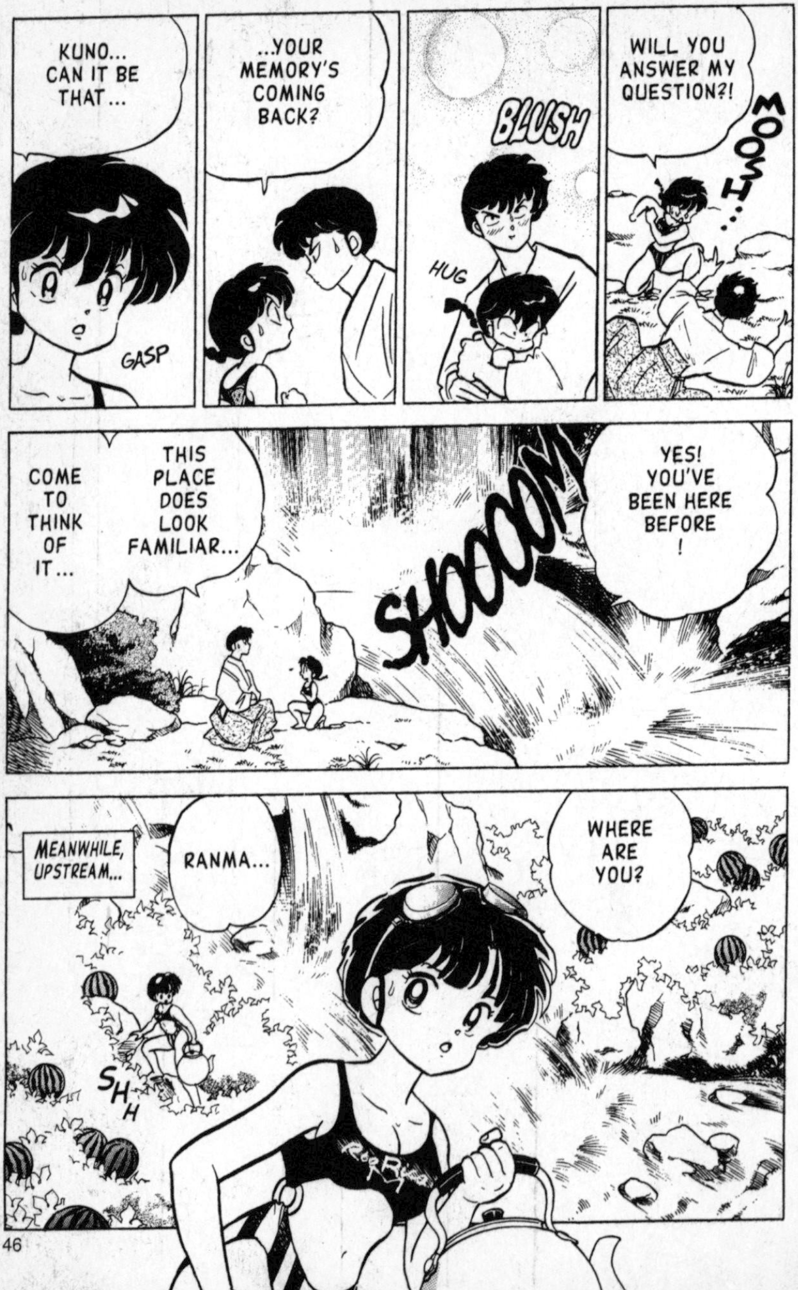
KUNO... CAN IT BE THAT...
GASP
...YOUR MEMORY'S COMING BACK?
BLUSH
HUG
WILL YOU ANSWER MY QUESTION?!
WOOSH...
COME TO THINK OF IT...
THIS PLACE DOES LOOK FAMILIAR...
SHOOOOM
YES! YOU'VE BEEN HERE BEFORE!
MEANWHILE, UPSTREAM...
RANMA...
WHERE ARE YOU?
SHH

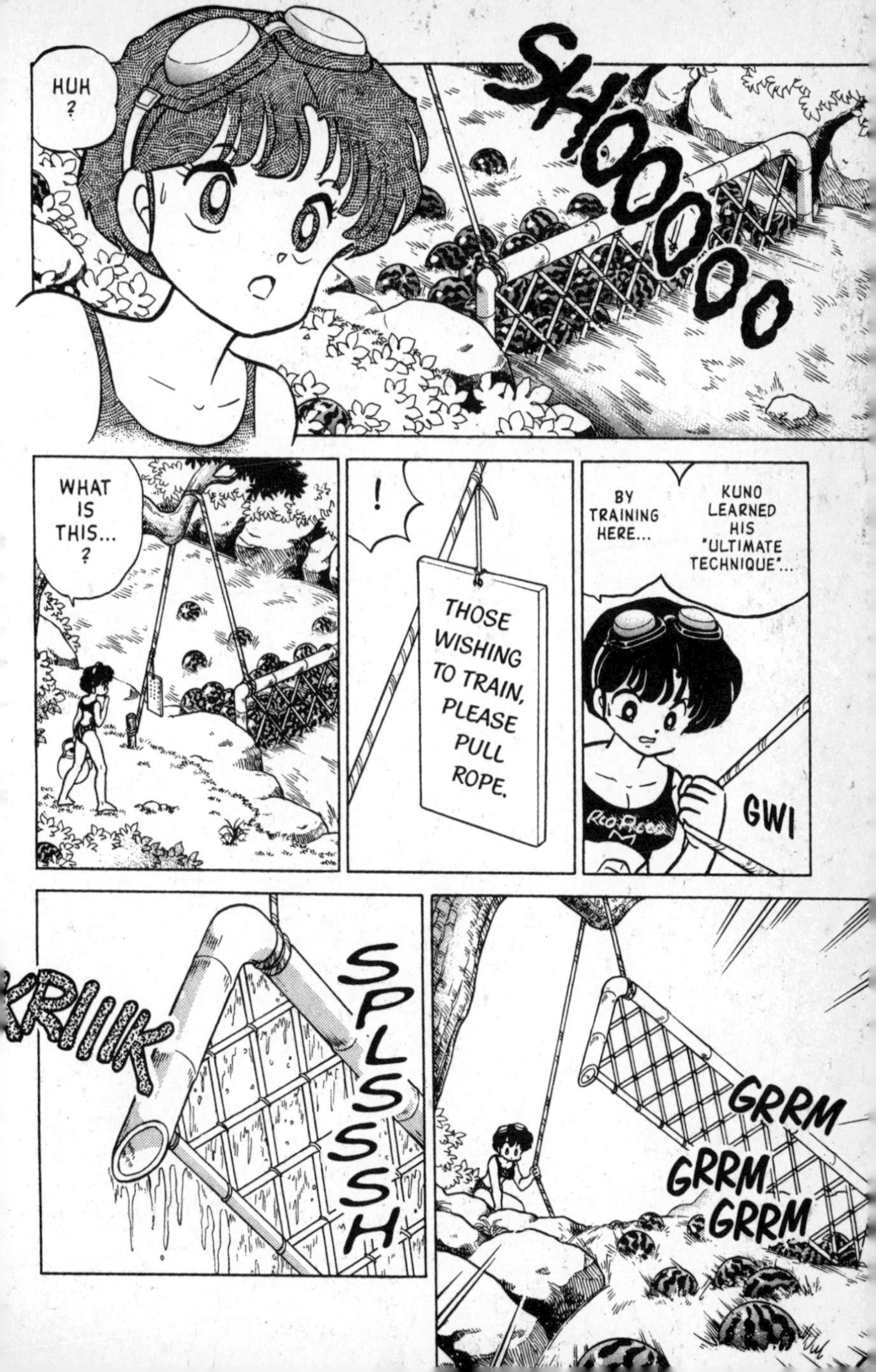
HUH?
SHOOOOOO
WHAT IS THIS...?
!
THOSE WISHING TO TRAIN, PLEASE PULL ROPE.
BY TRAINING HERE...
KUNO LEARNED HIS "ULTIMATE TECHNIQUE"...
GWI
KRIIIK
SPLSSSH
GRRM
GRRM
GRRM

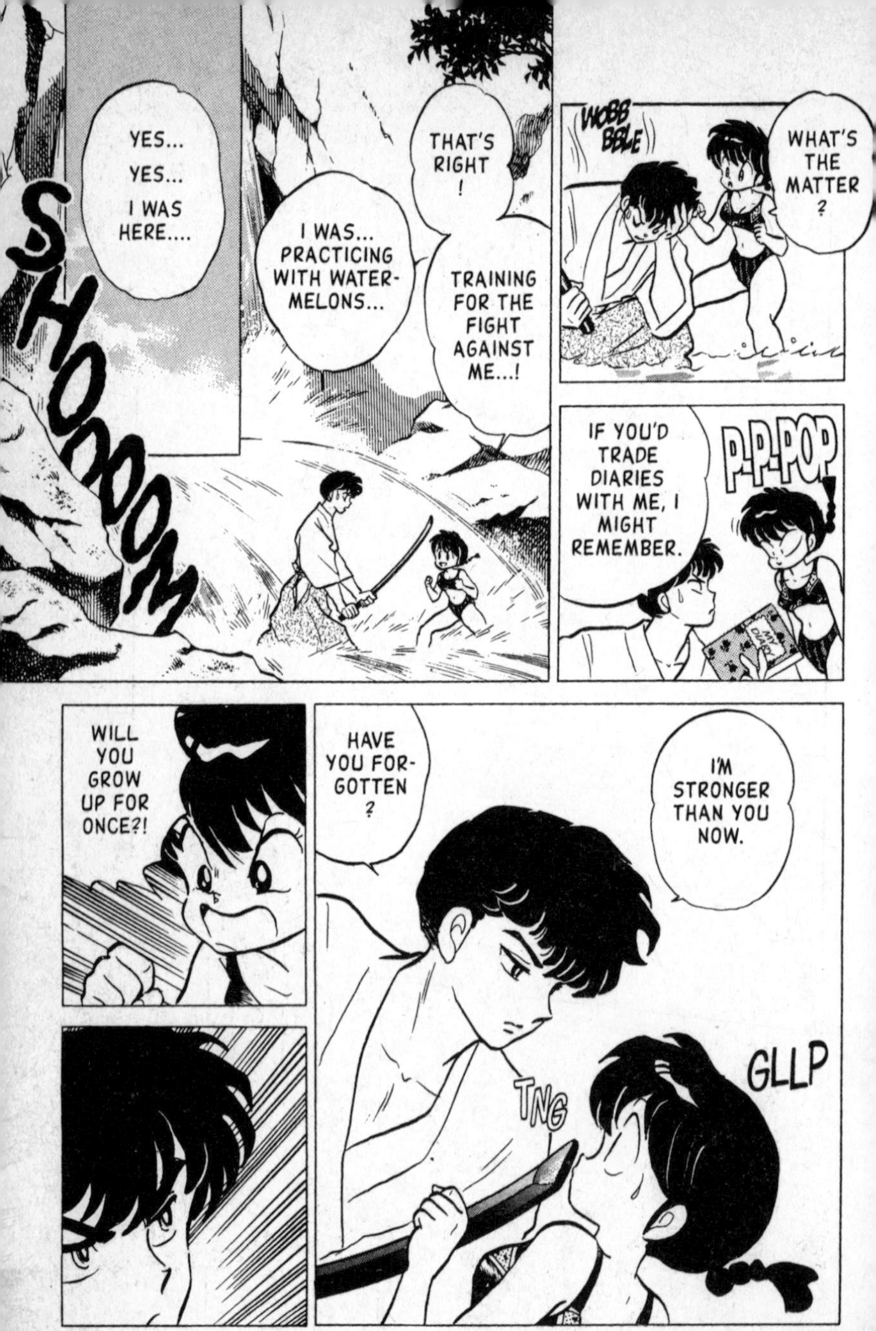
SHOOOOM
YES... YES... I WAS HERE....
THAT'S RIGHT!
I WAS... PRACTICING WITH WATER-MELONS...
TRAINING FOR THE FIGHT AGAINST ME...!
WOBBBBLE
WHAT'S THE MATTER?
IF YOU'D TRADE DIARIES WITH ME, I MIGHT REMEMBER.
P-P-POP
MY DIARY
WILL YOU GROW UP FOR ONCE?!
HAVE YOU FOR-GOTTEN?
I'M STRONGER THAN YOU NOW.
TNG
GLLP

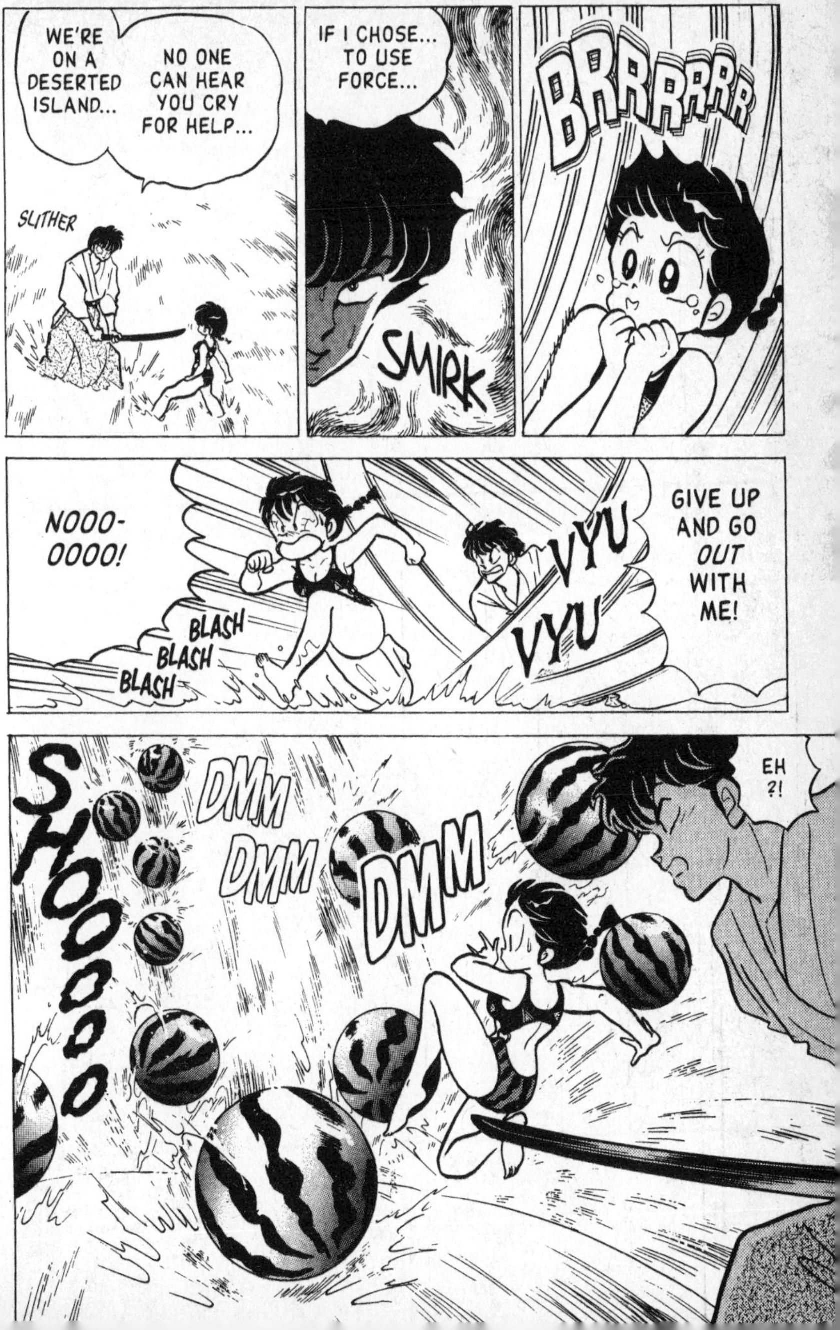
WE'RE ON A DESERTED ISLAND...
NO ONE CAN HEAR YOU CRY FOR HELP...
SLITHER
IF I CHOSE... TO USE FORCE...
SMIRK
BRRRRRR
NOOO-OOOO!
BLASH
BLASH
BLASH
VYU
VYU
GIVE UP AND GO *OUT* WITH ME!
SHOOOOOO
DMM
DMM
DMM
EH ?!

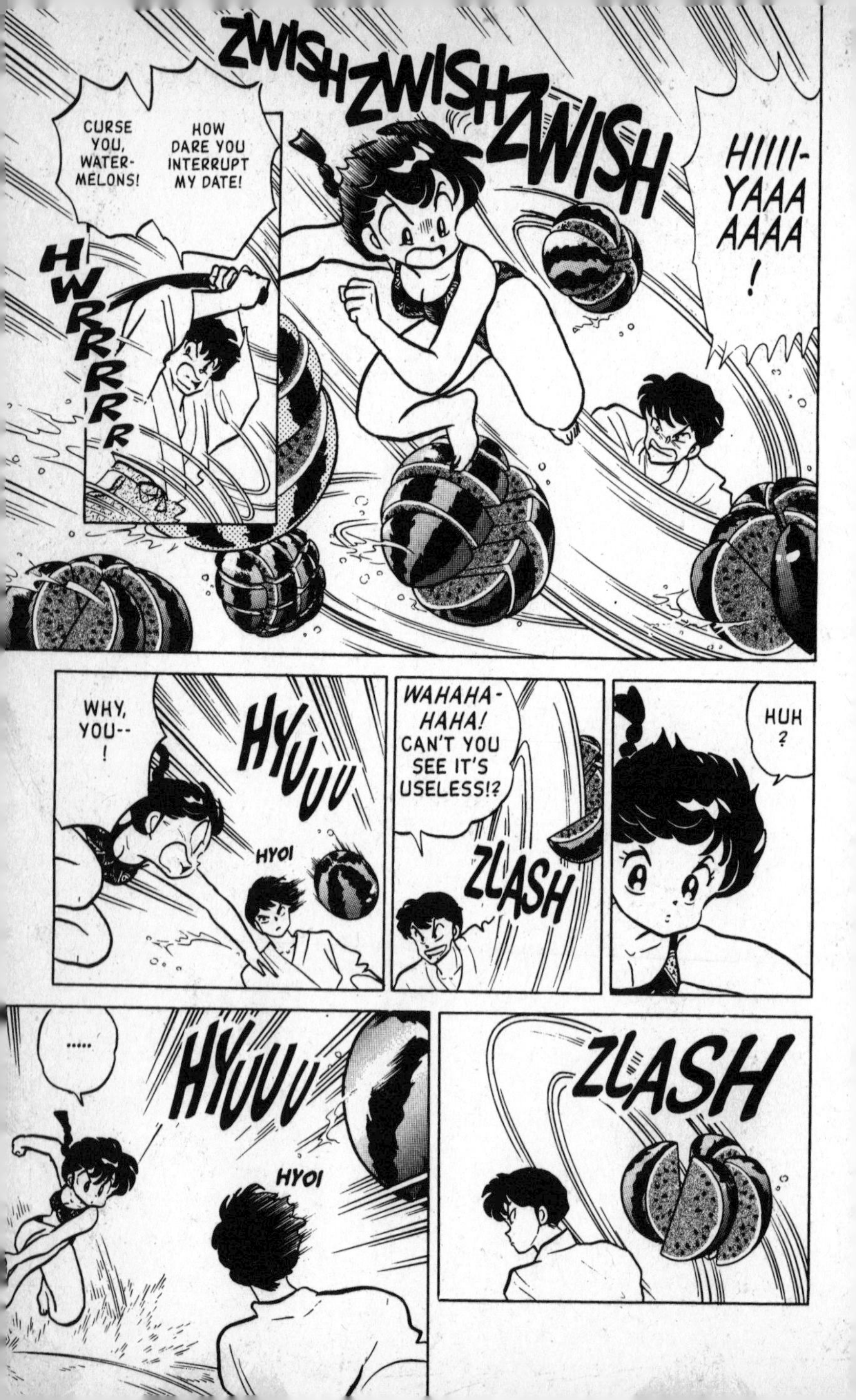
CURSE YOU, WATER-MELONS!
HOW DARE YOU INTERRUPT MY DATE!
ZWISH ZWISH ZWISH ZWISH
HIIII-YAAAAAAA!
HWRRRRRR
WHY, YOU--!
HYUUUU
HYOI
WAHAHA-HAHA! CAN'T YOU SEE IT'S USELESS!?
ZLASH
HUH?
......
HYUUUU
HYOI
ZLASH

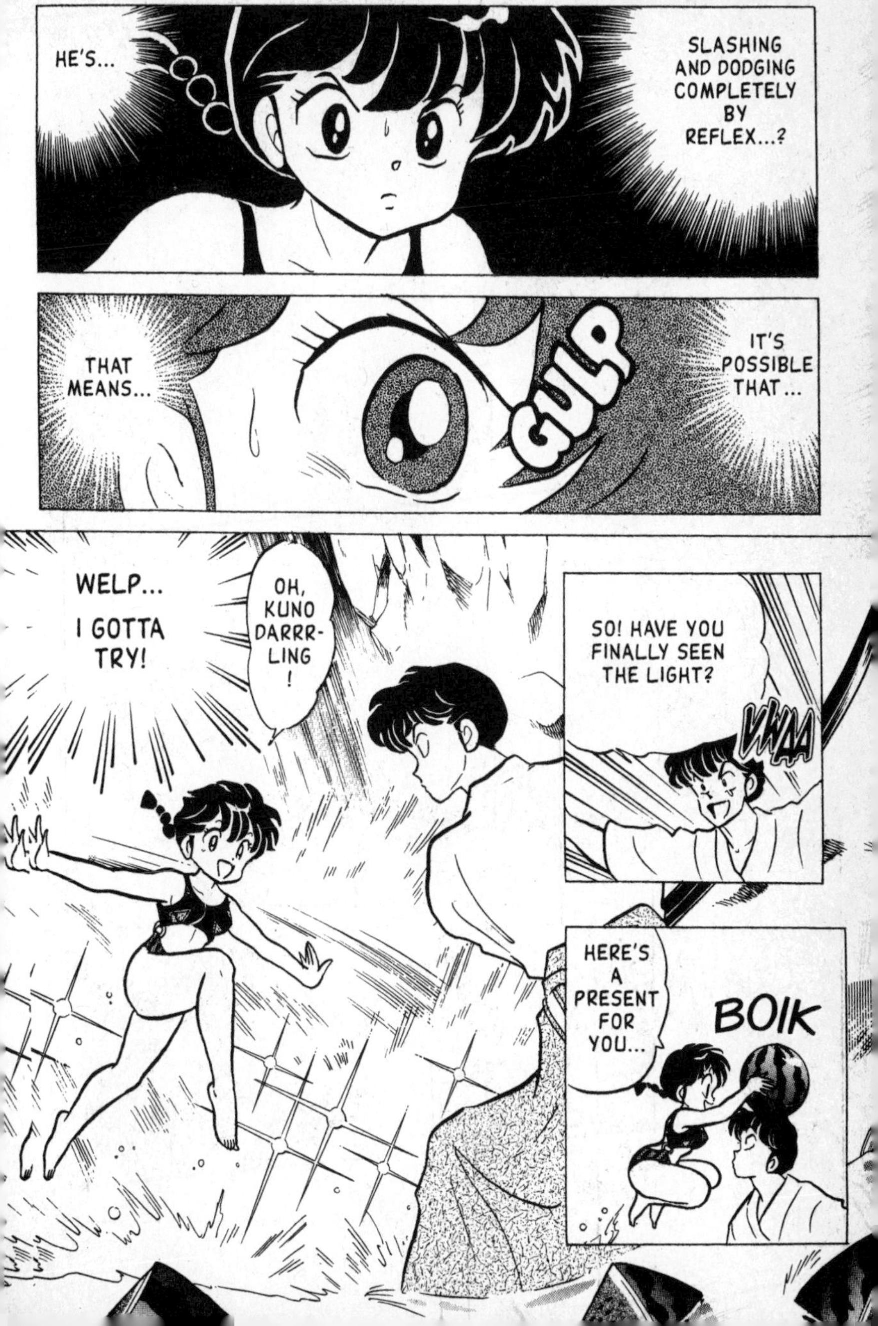
HE'S...
SLASHING AND DODGING COMPLETELY BY REFLEX...?
THAT MEANS...
GULP
IT'S POSSIBLE THAT...
WELP... I GOTTA TRY!
OH, KUNO DARRR-LING!
SO! HAVE YOU FINALLY SEEN THE LIGHT?
VWAA
HERE'S A PRESENT FOR YOU...
BOIK

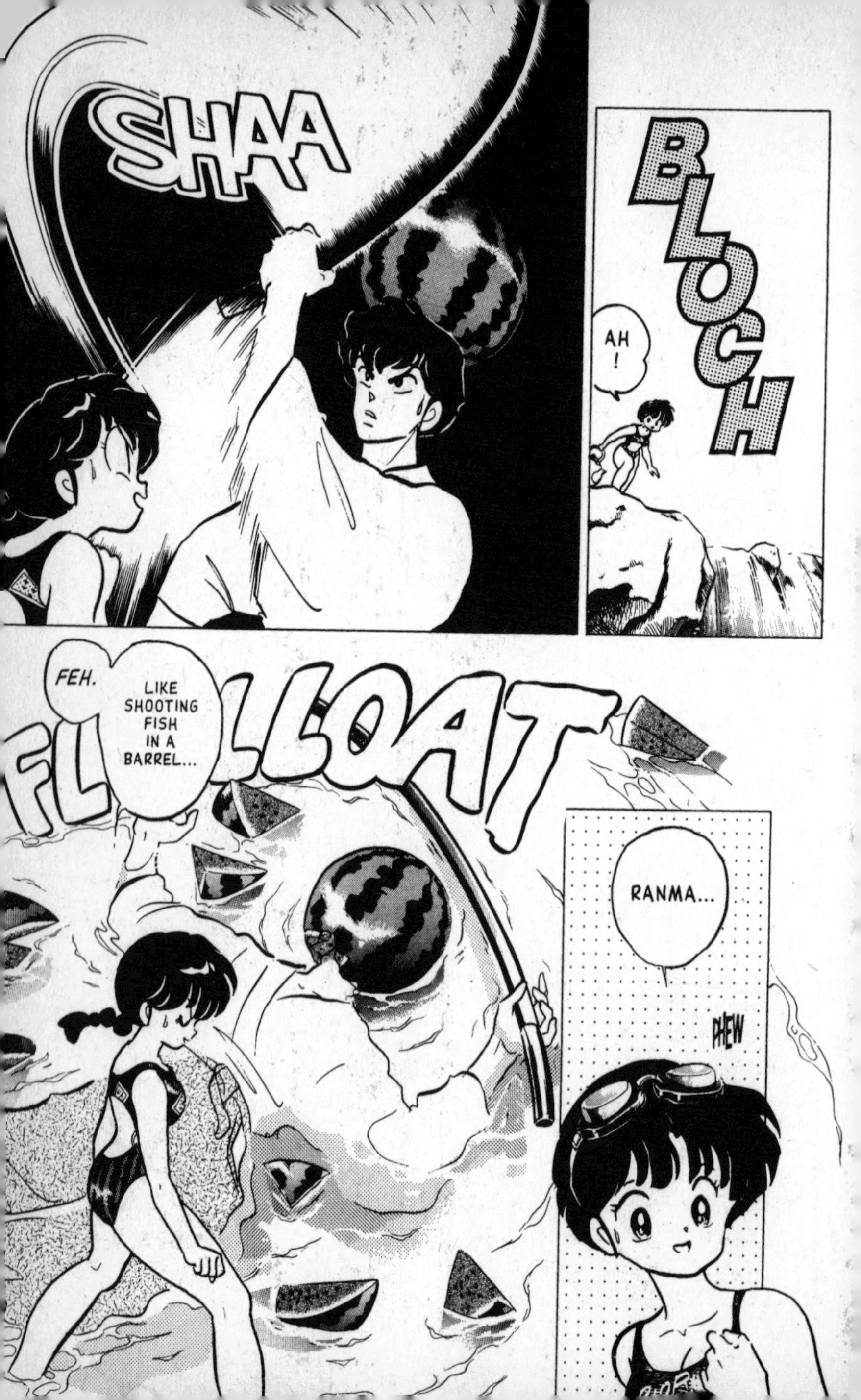
SHAA
BLOCH
AH!
FEH.
LIKE SHOOTING FISH IN A BARREL...
FLLOAT
RANMA...
PHEW

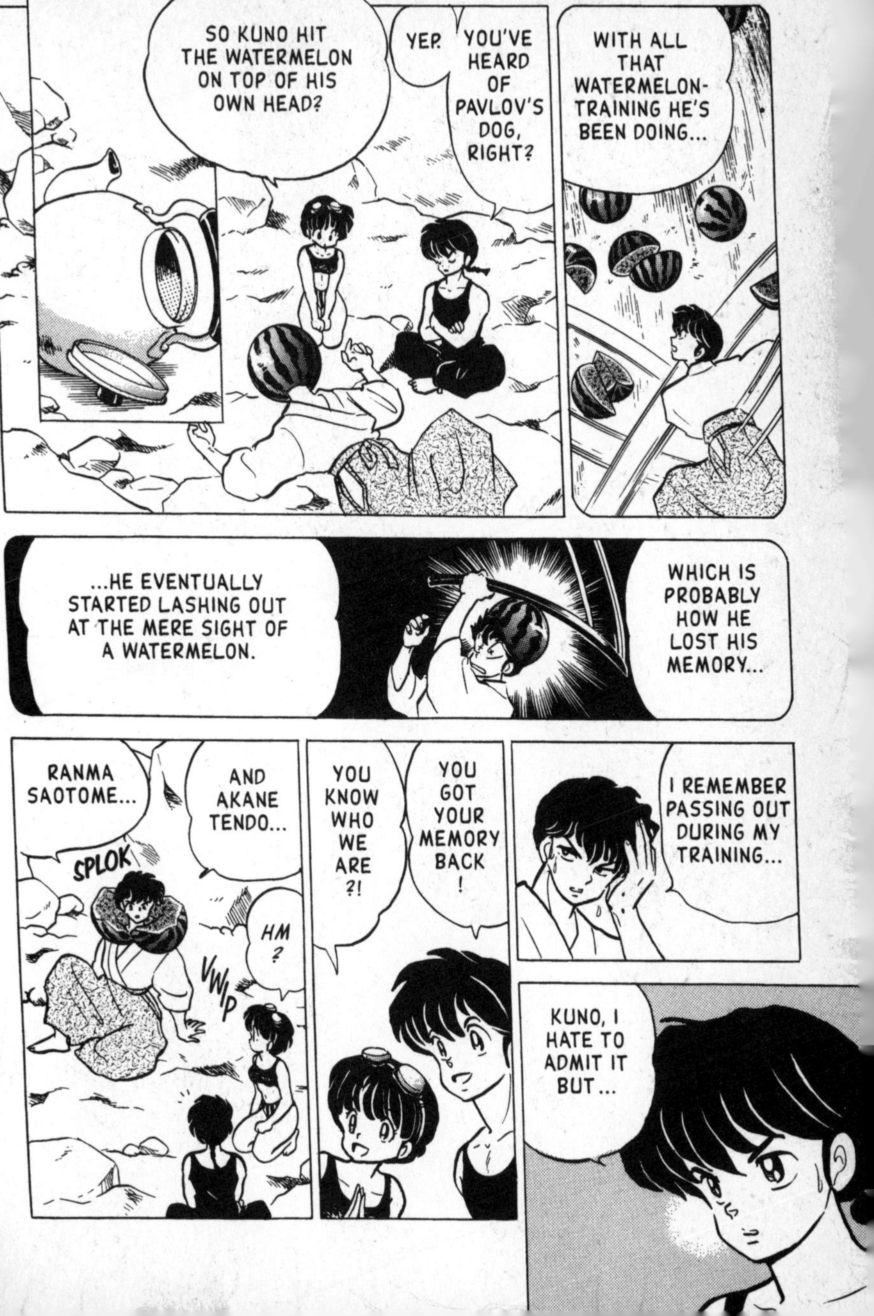
SO KUNO HIT THE WATERMELON ON TOP OF HIS OWN HEAD?
YEP.
YOU'VE HEARD OF PAVLOV'S DOG, RIGHT?
WITH ALL THAT WATERMELON-TRAINING HE'S BEEN DOING...
...HE EVENTUALLY STARTED LASHING OUT AT THE MERE SIGHT OF A WATERMELON.
WHICH IS PROBABLY HOW HE LOST HIS MEMORY...
RANMA SAOTOME...
AND AKANE TENDO...
SPLOK
HM?
VWIP
YOU KNOW WHO WE ARE?!
YOU GOT YOUR MEMORY BACK!
I REMEMBER PASSING OUT DURING MY TRAINING...
KUNO, I HATE TO ADMIT IT BUT...

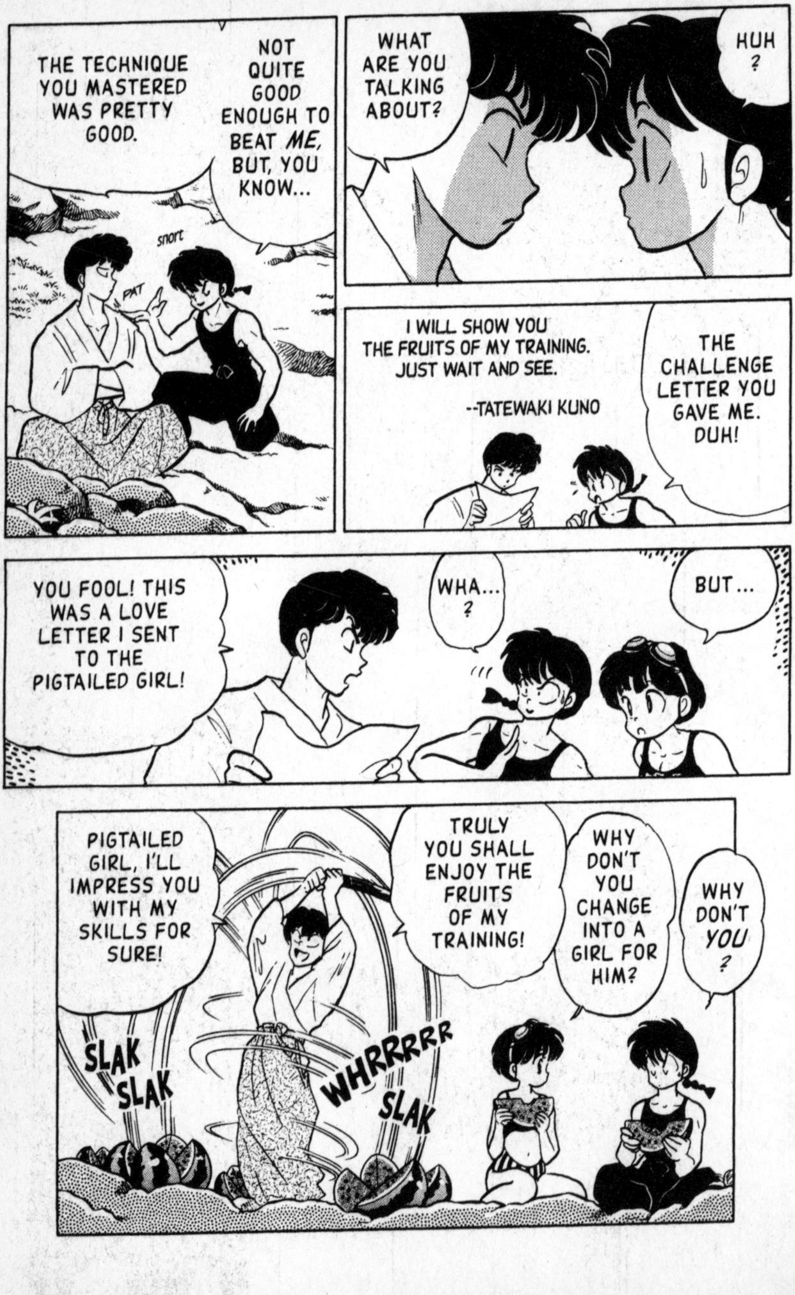
THE TECHNIQUE YOU MASTERED WAS PRETTY GOOD.
NOT QUITE GOOD ENOUGH TO BEAT *ME*, BUT, YOU KNOW...
snort
PAT
WHAT ARE YOU TALKING ABOUT?
HUH?
I WILL SHOW YOU THE FRUITS OF MY TRAINING. JUST WAIT AND SEE.
--TATEWAKI KUNO
THE CHALLENGE LETTER YOU GAVE ME. DUH!
YOU FOOL! THIS WAS A LOVE LETTER I SENT TO THE PIGTAILED GIRL!
WHA...?
BUT...
PIGTAILED GIRL, I'LL IMPRESS YOU WITH MY SKILLS FOR SURE!
TRULY YOU SHALL ENJOY THE FRUITS OF MY TRAINING!
WHY DON'T YOU CHANGE INTO A GIRL FOR HIM?
WHY DON'T *YOU*?
SLAK
SLAK
WHRRRRR
SLAK

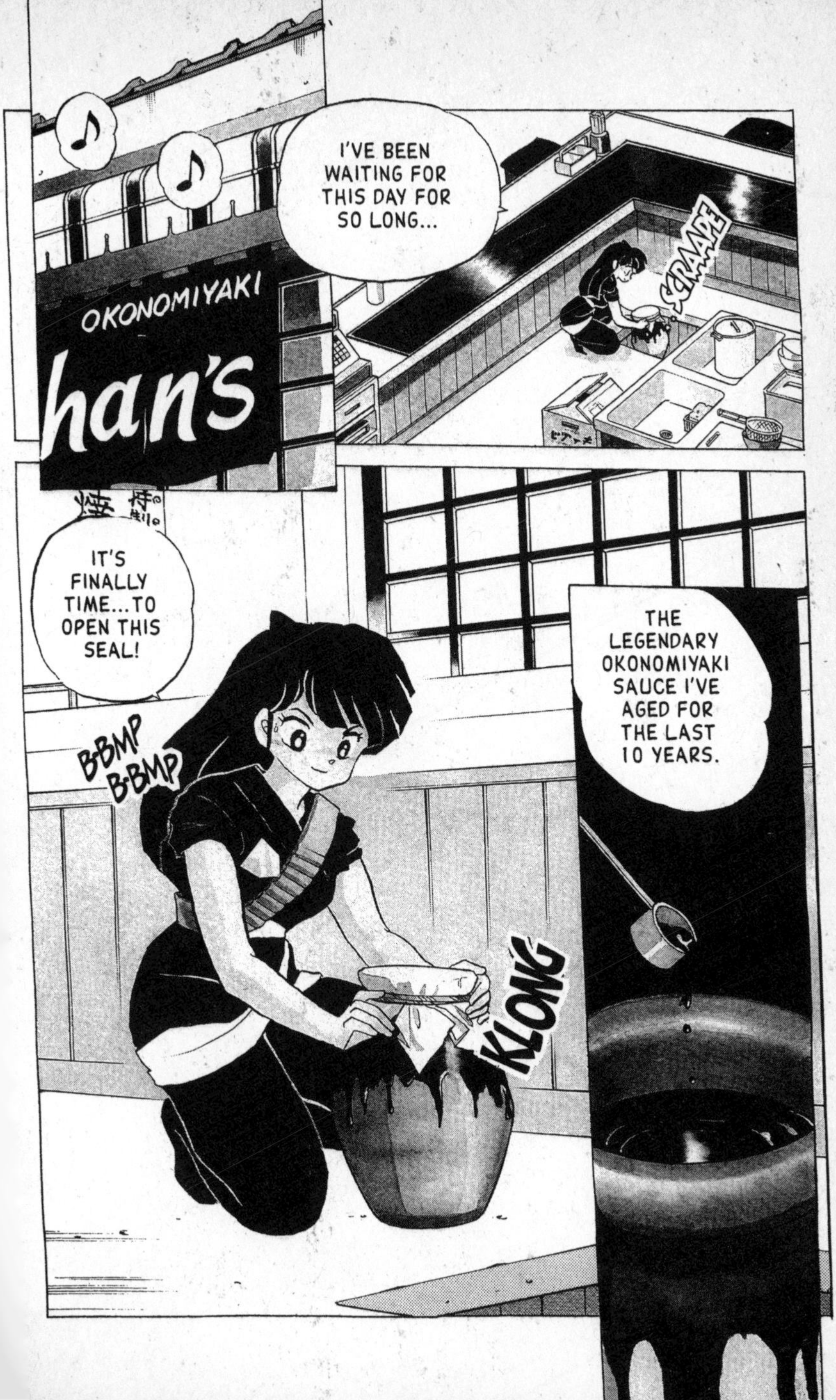

OKONOMIYAKI
han's
I'VE BEEN WAITING FOR THIS DAY FOR SO LONG...
SCRAAAPE
IT'S FINALLY TIME...TO OPEN THIS SEAL!
B-BMP B-BMP
KLONG
THE LEGENDARY OKONOMIYAKI SAUCE I'VE AGED FOR THE LAST 10 YEARS.

Part 4

THE SAUCE OF TEN YEARS

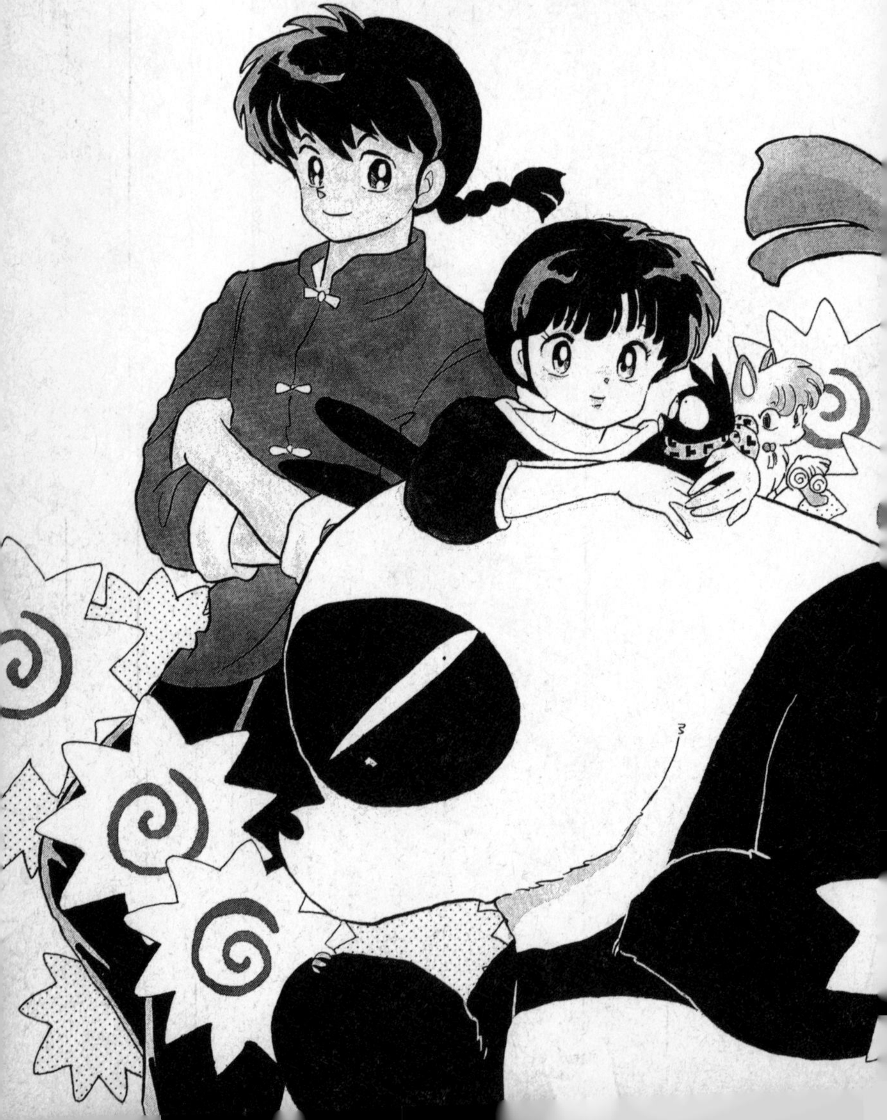

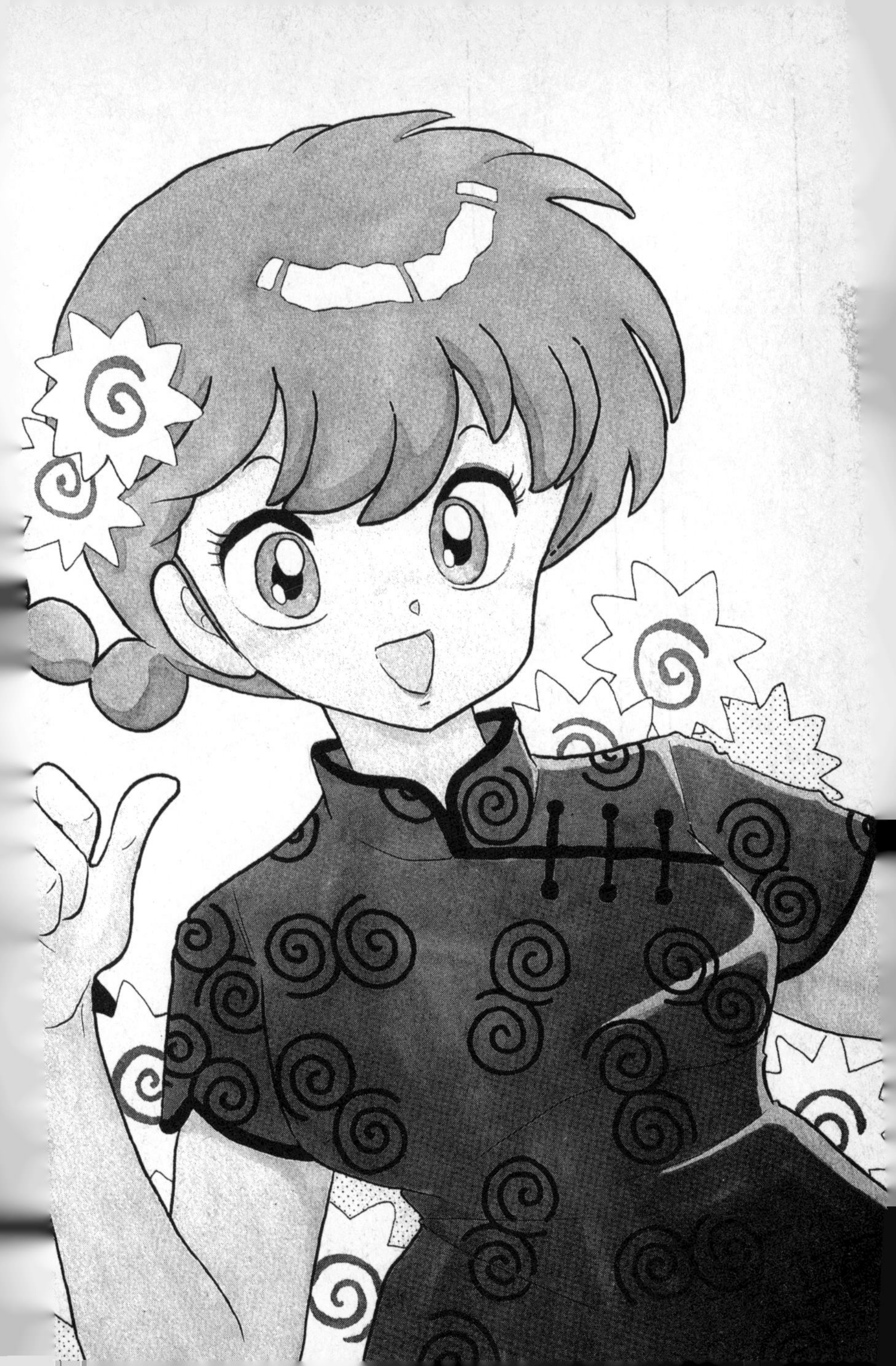

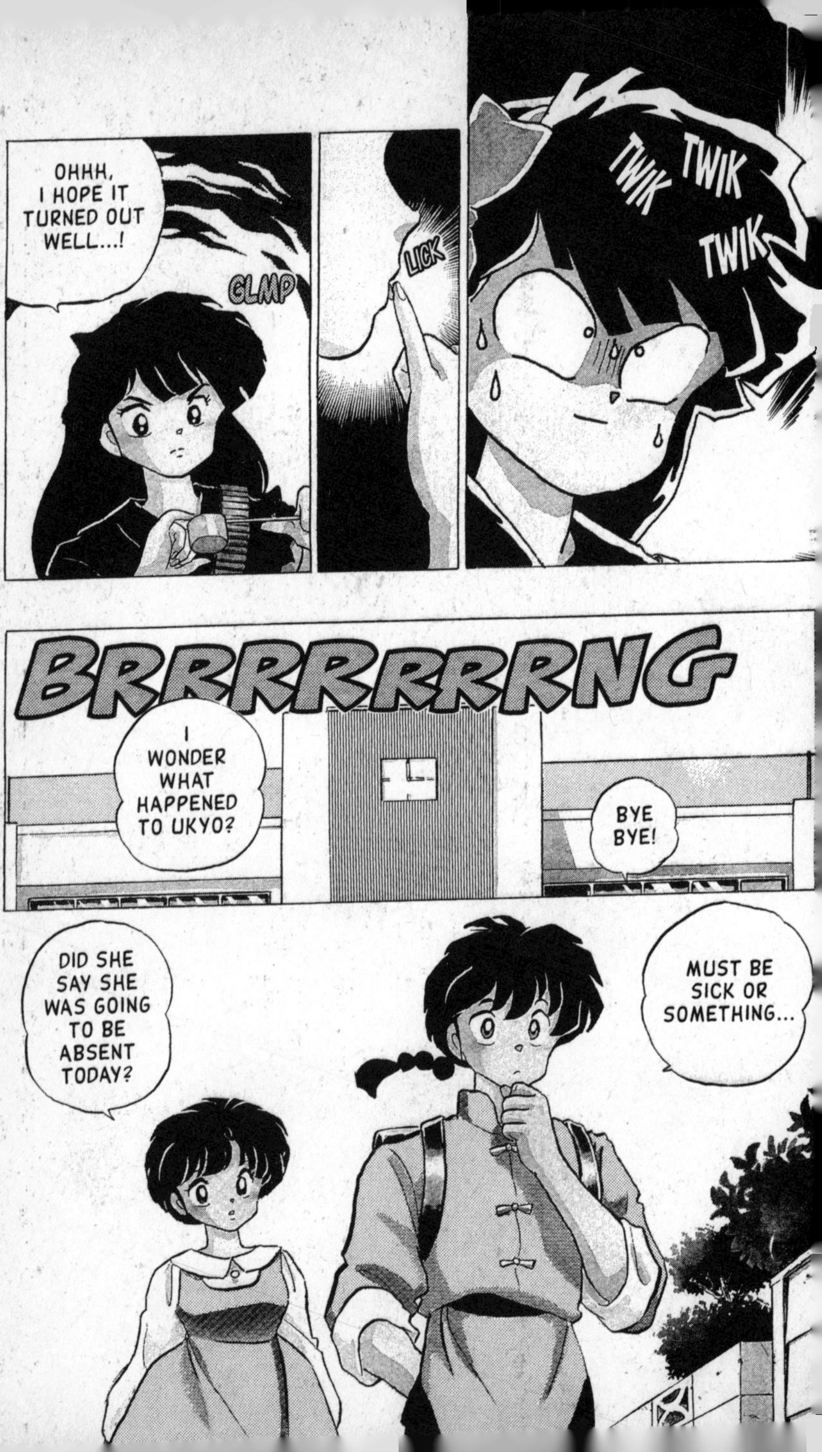
OHHH, I HOPE IT TURNED OUT WELL...!
GLMP
LICK
TWIK
TWIK
TWIK
BRRRRRRRNG
I WONDER WHAT HAPPENED TO UKYO?
BYE BYE!
DID SHE SAY SHE WAS GOING TO BE ABSENT TODAY?
MUST BE SICK OR SOMETHING...

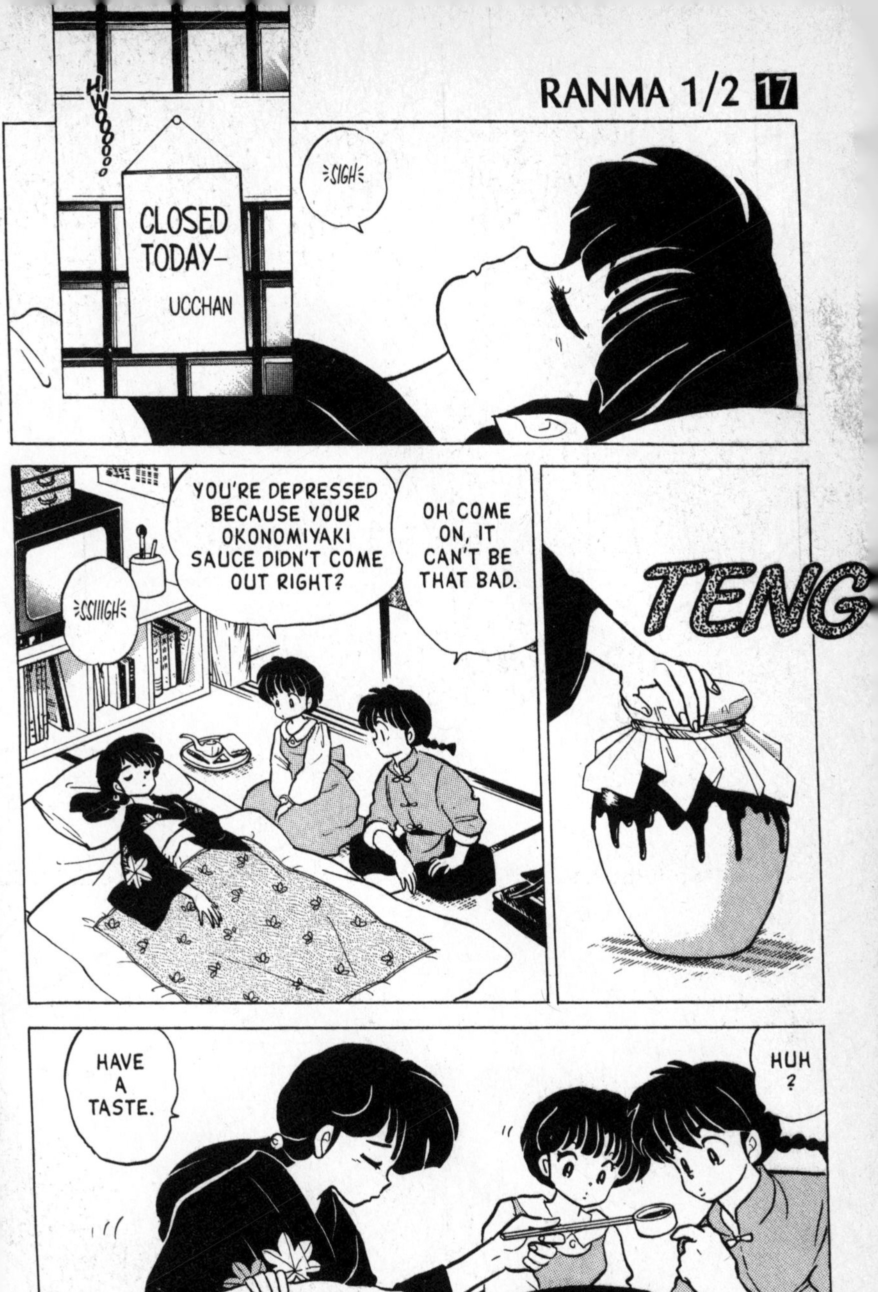
HWOOOOOOO
CLOSED TODAY- UCCHAN
SIGH
SSIIIGH
YOU'RE DEPRESSED BECAUSE YOUR OKONOMIYAKI SAUCE DIDN'T COME OUT RIGHT?
OH COME ON, IT CAN'T BE THAT BAD.
TENG
HAVE A TASTE.
HUH?

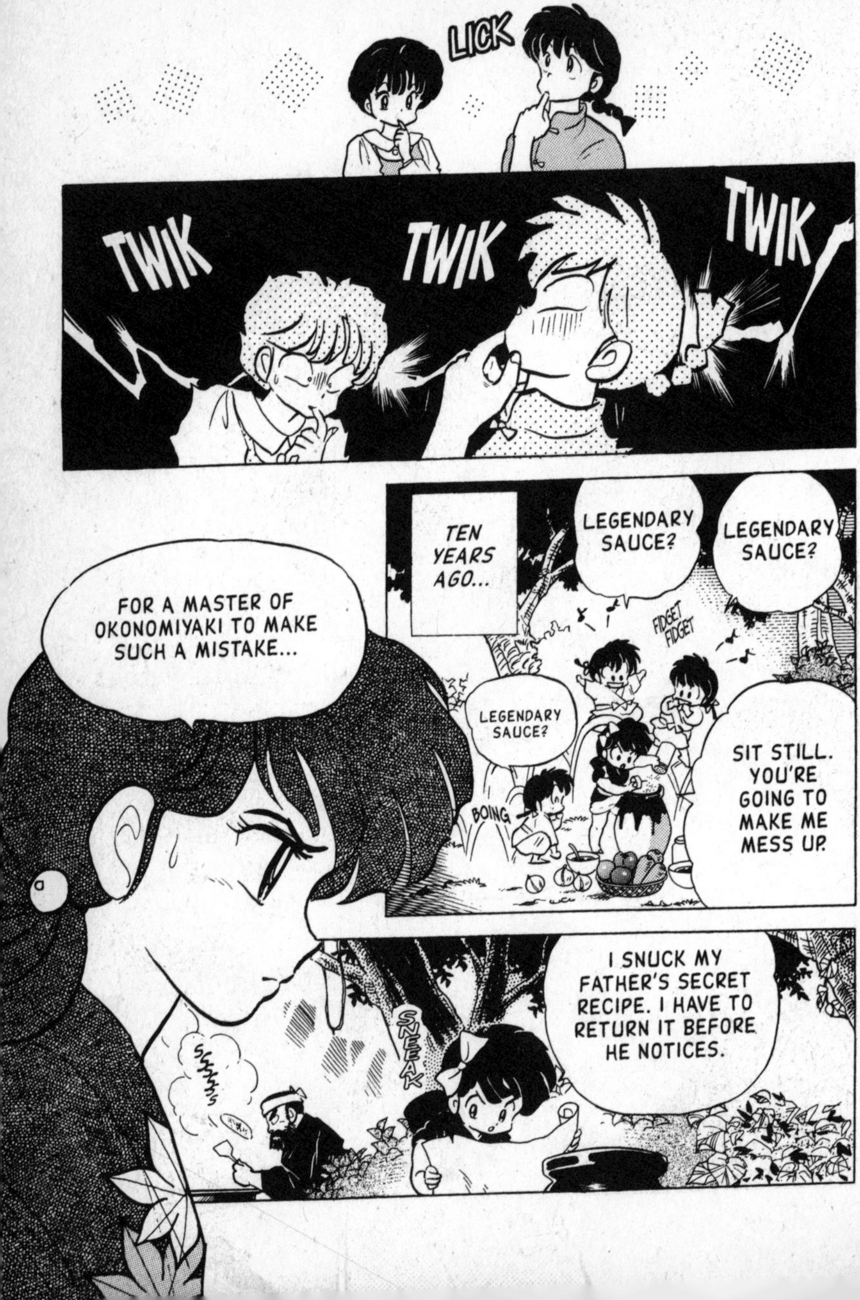
LICK
TWIK
TWIK
TWIK
FOR A MASTER OF OKONOMIYAKI TO MAKE SUCH A MISTAKE...
TEN YEARS AGO...
LEGENDARY SAUCE?
LEGENDARY SAUCE?
FIDGET FIDGET
LEGENDARY SAUCE?
BOING
SIT STILL. YOU'RE GOING TO MAKE ME MESS UP.
SNEEAK
I SNUCK MY FATHER'S SECRET RECIPE. I HAVE TO RETURN IT BEFORE HE NOTICES.

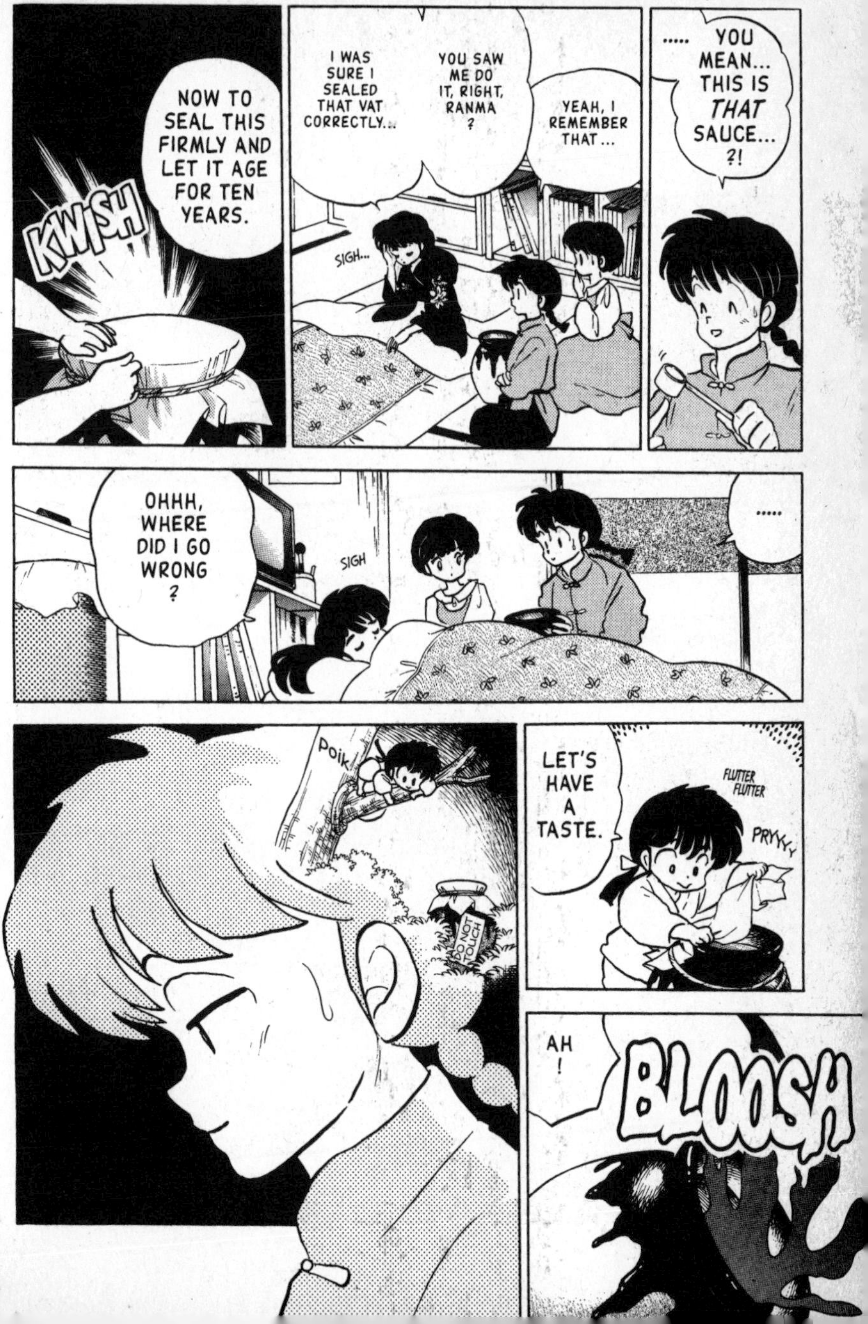
NOW TO SEAL THIS FIRMLY AND LET IT AGE FOR TEN YEARS.
KWISH
I WAS SURE I SEALED THAT VAT CORRECTLY...
YOU SAW ME DO IT, RIGHT, RANMA ?
SIGH...
YEAH, I REMEMBER THAT...
..... YOU MEAN... THIS IS THAT SAUCE... ?!
OHHH, WHERE DID I GO WRONG ?
SIGH
.....
Poik
DO NOT TOUCH
LET'S HAVE A TASTE.
FLUTTER FLUTTER
PRYYYY
AH !
BLOOSH

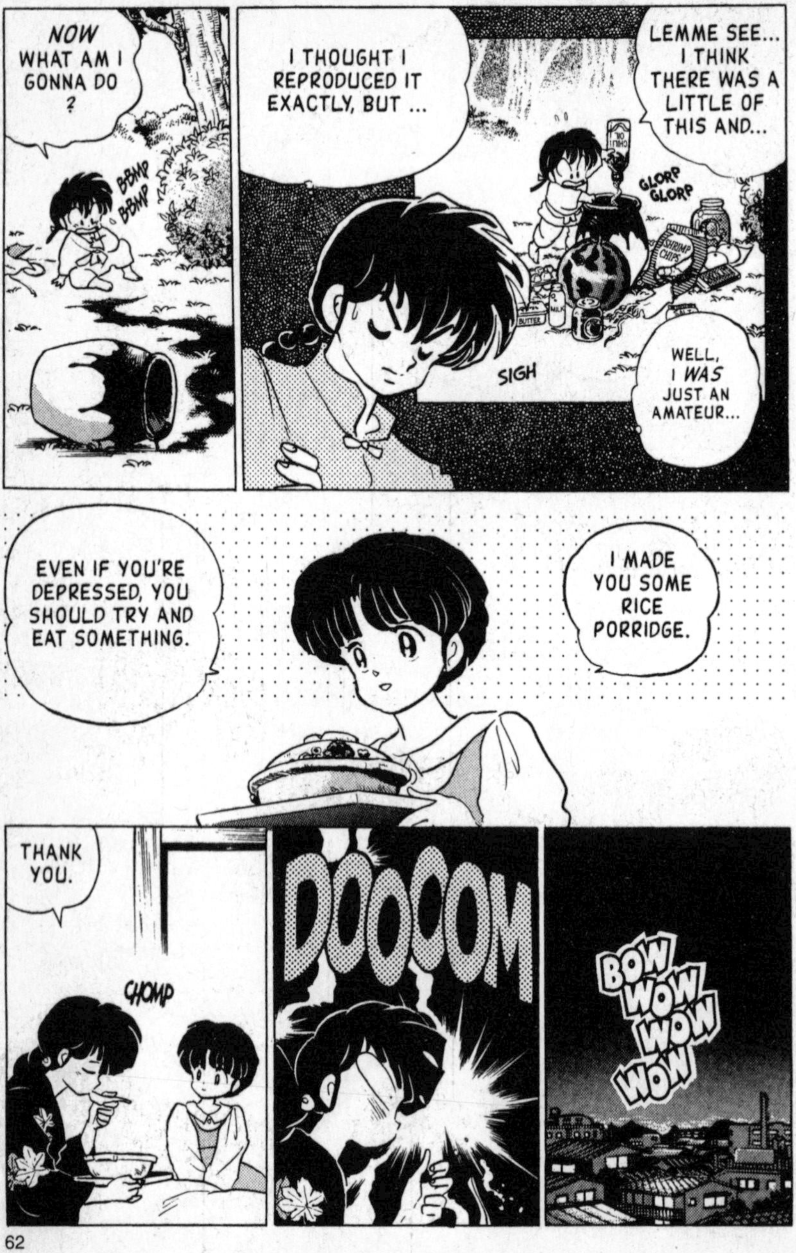
NOW WHAT AM I GONNA DO ?
B-BMP B-BMP
I THOUGHT I REPRODUCED IT EXACTLY, BUT ...
LEMME SEE... I THINK THERE WAS A LITTLE OF THIS AND...
CHILI OIL
GLORP GLORP
SHRIMP CHIPS
BUTTER
MILK
SIGH
WELL, I WAS JUST AN AMATEUR...
EVEN IF YOU'RE DEPRESSED, YOU SHOULD TRY AND EAT SOMETHING.
I MADE YOU SOME RICE PORRIDGE.
THANK YOU.
CHOMP
DOOOOM
BOW WOW WOW WOW

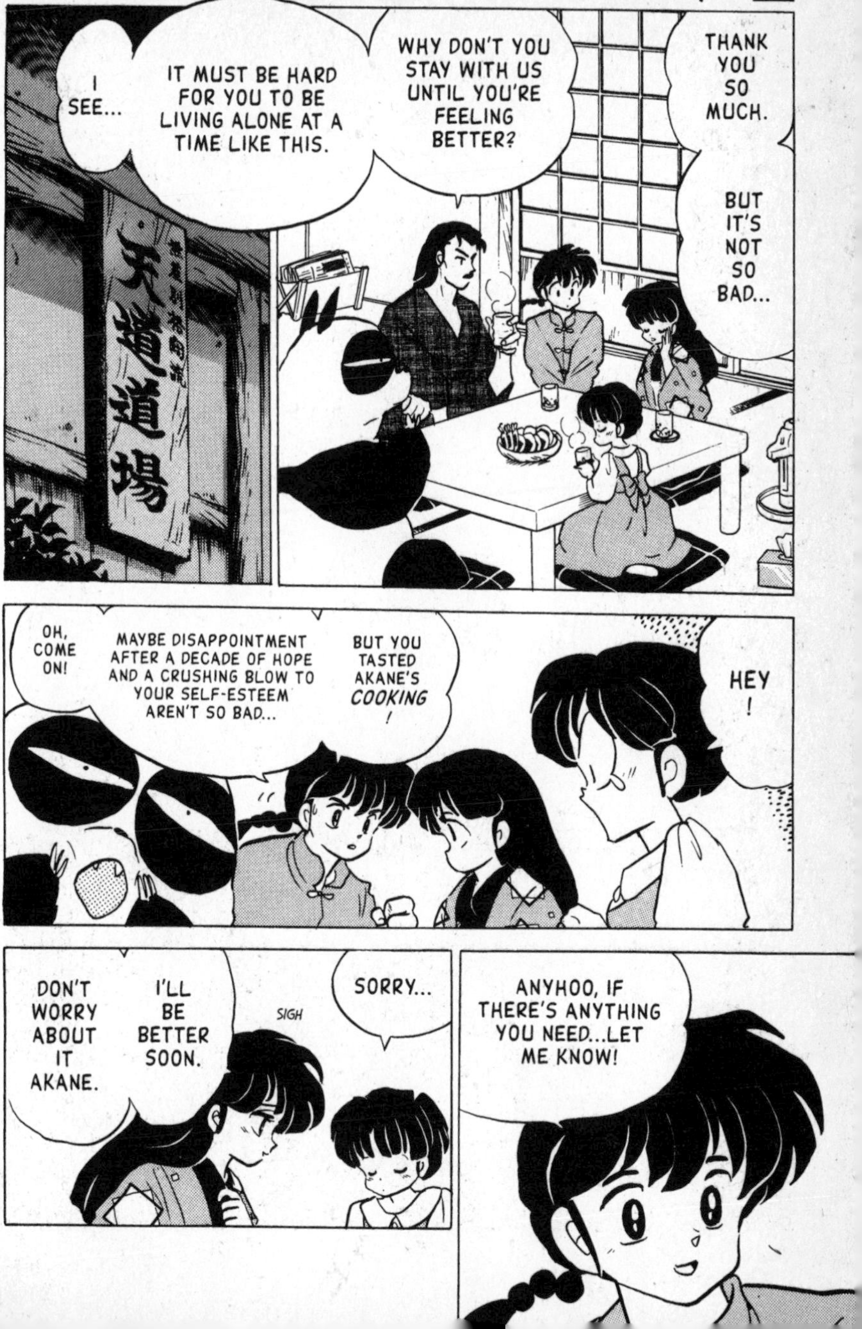
I SEE...
IT MUST BE HARD FOR YOU TO BE LIVING ALONE AT A TIME LIKE THIS.
WHY DON'T YOU STAY WITH US UNTIL YOU'RE FEELING BETTER?
THANK YOU SO MUCH.
BUT IT'S NOT SO BAD...
天道道場
OH, COME ON!
MAYBE DISAPPOINTMENT AFTER A DECADE OF HOPE AND A CRUSHING BLOW TO YOUR SELF-ESTEEM AREN'T SO BAD...
BUT YOU TASTED AKANE'S *COOKING*!
HEY!
DON'T WORRY ABOUT IT AKANE.
I'LL BE BETTER SOON.
SIGH
SORRY...
ANYHOO, IF THERE'S ANYTHING YOU NEED...LET ME KNOW!

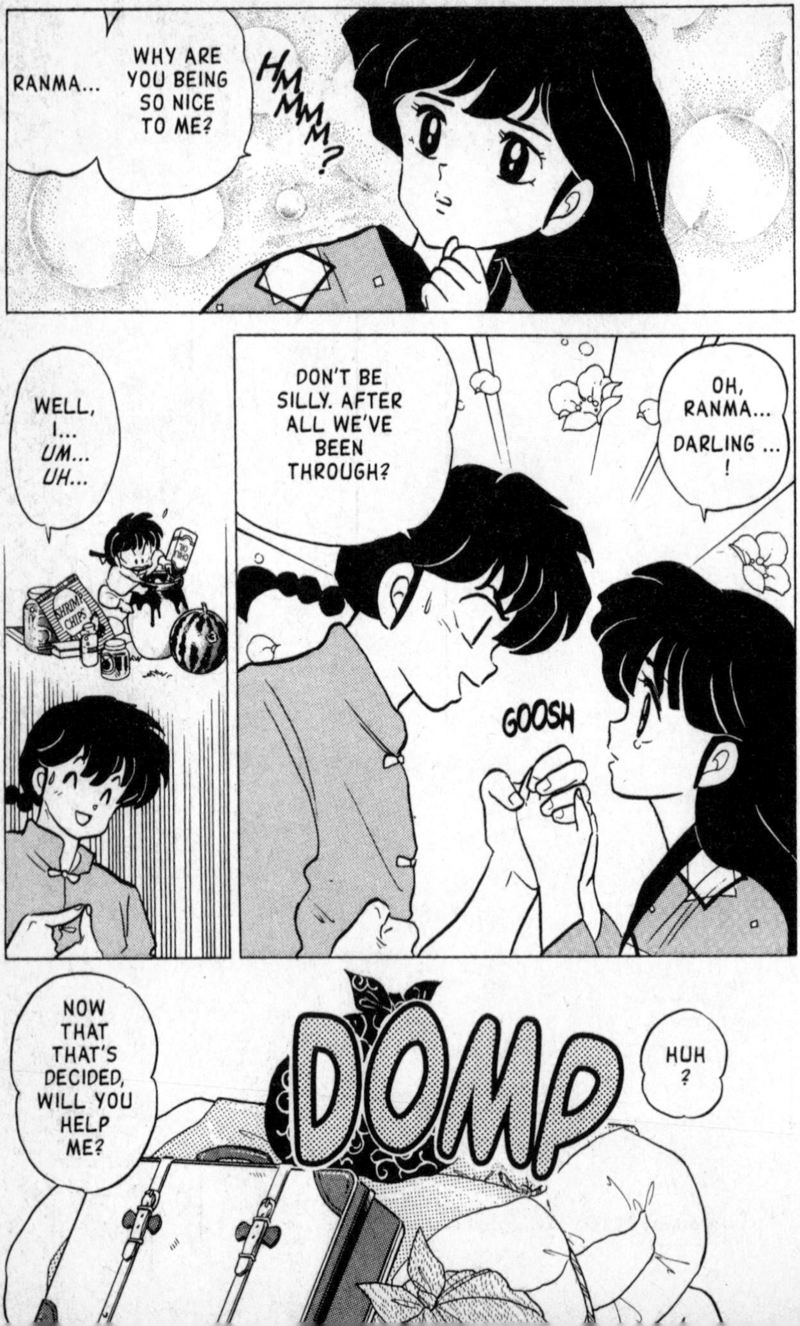
RANMA... WHY ARE YOU BEING SO NICE TO ME?
HMMMM?
WELL, I... UM... UH...
SHRIMP CHIPS
DON'T BE SILLY. AFTER ALL WE'VE BEEN THROUGH?
OH, RANMA... DARLING ...!
GOOSH
NOW THAT THAT'S DECIDED, WILL YOU HELP ME?
DOMP
HUH?

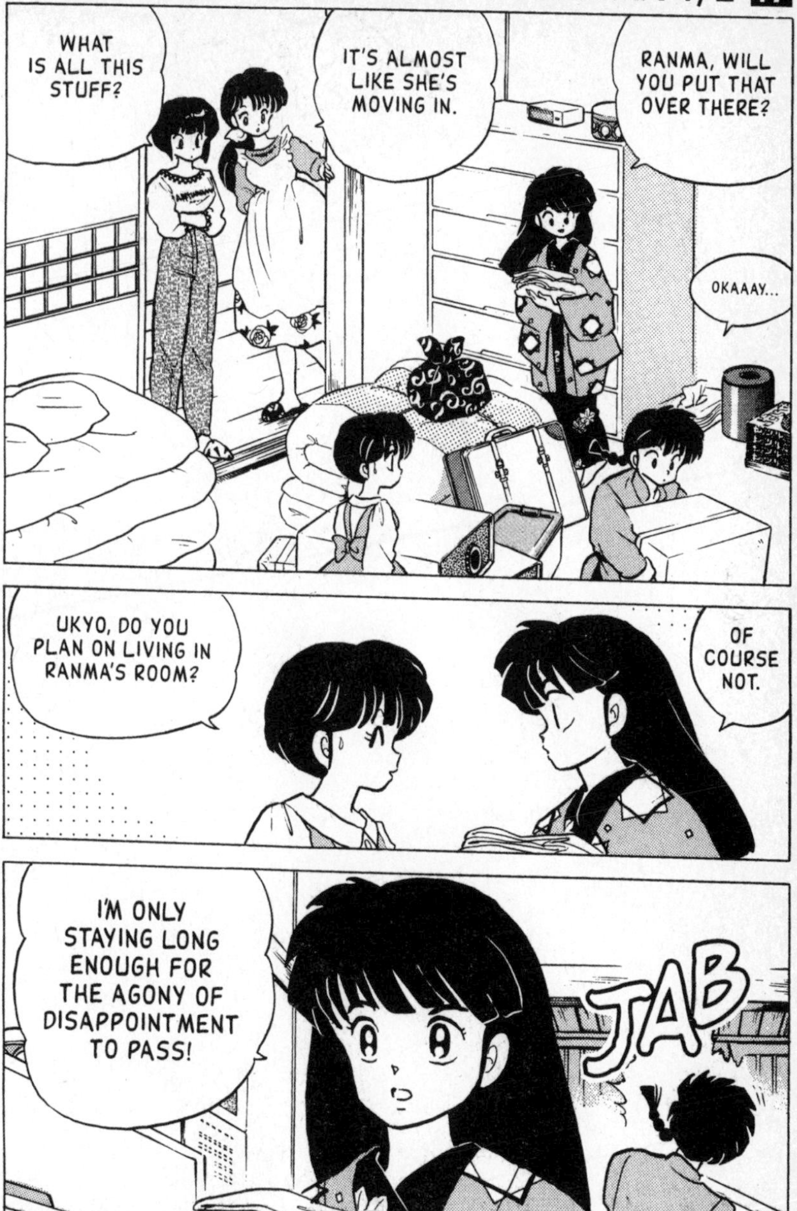
WHAT IS ALL THIS STUFF?
IT'S ALMOST LIKE SHE'S MOVING IN.
RANMA, WILL YOU PUT THAT OVER THERE?
OKAAAY...
UKYO, DO YOU PLAN ON LIVING IN RANMA'S ROOM?
OF COURSE NOT.
I'M ONLY STAYING LONG ENOUGH FOR THE AGONY OF DISAPPOINTMENT TO PASS!
JAB

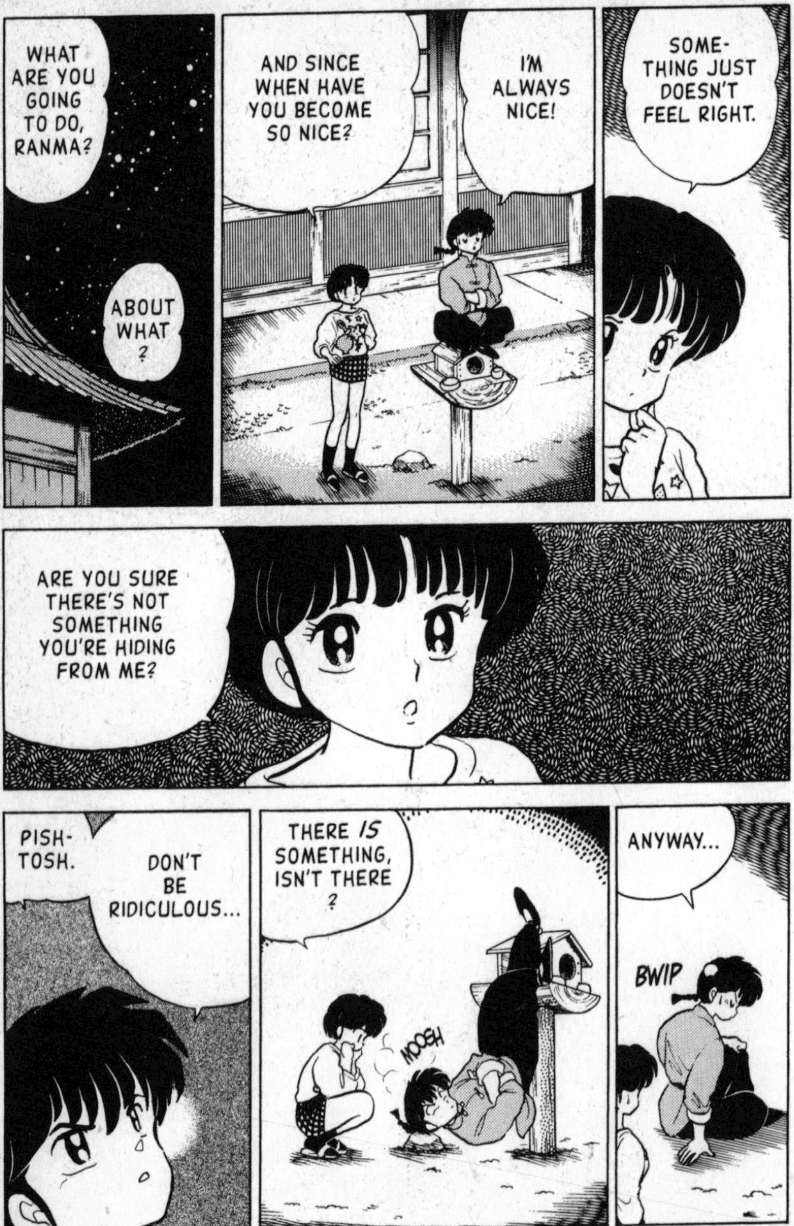
WHAT ARE YOU GOING TO DO, RANMA?
ABOUT WHAT?
AND SINCE WHEN HAVE YOU BECOME SO NICE?
I'M ALWAYS NICE!
SOME-THING JUST DOESN'T FEEL RIGHT.
ARE YOU SURE THERE'S NOT SOMETHING YOU'RE HIDING FROM ME?
PISH-TOSH.
DON'T BE RIDICULOUS...
THERE IS SOMETHING, ISN'T THERE?
MOOSH
ANYWAY...
BWIP

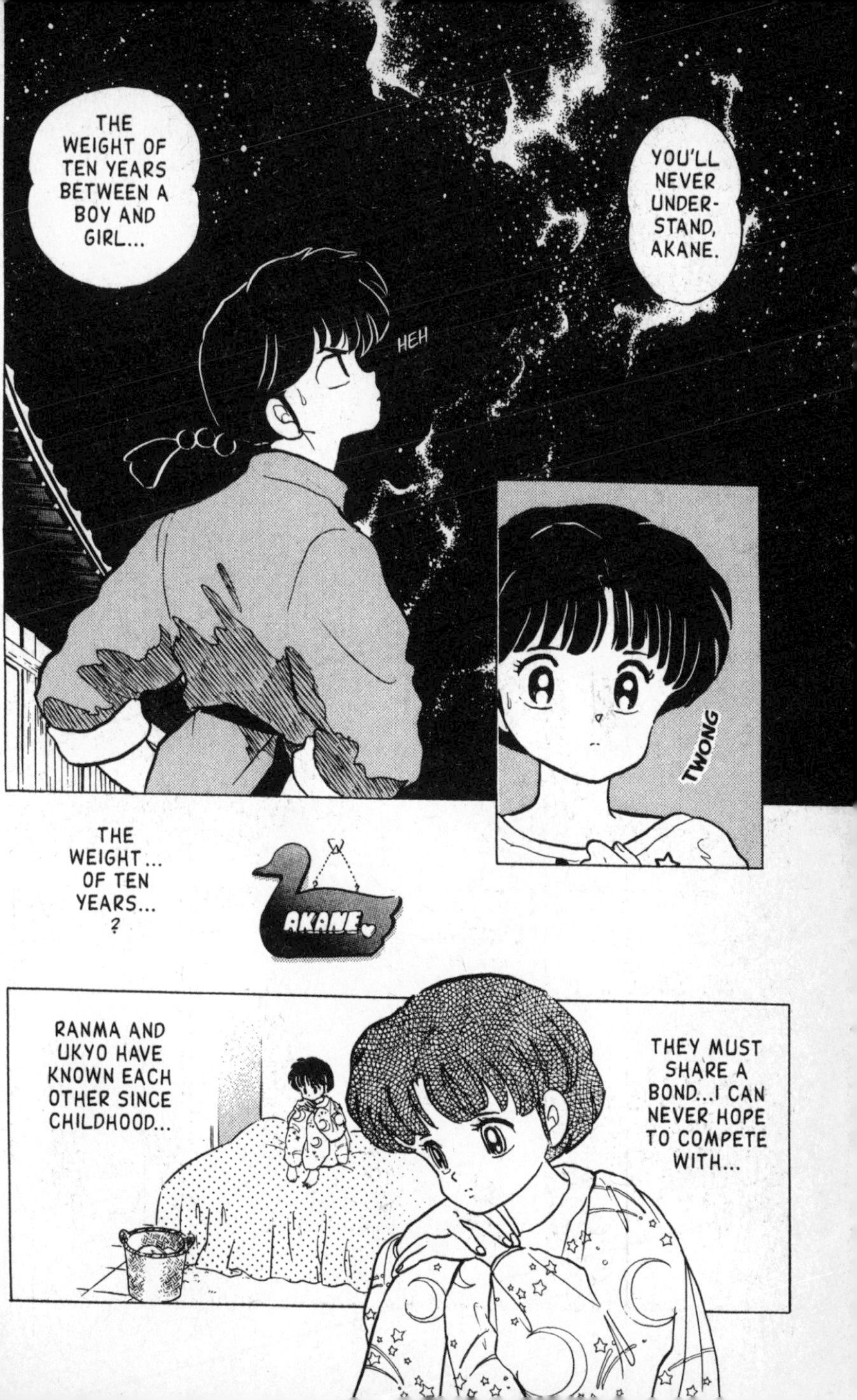
THE WEIGHT OF TEN YEARS BETWEEN A BOY AND GIRL...
YOU'LL NEVER UNDER-STAND, AKANE.
HEH
TWONG
THE WEIGHT... OF TEN YEARS...?
AKANE
RANMA AND UKYO HAVE KNOWN EACH OTHER SINCE CHILDHOOD...
THEY MUST SHARE A BOND...I CAN NEVER HOPE TO COMPETE WITH...

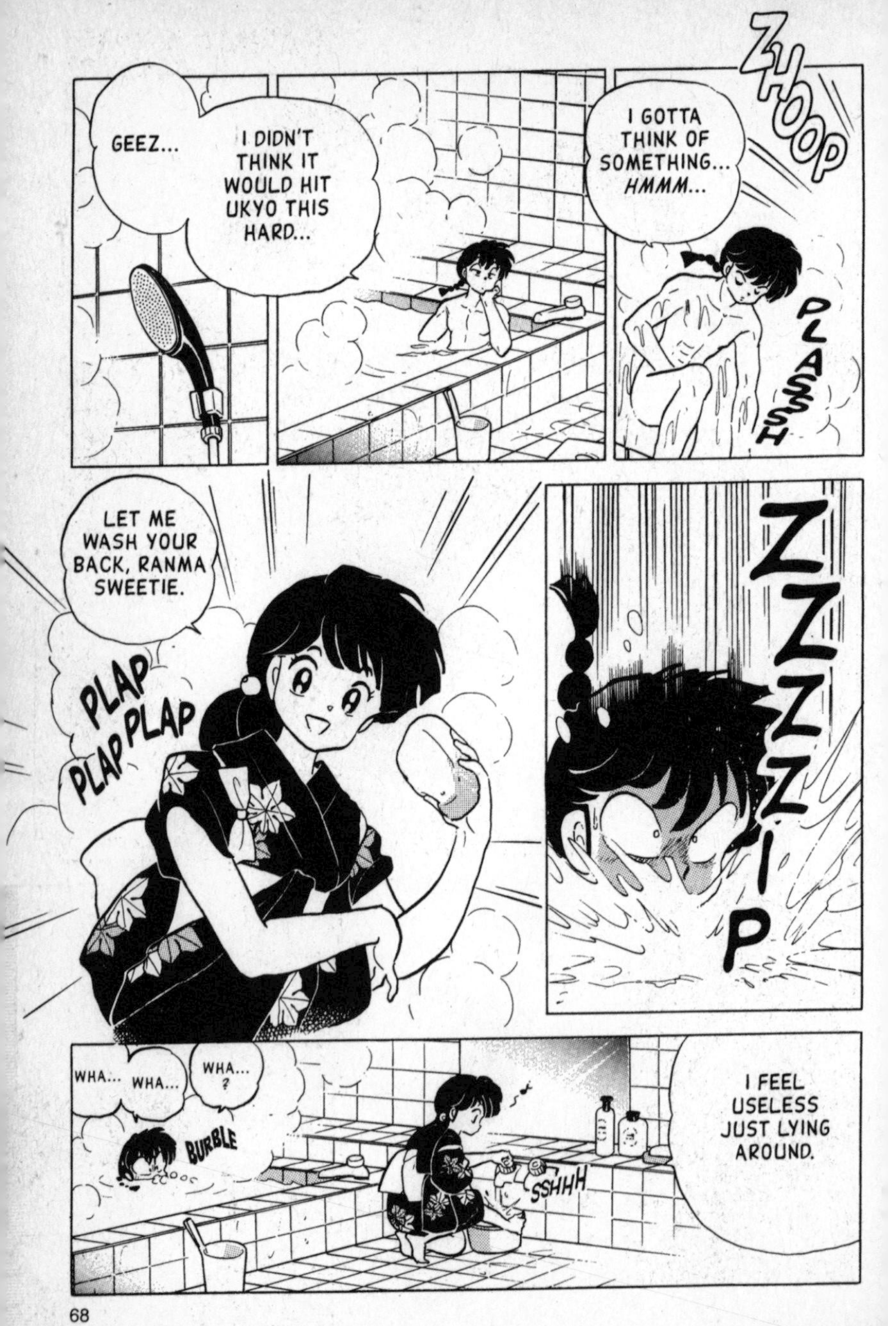
GEEZ...
I DIDN'T THINK IT WOULD HIT UKYO THIS HARD...
I GOTTA THINK OF SOMETHING... *HMMM...*
ZHOOP
PLASSSH
LET ME WASH YOUR BACK, RANMA SWEETIE.
PLAP PLAP PLAP
ZZZZIP
WHA... WHA...
WHA... ?
BURBLE
SSHHH
I FEEL USELESS JUST LYING AROUND.

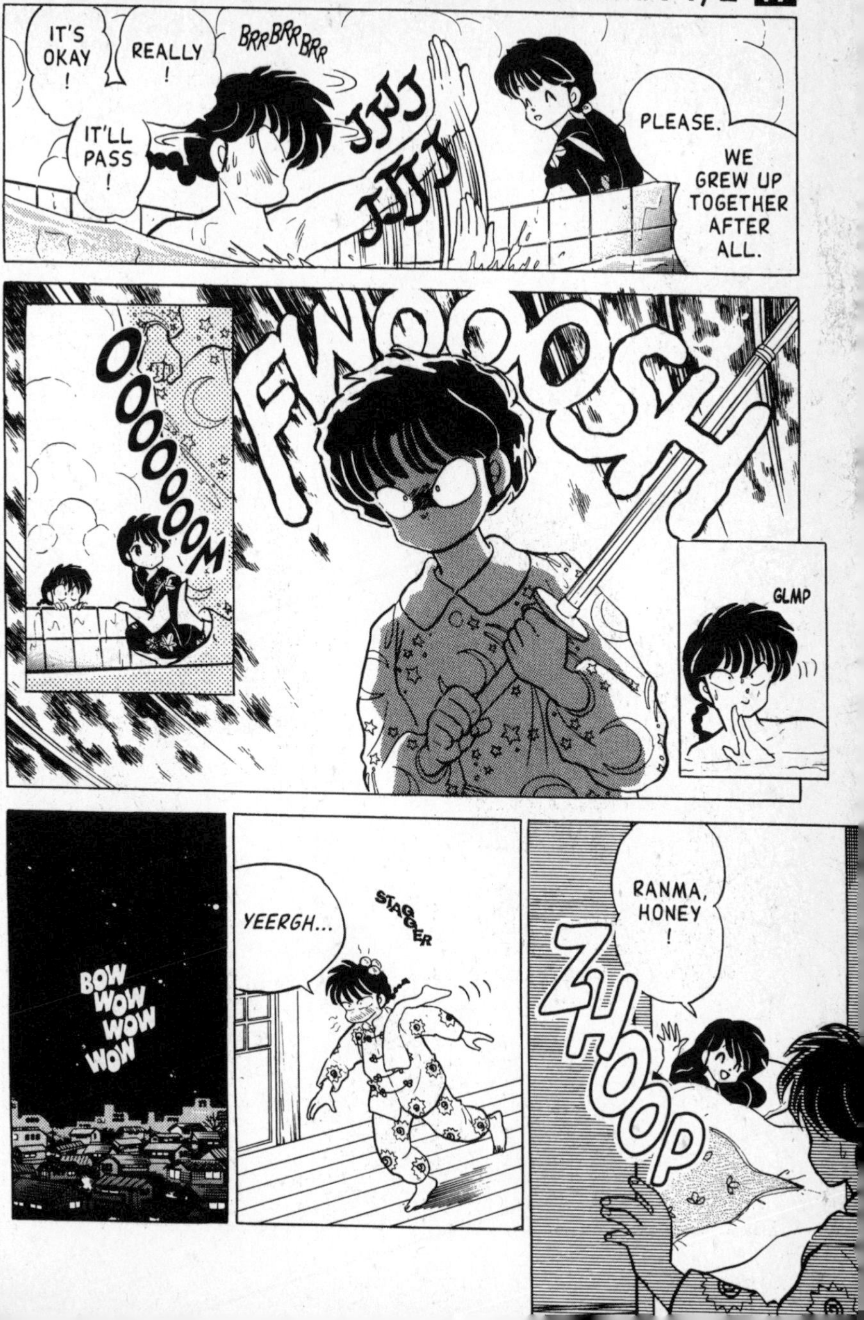
IT'S OKAY!
REALLY!
IT'LL PASS!
BRRBRRBRR
PLEASE.
WE GREW UP TOGETHER AFTER ALL.
OOOOOOOOM
FWOOOOSH
GLMP
BOW WOW WOW WOW
YEERGH...
STAGGER
RANMA, HONEY!
ZHOOP

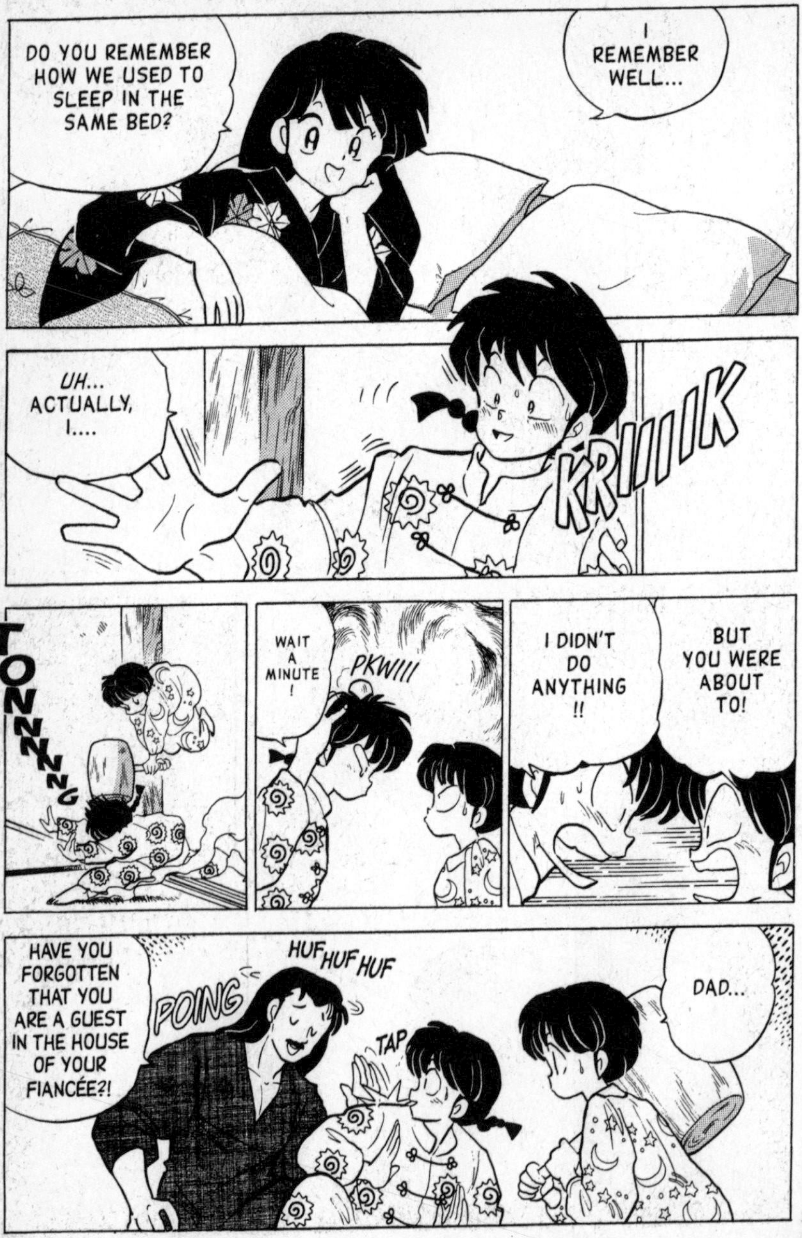
DO YOU REMEMBER HOW WE USED TO SLEEP IN THE SAME BED?
I REMEMBER WELL...
UH... ACTUALLY, I....
KRIIIIK
TONNNNG
WAIT A MINUTE!
PKWIII
I DIDN'T DO ANYTHING !!
BUT YOU WERE ABOUT TO!
HAVE YOU FORGOTTEN THAT YOU ARE A GUEST IN THE HOUSE OF YOUR FIANCÉE?!
HUF HUF HUF
POING
TAP
DAD...

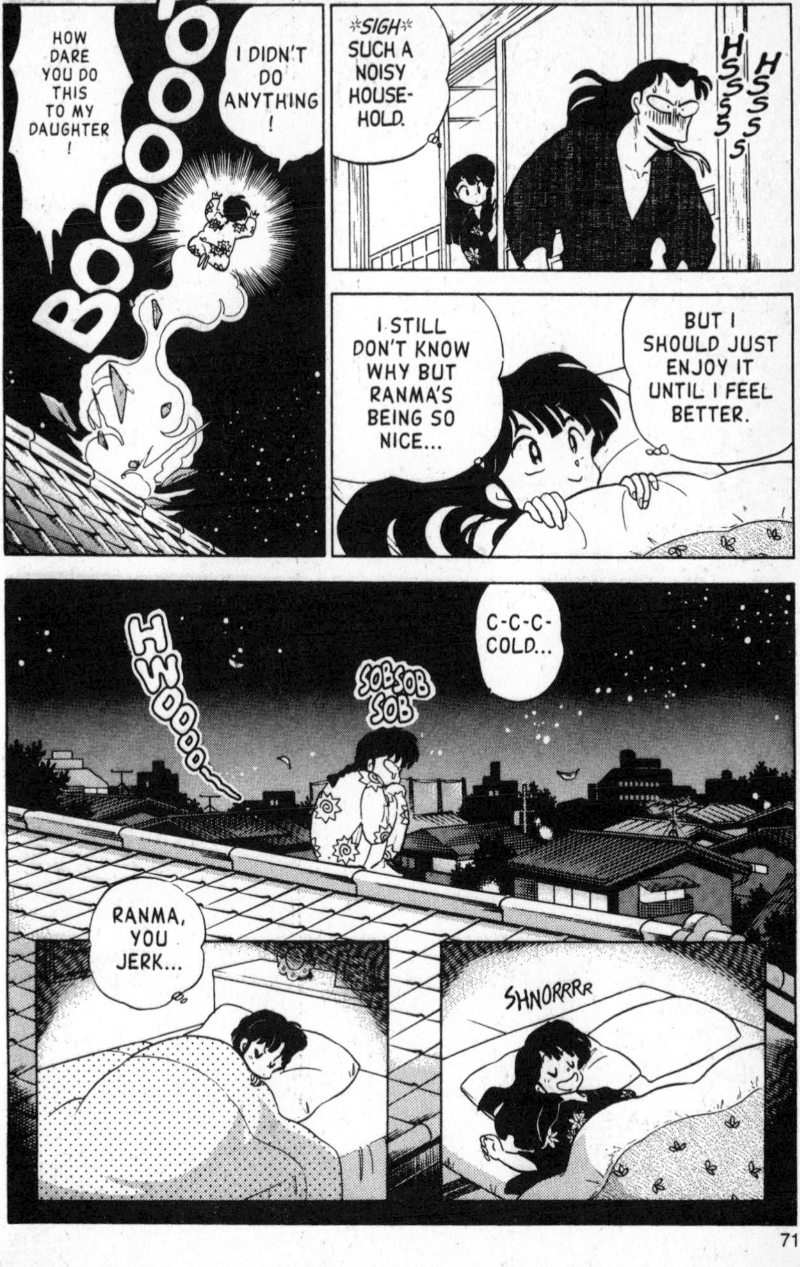
HOW DARE YOU DO THIS TO MY DAUGHTER!
I DIDN'T DO ANYTHING!
BOOOOOOOT
SIGH SUCH A NOISY HOUSE-HOLD.
HSSSSS
HSSSSS
I STILL DON'T KNOW WHY BUT RANMA'S BEING SO NICE...
BUT I SHOULD JUST ENJOY IT UNTIL I FEEL BETTER.
HWOOOOO
SOBSOB SOB
C-C-C-COLD...
RANMA, YOU JERK...
SHNORRRR

Part 5
FOR THE LOVE OF SAUCE

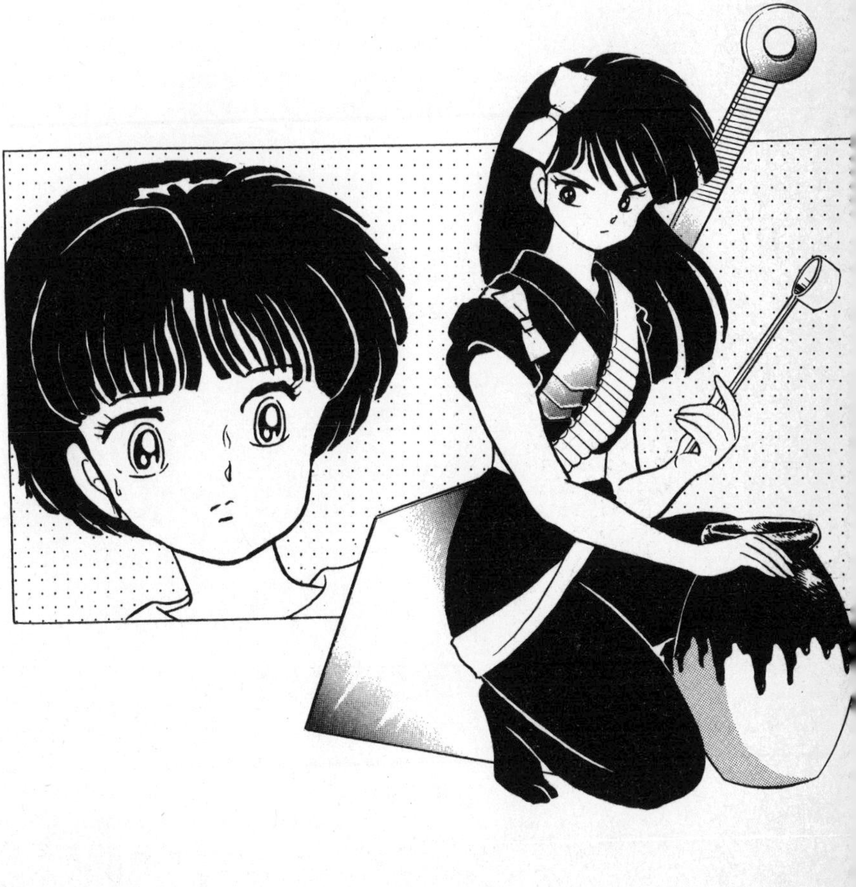

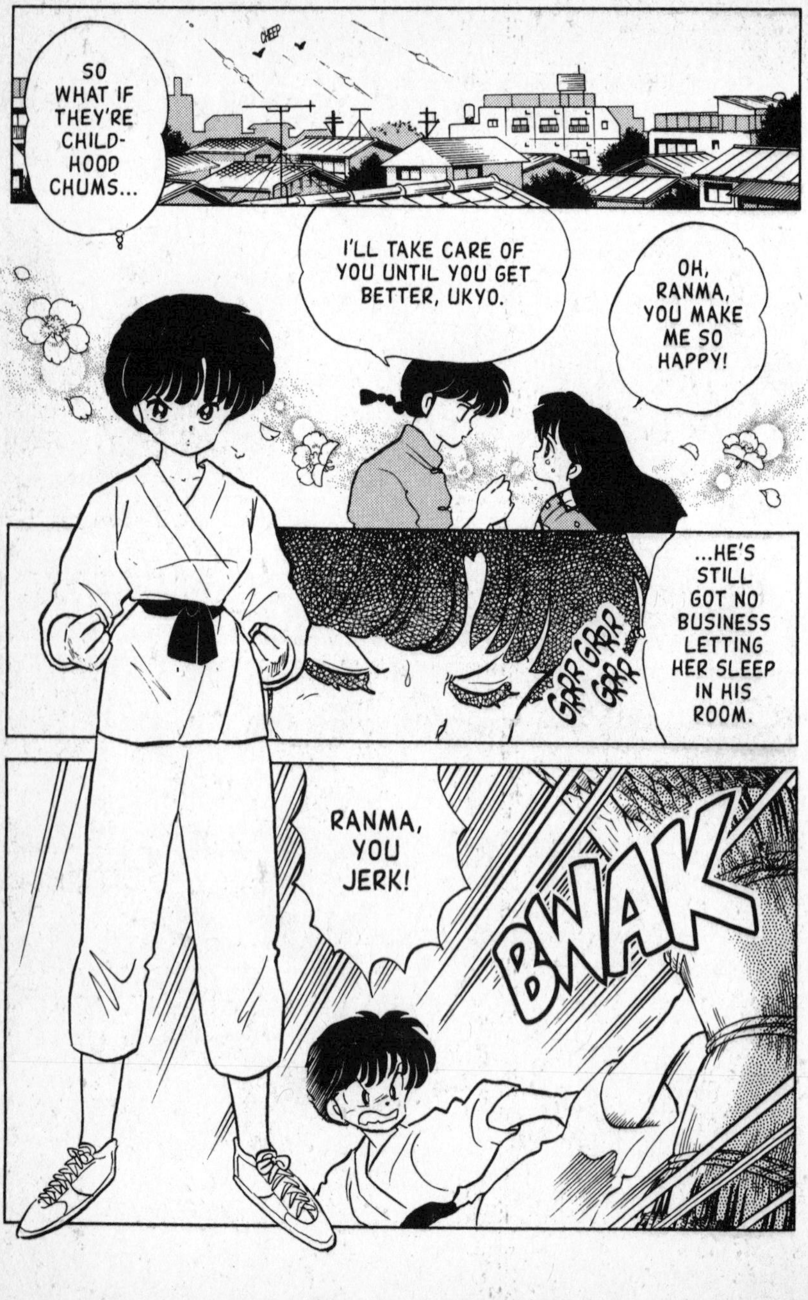
CHEEP
SO WHAT IF THEY'RE CHILD-HOOD CHUMS...
I'LL TAKE CARE OF YOU UNTIL YOU GET BETTER, UKYO.
OH, RANMA, YOU MAKE ME SO HAPPY!
...HE'S STILL GOT NO BUSINESS LETTING HER SLEEP IN HIS ROOM.
GRRR GRRR GRRR
RANMA, YOU JERK!
BWAK

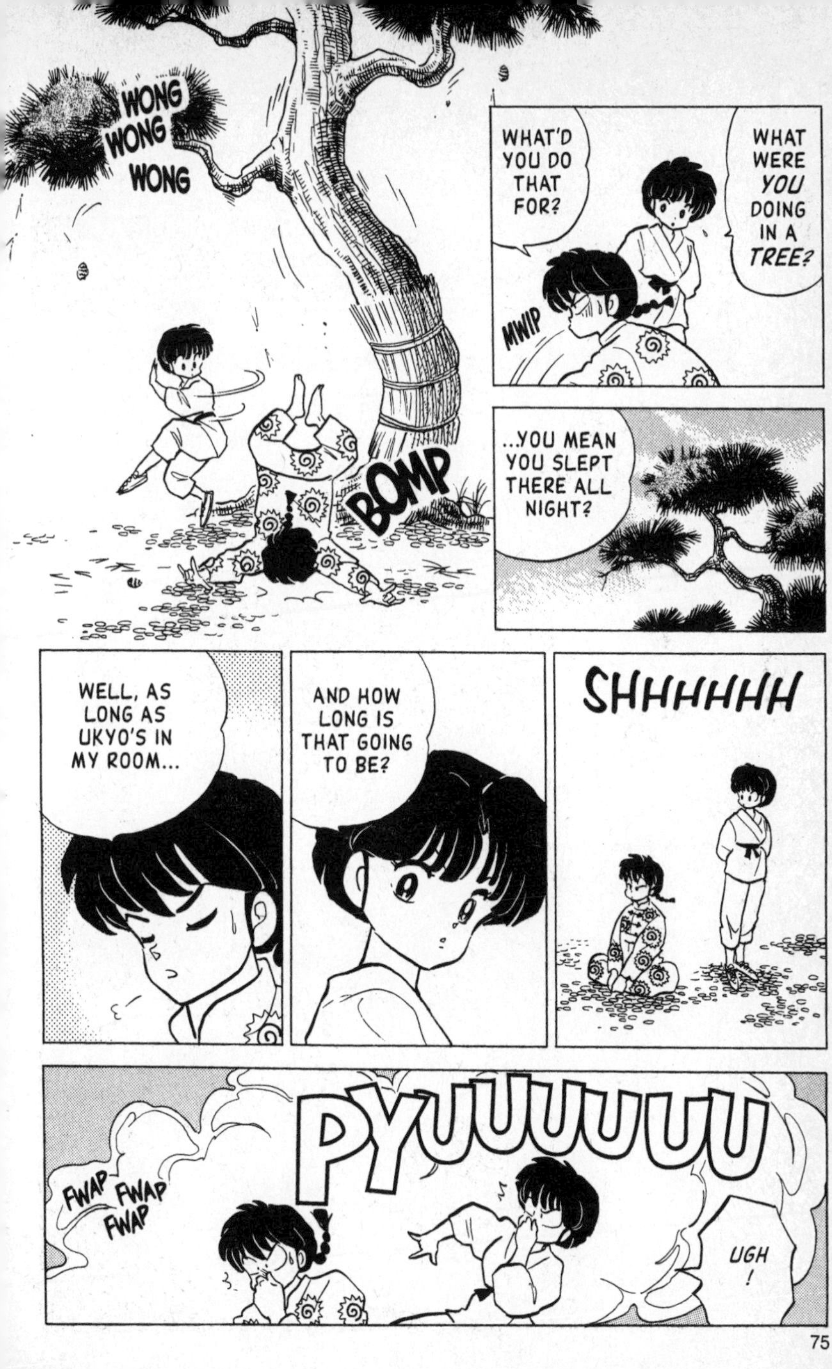
WONG
WONG
WONG
BOMP
WHAT'D YOU DO THAT FOR?
MWIP
WHAT WERE YOU DOING IN A TREE?
...YOU MEAN YOU SLEPT THERE ALL NIGHT?
WELL, AS LONG AS UKYO'S IN MY ROOM...
AND HOW LONG IS THAT GOING TO BE?
SHHHHHH
FWAP FWAP FWAP
PYUUUUUU
UGH!

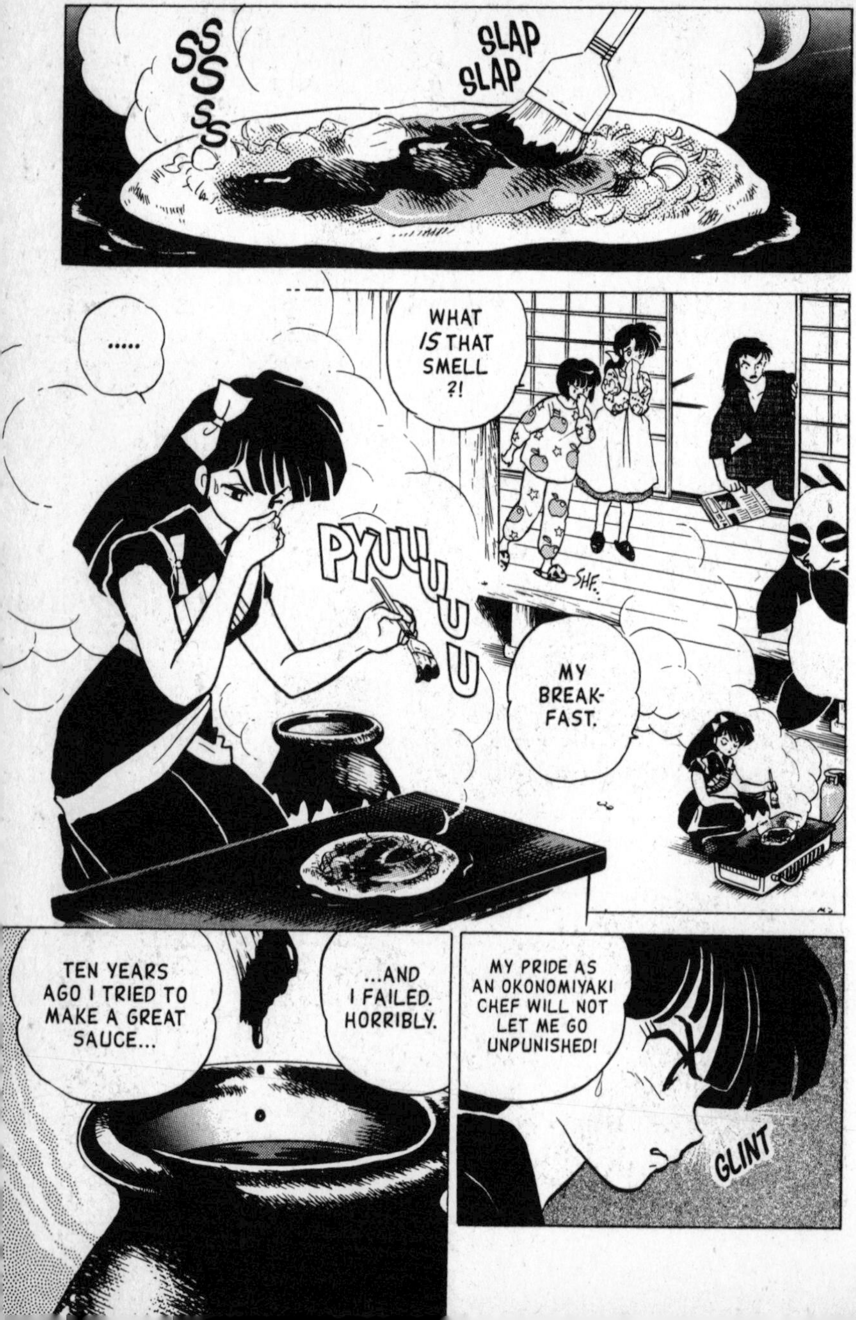
SSSSSS
SLAP SLAP
.....
WHAT *IS* THAT SMELL ?!
PYUUUUUU
SHF...
MY BREAK-FAST.
TEN YEARS AGO I TRIED TO MAKE A GREAT SAUCE...
...AND I FAILED. HORRIBLY.
MY PRIDE AS AN OKONOMIYAKI CHEF WILL NOT LET ME GO UNPUNISHED!
GLINT

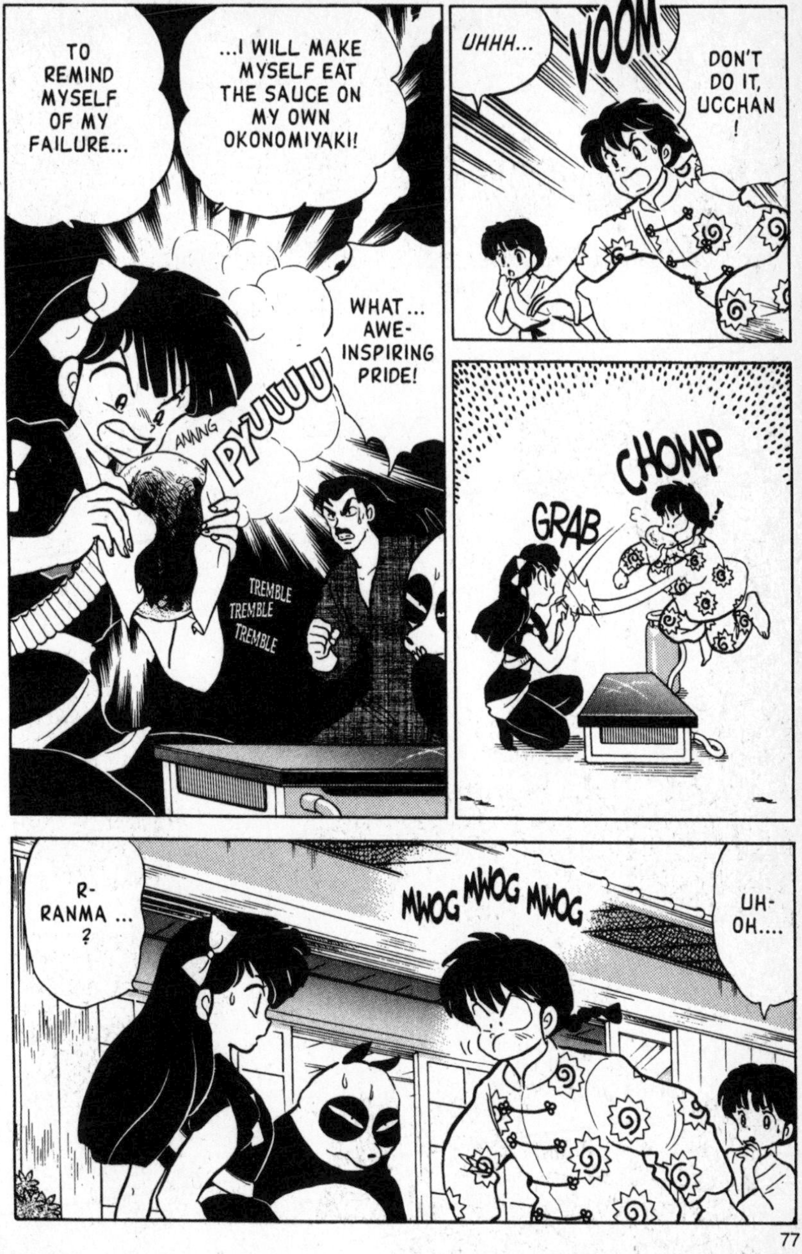
TO REMIND MYSELF OF MY FAILURE...
...I WILL MAKE MYSELF EAT THE SAUCE ON MY OWN OKONOMIYAKI!
WHAT ... AWE-INSPIRING PRIDE!
ANNNG
PYUUUU
TREMBLE TREMBLE TREMBLE
UHHH...
VOOM
DON'T DO IT, UCCHAN!
CHOMP
GRAB
R-RANMA ...?
MWOG MWOG MWOG
UH-OH....

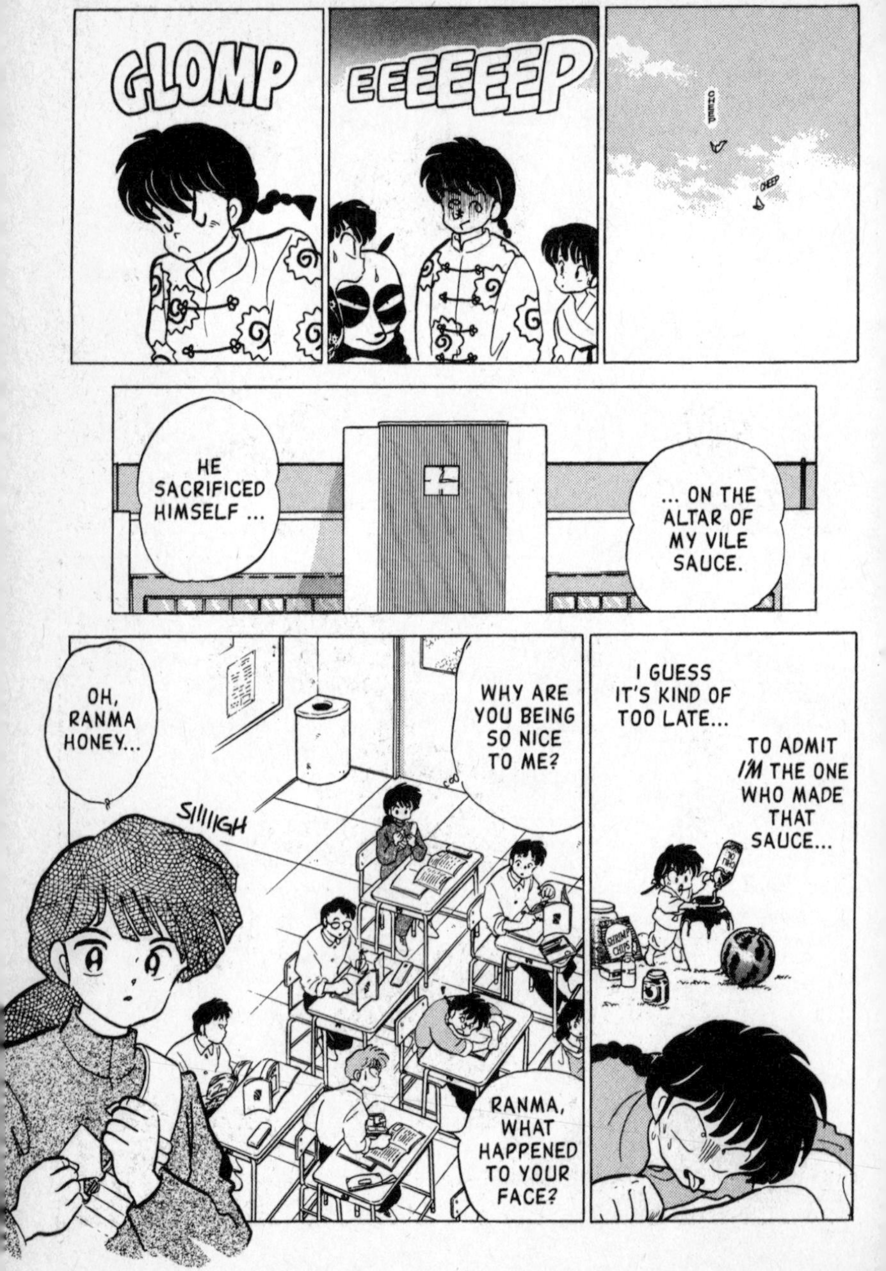
GLOMP
EEEEEEEP
CHEEP
CHEEP
HE SACRIFICED HIMSELF ...
... ON THE ALTAR OF MY VILE SAUCE.
OH, RANMA HONEY...
SIIIIGH
WHY ARE YOU BEING SO NICE TO ME?
RANMA, WHAT HAPPENED TO YOUR FACE?
I GUESS IT'S KIND OF TOO LATE...
TO ADMIT *I'M* THE ONE WHO MADE THAT SAUCE...
SHRIMP CHIPS

UKYO MUST HAVE SOMETHING ON HIM...

SOME KIND OF BLACK-MAIL...

WHAT DID YOU WANT TO TALK TO ME ABOUT, AKANE?

WELL...

MATH 1

IT'S ABOUT RANMA...

DON'T YOU THINK HE'S ACTING DIFFERENT LATELY?

YES...

I WAS THINKING SO MYSELF...

ANY IDEA WHY?

HMM....

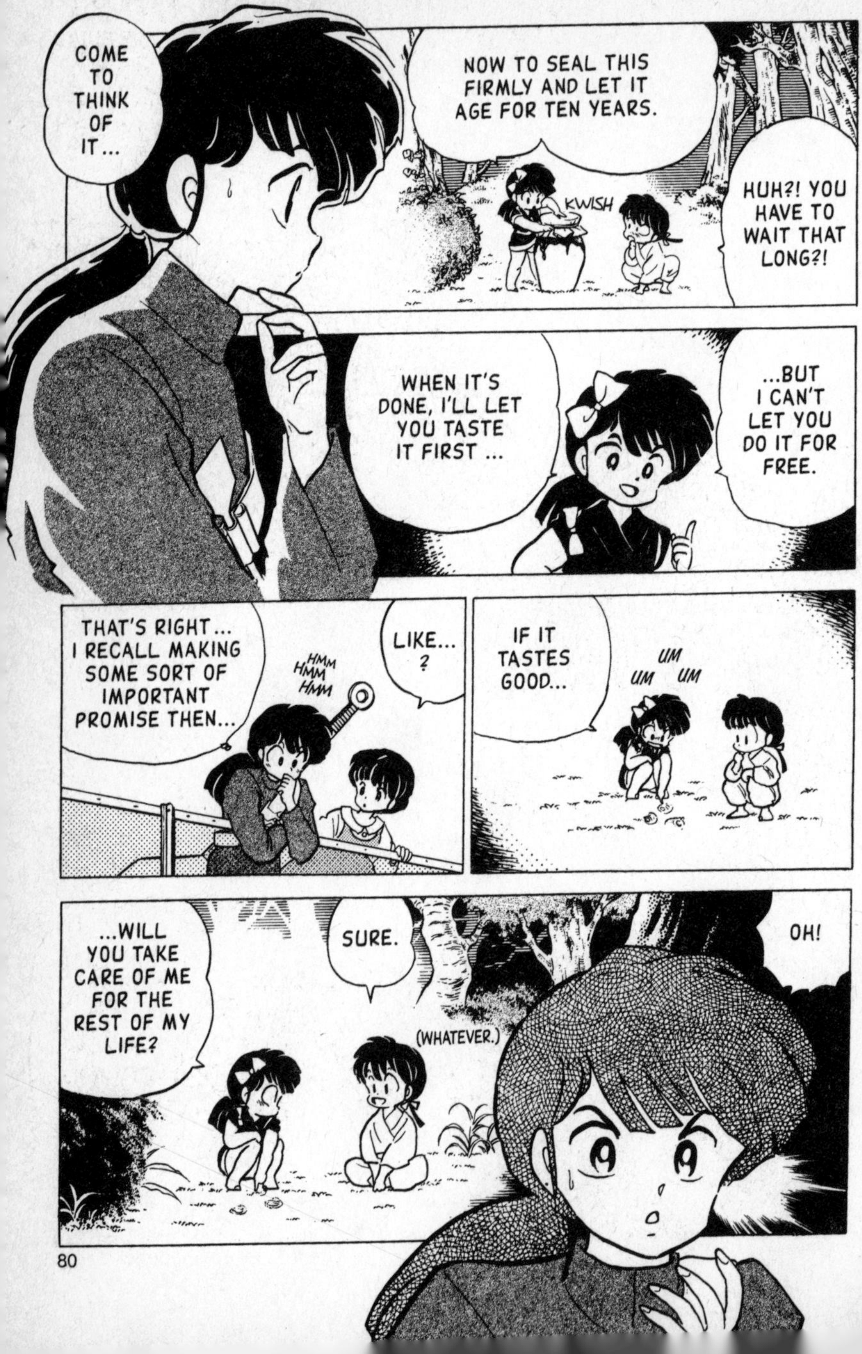
COME TO THINK OF IT...
NOW TO SEAL THIS FIRMLY AND LET IT AGE FOR TEN YEARS.
KWISH
HUH?! YOU HAVE TO WAIT THAT LONG?!
WHEN IT'S DONE, I'LL LET YOU TASTE IT FIRST ...
...BUT I CAN'T LET YOU DO IT FOR FREE.
THAT'S RIGHT ... I RECALL MAKING SOME SORT OF IMPORTANT PROMISE THEN...
HMM HMM HMM
LIKE... ?
IF IT TASTES GOOD...
UM UM UM
...WILL YOU TAKE CARE OF ME FOR THE REST OF MY LIFE?
SURE.
(WHATEVER.)
OH!

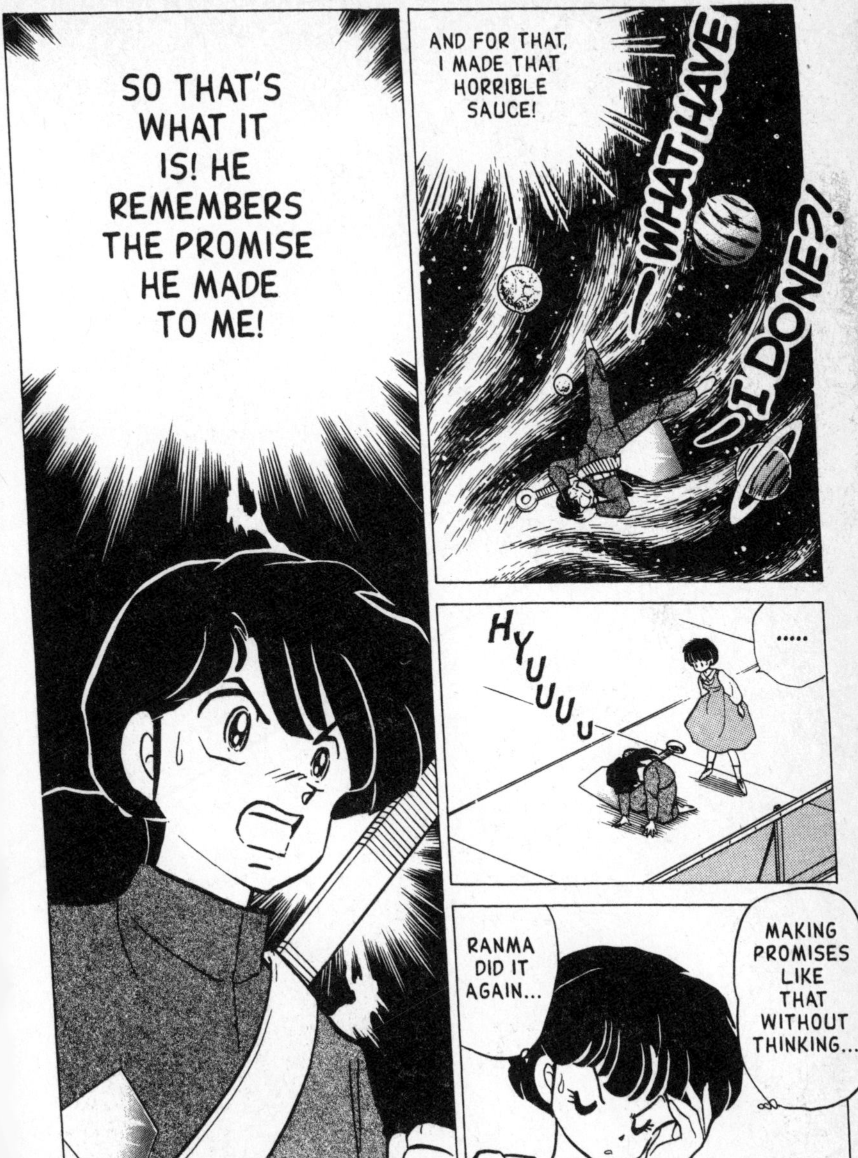
SO THAT'S WHAT IT IS! HE REMEMBERS THE PROMISE HE MADE TO ME!
AND FOR THAT, I MADE THAT HORRIBLE SAUCE!
—WHAT HAVE I DONE?!
HYUUUUU
.....
RANMA DID IT AGAIN...
MAKING PROMISES LIKE THAT WITHOUT THINKING...

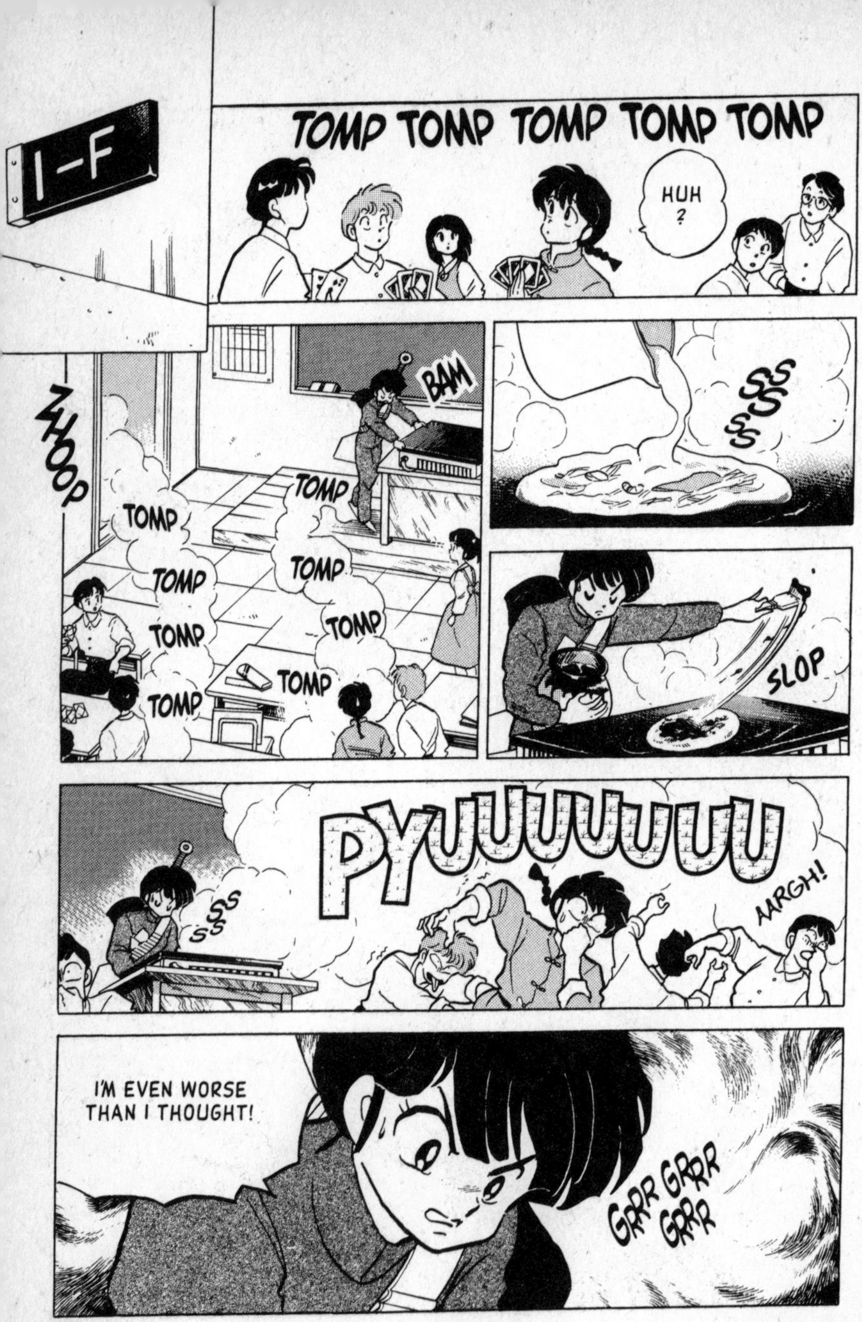
1-F
TOMP TOMP TOMP TOMP TOMP
HUH?
ZHOOP
BAM
TOMP
TOMP
TOMP
TOMP
TOMP
TOMP
TOMP
TOMP
SSSSS
SLOP
SSS
PYUUUUUUU
AARGH!
I'M EVEN WORSE THAN I THOUGHT!
GRRR GRRR GRRR

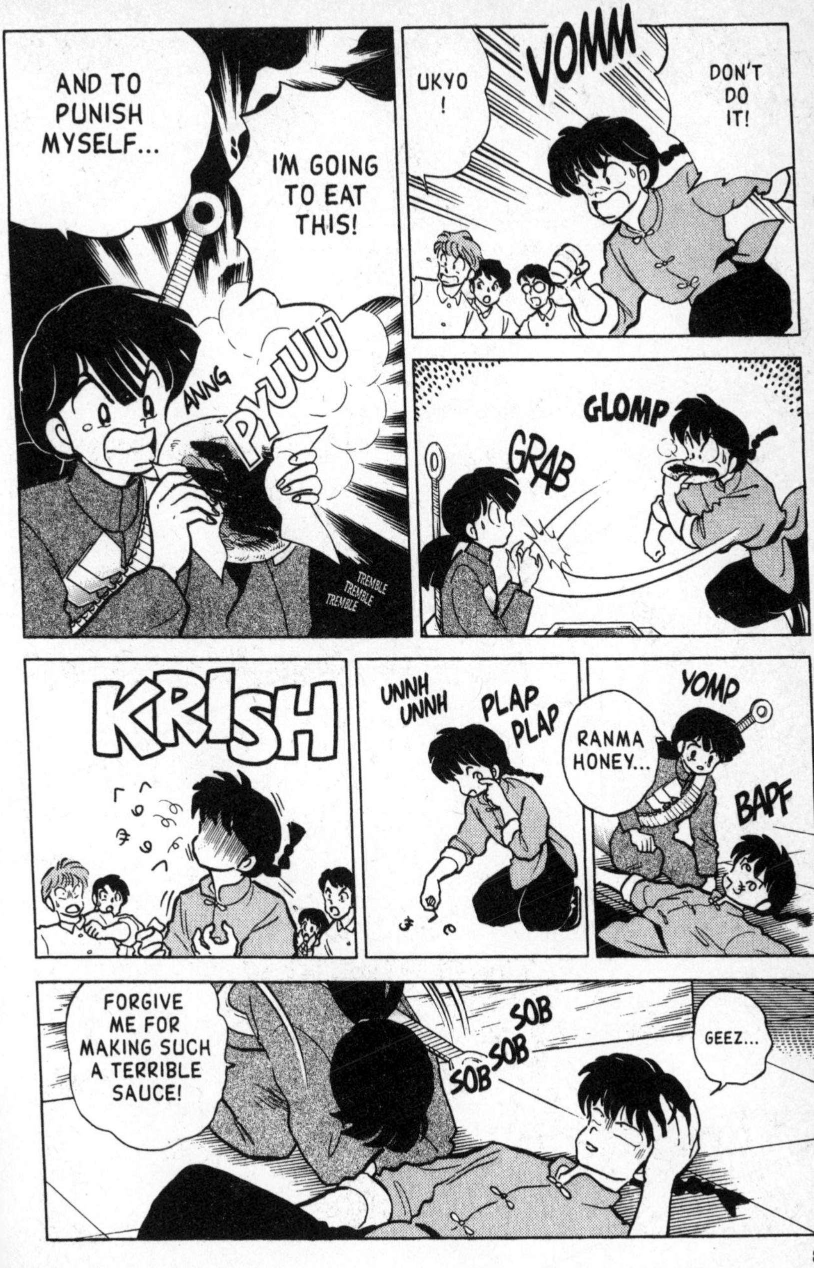
AND TO PUNISH MYSELF...
I'M GOING TO EAT THIS!
ANNG
PYUUU
TREMBLE TREMBLE TREMBLE
UKYO!
VOMM
DON'T DO IT!
GLOMP
GRAB
KRISH
UNNH UNNH
PLAP PLAP
YOMP
RANMA HONEY...
BAPF
FORGIVE ME FOR MAKING SUCH A TERRIBLE SAUCE!
SOB SOB SOB
GEEZ...

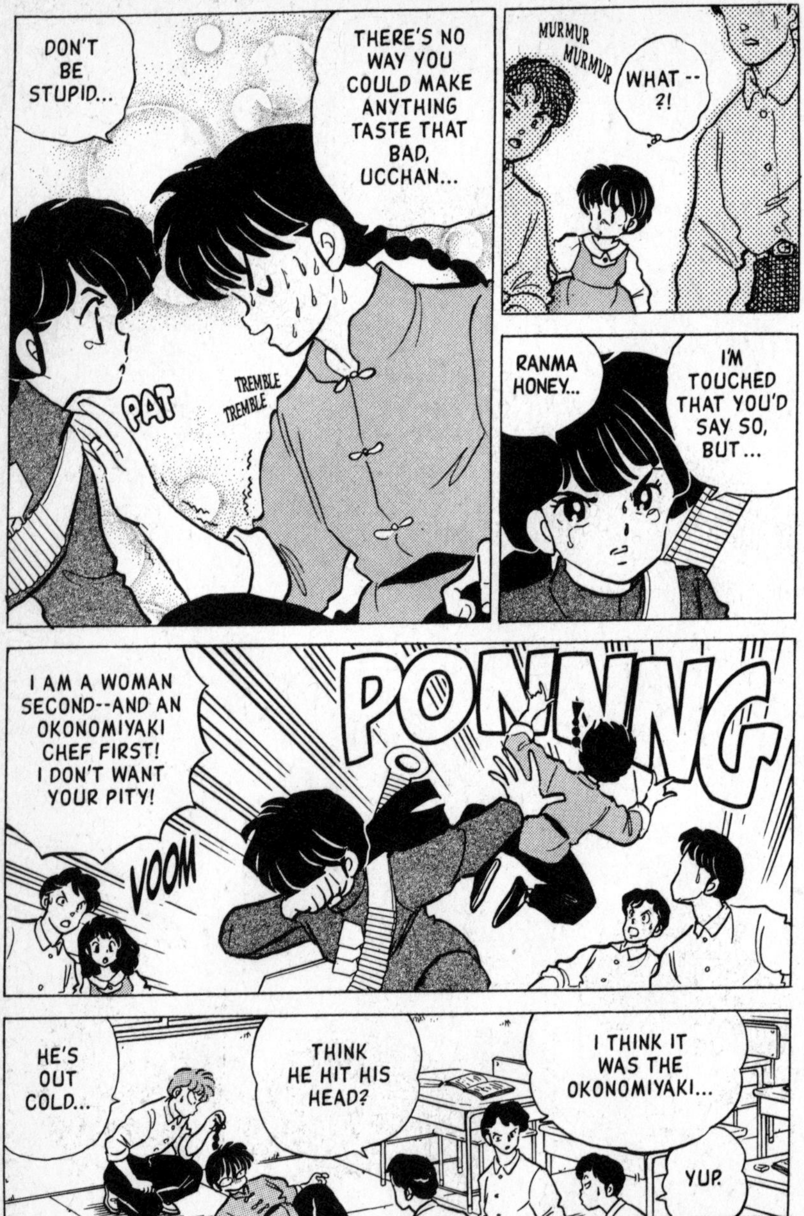
DON'T BE STUPID...
THERE'S NO WAY YOU COULD MAKE ANYTHING TASTE THAT BAD, UCCHAN...
PAT
TREMBLE TREMBLE
MURMUR
MURMUR
WHAT -- ?!
RANMA HONEY...
I'M TOUCHED THAT YOU'D SAY SO, BUT...
I AM A WOMAN SECOND--AND AN OKONOMIYAKI CHEF FIRST! I DON'T WANT YOUR PITY!
PONNNG
VOOM
HE'S OUT COLD...
THINK HE HIT HIS HEAD?
I THINK IT WAS THE OKONOMIYAKI...
YUP.

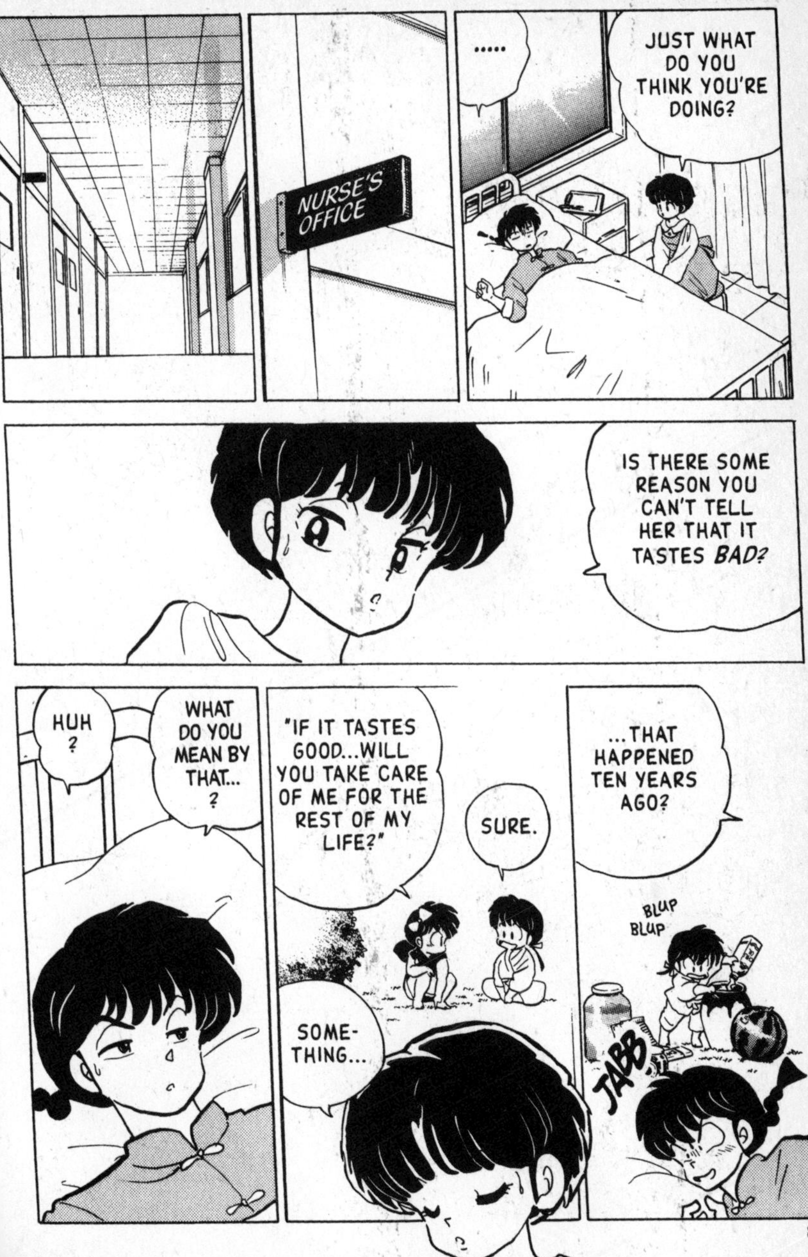
NURSE'S OFFICE
.....
JUST WHAT DO YOU THINK YOU'RE DOING?
IS THERE SOME REASON YOU CAN'T TELL HER THAT IT TASTES *BAD?*
HUH ?
WHAT DO YOU MEAN BY THAT... ?
"IF IT TASTES GOOD...WILL YOU TAKE CARE OF ME FOR THE REST OF MY LIFE?"
SURE.
SOME-THING...
...THAT HAPPENED TEN YEARS AGO?
BLUP BLUP
JABB

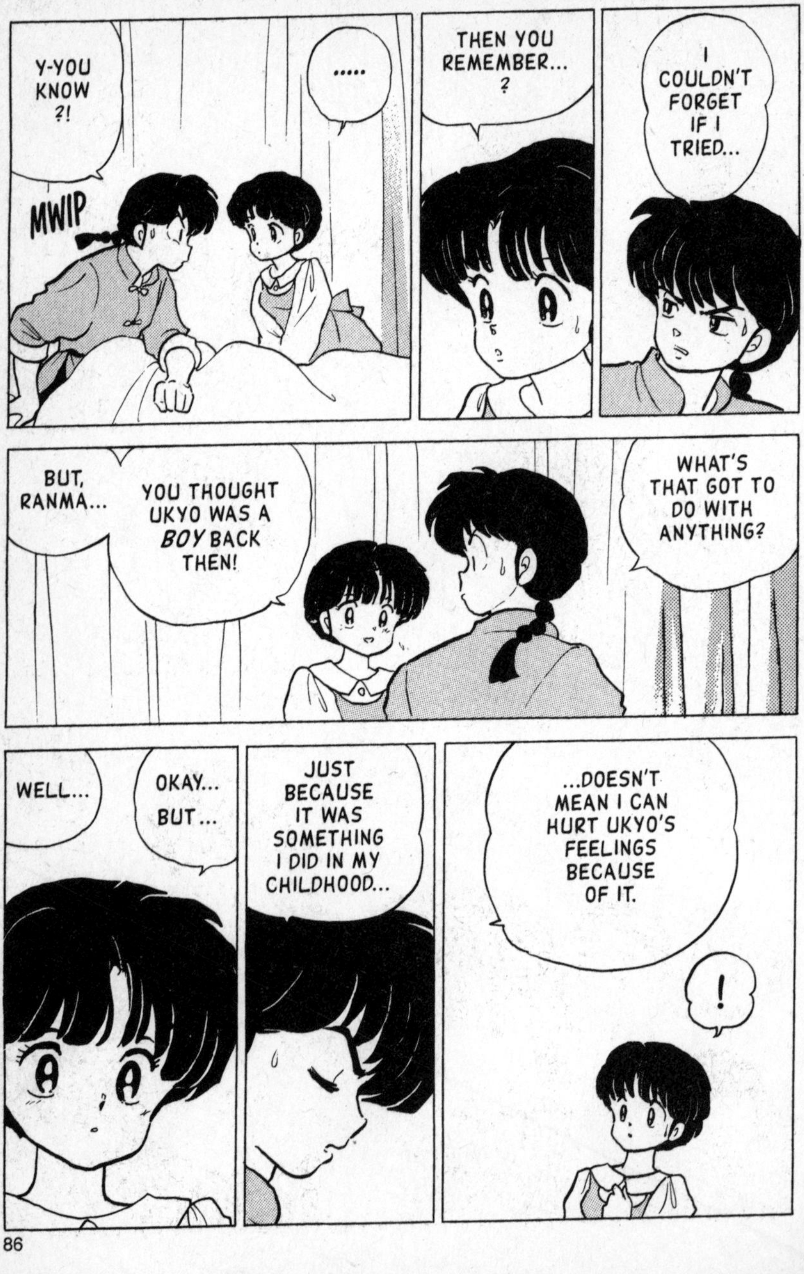

Y-YOU KNOW ?!
MWIP
.....
THEN YOU REMEMBER...?
I COULDN'T FORGET IF I TRIED...
BUT, RANMA...
YOU THOUGHT UKYO WAS A *BOY* BACK THEN!
WHAT'S THAT GOT TO DO WITH ANYTHING?
WELL...
OKAY... BUT...
JUST BECAUSE IT WAS SOMETHING I DID IN MY CHILDHOOD...
...DOESN'T MEAN I CAN HURT UKYO'S FEELINGS BECAUSE OF IT.
!

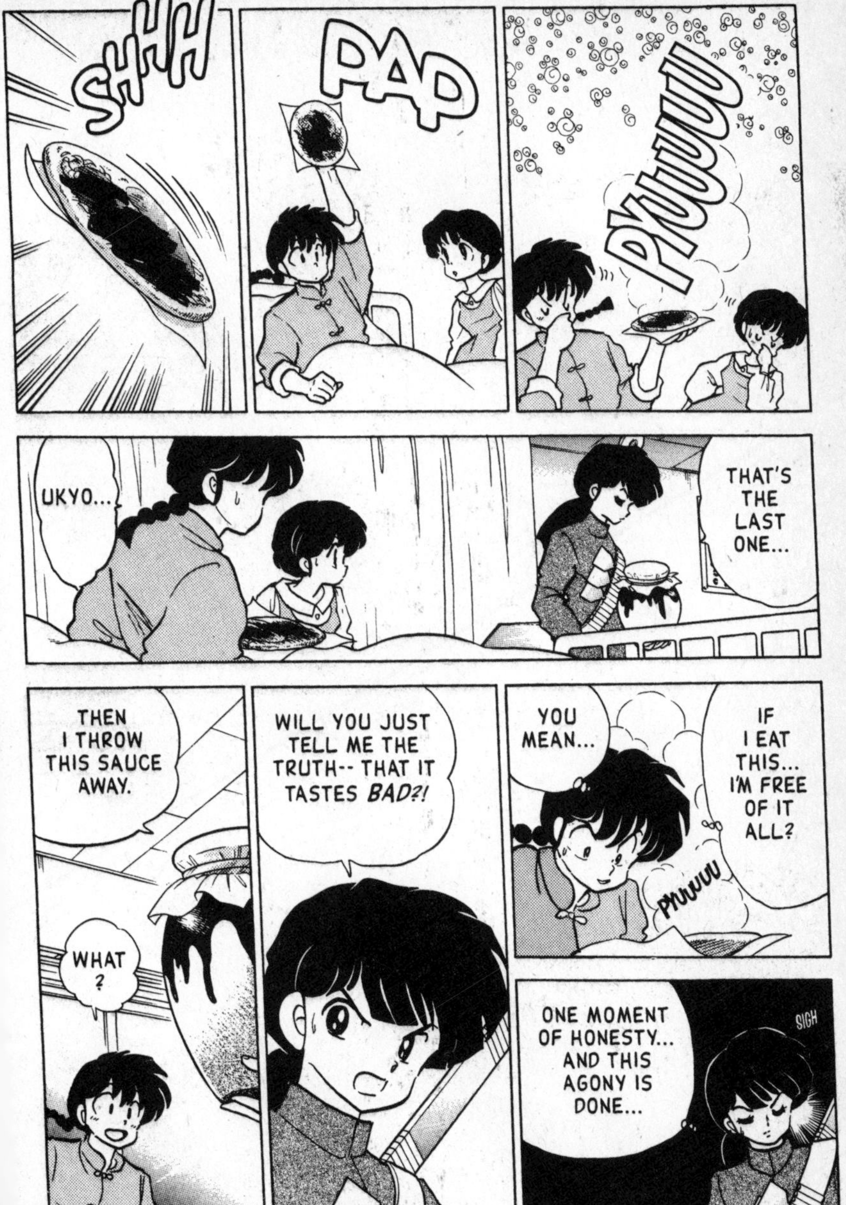
SHHH
PAP
PYUUUUU
UKYO...
THAT'S THE LAST ONE...
THEN I THROW THIS SAUCE AWAY.
WHAT ?
WILL YOU JUST TELL ME THE TRUTH-- THAT IT TASTES *BAD?!*
YOU MEAN...
IF I EAT THIS... I'M FREE OF IT ALL?
PYUUUU
ONE MOMENT OF HONESTY... AND THIS AGONY IS DONE...
SIGH

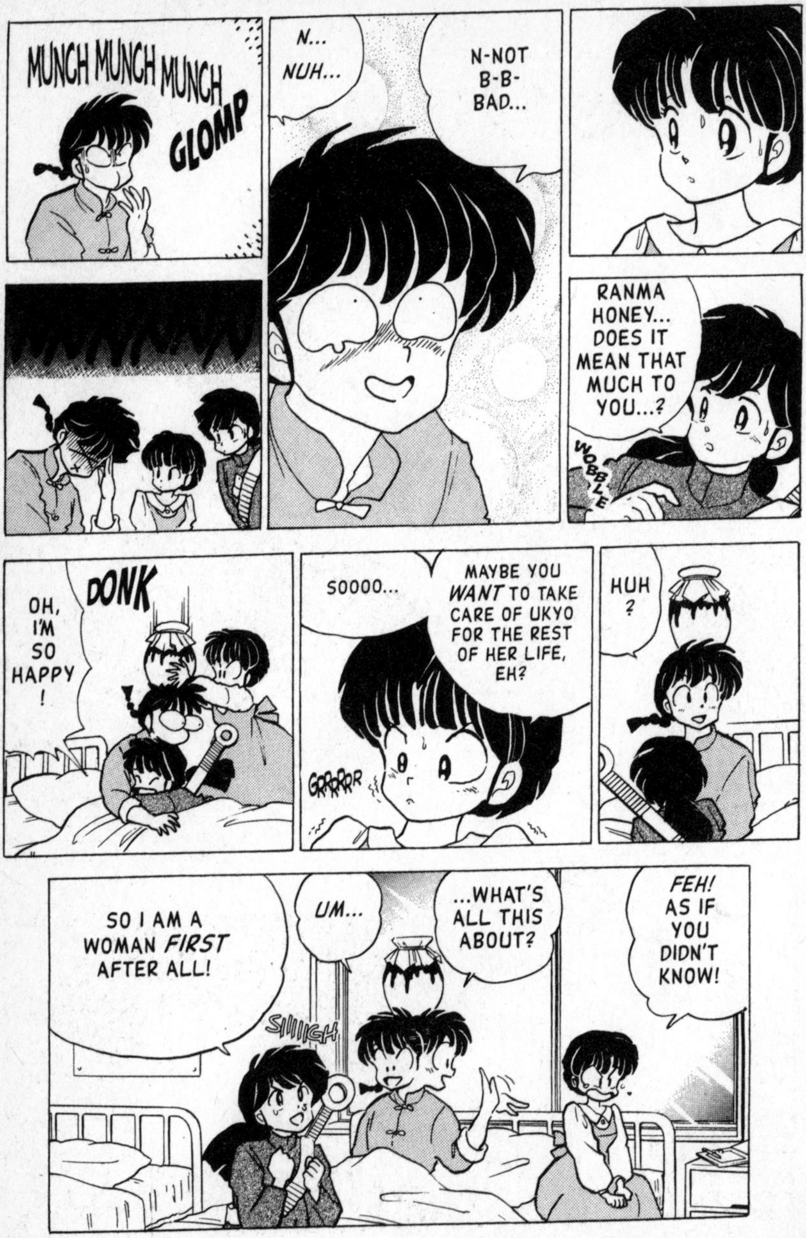
MUNCH MUNCH MUNCH
GLOMP
N... NUH...
N-NOT B-B-BAD...
RANMA HONEY... DOES IT MEAN THAT MUCH TO YOU...?
WOBBLE
DONK
OH, I'M SO HAPPY!
SOOOO...
MAYBE YOU *WANT* TO TAKE CARE OF UKYO FOR THE REST OF HER LIFE, EH?
GRRRRR
HUH?
SO I AM A WOMAN *FIRST* AFTER ALL!
SIIIIGH
UM...
...WHAT'S ALL THIS ABOUT?
FEH! AS IF YOU DIDN'T KNOW!

Part 6
THE TRUTH ABOUT THE TRUTH

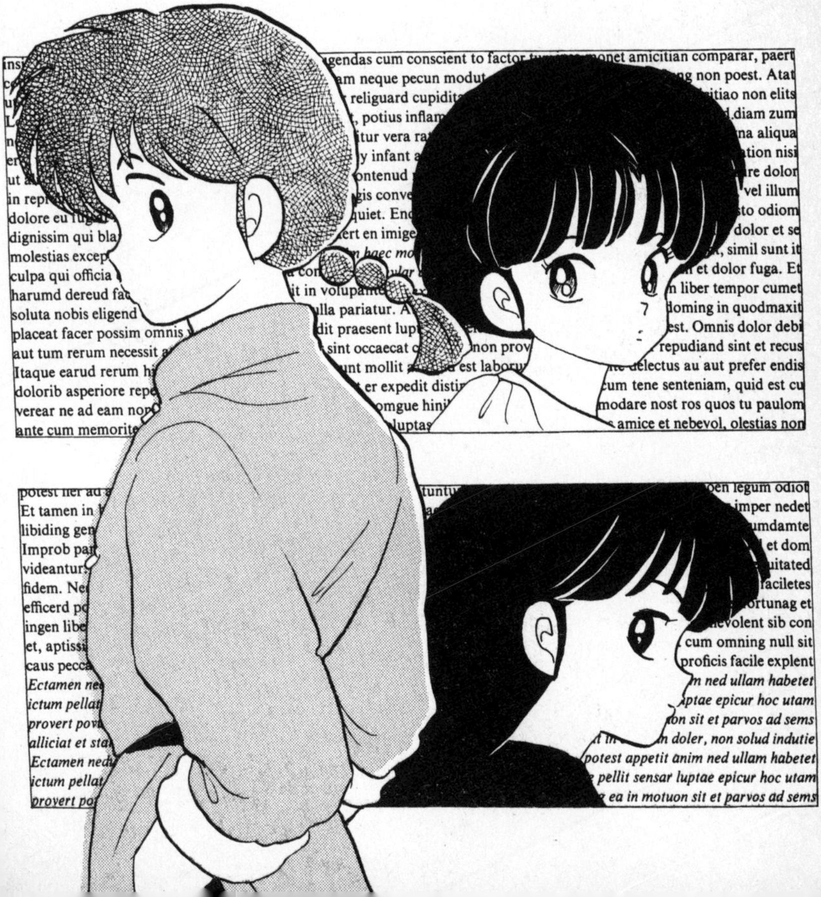

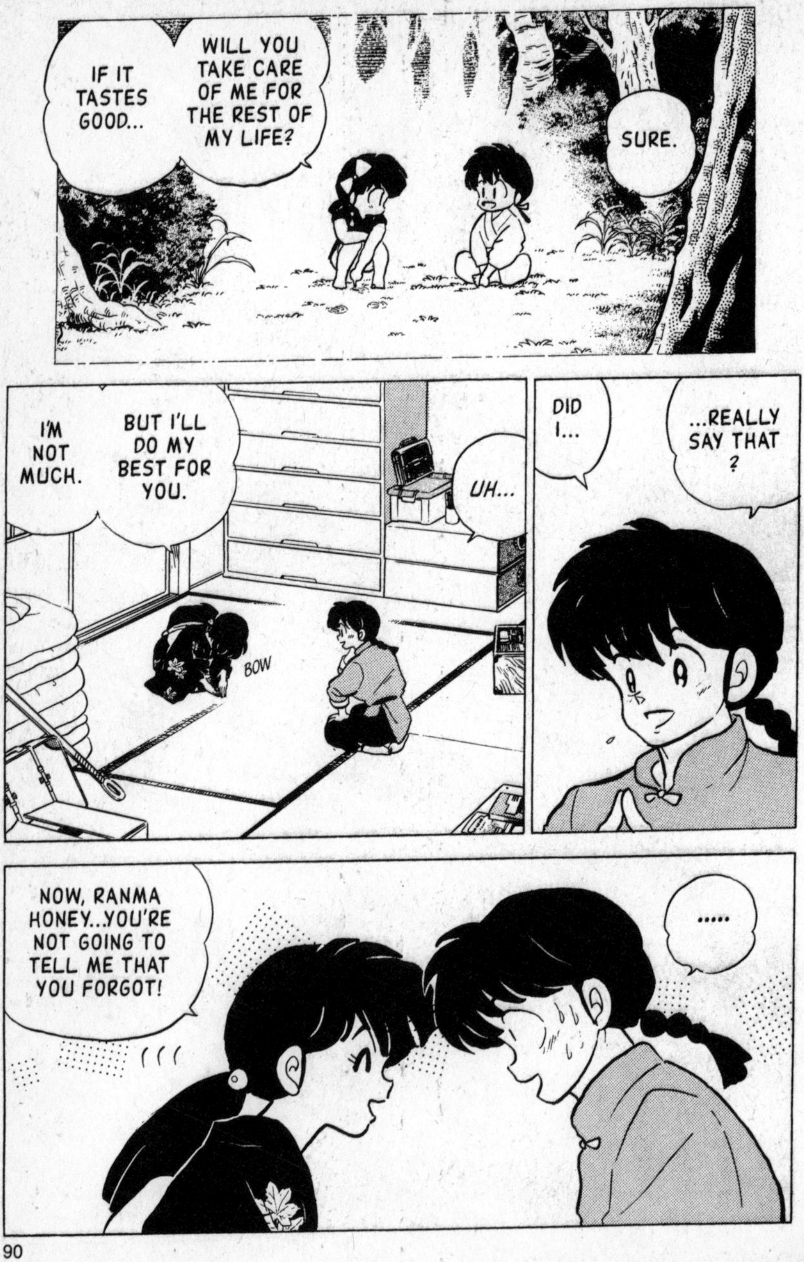
IF IT TASTES GOOD...
WILL YOU TAKE CARE OF ME FOR THE REST OF MY LIFE?
SURE.
I'M NOT MUCH.
BUT I'LL DO MY BEST FOR YOU.
UH...
BOW
DID I...
...REALLY SAY THAT?
NOW, RANMA HONEY...YOU'RE NOT GOING TO TELL ME THAT YOU FORGOT!
......

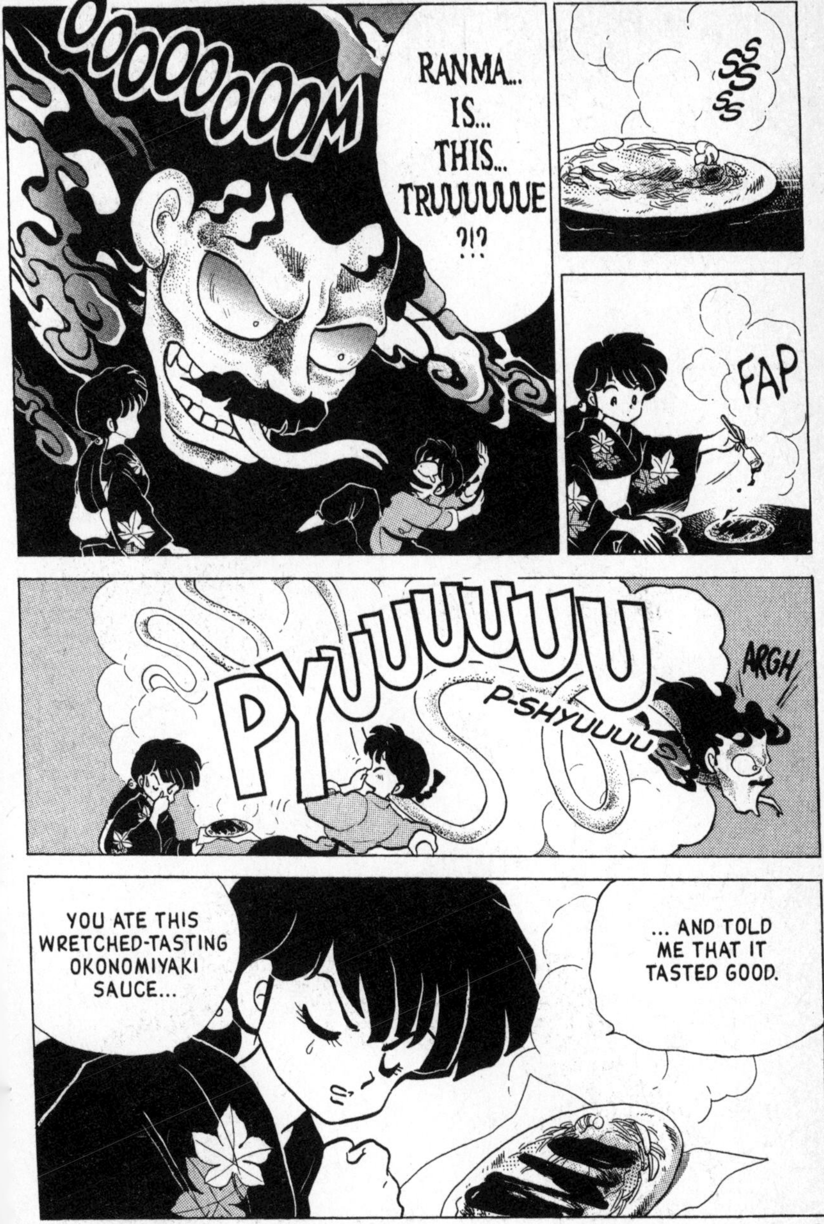
OOOOOOOOM
RANMA... IS... THIS... TRUUUUUE ?!?
SSSSS
FAP
PYUUUUUU
P-SHYUUUUU
ARGH
YOU ATE THIS WRETCHED-TASTING OKONOMIYAKI SAUCE...
... AND TOLD ME THAT IT TASTED GOOD.

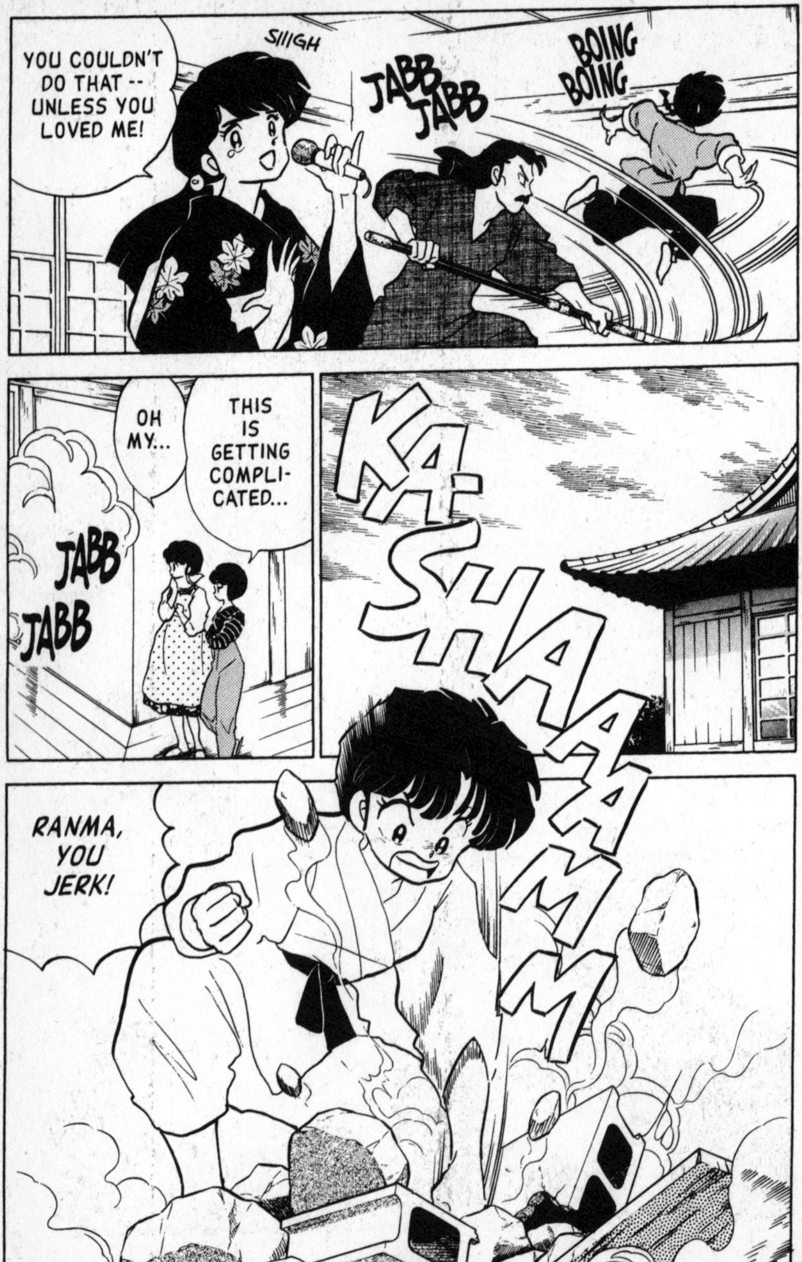
YOU COULDN'T DO THAT -- UNLESS YOU LOVED ME!
SIIIGH
JABB JABB
BOING BOING
OH MY...
THIS IS GETTING COMPLI-CATED...
JABB
JABB
KA-SHAAAAMMM
RANMA, YOU JERK!

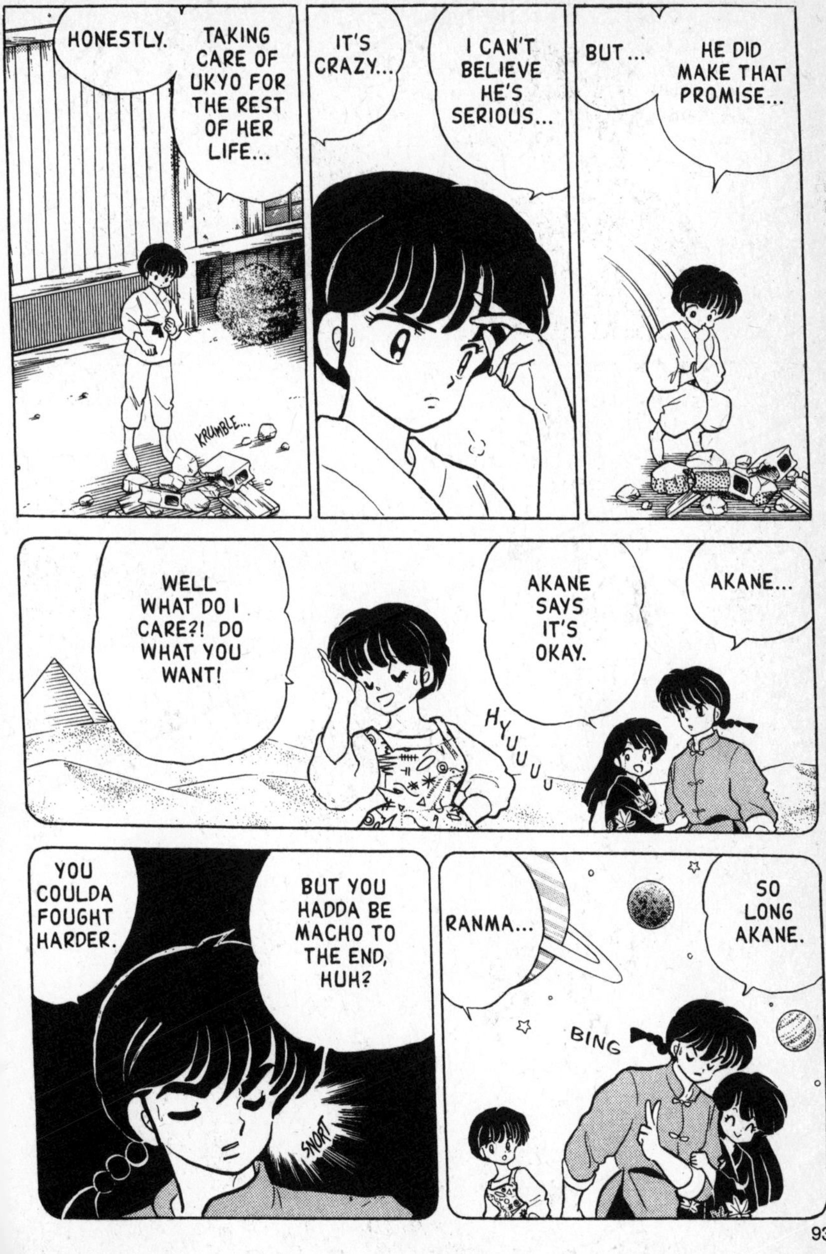
HONESTLY.
TAKING CARE OF UKYO FOR THE REST OF HER LIFE...
KRUMBLE...
IT'S CRAZY...
I CAN'T BELIEVE HE'S SERIOUS...
BUT...
HE DID MAKE THAT PROMISE...
WELL WHAT DO I CARE?! DO WHAT YOU WANT!
HYUUUUU
AKANE SAYS IT'S OKAY.
AKANE...
YOU COULDA FOUGHT HARDER.
BUT YOU HADDA BE MACHO TO THE END, HUH?
SNORT
RANMA...
SO LONG AKANE.
BING

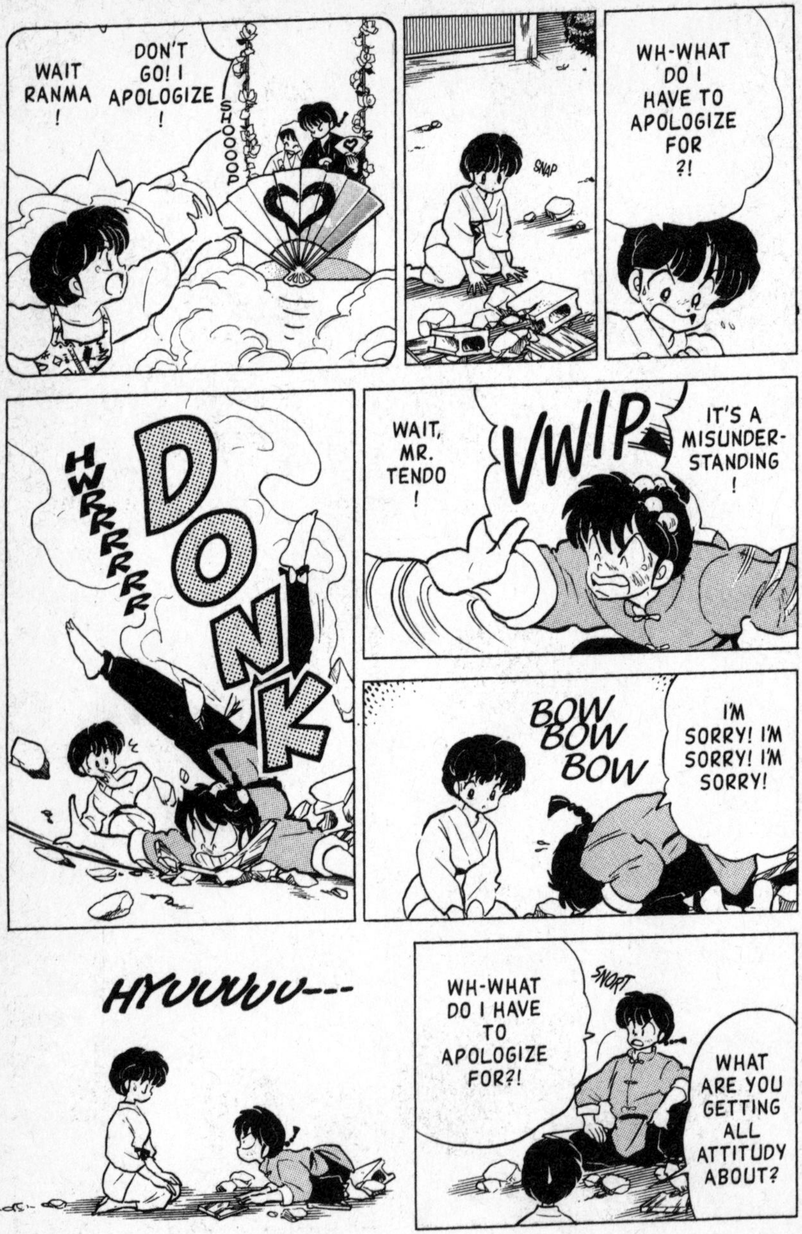
WAIT RANMA!
DON'T GO! I APOLOGIZE!
SHOOOOP
SNAP
WH-WHAT DO I HAVE TO APOLOGIZE FOR?!
HWRRRRRR
DONK
WAIT, MR. TENDO!
VWIP
IT'S A MISUNDERSTANDING!
BOW BOW BOW
I'M SORRY! I'M SORRY! I'M SORRY!
HYUUUUU---
WH-WHAT DO I HAVE TO APOLOGIZE FOR?!
SNORT
WHAT ARE YOU GETTING ALL ATTITUDY ABOUT?

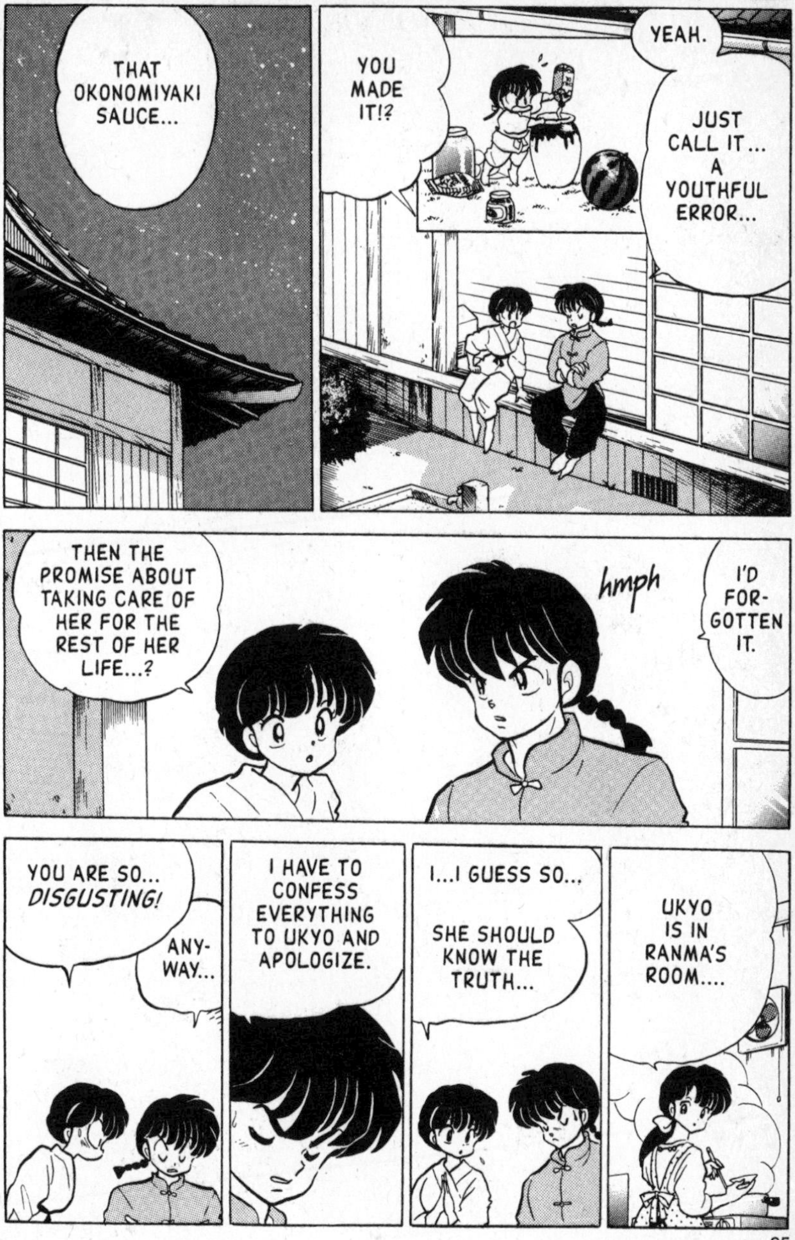
THAT OKONOMIYAKI SAUCE...
YOU MADE IT!?
YEAH.
JUST CALL IT... A YOUTHFUL ERROR...
THEN THE PROMISE ABOUT TAKING CARE OF HER FOR THE REST OF HER LIFE...?
hmph
I'D FOR-GOTTEN IT.
YOU ARE SO... *DISGUSTING!*
ANY-WAY...
I HAVE TO CONFESS EVERYTHING TO UKYO AND APOLOGIZE.
I...I GUESS SO...
SHE SHOULD KNOW THE TRUTH...
UKYO IS IN RANMA'S ROOM....

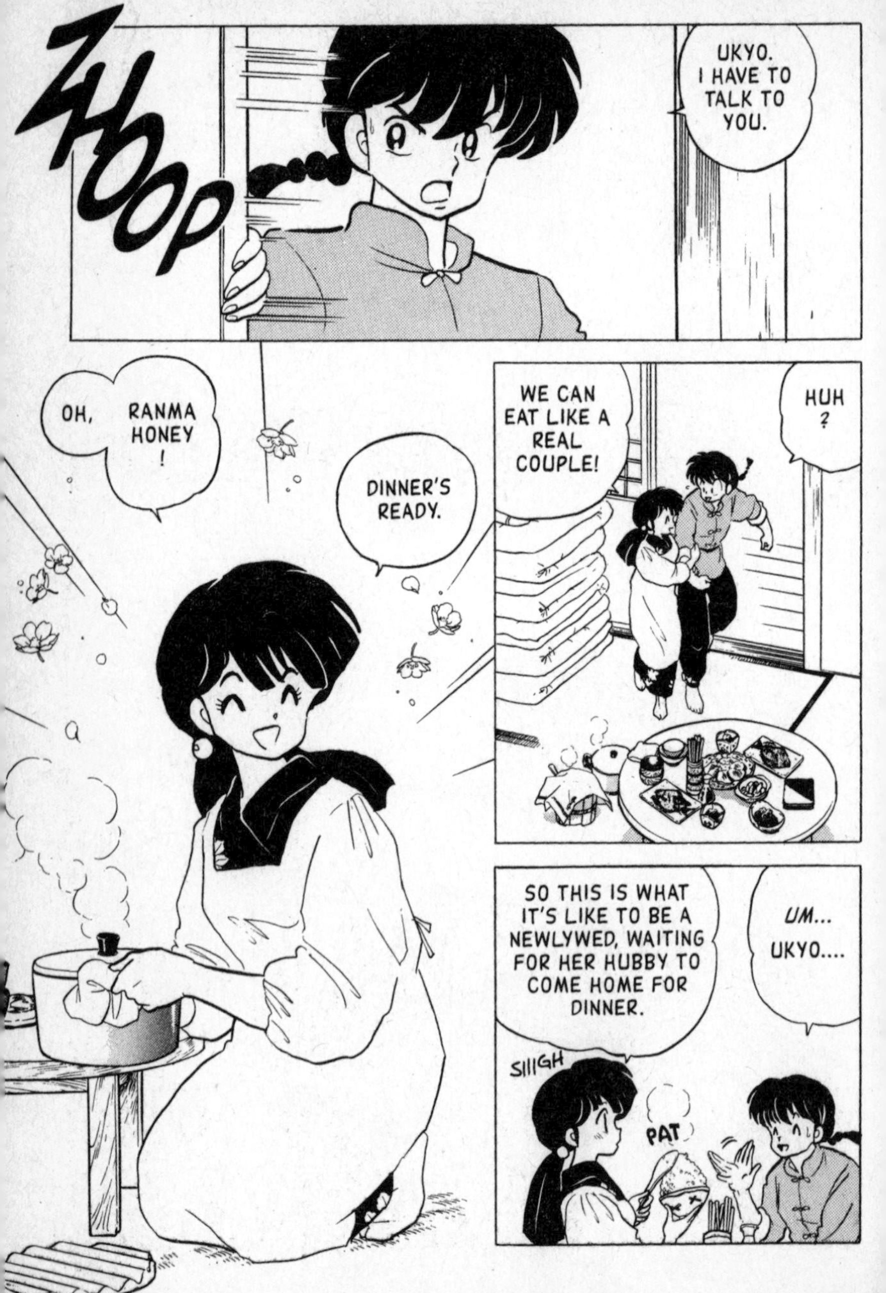
ZHOOP
UKYO. I HAVE TO TALK TO YOU.
OH, RANMA HONEY!
DINNER'S READY.
WE CAN EAT LIKE A REAL COUPLE!
HUH?
SO THIS IS WHAT IT'S LIKE TO BE A NEWLYWED, WAITING FOR HER HUBBY TO COME HOME FOR DINNER.
UM... UKYO....
SIIIGH
PAT

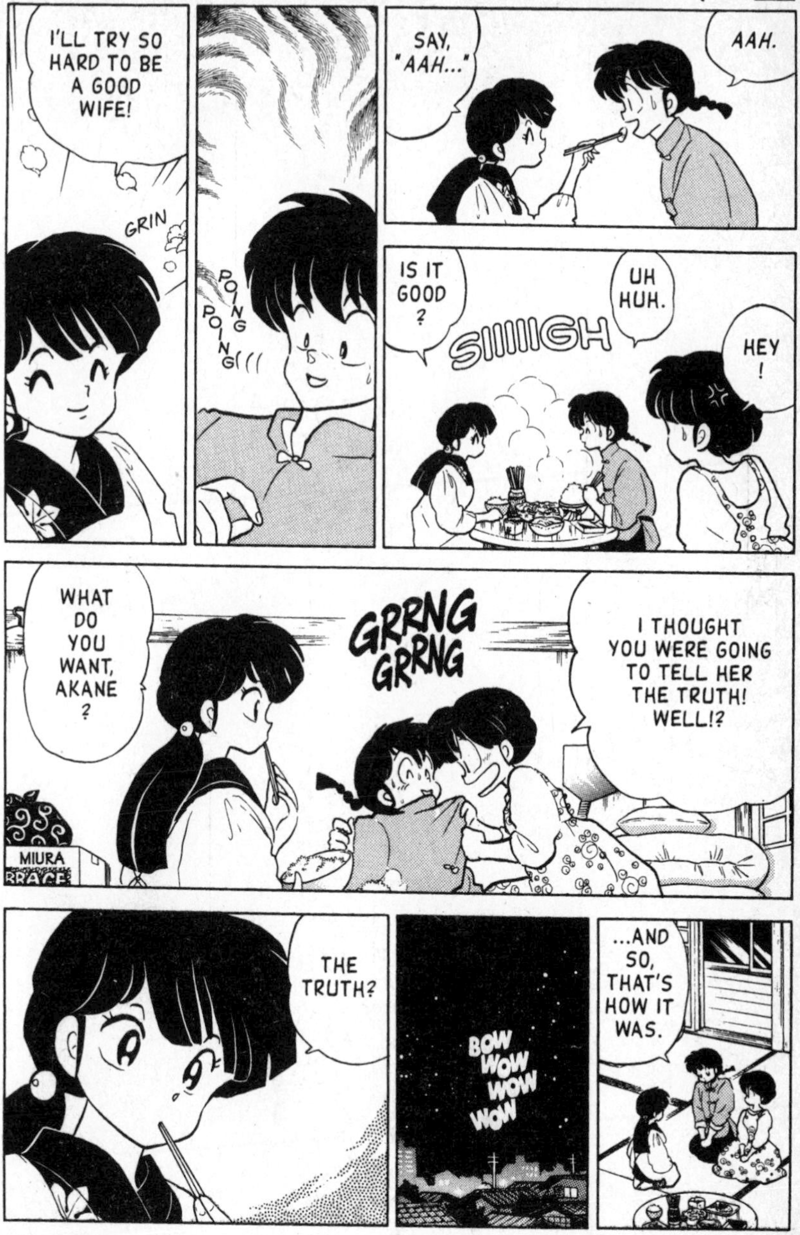
I'LL TRY SO HARD TO BE A GOOD WIFE!
GRIN
POING POING
SAY, "AAH..."
AAH.
IS IT GOOD?
UH HUH.
SIIIIIGH
HEY!
WHAT DO YOU WANT, AKANE?
GRRNG GRRNG
I THOUGHT YOU WERE GOING TO TELL HER THE TRUTH! WELL!?
MIURA
THE TRUTH?
BOW WOW WOW WOW
...AND SO, THAT'S HOW IT WAS.

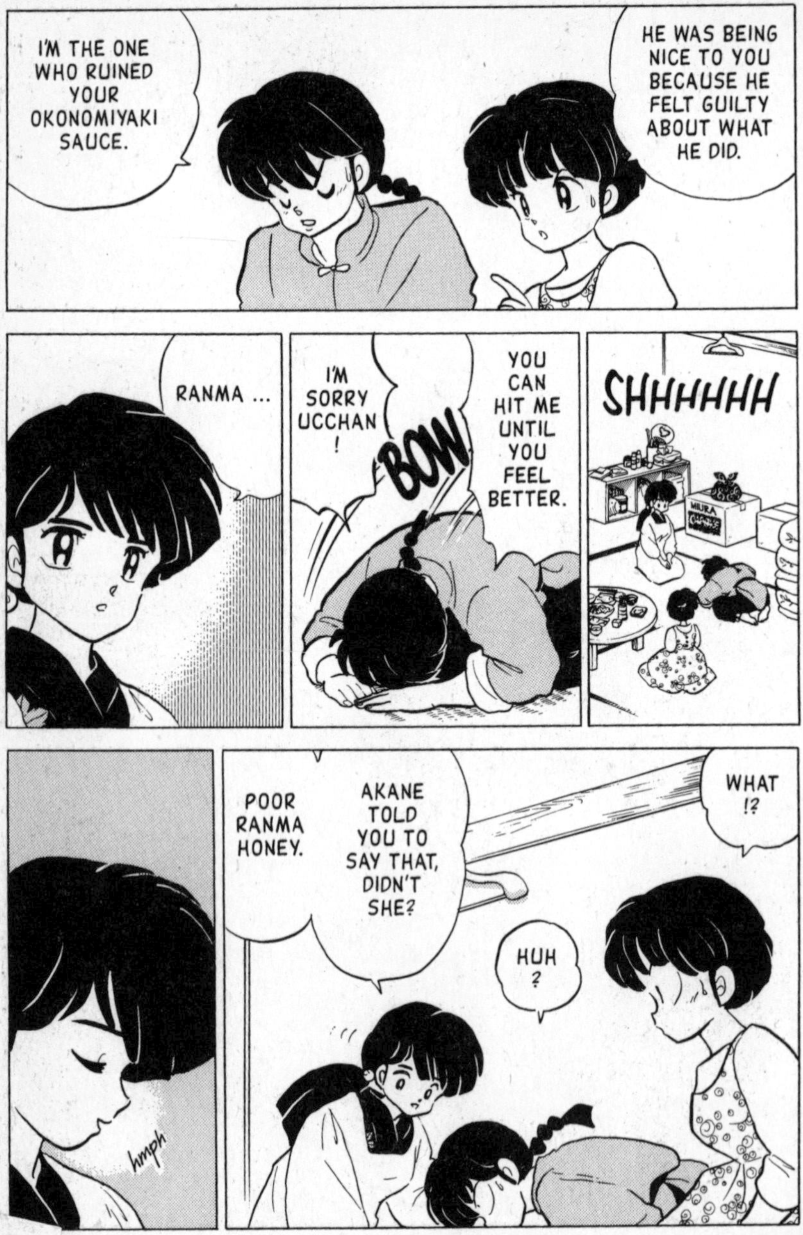
I'M THE ONE WHO RUINED YOUR OKONOMIYAKI SAUCE.
HE WAS BEING NICE TO YOU BECAUSE HE FELT GUILTY ABOUT WHAT HE DID.
RANMA ...
I'M SORRY UCCHAN !
BOW
YOU CAN HIT ME UNTIL YOU FEEL BETTER.
SHHHHHH
MIURA
hmph
POOR RANMA HONEY.
AKANE TOLD YOU TO SAY THAT, DIDN'T SHE?
HUH ?
WHAT !?

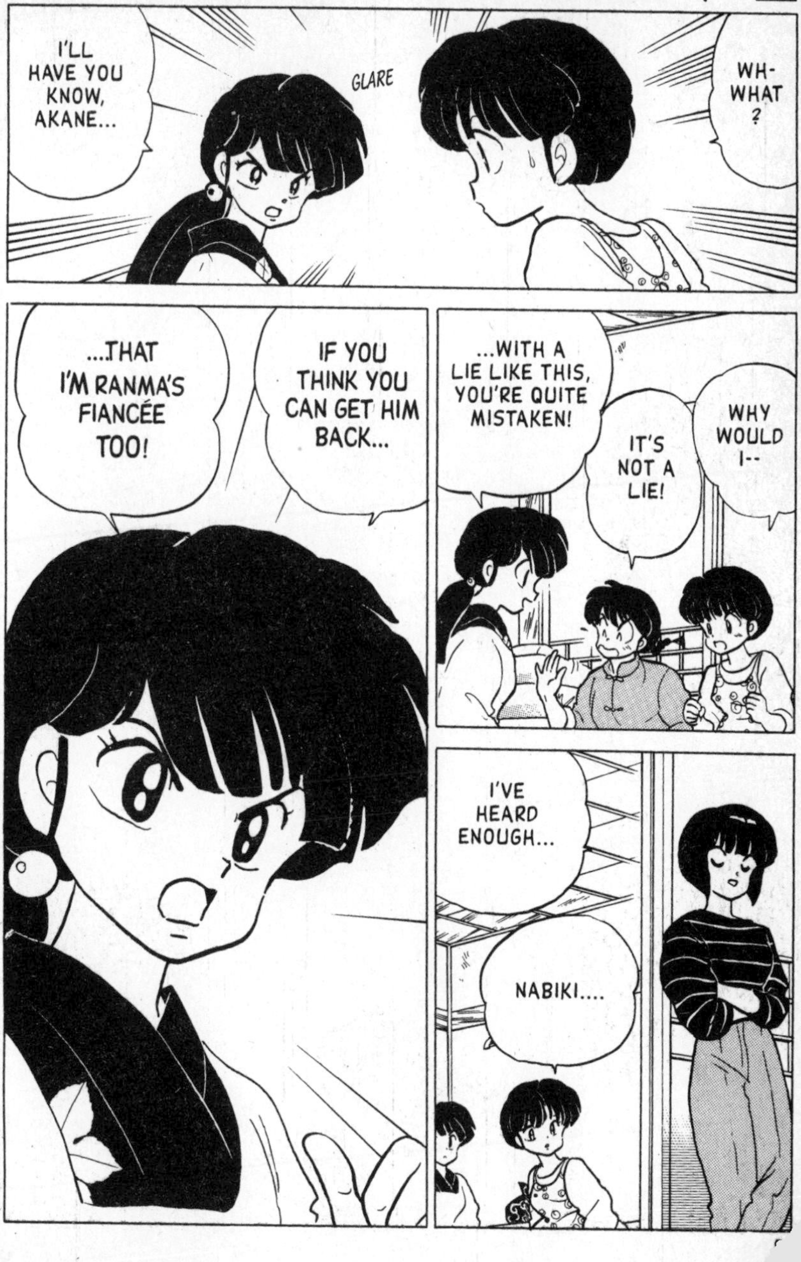
I'LL HAVE YOU KNOW, AKANE...
GLARE
WH- WHAT?
...THAT I'M RANMA'S FIANCÉE TOO!
IF YOU THINK YOU CAN GET HIM BACK...
...WITH A LIE LIKE THIS, YOU'RE QUITE MISTAKEN!
IT'S NOT A LIE!
WHY WOULD I--
I'VE HEARD ENOUGH...
NABIKI....

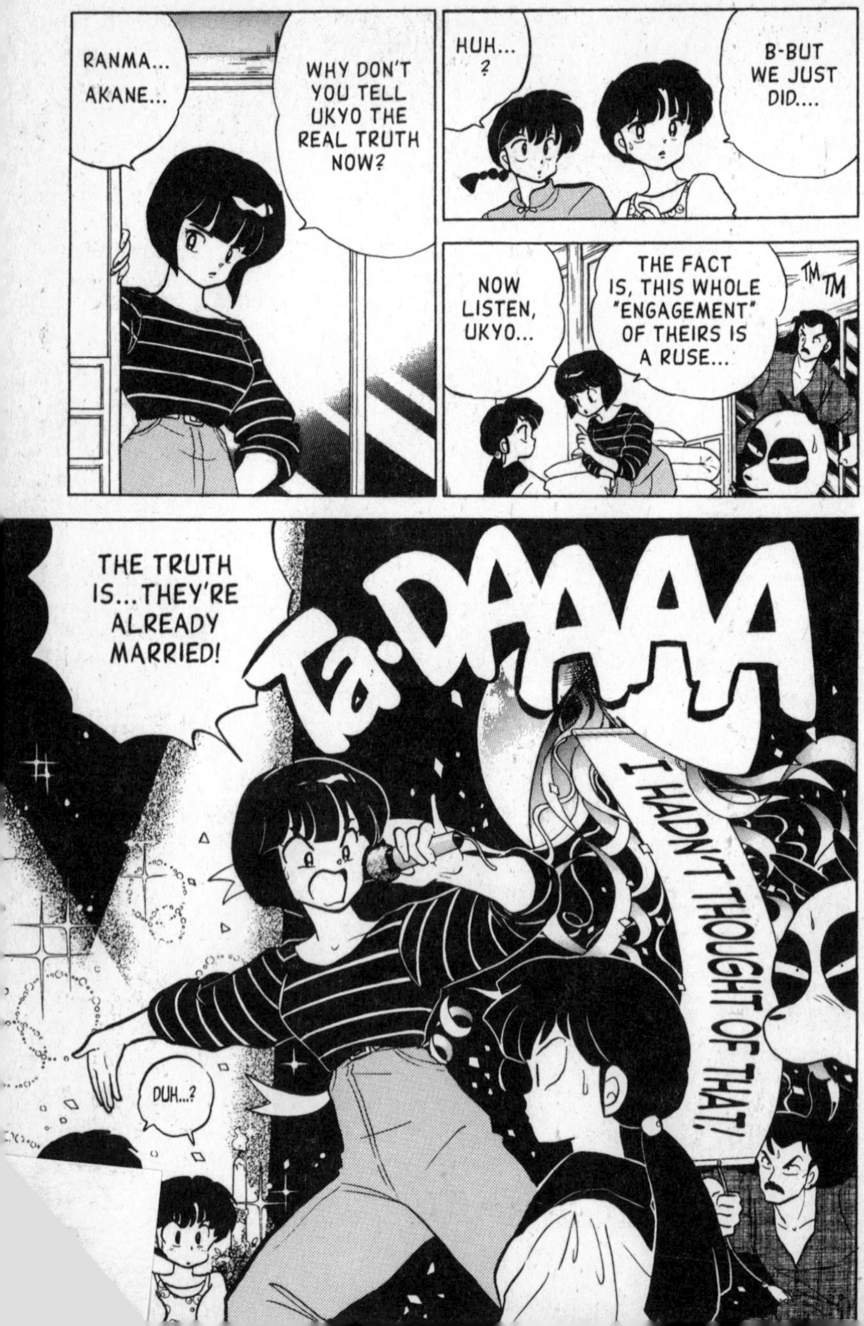
RANMA... AKANE...
WHY DON'T YOU TELL UKYO THE REAL TRUTH NOW?
HUH... ?
B-BUT WE JUST DID....
NOW LISTEN, UKYO...
THE FACT IS, THIS WHOLE "ENGAGEMENT" OF THEIRS IS A RUSE...
TM TM
THE TRUTH IS...THEY'RE ALREADY MARRIED!
TA-DAAAA
I HADN'T THOUGHT OF THAT!
DUH...?

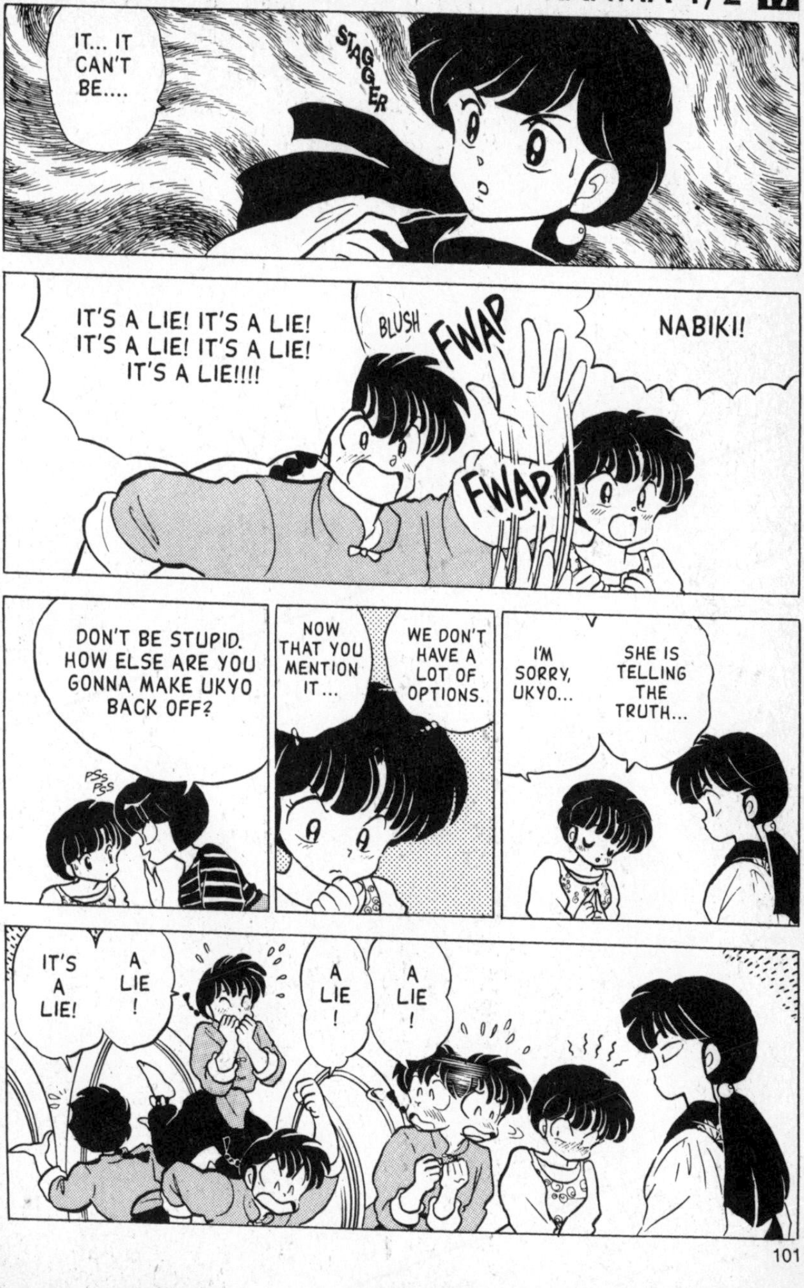
IT... IT CAN'T BE....
STAGGER
IT'S A LIE! IT'S A LIE! IT'S A LIE! IT'S A LIE! IT'S A LIE!!!!
BLUSH
FWAP
NABIKI!
FWAP
DON'T BE STUPID. HOW ELSE ARE YOU GONNA MAKE UKYO BACK OFF?
PSS PSS
NOW THAT YOU MENTION IT...
WE DON'T HAVE A LOT OF OPTIONS.
I'M SORRY, UKYO...
SHE IS TELLING THE TRUTH...
IT'S A LIE!
A LIE!
A LIE!
A LIE!

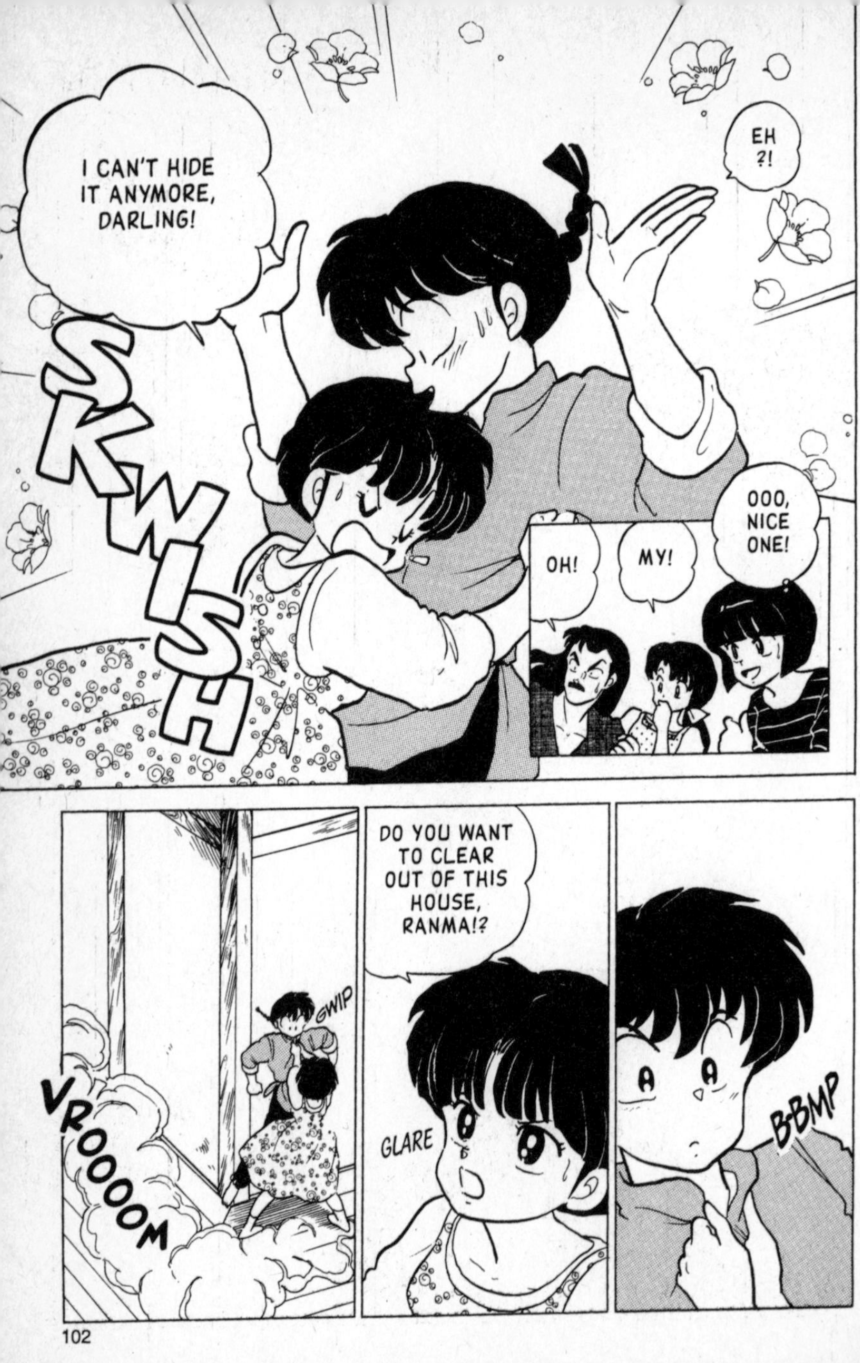
I CAN'T HIDE IT ANYMORE, DARLING!
SKWISH
EH ?!
OH!
MY!
OOO, NICE ONE!
GWIP
VROOOOM
DO YOU WANT TO CLEAR OUT OF THIS HOUSE, RANMA!?
GLARE
B-BMP

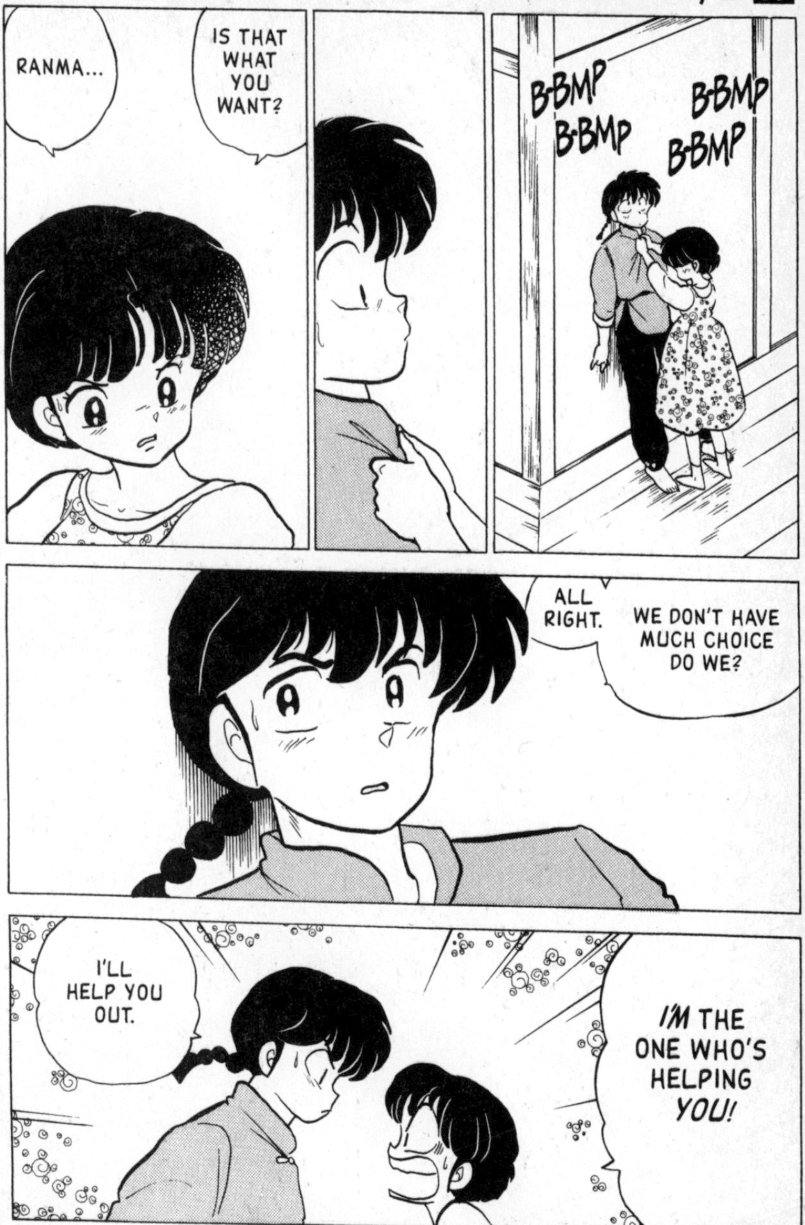
RANMA...
IS THAT WHAT YOU WANT?
B-BMP
B-BMP
B-BMP
B-BMP
ALL RIGHT.
WE DON'T HAVE MUCH CHOICE DO WE?
I'LL HELP YOU OUT.
I'M THE ONE WHO'S HELPING *YOU!*

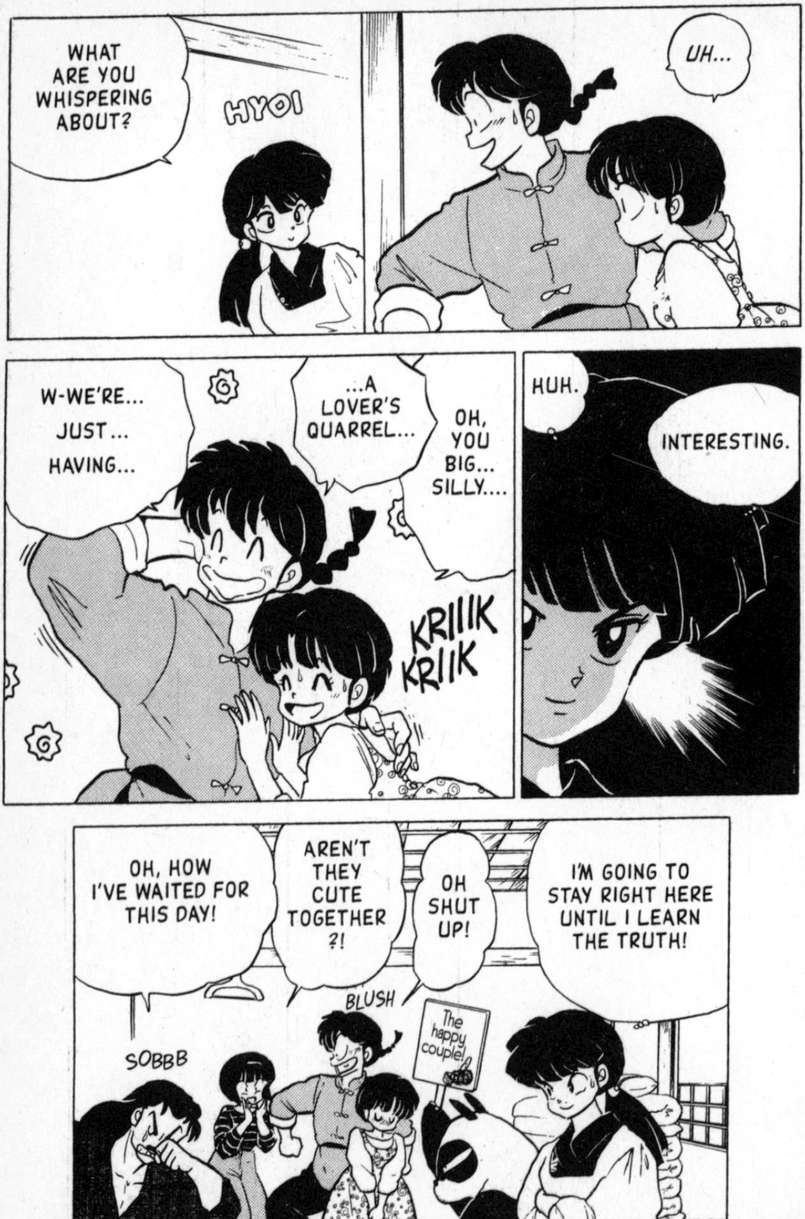
WHAT ARE YOU WHISPERING ABOUT?
HYOI
UH...
W-WE'RE... JUST... HAVING...
...A LOVER'S QUARREL...
OH, YOU BIG... SILLY....
KRIIIK KRIIK
HUH.
INTERESTING.
OH, HOW I'VE WAITED FOR THIS DAY!
SOBBB
AREN'T THEY CUTE TOGETHER?!
OH SHUT UP!
BLUSH
The happy couple!
I'M GOING TO STAY RIGHT HERE UNTIL I LEARN THE TRUTH!

Part 7
THE HONEYMOON PERIOD

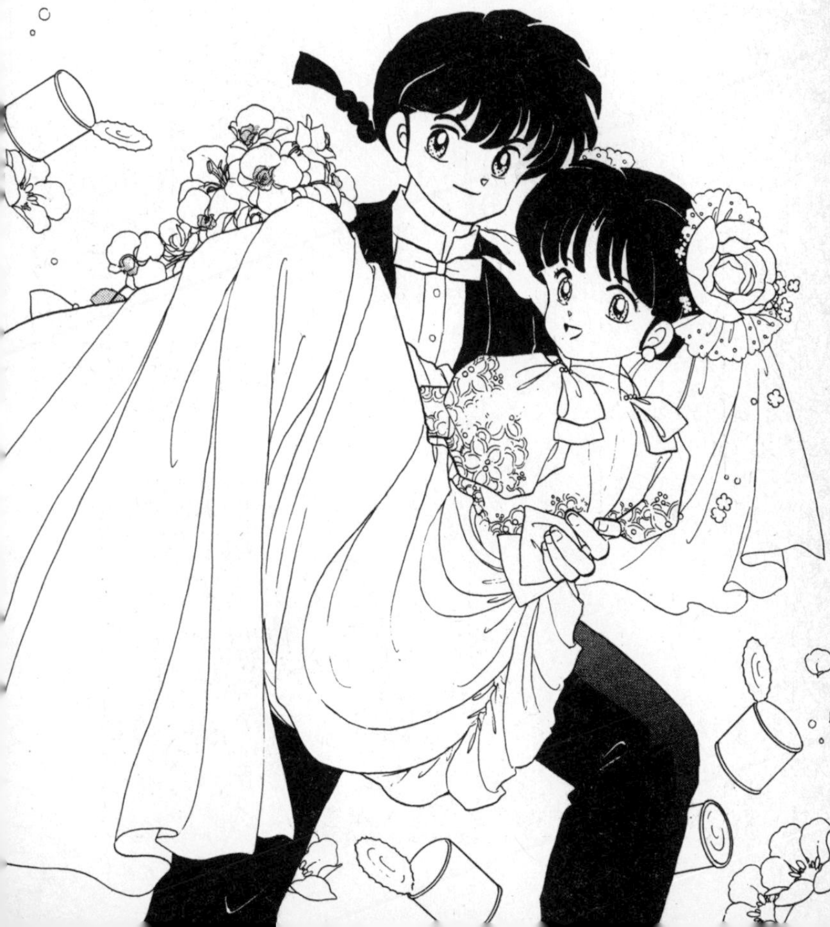

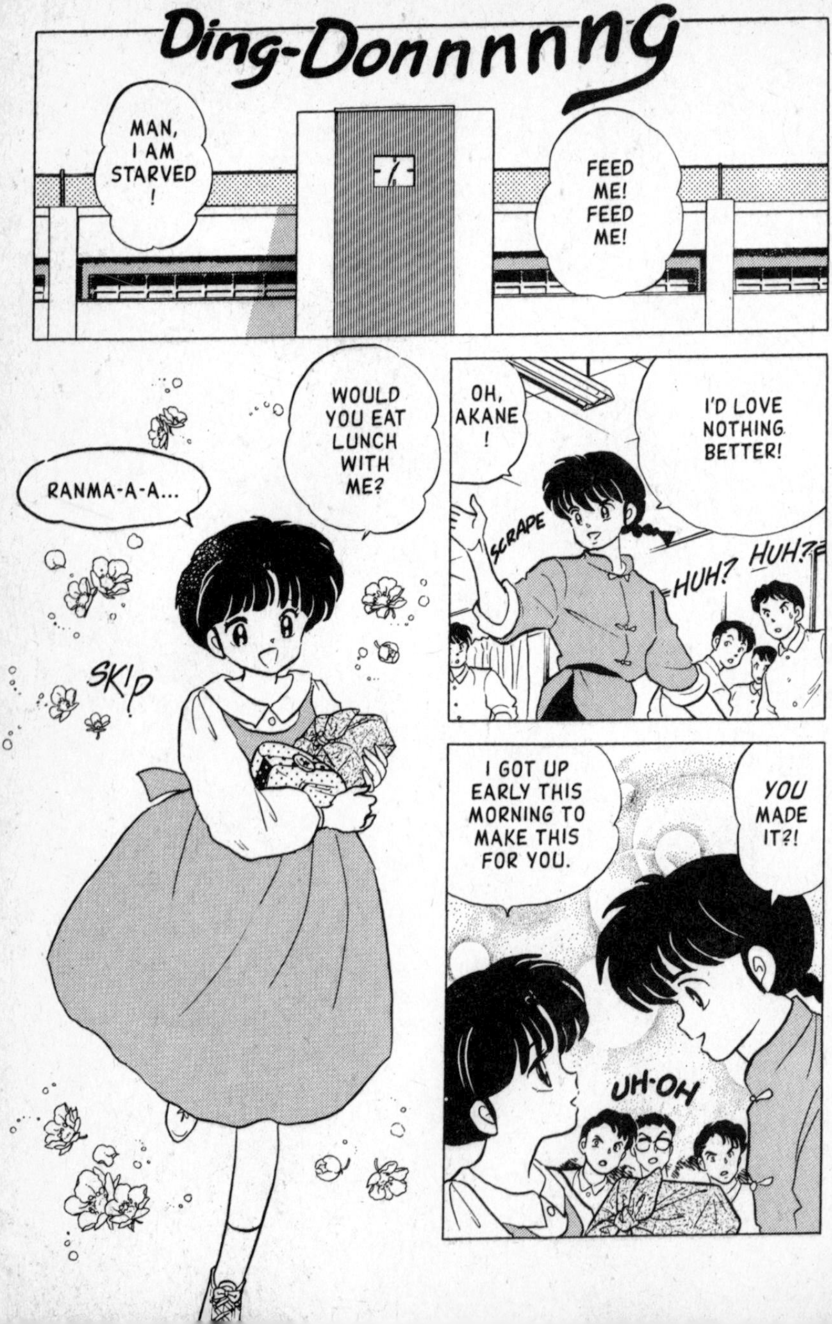
Ding-Donnnnng
MAN, I AM STARVED!
FEED ME! FEED ME!
RANMA-A-A...
WOULD YOU EAT LUNCH WITH ME?
SKIP
OH, AKANE!
I'D LOVE NOTHING BETTER!
SCRAPE
HUH? HUH??
I GOT UP EARLY THIS MORNING TO MAKE THIS FOR YOU.
YOU MADE IT?!
UH-OH

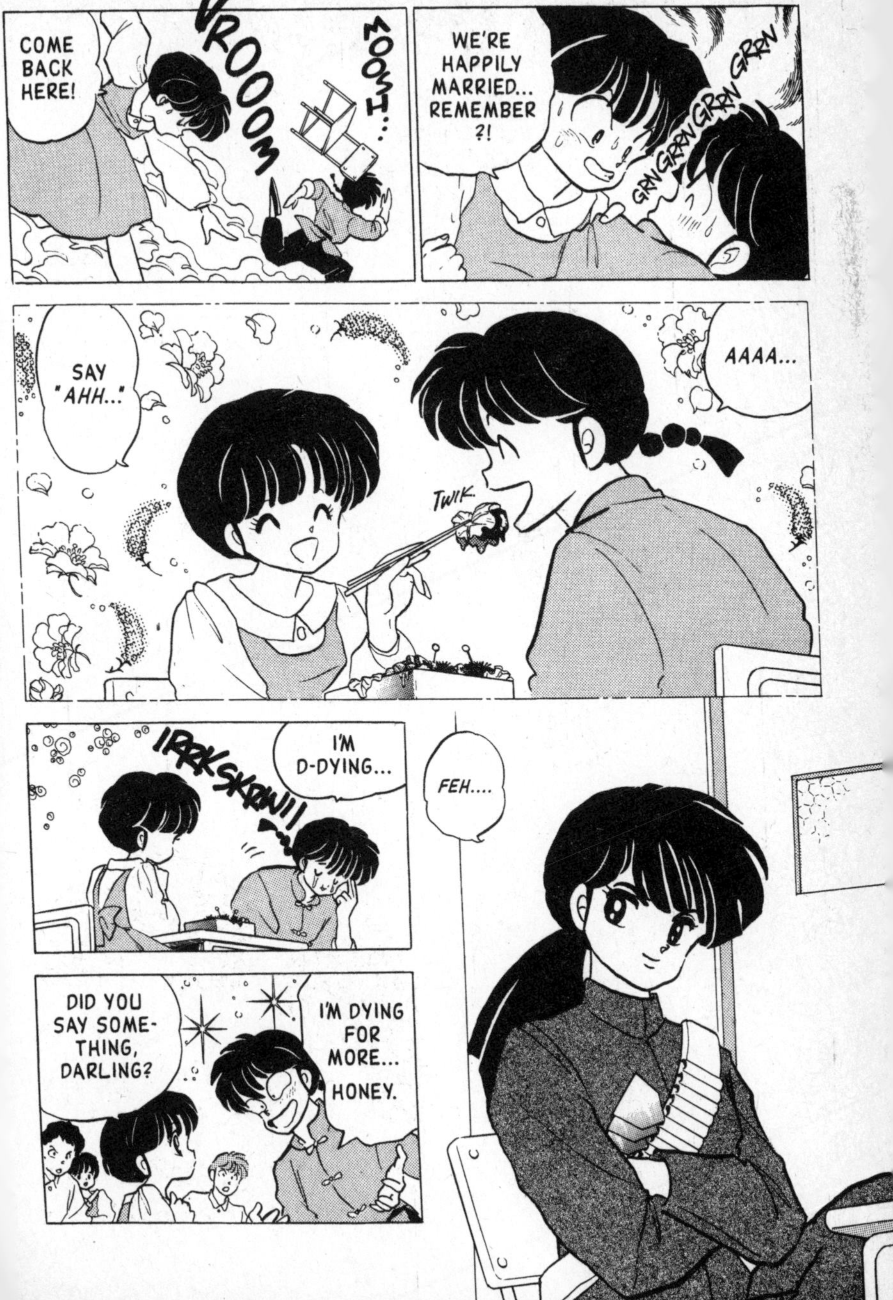
COME BACK HERE!
VROOOOM
WOOSH...
WE'RE HAPPILY MARRIED... REMEMBER?!
GRRN GRRN GRRN GRRN
SAY "AHH..."
TWIK
AAAA...
I'M D-DYING...
!RRKSKRN!!
DID YOU SAY SOMETHING, DARLING?
I'M DYING FOR MORE... HONEY.
FEH....

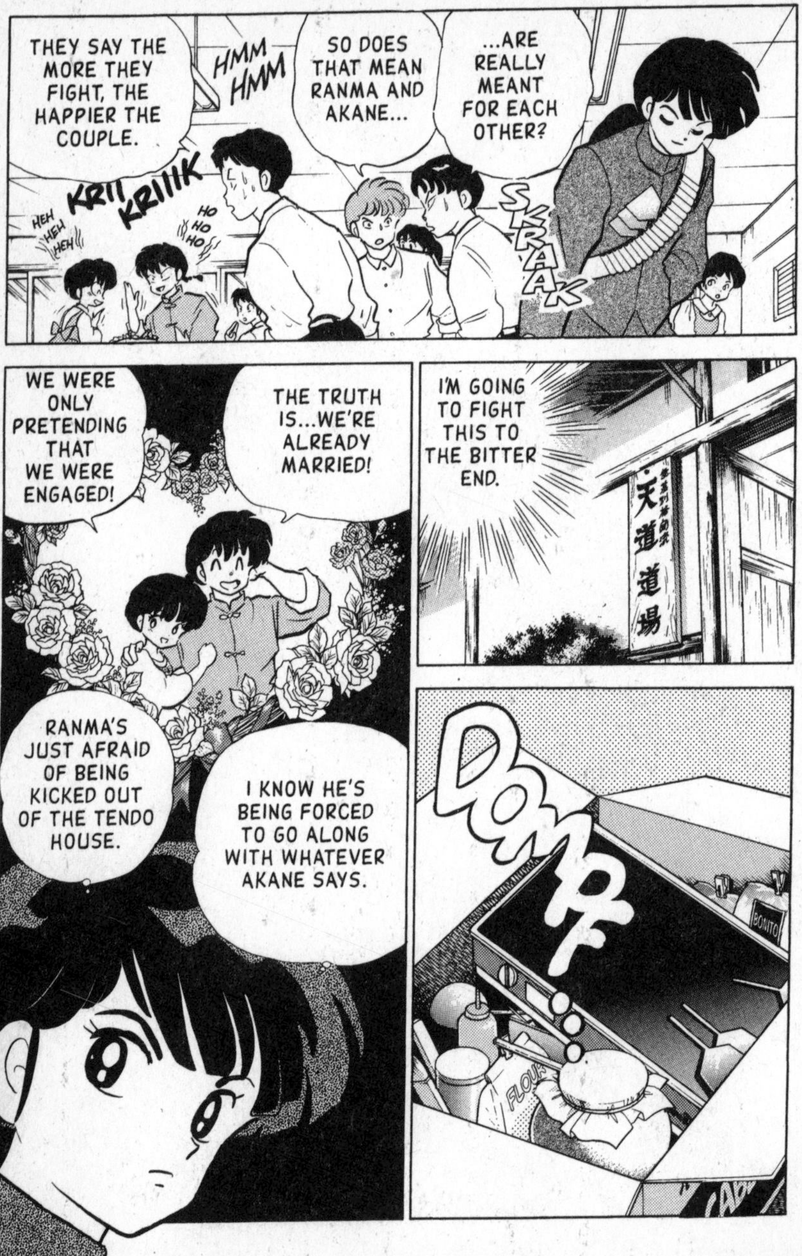
THEY SAY THE MORE THEY FIGHT, THE HAPPIER THE COUPLE.
HMM HMM
SO DOES THAT MEAN RANMA AND AKANE...
...ARE REALLY MEANT FOR EACH OTHER?
KRII KRIIIK
HEH HEH HEH
HO HO HO
SKRAAK
WE WERE ONLY PRETENDING THAT WE WERE ENGAGED!
THE TRUTH IS...WE'RE ALREADY MARRIED!
RANMA'S JUST AFRAID OF BEING KICKED OUT OF THE TENDO HOUSE.
I KNOW HE'S BEING FORCED TO GO ALONG WITH WHATEVER AKANE SAYS.
I'M GOING TO FIGHT THIS TO THE BITTER END.
天道道場
DOMPF...
BONITO
FLOUR

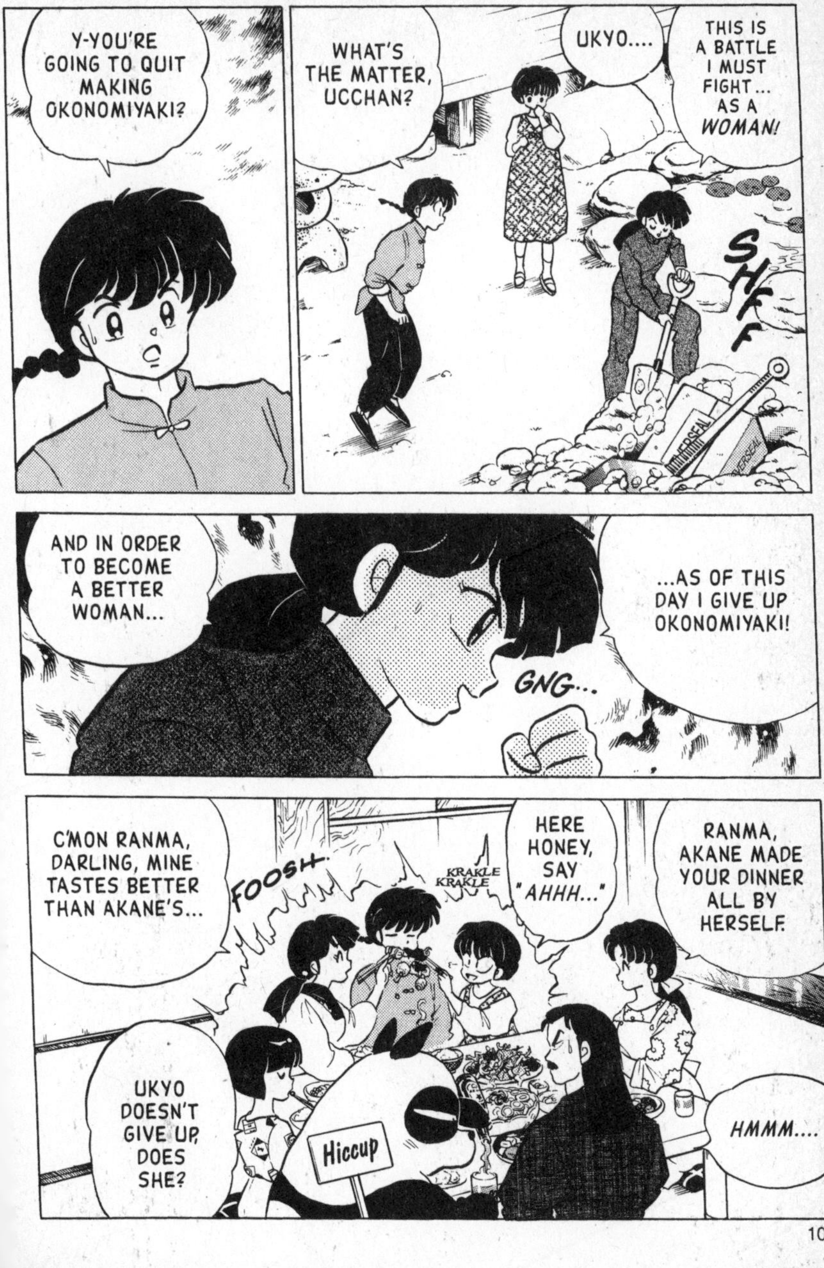
Y-YOU'RE GOING TO QUIT MAKING OKONOMIYAKI?
WHAT'S THE MATTER, UCCHAN?
UKYO....
THIS IS A BATTLE I MUST FIGHT... AS A *WOMAN!*
SHFF
AND IN ORDER TO BECOME A BETTER WOMAN...
...AS OF THIS DAY I GIVE UP OKONOMIYAKI!
GNG...
C'MON RANMA, DARLING, MINE TASTES BETTER THAN AKANE'S...
FOOSH
KRAKLE KRAKLE
HERE HONEY, SAY "AHHH..."
RANMA, AKANE MADE YOUR DINNER ALL BY HERSELF.
UKYO DOESN'T GIVE UP, DOES SHE?
Hiccup
HMMM....

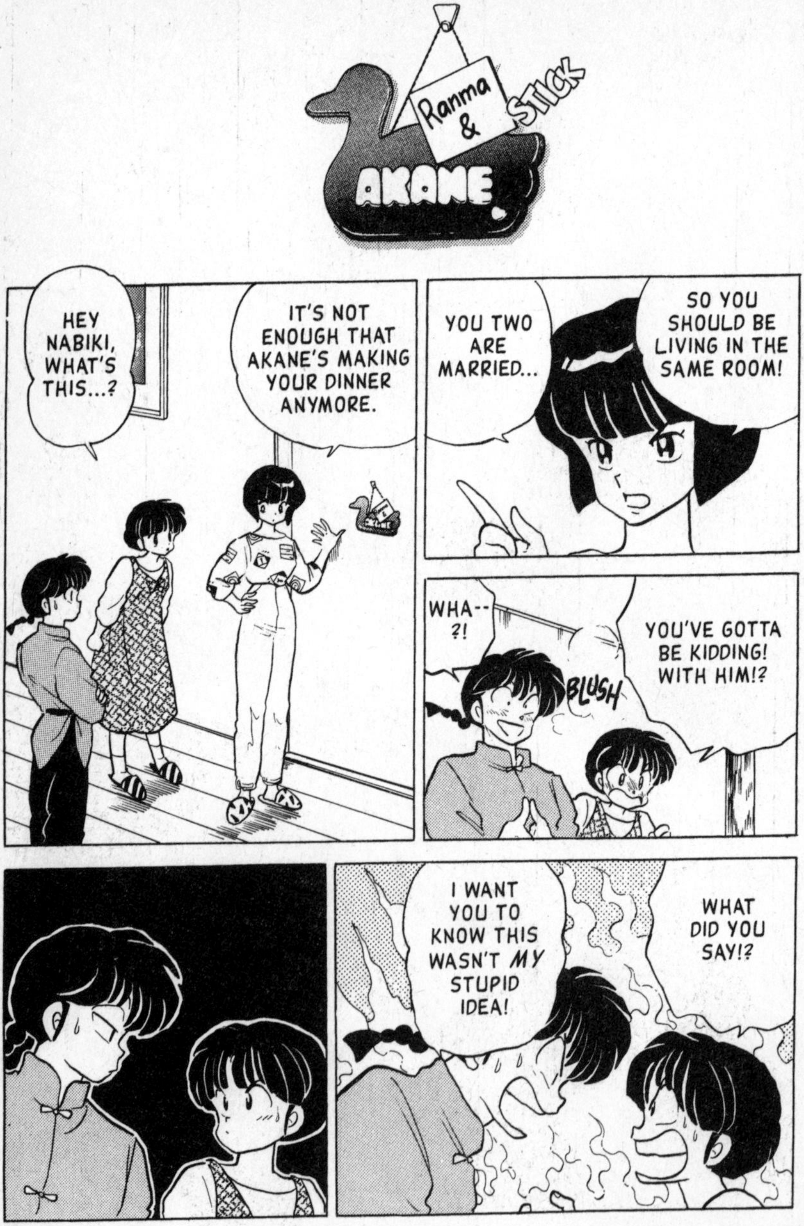

Ranma & Akane STICK
HEY NABIKI, WHAT'S THIS...?
IT'S NOT ENOUGH THAT AKANE'S MAKING YOUR DINNER ANYMORE.
YOU TWO ARE MARRIED...
SO YOU SHOULD BE LIVING IN THE SAME ROOM!
WHA-- ?!
BLUSH
YOU'VE GOTTA BE KIDDING! WITH HIM!?
I WANT YOU TO KNOW THIS WASN'T *MY* STUPID IDEA!
WHAT DID YOU SAY!?

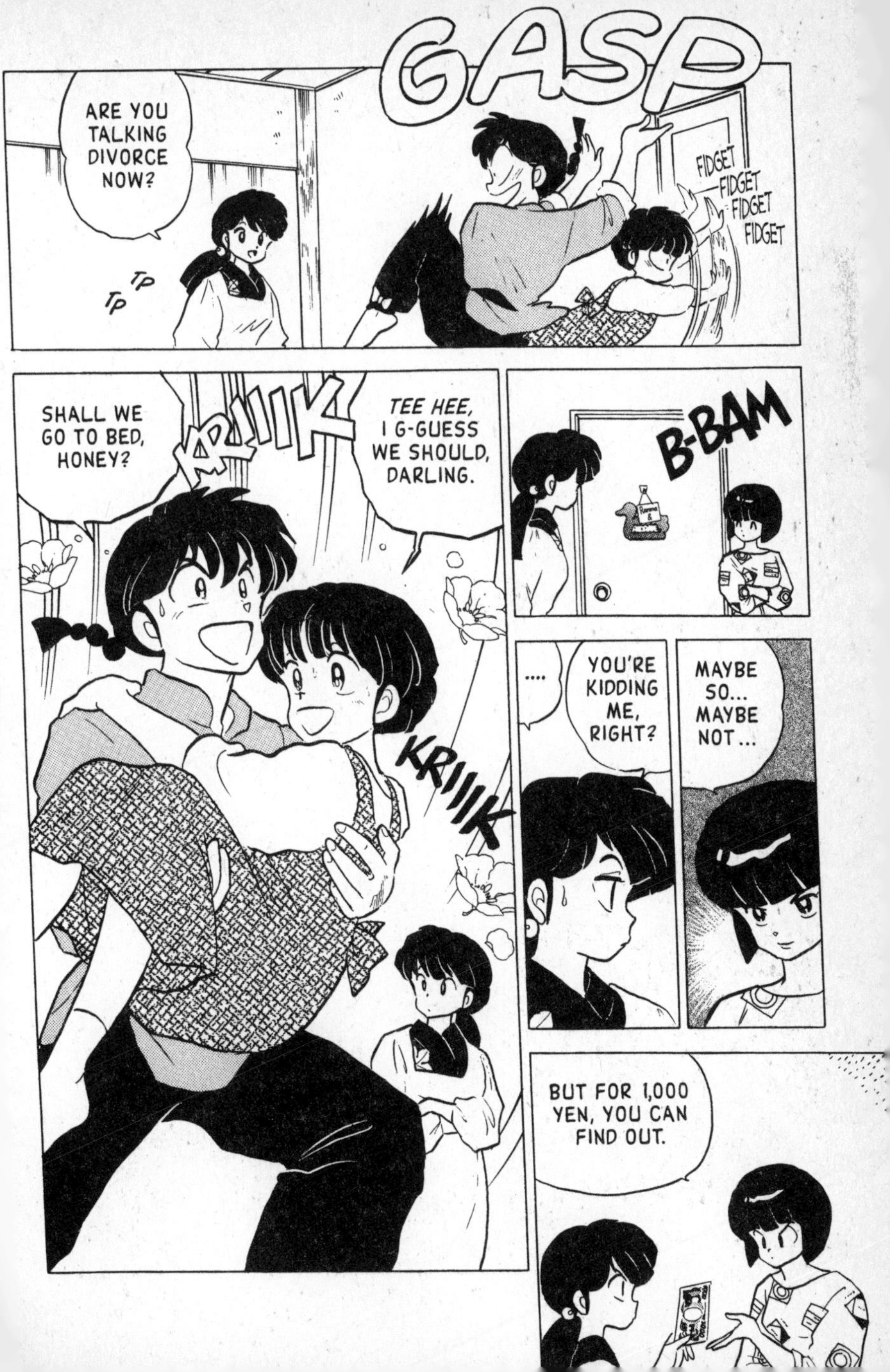
ARE YOU TALKING DIVORCE NOW?
TP TP
GASP
FIDGET FIDGET FIDGET FIDGET
SHALL WE GO TO BED, HONEY?
KRIIIK
TEE HEE, I G-GUESS WE SHOULD, DARLING.
KRIIIK
B-BAM
....
YOU'RE KIDDING ME, RIGHT?
MAYBE SO... MAYBE NOT...
BUT FOR 1,000 YEN, YOU CAN FIND OUT.

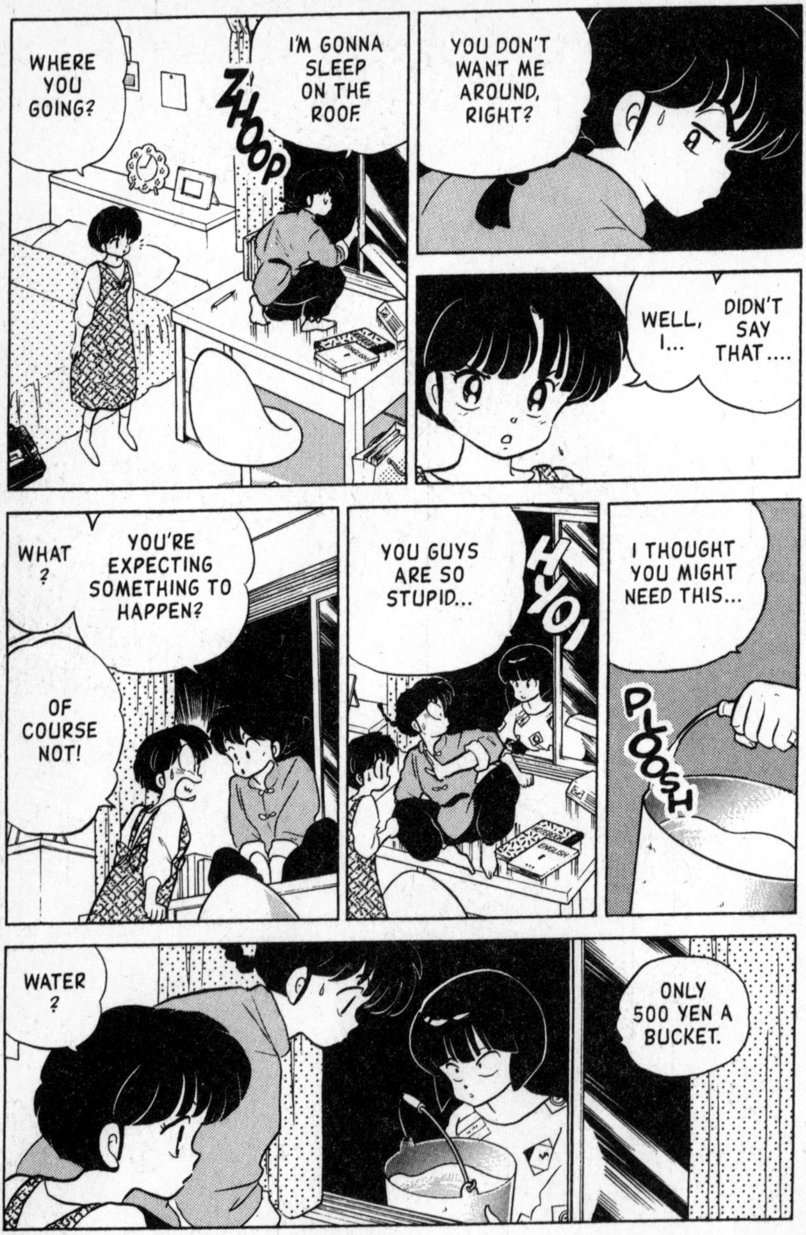
WHERE YOU GOING?
I'M GONNA SLEEP ON THE ROOF.
ZHOOP
YOU DON'T WANT ME AROUND, RIGHT?
WELL, I...
DIDN'T SAY THAT....
WHAT?
YOU'RE EXPECTING SOMETHING TO HAPPEN?
OF COURSE NOT!
YOU GUYS ARE SO STUPID...
HYOI
I THOUGHT YOU MIGHT NEED THIS...
PLOOSH
WATER?
ONLY 500 YEN A BUCKET.

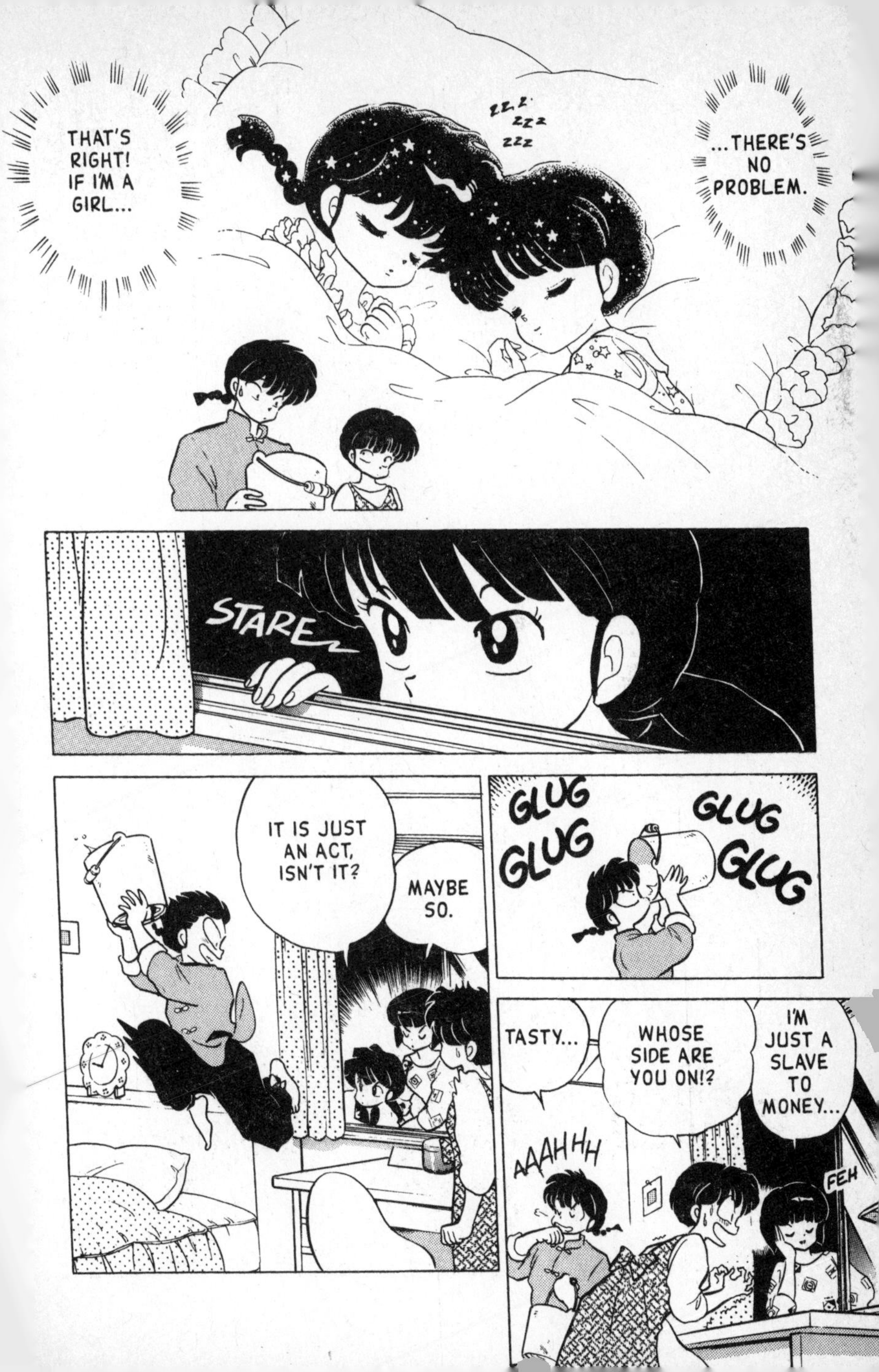
THAT'S RIGHT! IF I'M A GIRL...
ZZZ ZZZ ZZZ
...THERE'S NO PROBLEM.
STARE
IT IS JUST AN ACT, ISN'T IT?
MAYBE SO.
GLUG GLUG
GLUG GLUG
TASTY...
WHOSE SIDE ARE YOU ON!?
I'M JUST A SLAVE TO MONEY...
AAAHHH
FEH

BOW WOW WOW

TIK TIK TIK TIK

B-BMP B-BMP B-BMP
B-BMP
B-BMP

B-BMP B-BMP B-BMP

B-BMP B-BMP

B-BMP B-BMP
B-BMP

KRIIIIII

CKONG

STOP LISTENING IN!

GASHUNNG TONG-KLARA

SHEESH!

BAM

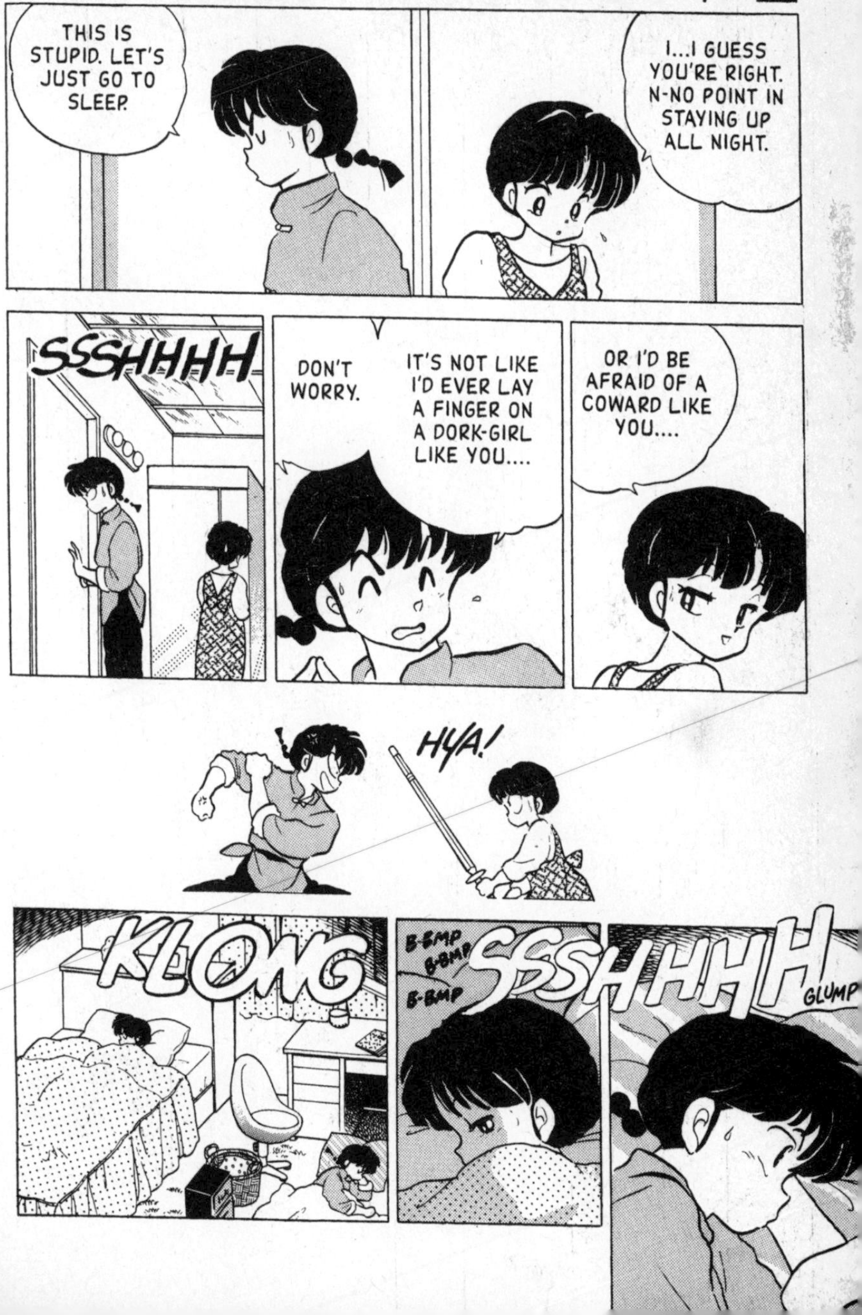
THIS IS STUPID. LET'S JUST GO TO SLEEP.
I...I GUESS YOU'RE RIGHT. N-NO POINT IN STAYING UP ALL NIGHT.
SSSHHHH
DON'T WORRY.
IT'S NOT LIKE I'D EVER LAY A FINGER ON A DORK-GIRL LIKE YOU....
OR I'D BE AFRAID OF A COWARD LIKE YOU....
HYA!
KLONG
B-BMP
B-BMP
B-BMP
SSSHHHH
GLUMP

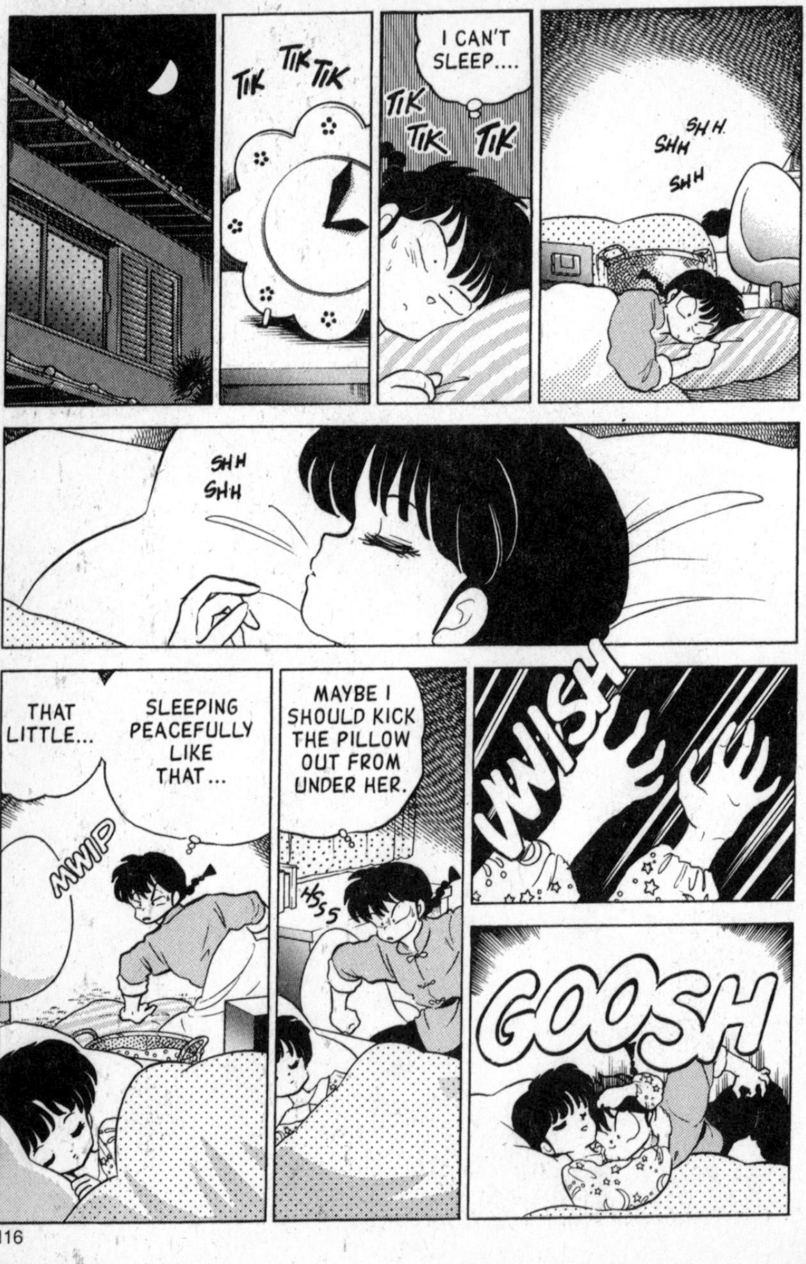

TIK
TIK
TIK
I CAN'T SLEEP....
TIK
TIK
TIK
SHH
SHH
SHH
SHH
SHH
THAT LITTLE...
SLEEPING PEACEFULLY LIKE THAT...
MWIP
MAYBE I SHOULD KICK THE PILLOW OUT FROM UNDER HER.
HSSS
VWISH
GOOSH

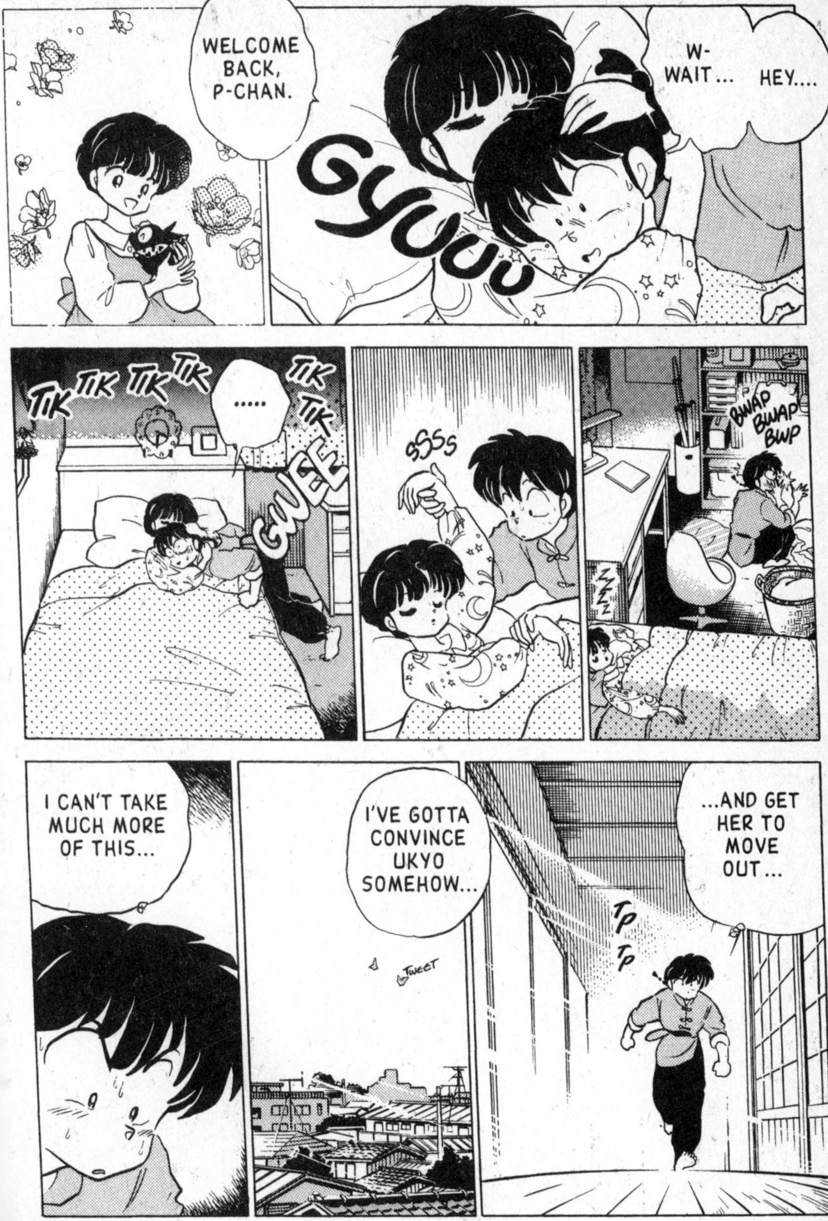
WELCOME BACK, P-CHAN.
GYUUU
W- WAIT... HEY....
TIK TIK TIK TIK
......
TIK TIK
GWEE
SSSS
BWAP BWAP BWP
I CAN'T TAKE MUCH MORE OF THIS...
I'VE GOTTA CONVINCE UKYO SOMEHOW...
TWEET
TP TP
...AND GET HER TO MOVE OUT...

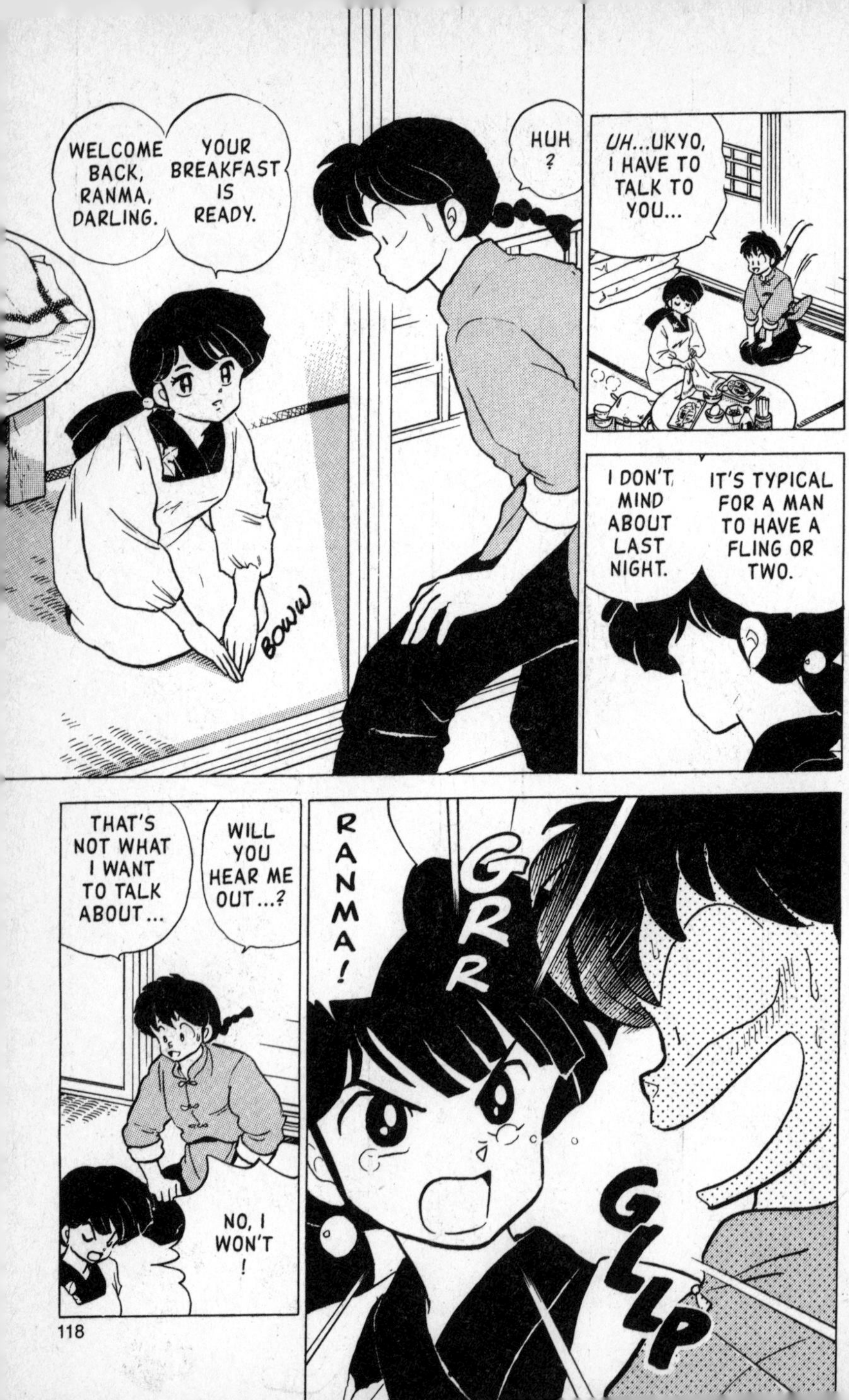
WELCOME BACK, RANMA, DARLING.
YOUR BREAKFAST IS READY.
BOWW
HUH?
UH...UKYO, I HAVE TO TALK TO YOU...
I DON'T MIND ABOUT LAST NIGHT.
IT'S TYPICAL FOR A MAN TO HAVE A FLING OR TWO.
THAT'S NOT WHAT I WANT TO TALK ABOUT...
WILL YOU HEAR ME OUT...?
NO, I WON'T!
RANMA!
GRR
GLLP

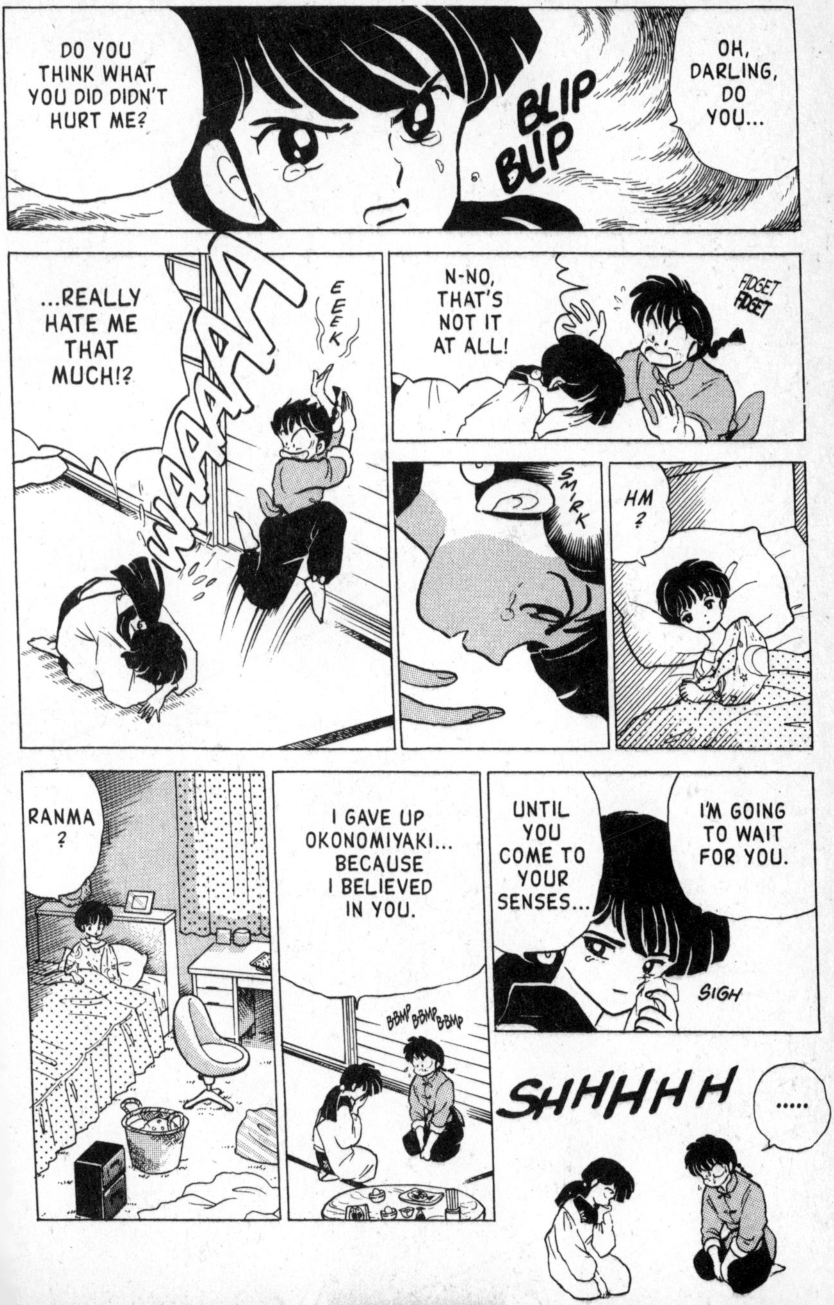
DO YOU THINK WHAT YOU DID DIDN'T HURT ME?
BLIP BLIP
OH, DARLING, DO YOU...
...REALLY HATE ME THAT MUCH!?
WAAAAH
EEEK
N-NO, THAT'S NOT IT AT ALL!
FIDGET FIDGET
SMIRK
HM ?
RANMA ?
I GAVE UP OKONOMIYAKI... BECAUSE I BELIEVED IN YOU.
UNTIL YOU COME TO YOUR SENSES...
I'M GOING TO WAIT FOR YOU.
SIGH
SHHHHH
.....

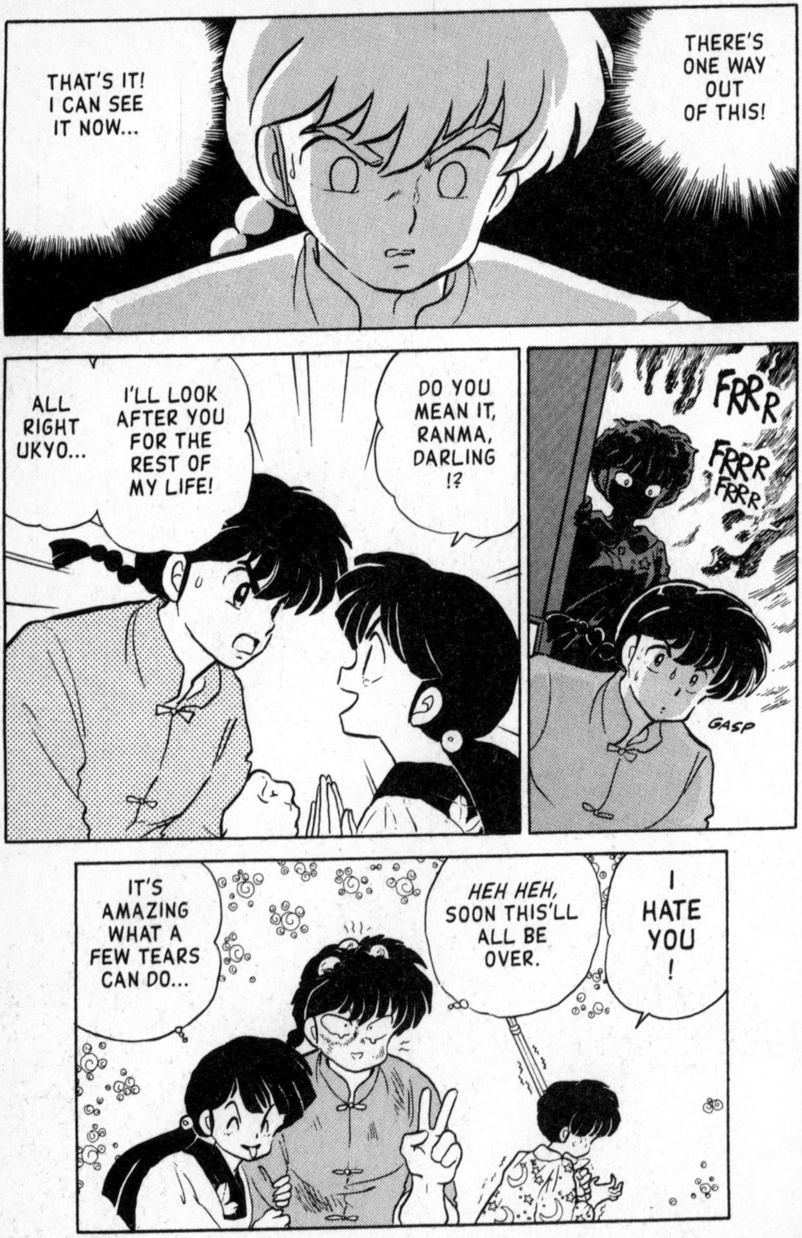
THAT'S IT! I CAN SEE IT NOW...
THERE'S ONE WAY OUT OF THIS!
ALL RIGHT UKYO...
I'LL LOOK AFTER YOU FOR THE REST OF MY LIFE!
DO YOU MEAN IT, RANMA, DARLING !?
FRRR
FRRR FRRR
GASP
IT'S AMAZING WHAT A FEW TEARS CAN DO...
HEH HEH, SOON THIS'LL ALL BE OVER.
I HATE YOU !

Part 8
PLEASE HATE ME

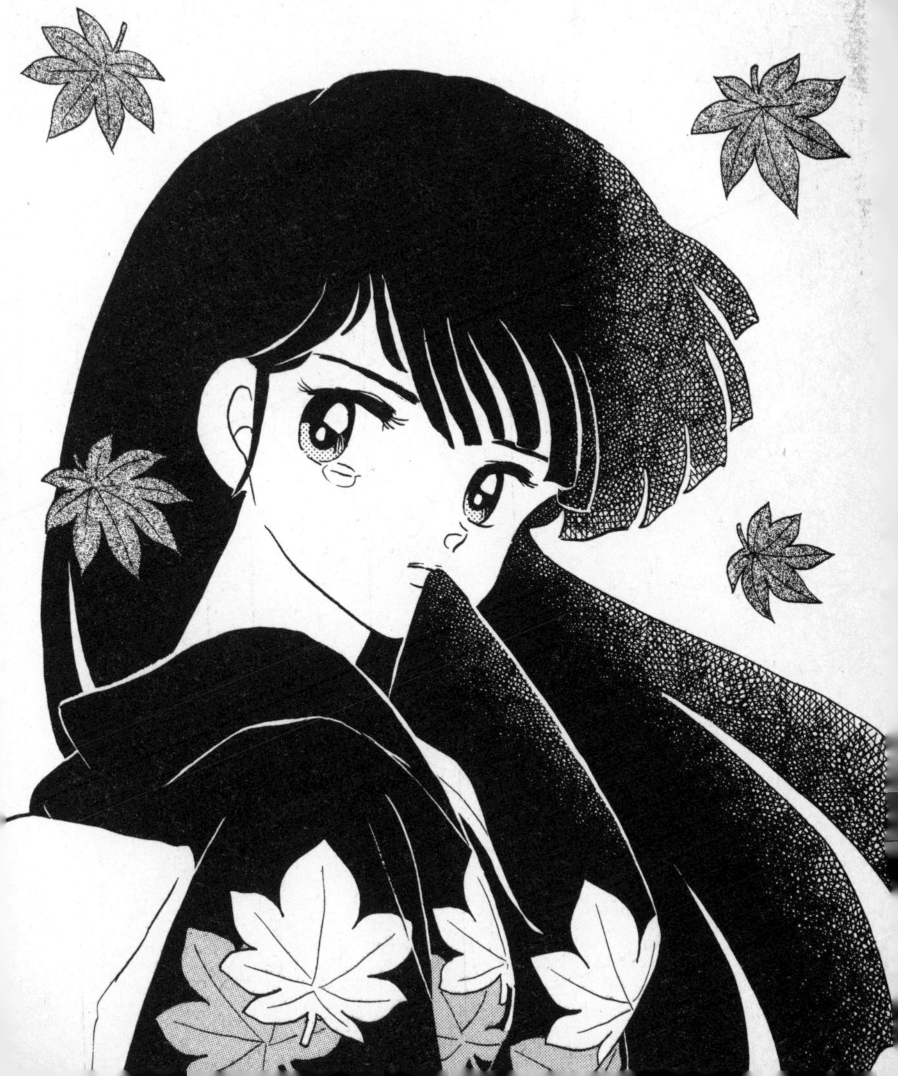

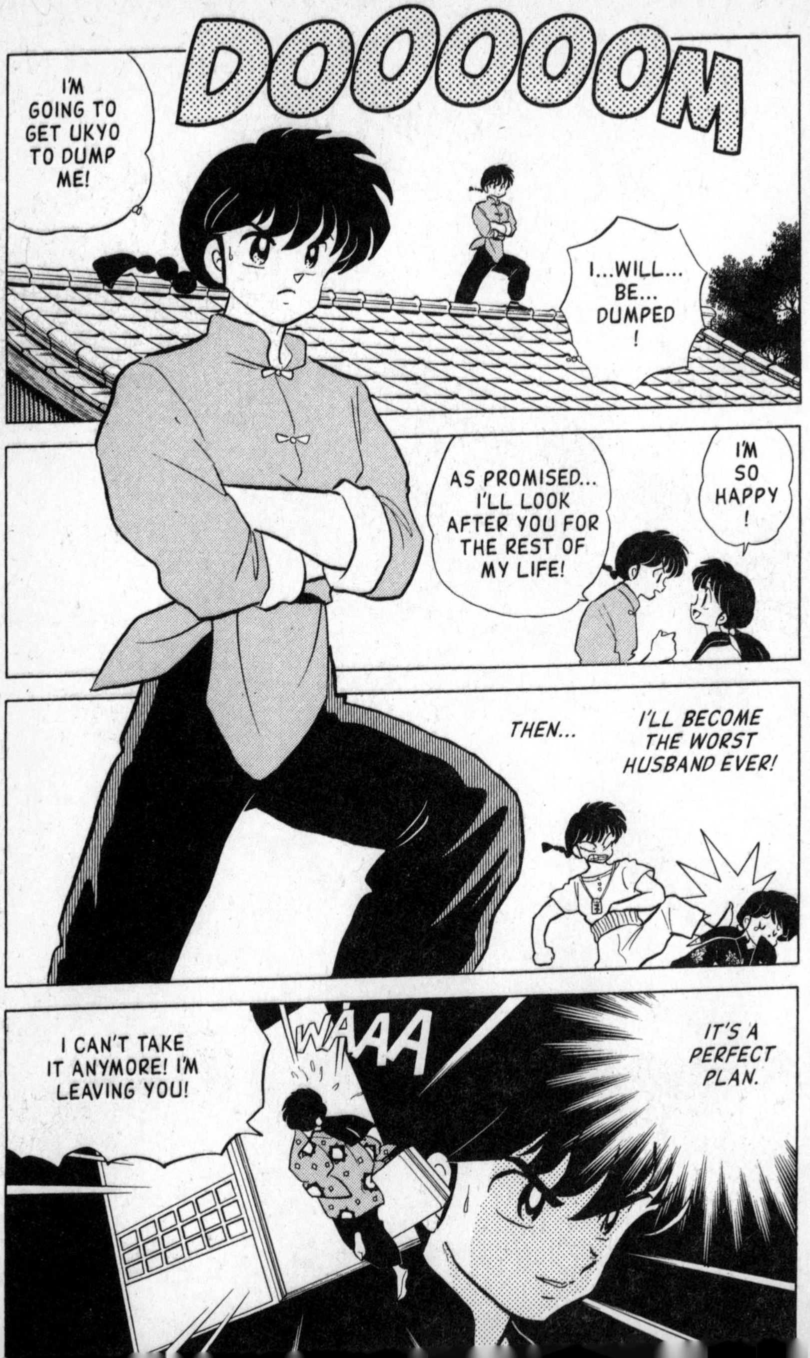
DOOOOOOM
I'M GOING TO GET UKYO TO DUMP ME!
I...WILL... BE... DUMPED !
AS PROMISED... I'LL LOOK AFTER YOU FOR THE REST OF MY LIFE!
I'M SO HAPPY !
THEN...
I'LL BECOME THE WORST HUSBAND EVER!
I CAN'T TAKE IT ANYMORE! I'M LEAVING YOU!
WAAA
IT'S A PERFECT PLAN.

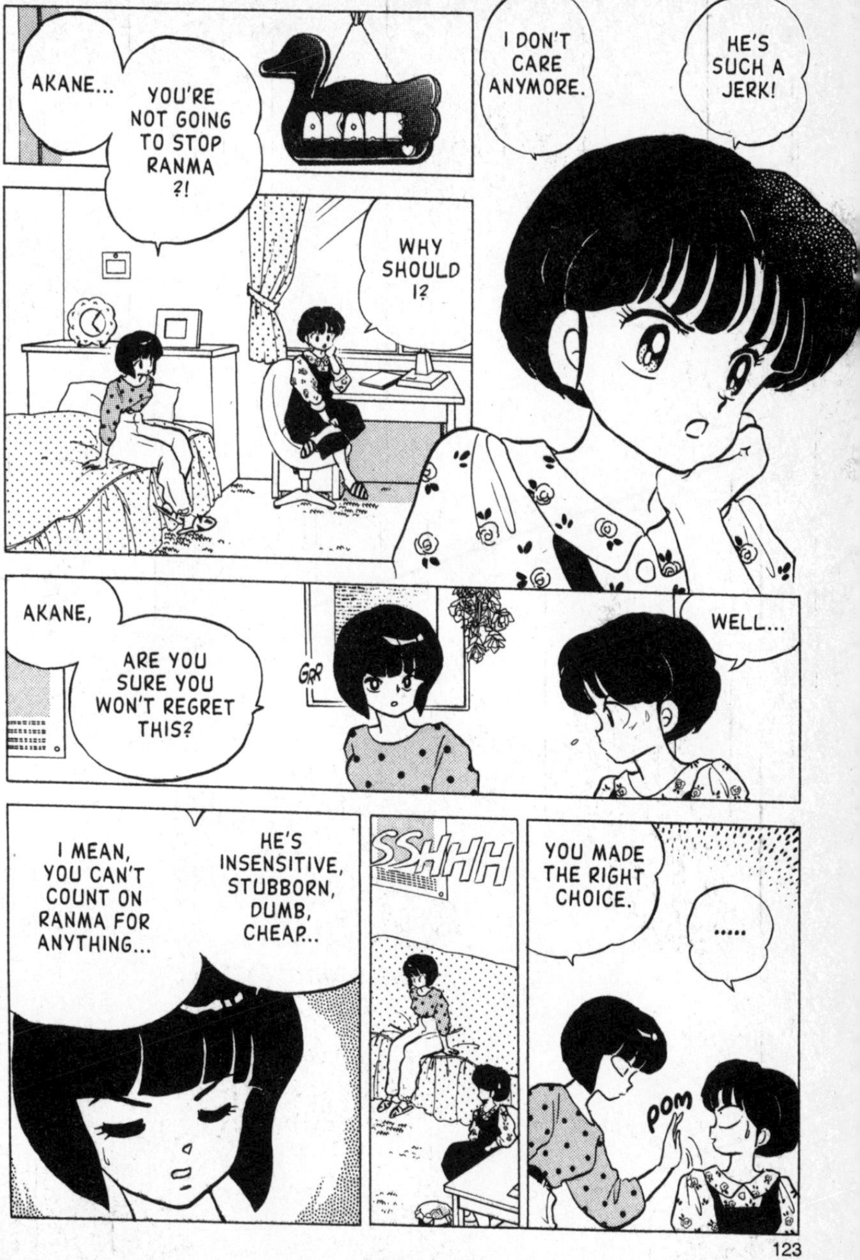
AKANE...
YOU'RE NOT GOING TO STOP RANMA ?!
WHY SHOULD I?
I DON'T CARE ANYMORE.
HE'S SUCH A JERK!
AKANE,
ARE YOU SURE YOU WON'T REGRET THIS?
GRR
WELL...
I MEAN, YOU CAN'T COUNT ON RANMA FOR ANYTHING...
HE'S INSENSITIVE, STUBBORN, DUMB, CHEAP...
SSHHH
YOU MADE THE RIGHT CHOICE.
.....
POM

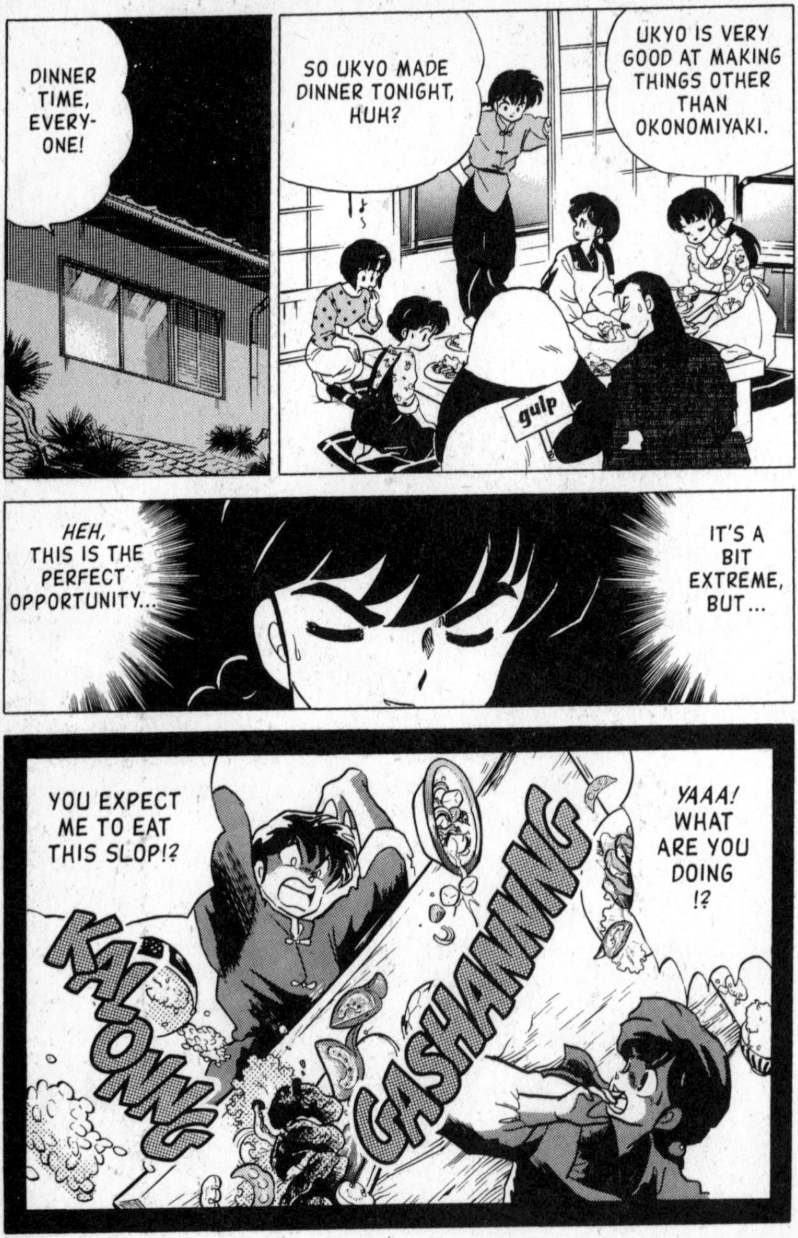
DINNER TIME, EVERY-ONE!
SO UKYO MADE DINNER TONIGHT, HUH?
UKYO IS VERY GOOD AT MAKING THINGS OTHER THAN OKONOMIYAKI.
gulp
HEH, THIS IS THE PERFECT OPPORTUNITY...
IT'S A BIT EXTREME, BUT...
YOU EXPECT ME TO EAT THIS SLOP!?
KALONNG
GASHANNG
YAAA! WHAT ARE YOU DOING !?

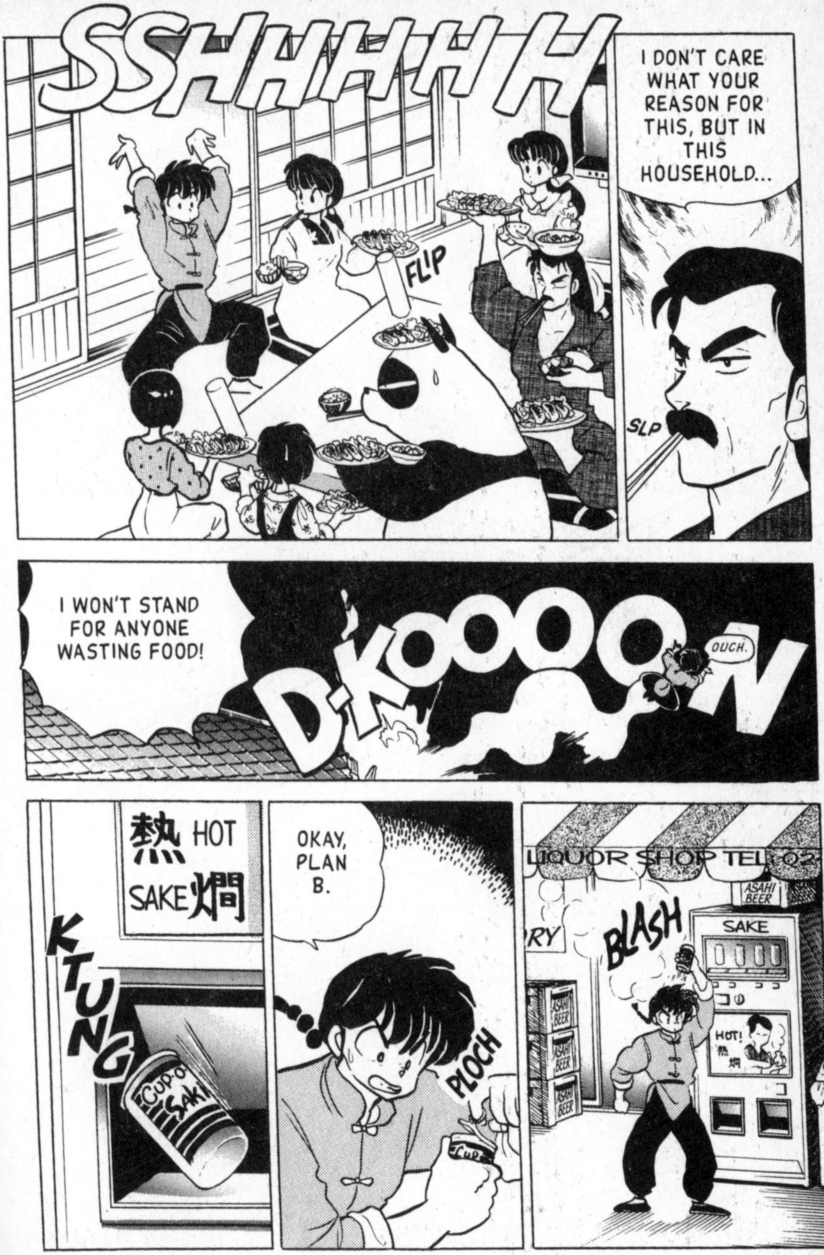
SSHHHHH
FLIP
SLP
I DON'T CARE WHAT YOUR REASON FOR THIS, BUT IN THIS HOUSEHOLD...
I WON'T STAND FOR ANYONE WASTING FOOD!
D-KOOOOON
OUCH.
熱 HOT
SAKE 燗
KTUNG
CUP-O-SAKI
OKAY, PLAN B.
PLOCH
LIQUOR SHOP TEL: 02-
ASAHI BEER
SAKE
BLASH
HOT! 熱 燗

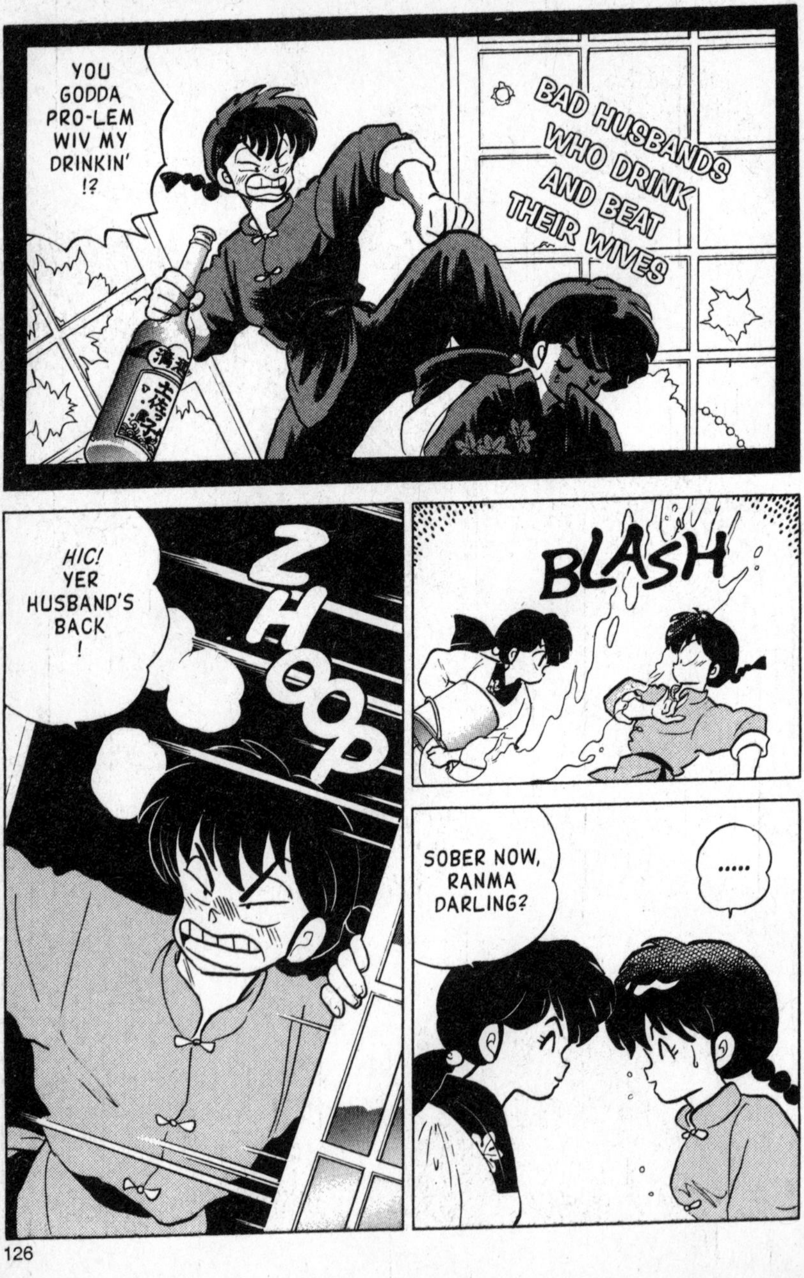
YOU GODDA PRO-LEM WIV MY DRINKIN' !?
BAD HUSBANDS WHO DRINK AND BEAT THEIR WIVES
HIC! YER HUSBAND'S BACK !
ZHOOP
BLASH
SOBER NOW, RANMA DARLING?
......

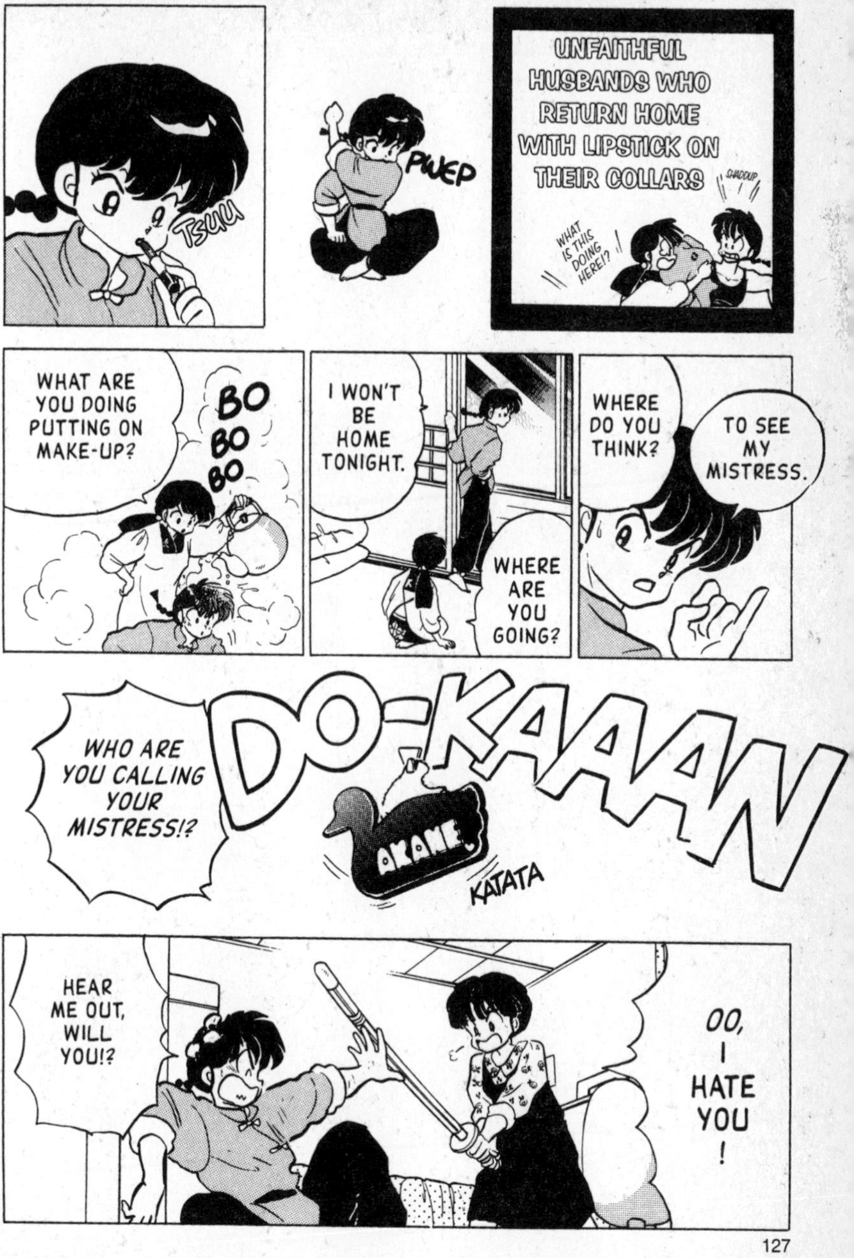

TSUU
PWEP
UNFAITHFUL HUSBANDS WHO RETURN HOME WITH LIPSTICK ON THEIR COLLARS
WHAT IS THIS DOING HERE!?
SHADDUP
WHAT ARE YOU DOING PUTTING ON MAKE-UP?
BO BO BO
I WON'T BE HOME TONIGHT.
WHERE ARE YOU GOING?
WHERE DO YOU THINK?
TO SEE MY MISTRESS.
WHO ARE YOU CALLING YOUR MISTRESS!?
DO-KAAAAN
AKANE
KATATA
HEAR ME OUT, WILL YOU!?
OO, I HATE YOU!

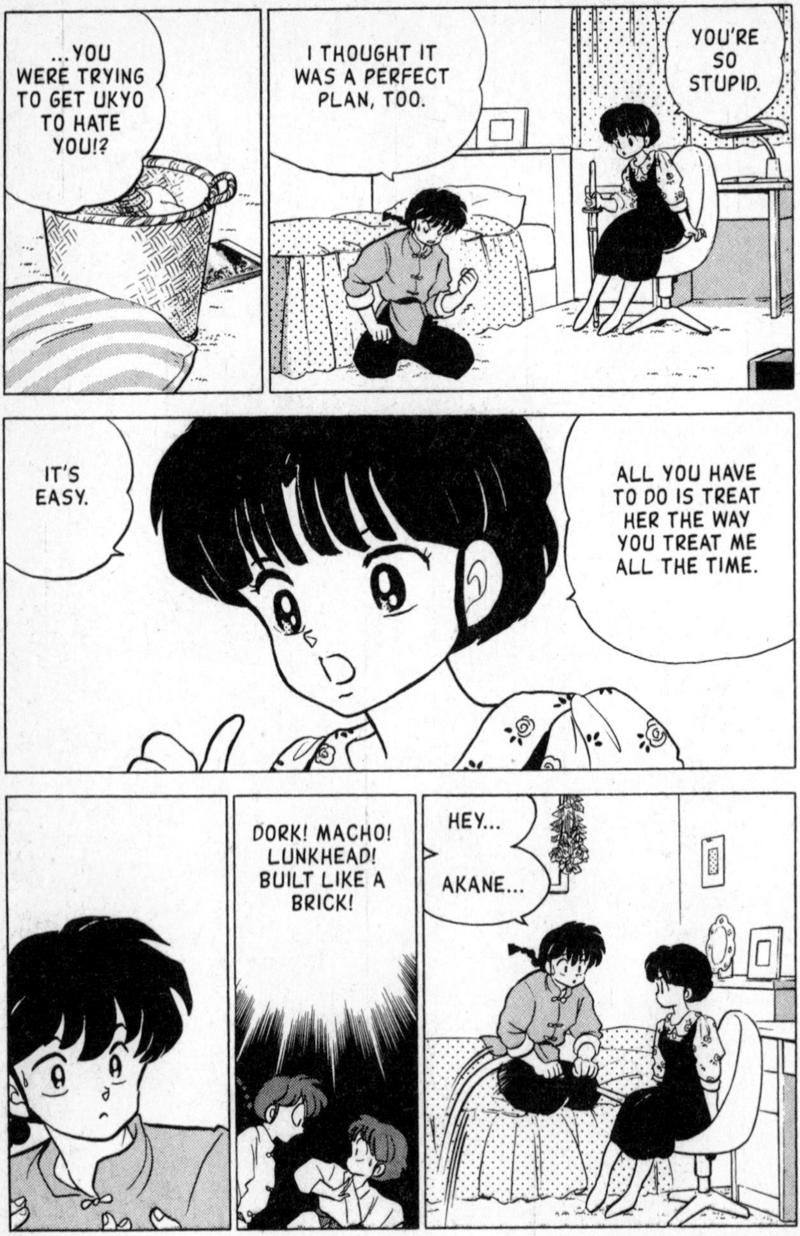
...YOU WERE TRYING TO GET UKYO TO HATE YOU!?
I THOUGHT IT WAS A PERFECT PLAN, TOO.
YOU'RE SO STUPID.
IT'S EASY.
ALL YOU HAVE TO DO IS TREAT HER THE WAY YOU TREAT ME ALL THE TIME.
DORK! MACHO! LUNKHEAD! BUILT LIKE A BRICK!
HEY...
AKANE...

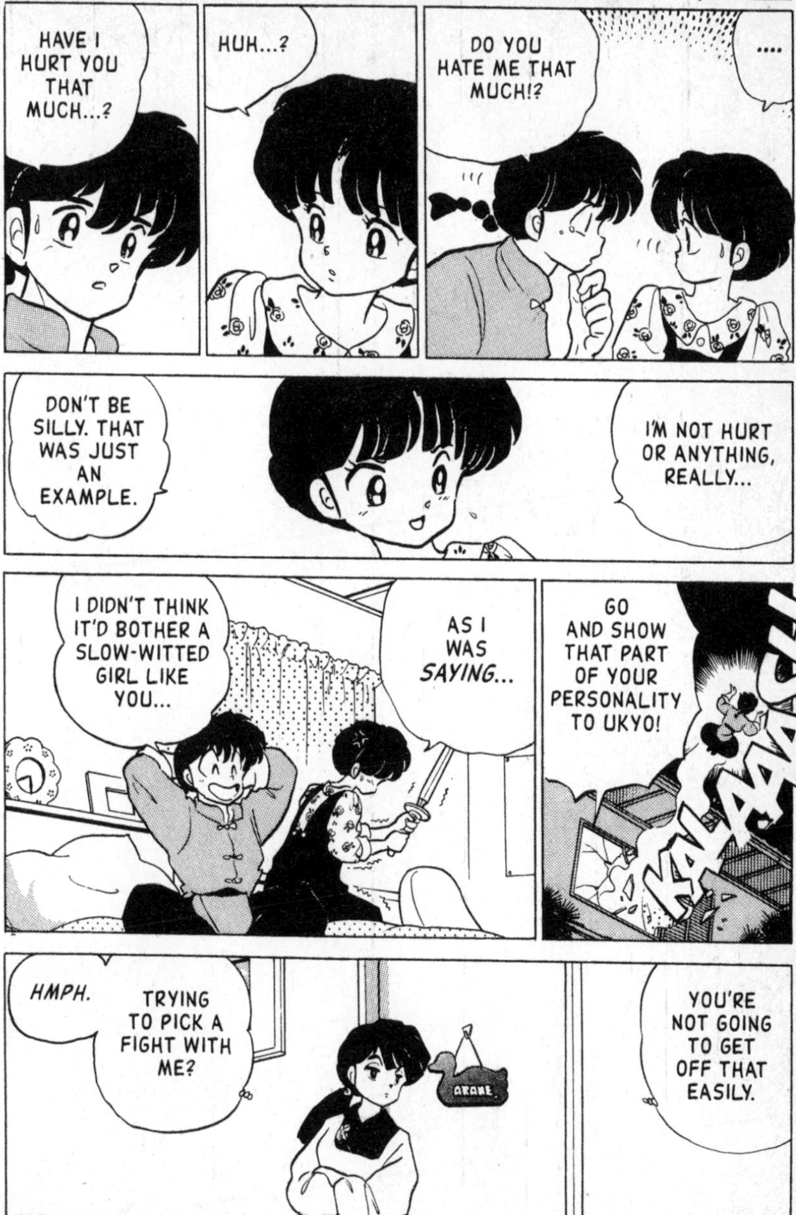
HAVE I HURT YOU THAT MUCH...?
HUH...?
DO YOU HATE ME THAT MUCH!?
....
DON'T BE SILLY. THAT WAS JUST AN EXAMPLE.
I'M NOT HURT OR ANYTHING, REALLY...
I DIDN'T THINK IT'D BOTHER A SLOW-WITTED GIRL LIKE YOU...
AS I WAS *SAYING*...
GO AND SHOW THAT PART OF YOUR PERSONALITY TO UKYO!
KA-BAAASH
HMPH.
TRYING TO PICK A FIGHT WITH ME?
AKANE
YOU'RE NOT GOING TO GET OFF THAT EASILY.

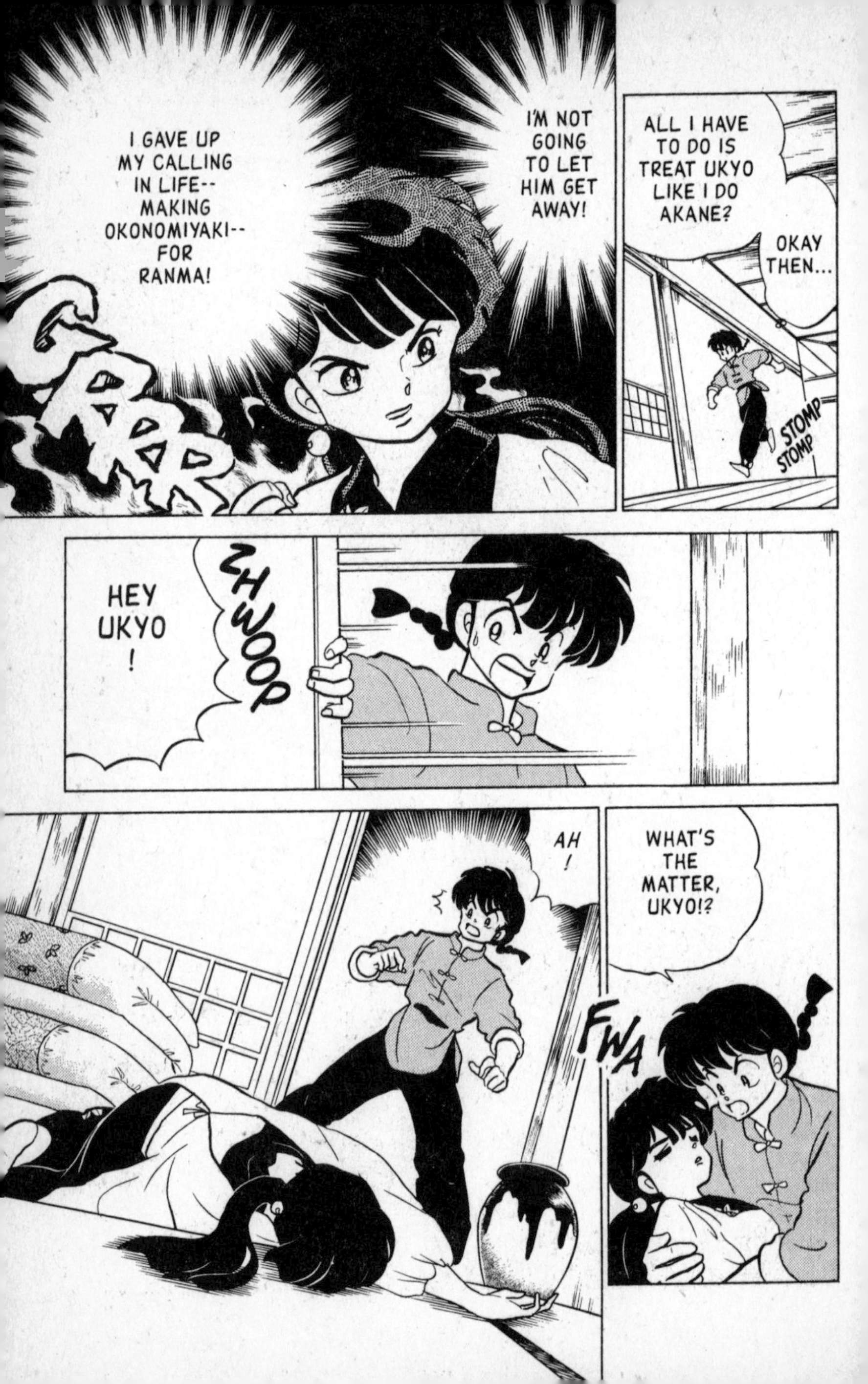
GRRRR
I GAVE UP MY CALLING IN LIFE-- MAKING OKONOMIYAKI-- FOR RANMA!
I'M NOT GOING TO LET HIM GET AWAY!
ALL I HAVE TO DO IS TREAT UKYO LIKE I DO AKANE?
OKAY THEN...
STOMP STOMP
HEY UKYO!
ZHWOOP
AH!
WHAT'S THE MATTER, UKYO!?
FWA

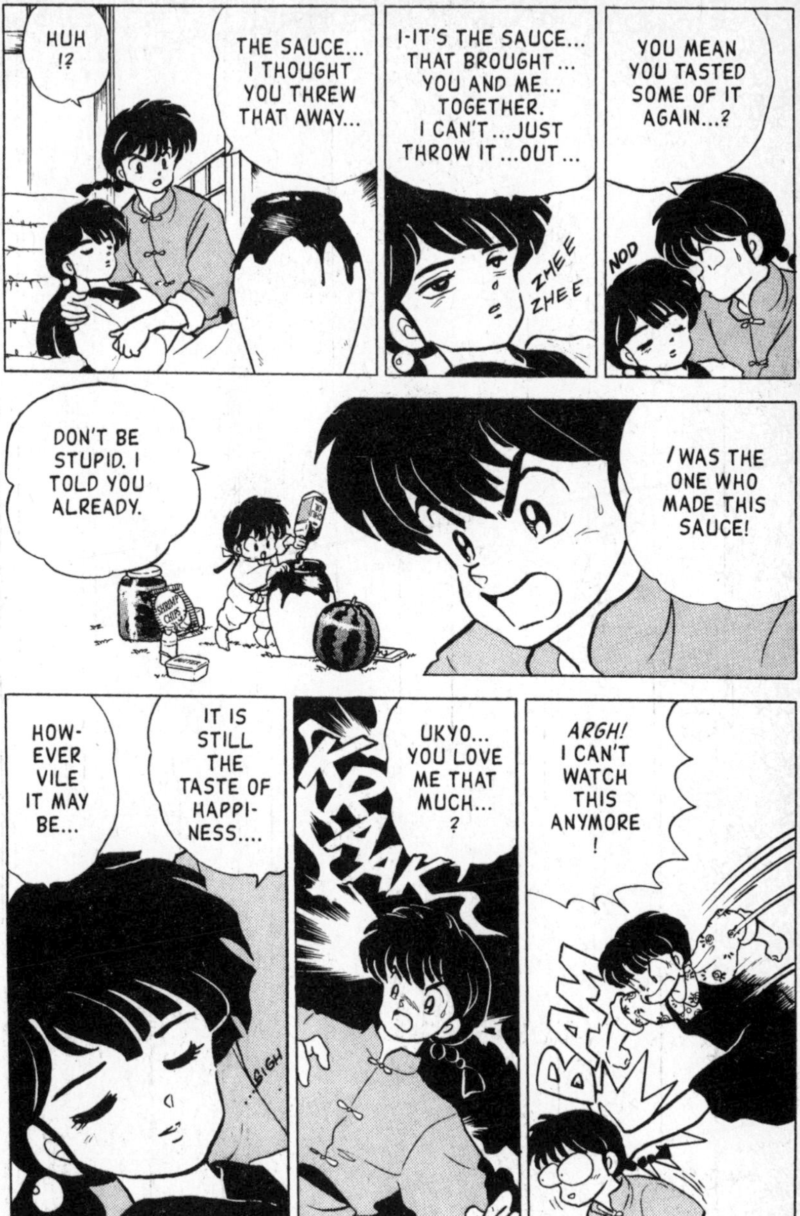
HUH !?
THE SAUCE... I THOUGHT YOU THREW THAT AWAY...
I-IT'S THE SAUCE... THAT BROUGHT... YOU AND ME... TOGETHER. I CAN'T ...JUST THROW IT ...OUT...
ZHEE ZHEE
YOU MEAN YOU TASTED SOME OF IT AGAIN...?
NOD
DON'T BE STUPID. I TOLD YOU ALREADY.
SHRIMP CHIPS
I WAS THE ONE WHO MADE THIS SAUCE!
HOW-EVER VILE IT MAY BE...
IT IS STILL THE TASTE OF HAPPI-NESS....
...SIGH
KRAAAK
UKYO... YOU LOVE ME THAT MUCH...?
ARGH! I CAN'T WATCH THIS ANYMORE!
BAM

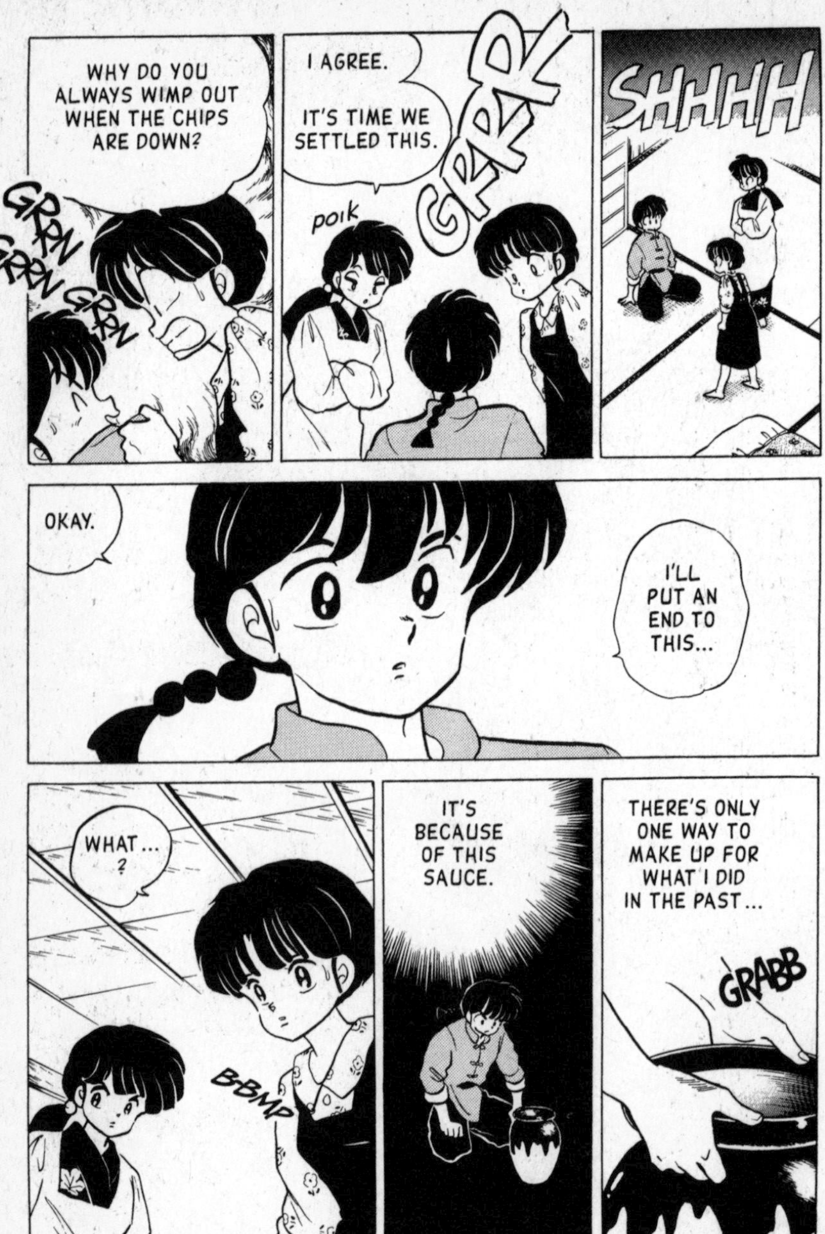
WHY DO YOU ALWAYS WIMP OUT WHEN THE CHIPS ARE DOWN?
GRRN GRRN GRRN GRRN
I AGREE.
IT'S TIME WE SETTLED THIS.
poik
GRRR
SHHHH
OKAY.
I'LL PUT AN END TO THIS...
WHAT... ?
B-BMP
IT'S BECAUSE OF THIS SAUCE.
THERE'S ONLY ONE WAY TO MAKE UP FOR WHAT I DID IN THE PAST...
GRABB

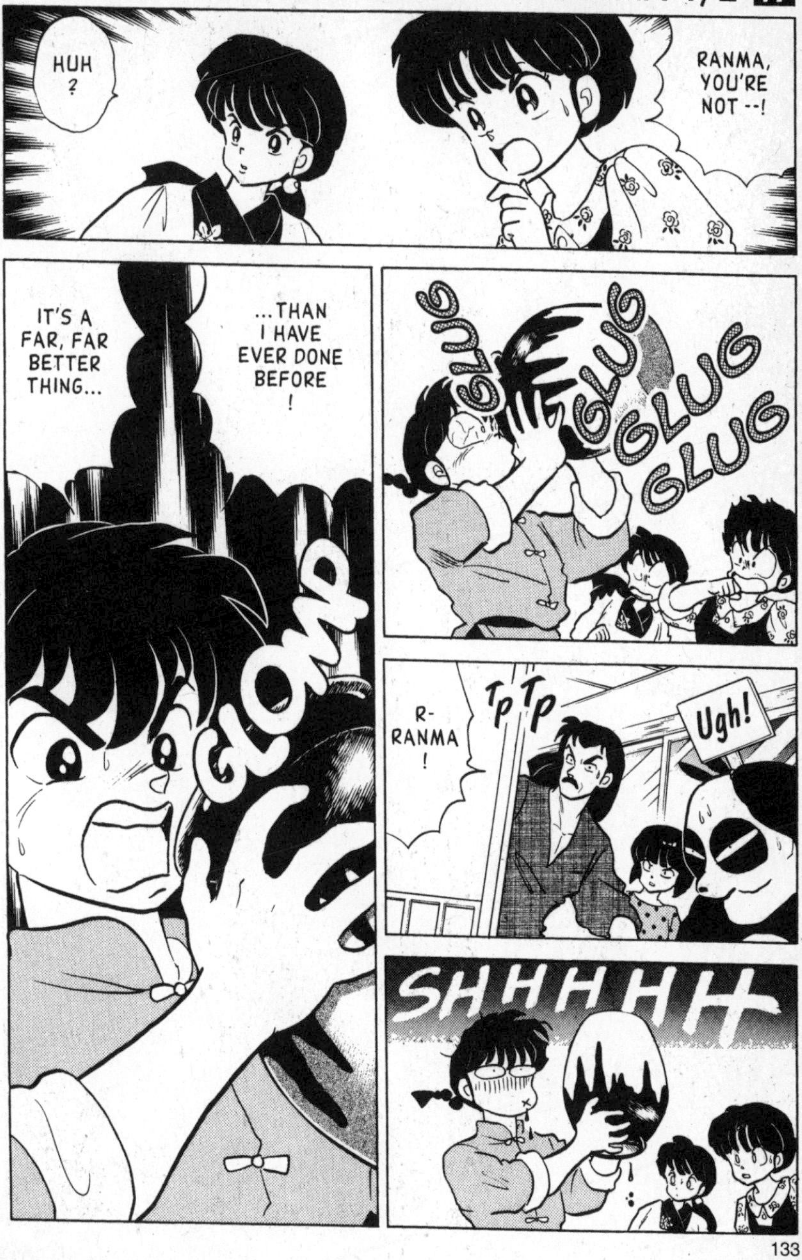
HUH ?
RANMA, YOU'RE NOT --!
IT'S A FAR, FAR BETTER THING...
...THAN I HAVE EVER DONE BEFORE !
GLOMP
GLUG
GLUG
GLUG
GLUG
R-RANMA !
Tp Tp
Ugh!
SHHHHHH

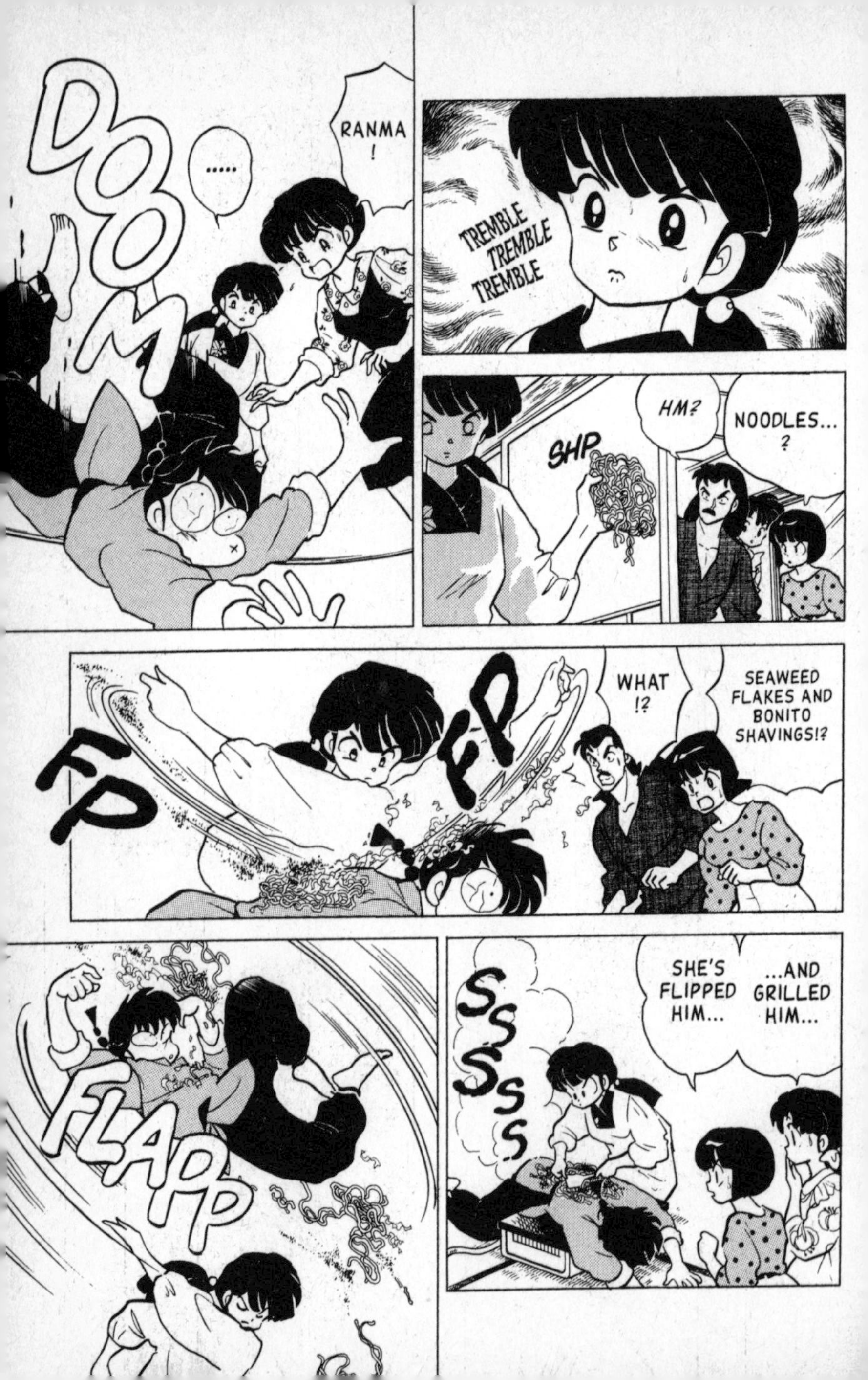
DOOM
......
RANMA!
TREMBLE TREMBLE TREMBLE
SHP
HM?
NOODLES...?
FP
FP
WHAT!?
SEAWEED FLAKES AND BONITO SHAVINGS!?
FLAPP
SSSSS
SHE'S FLIPPED HIM...
...AND GRILLED HIM...

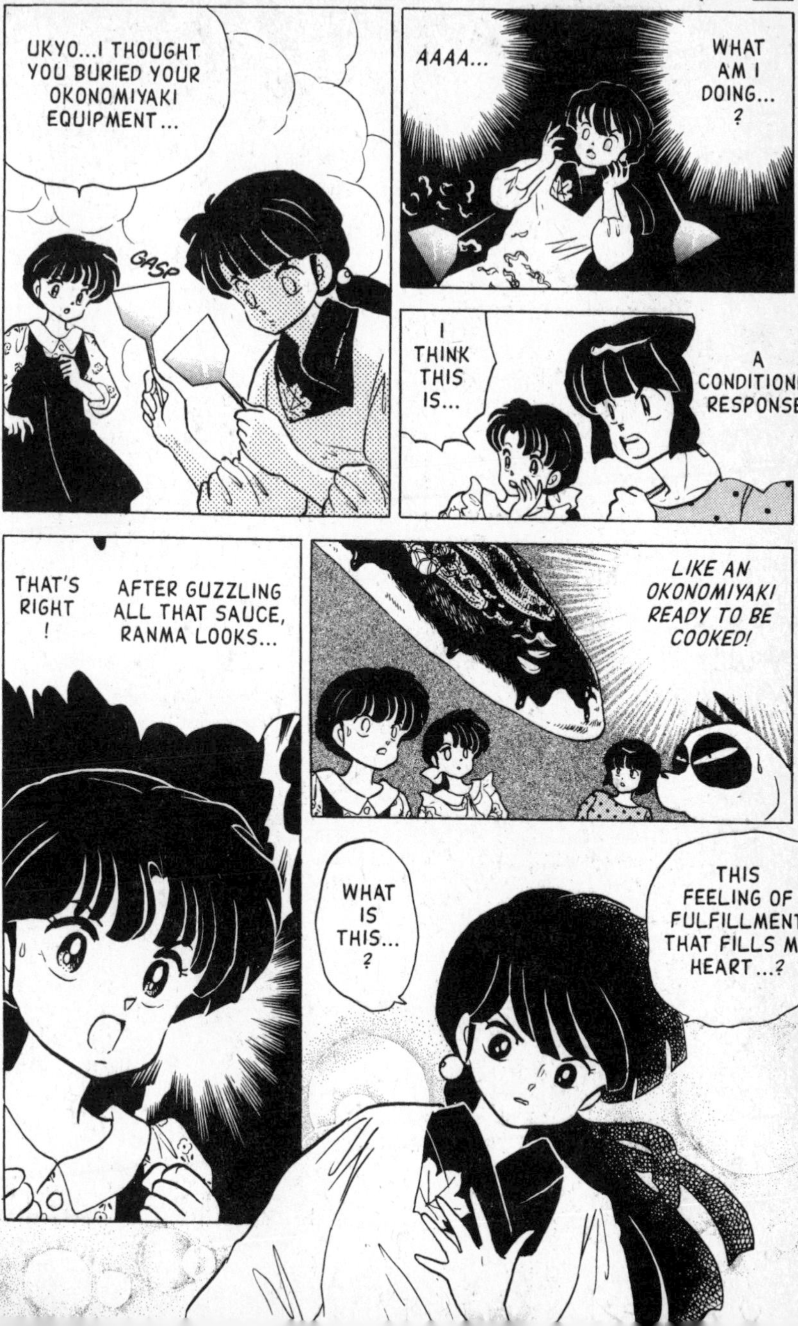
UKYO...I THOUGHT YOU BURIED YOUR OKONOMIYAKI EQUIPMENT...
GASP
AAAA...
WHAT AM I DOING...?
I THINK THIS IS...
A CONDITIONED RESPONSE!
THAT'S RIGHT!
AFTER GUZZLING ALL THAT SAUCE, RANMA LOOKS...
LIKE AN OKONOMIYAKI READY TO BE COOKED!
WHAT IS THIS...?
THIS FEELING OF FULFILLMENT THAT FILLS MY HEART...?

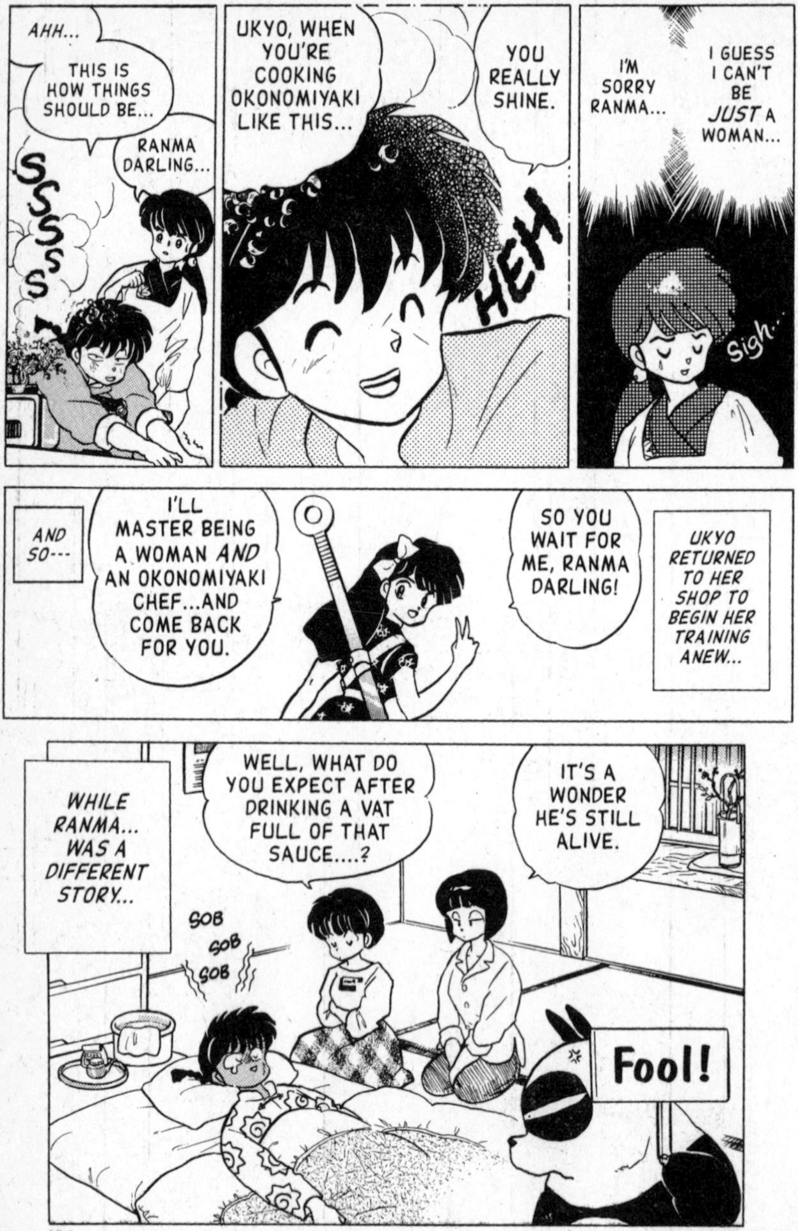
AHH...
THIS IS HOW THINGS SHOULD BE...
RANMA DARLING...
SSSSSS
UKYO, WHEN YOU'RE COOKING OKONOMIYAKI LIKE THIS...
YOU REALLY SHINE.
HEH
I'M SORRY RANMA...
I GUESS I CAN'T BE JUST A WOMAN...
Sigh...
AND SO---
I'LL MASTER BEING A WOMAN AND AN OKONOMIYAKI CHEF...AND COME BACK FOR YOU.
SO YOU WAIT FOR ME, RANMA DARLING!
UKYO RETURNED TO HER SHOP TO BEGIN HER TRAINING ANEW...
WHILE RANMA... WAS A DIFFERENT STORY...
WELL, WHAT DO YOU EXPECT AFTER DRINKING A VAT FULL OF THAT SAUCE....?
IT'S A WONDER HE'S STILL ALIVE.
SOB SOB SOB
Fool!

Part 9
NIGHTMARE ON HOT SPRINGS STREET

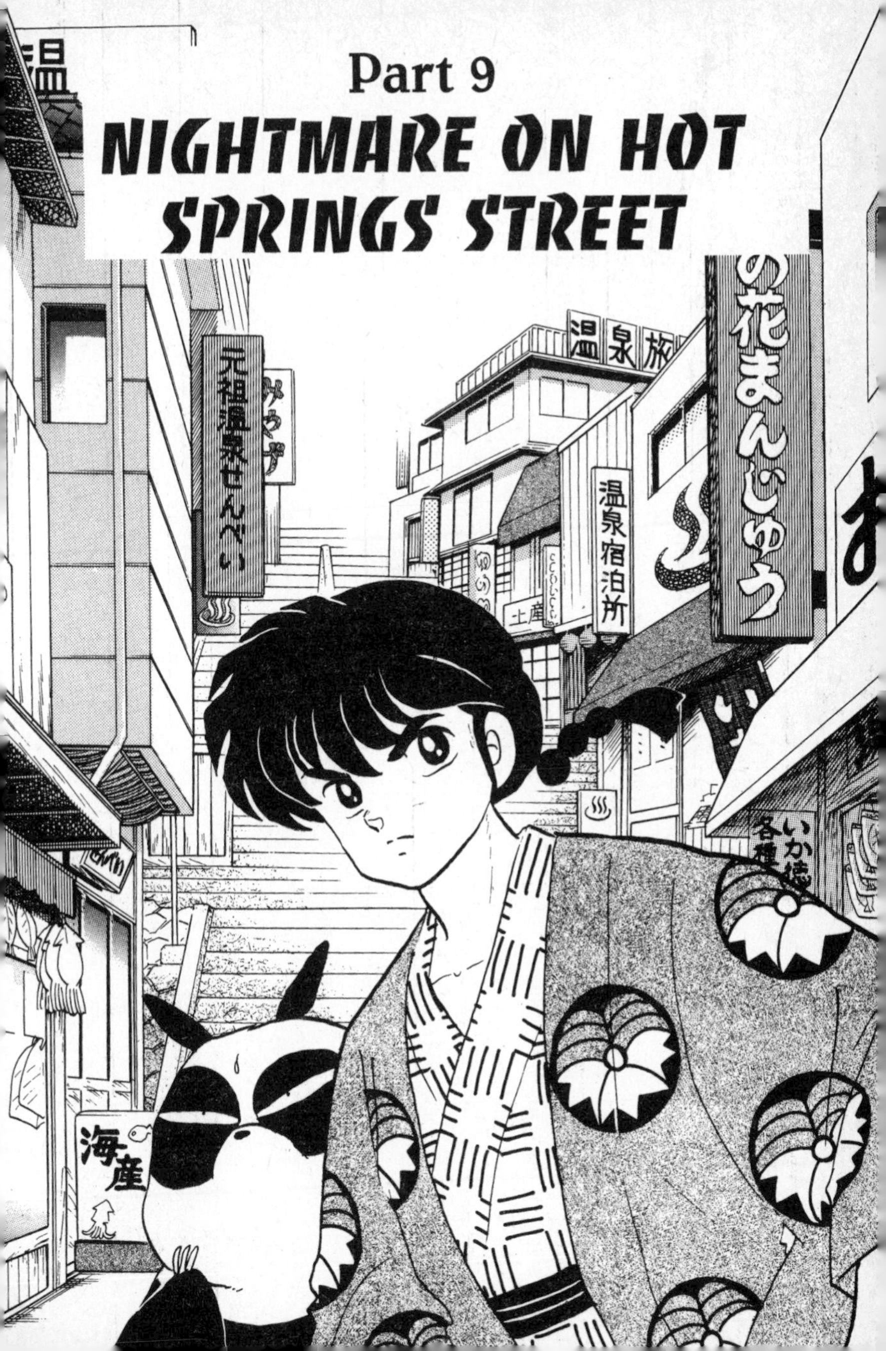

温
元祖温泉せんべい
温泉旅
の花まんじゅう
温泉宿泊所
土産
いか徳
各種
海産

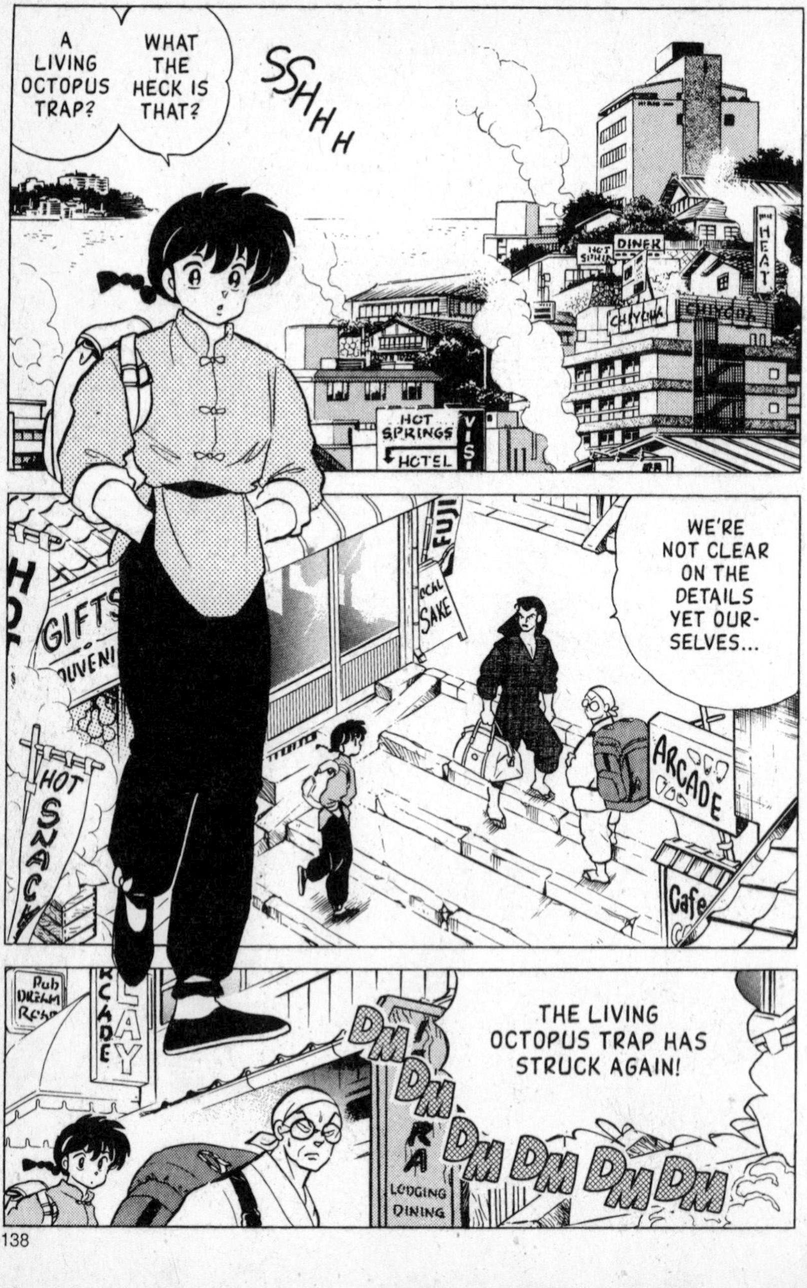
A LIVING OCTOPUS TRAP?
WHAT THE HECK IS THAT?
SSHHHH
DINER
HEAT
HOT SPRINGS
HOTEL
GIFTS
HOT SNACK
SAKE
WE'RE NOT CLEAR ON THE DETAILS YET OUR-SELVES...
ARCADE
Cafe
ARCADE
THE LIVING OCTOPUS TRAP HAS STRUCK AGAIN!
DM DM DM DM DM DM DM DM
LODGING
DINING

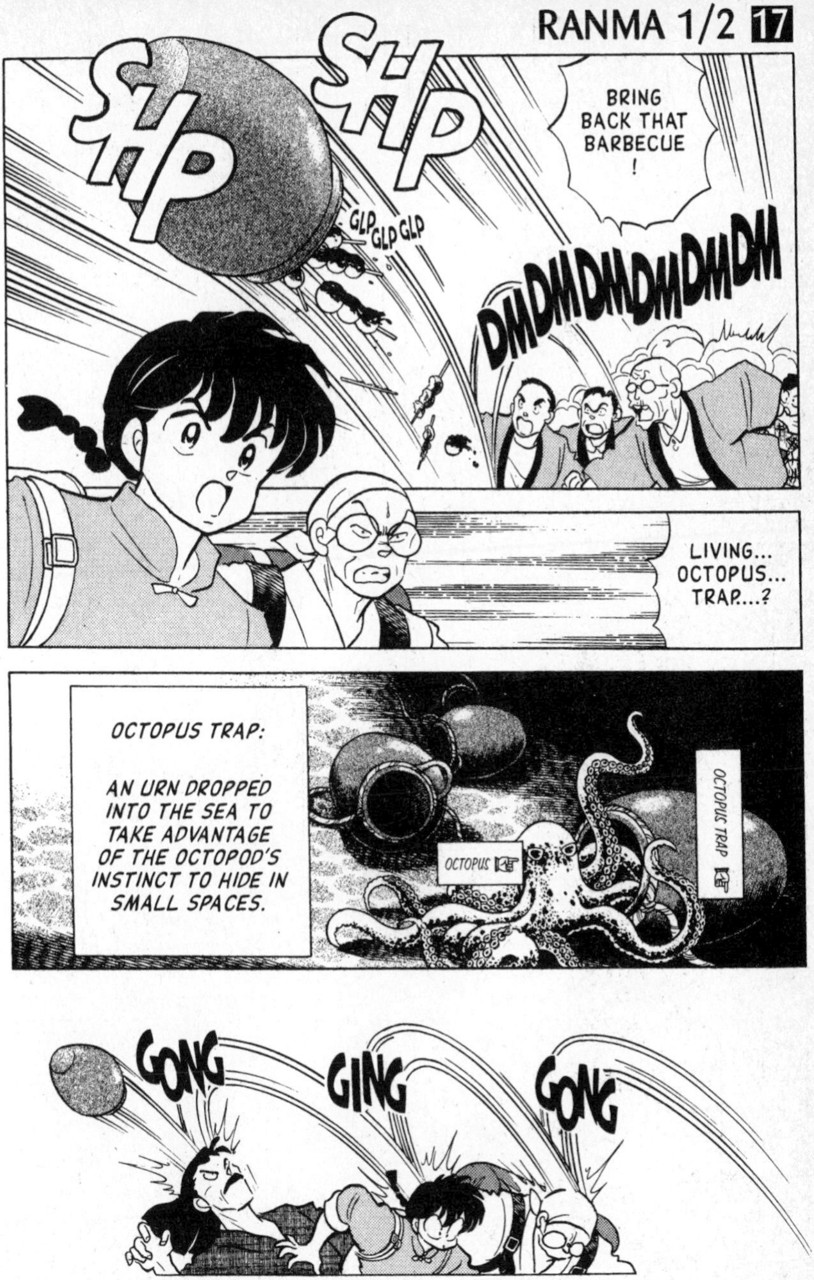
SHP
SHP
GLP GLP GLP
BRING BACK THAT BARBECUE !
DMDMDMDMDMDM
LIVING... OCTOPUS... TRAP....?
OCTOPUS TRAP:
AN URN DROPPED INTO THE SEA TO TAKE ADVANTAGE OF THE OCTOPOD'S INSTINCT TO HIDE IN SMALL SPACES.
OCTOPUS
OCTOPUS TRAP
GONG
GING
GONG

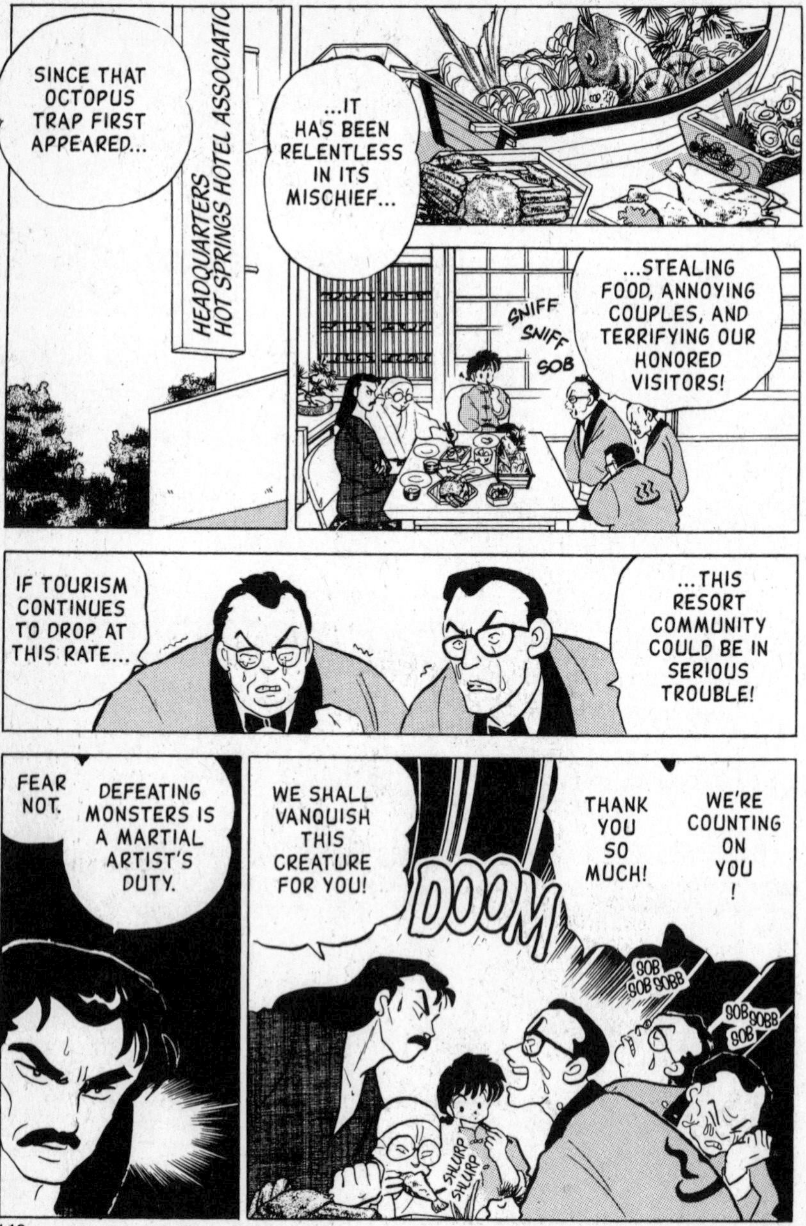
SINCE THAT OCTOPUS TRAP FIRST APPEARED...
HEADQUARTERS HOT SPRINGS HOTEL ASSOCIATIO
...IT HAS BEEN RELENTLESS IN ITS MISCHIEF...
SNIFF SNIFF SOB
...STEALING FOOD, ANNOYING COUPLES, AND TERRIFYING OUR HONORED VISITORS!
IF TOURISM CONTINUES TO DROP AT THIS RATE...
...THIS RESORT COMMUNITY COULD BE IN SERIOUS TROUBLE!
FEAR NOT.
DEFEATING MONSTERS IS A MARTIAL ARTIST'S DUTY.
WE SHALL VANQUISH THIS CREATURE FOR YOU!
DOOM
THANK YOU SO MUCH!
WE'RE COUNTING ON YOU!
SOB SOB SOBB
SOB SOBB SOB
SHLURP SHLURP

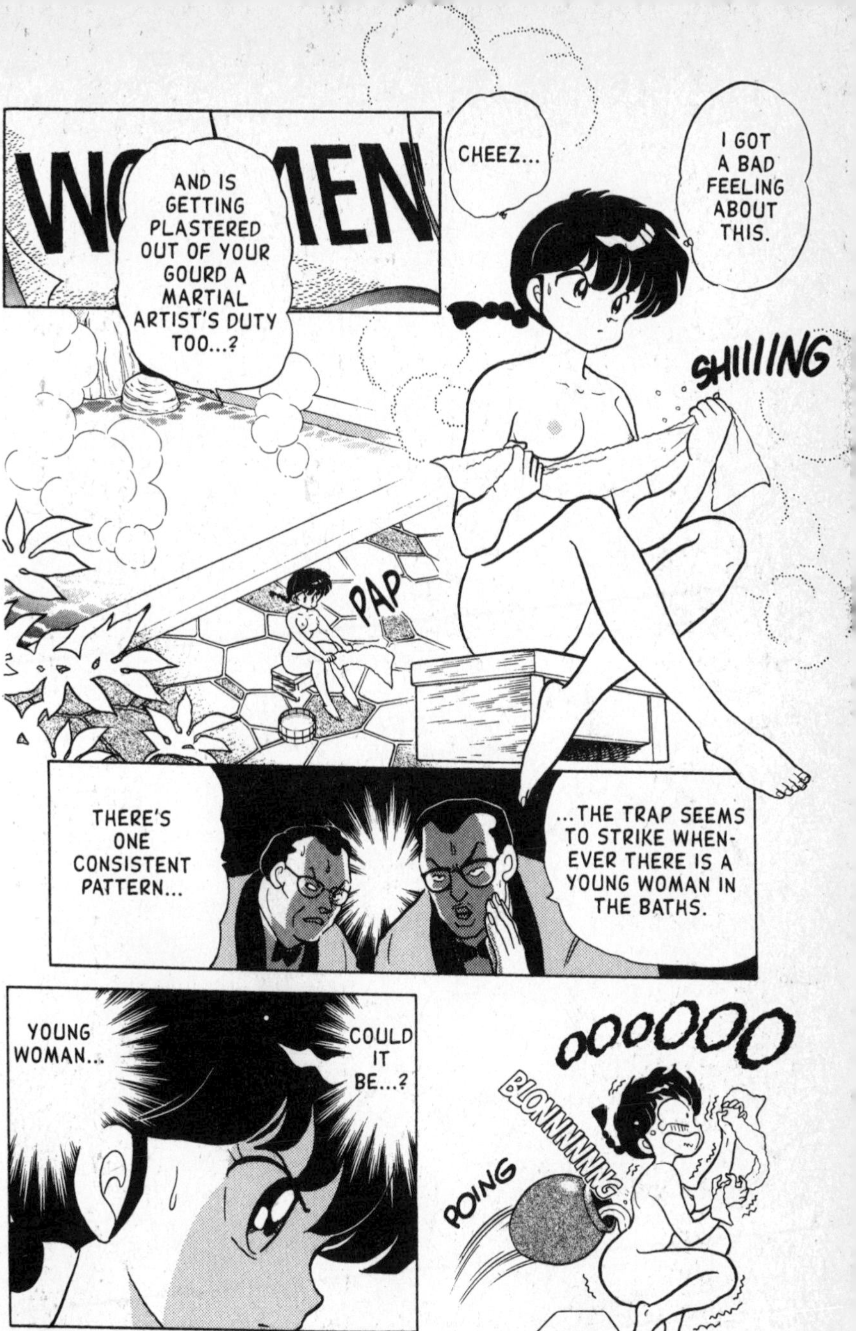
AND IS GETTING PLASTERED OUT OF YOUR GOURD A MARTIAL ARTIST'S DUTY TOO...?
CHEEZ...
I GOT A BAD FEELING ABOUT THIS.
SHIIIING
PAP
THERE'S ONE CONSISTENT PATTERN...
...THE TRAP SEEMS TO STRIKE WHEN-EVER THERE IS A YOUNG WOMAN IN THE BATHS.
YOUNG WOMAN...
COULD IT BE...?
OOOOOO
BLONNNNNNG
POING

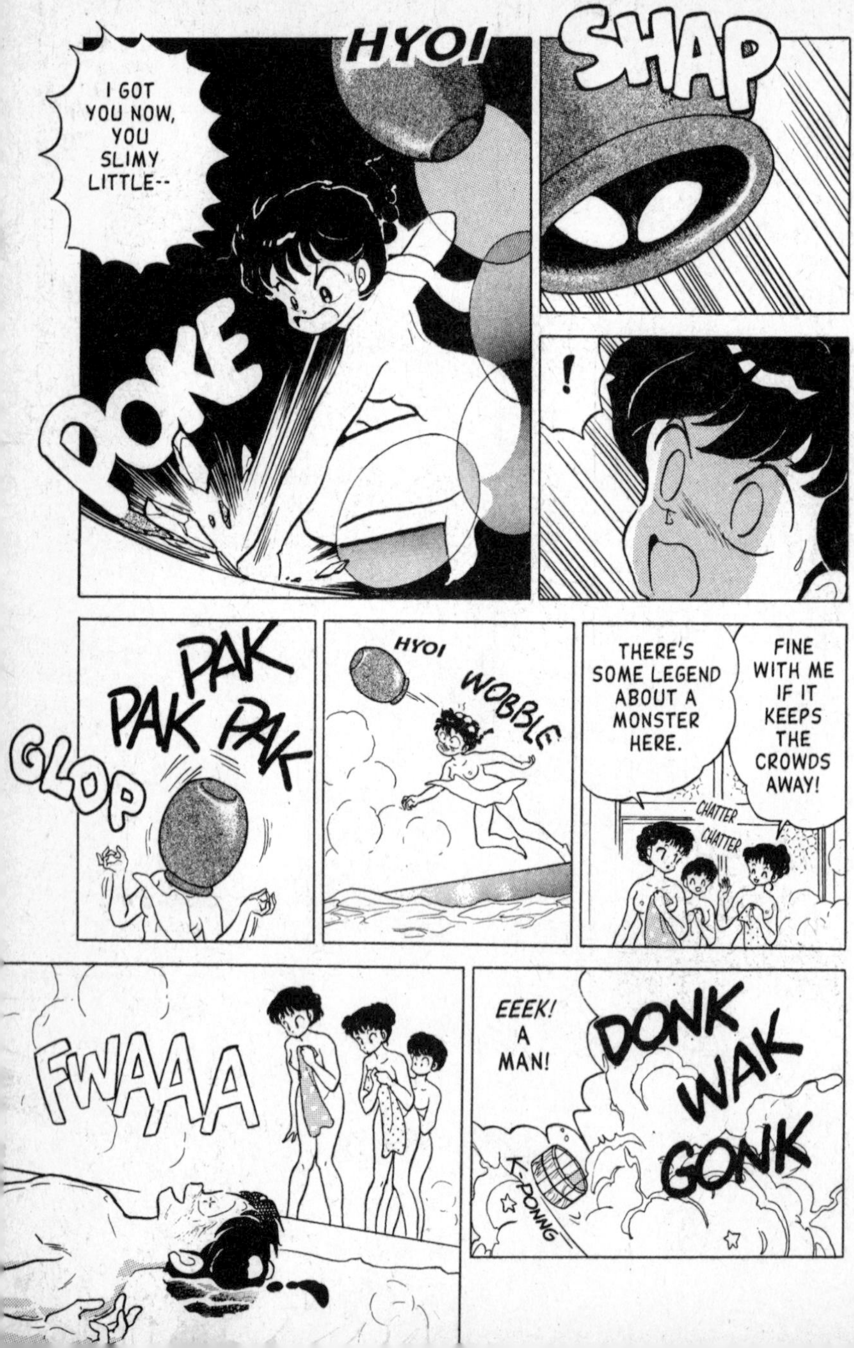
HYOI
I GOT YOU NOW, YOU SLIMY LITTLE--
POKE
SHAP
!
PAK PAK PAK PAK
GLOP
HYOI
WOBBLE
THERE'S SOME LEGEND ABOUT A MONSTER HERE.
FINE WITH ME IF IT KEEPS THE CROWDS AWAY!
CHATTER CHATTER
FWAAA
EEEK! A MAN!
DONK WAK GONK
K-PONNG

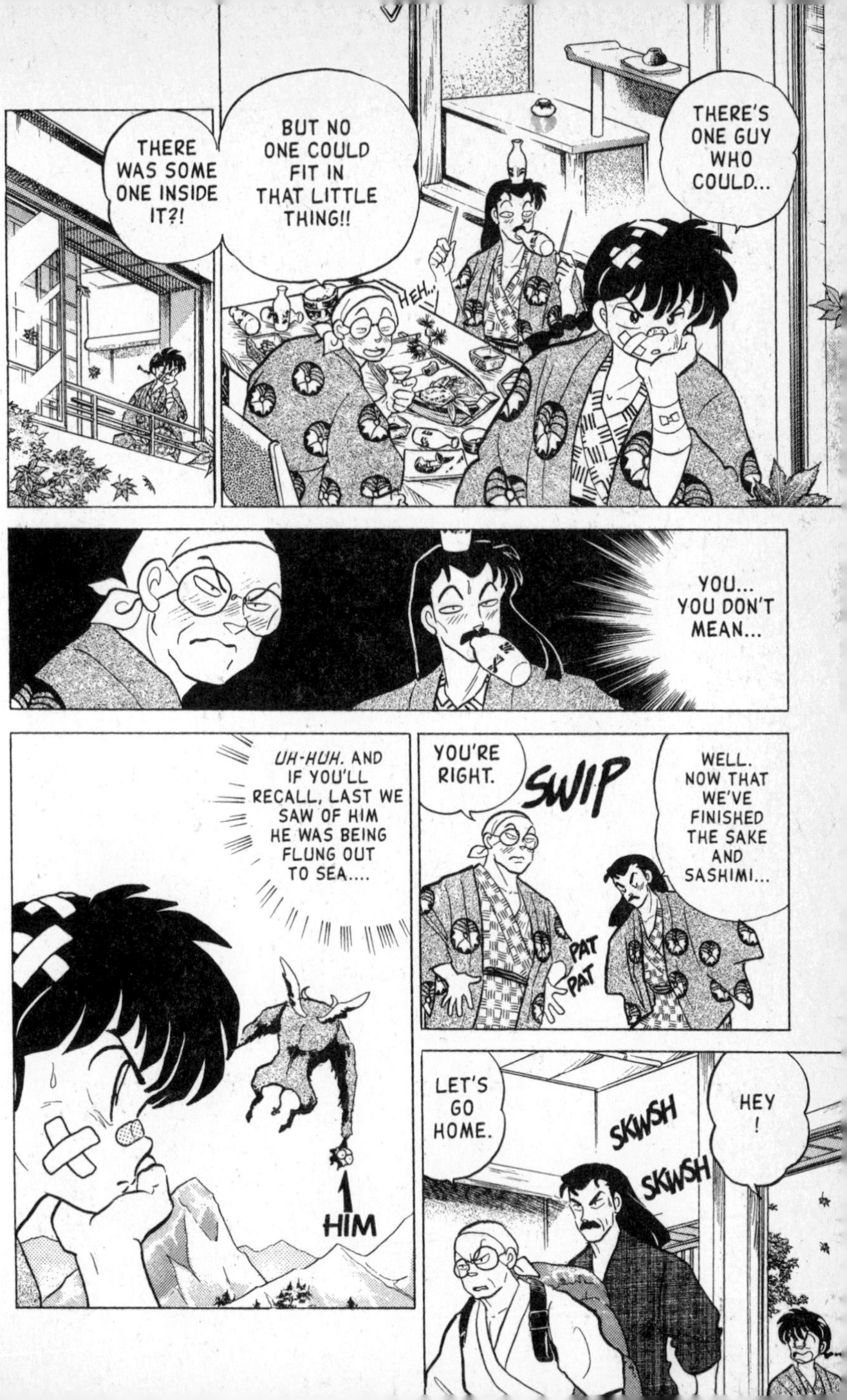
THERE WAS SOME ONE INSIDE IT?!
BUT NO ONE COULD FIT IN THAT LITTLE THING!!
HEH...
THERE'S ONE GUY WHO COULD...
YOU... YOU DON'T MEAN...
UH-HUH. AND IF YOU'LL RECALL, LAST WE SAW OF HIM HE WAS BEING FLUNG OUT TO SEA....
HIM
YOU'RE RIGHT.
SWIP
WELL. NOW THAT WE'VE FINISHED THE SAKE AND SASHIMI...
PAT
PAT
LET'S GO HOME.
SKWSH
SKWSH
HEY !

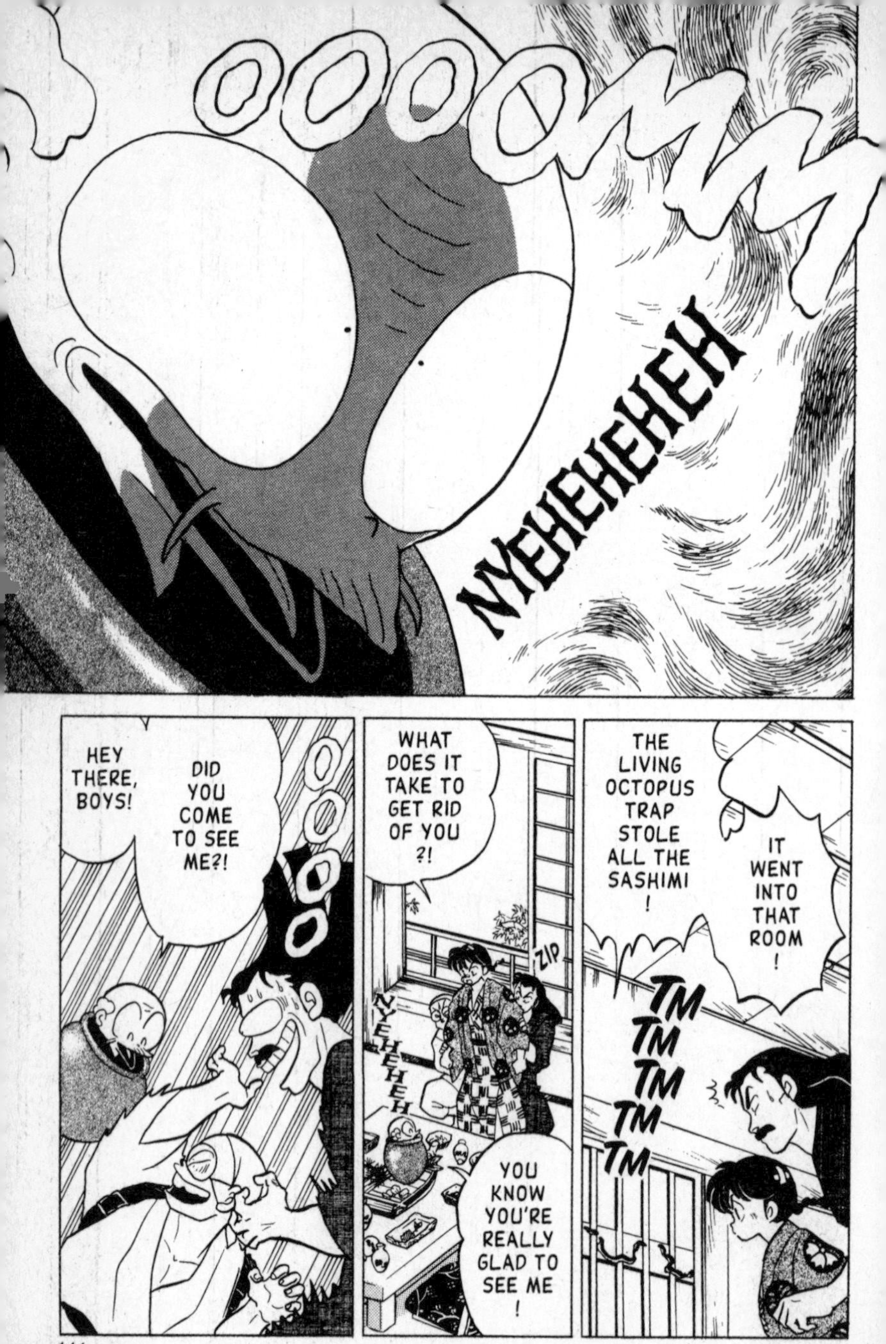
OOOOMM
NYEHEHEHEH
HEY THERE, BOYS!
DID YOU COME TO SEE ME?!
WHAT DOES IT TAKE TO GET RID OF YOU ?!
ZIP
NYEHEHEHEH
YOU KNOW YOU'RE REALLY GLAD TO SEE ME !
THE LIVING OCTOPUS TRAP STOLE ALL THE SASHIMI !
IT WENT INTO THAT ROOM !
TM TM TM TM TM

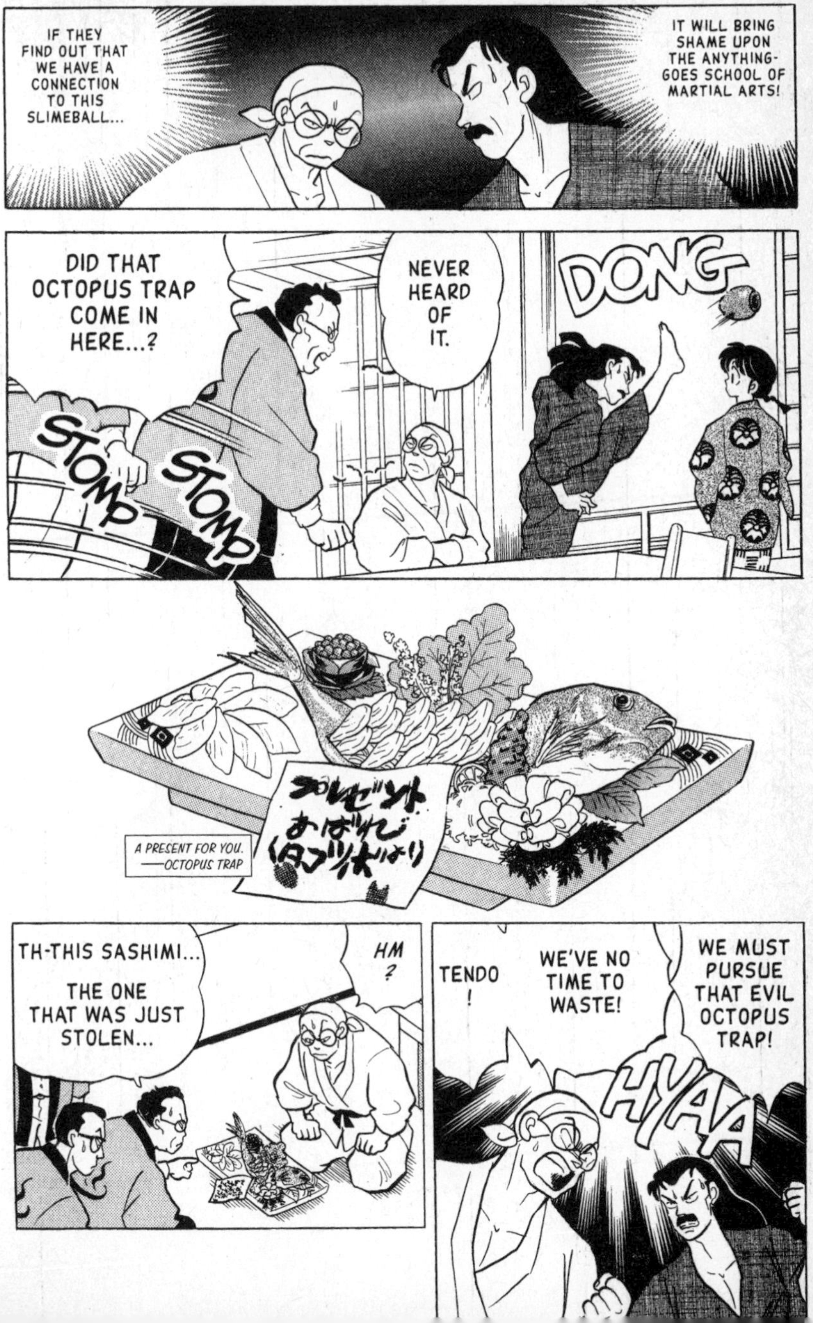
IF THEY FIND OUT THAT WE HAVE A CONNECTION TO THIS SLIMEBALL...
IT WILL BRING SHAME UPON THE ANYTHING-GOES SCHOOL OF MARTIAL ARTS!
DID THAT OCTOPUS TRAP COME IN HERE...?
STOMP STOMP
NEVER HEARD OF IT.
DONG
プレゼント おばれ 八宝菜なり
A PRESENT FOR YOU. ——OCTOPUS TRAP
TH-THIS SASHIMI...
THE ONE THAT WAS JUST STOLEN...
HM?
TENDO!
WE'VE NO TIME TO WASTE!
WE MUST PURSUE THAT EVIL OCTOPUS TRAP!
HYAA

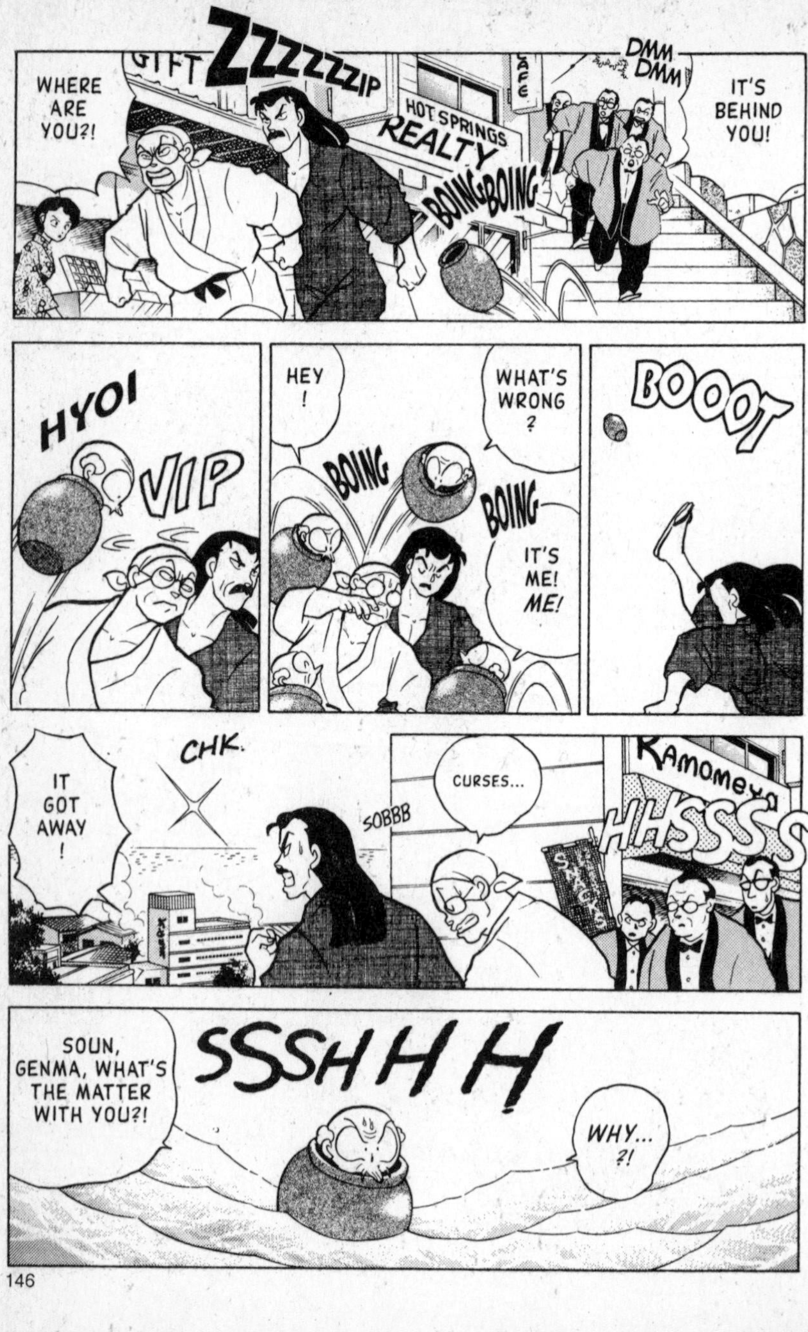
ZZZZZZZIP
GIFT
HOT SPRINGS REALTY
CAFE
WHERE ARE YOU?!
DMM DMM
IT'S BEHIND YOU!
BOING BOING
HYOI
VIP
HEY!
BOING
WHAT'S WRONG?
BOING
IT'S ME! ME!
BOOOT
CHK.
IT GOT AWAY!
SOBBB
CURSES...
KAMOMEYA
HHSSSS
SOUN, GENMA, WHAT'S THE MATTER WITH YOU?!
SSSHHH
WHY...?!

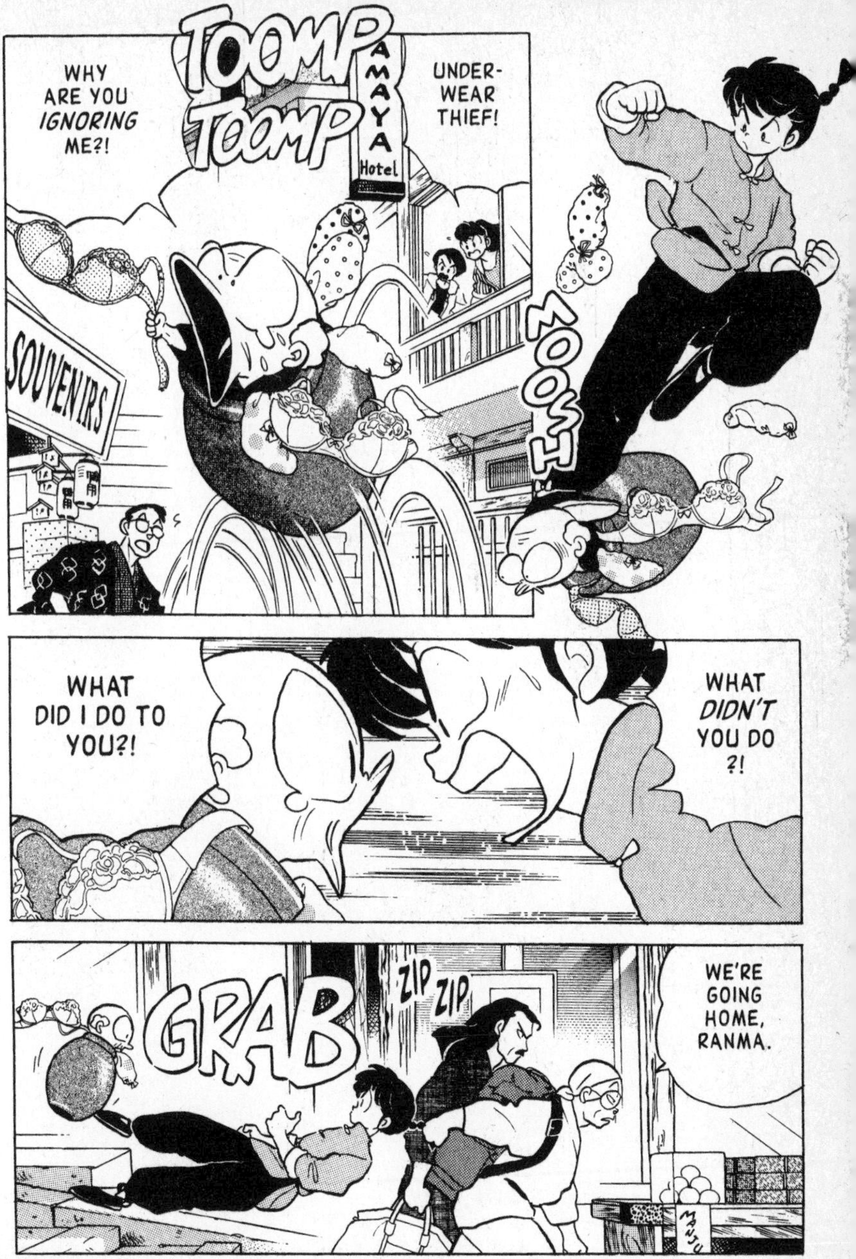
TOOMP TOOMP
AMAYA Hotel
WHY ARE YOU *IGNORING* ME?!
UNDER-WEAR THIEF!
SOUVENIRS
WOOSH
WHAT DID I DO TO YOU?!
WHAT *DIDN'T* YOU DO?!
GRAB
ZIP ZIP
WE'RE GOING HOME, RANMA.
MANJU

WE CAN'T JUST LEAVE THAT OLD FREAK HERE!

ZOOOMM

WHAT ARE YOU TALKING ABOUT?

WHAT OLD PERVERT?

OH, SO THAT'S HOW IT IS?!

Cuttle Fish Cafe

WHY YOU...!

RRRR

HAPPO FIRE BURST!

DROP DROP

DAA DOOOM

DOOOM

DWAH!

PFFFFF

GIFTS

TM TM

KOFF

Hotel YAMA

W-WAIT UP...

PPFFFFFF

SOB
SOB
SOB
SNIF
SNIF

SOMETHING'S NOT RIGHT WITH THE OLD FREAK...

NORMALLY HE'D BE AFTER US WITH A VENGEANCE...

Sale

ced

FRESH FISH

HYOI!

HOT SPRINGS BUNS

HEY!

RANMA!

HEY, OLD GOAT...

SNIF
SNIF
SNIF
SOB
SOB

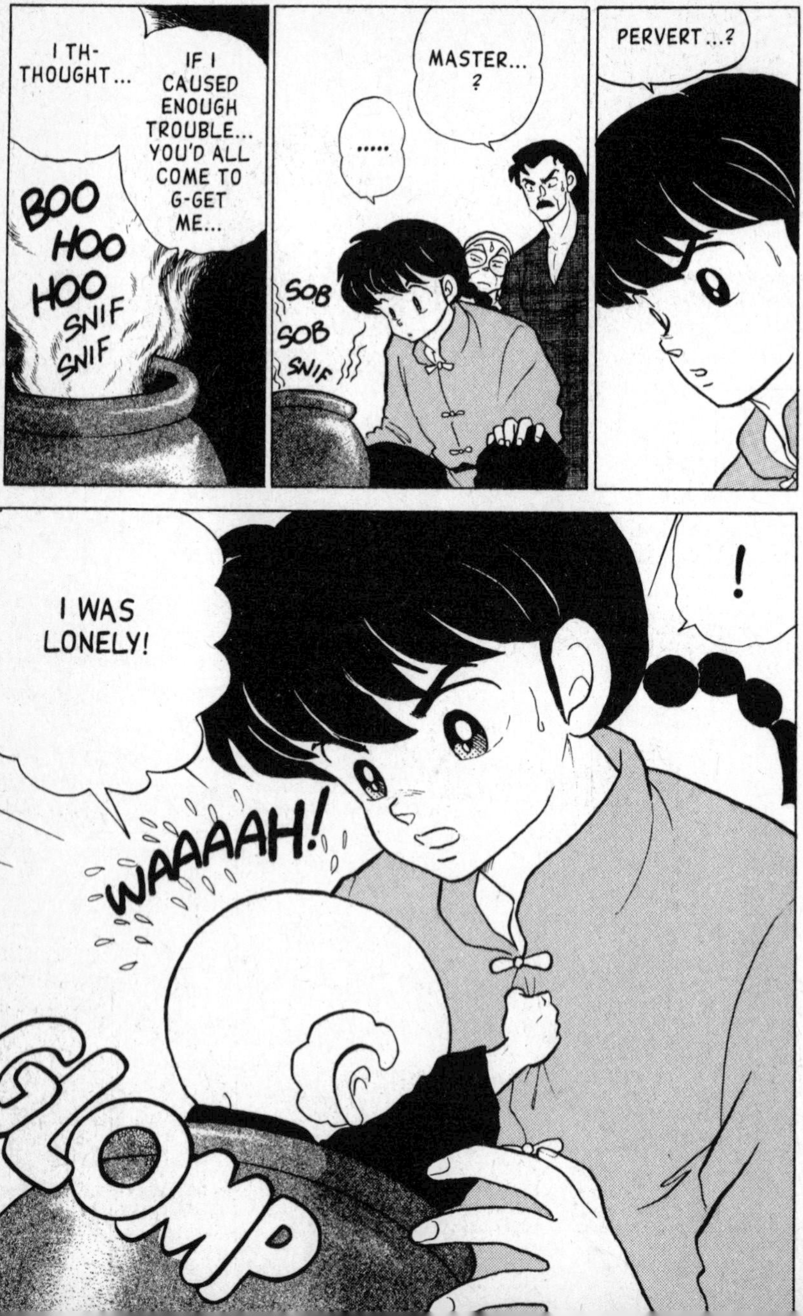
I TH-
THOUGHT...
IF I CAUSED ENOUGH TROUBLE... YOU'D ALL COME TO G-GET ME...
BOO HOO HOO SNIF SNIF
......
MASTER... ?
SOB SOB SNIF
PERVERT...?
I WAS LONELY!
WAAAAH!
GLOMP
!

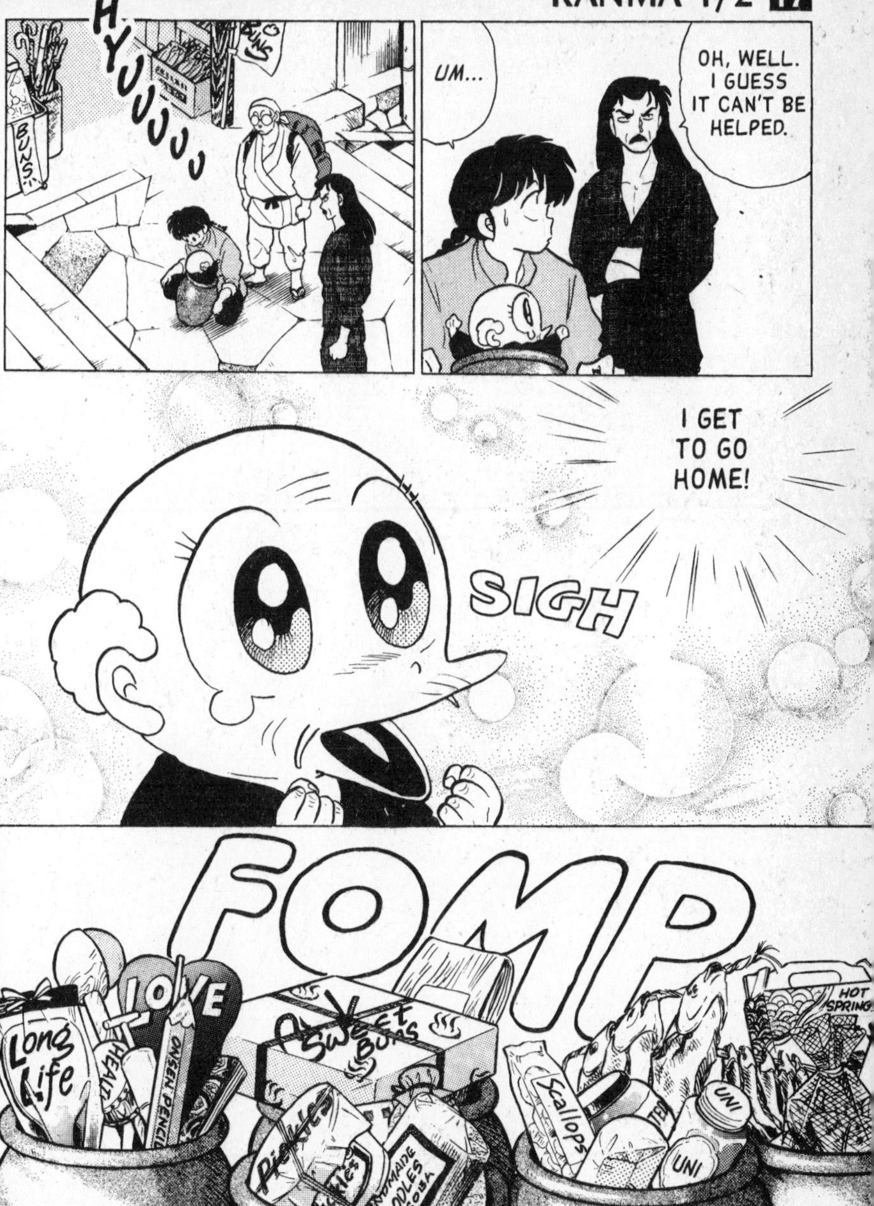
HYUUUUU
BUNS
BUNS
UM...
OH, WELL. I GUESS IT CAN'T BE HELPED.
I GET TO GO HOME!
SIGH
FOMP
LOVE
Long Life
ONSEN PENCIL
Sweet Buns
Pickles
HANDMADE NOODLES SOBA
Scallops
UNI
UNI
HOT SPRING

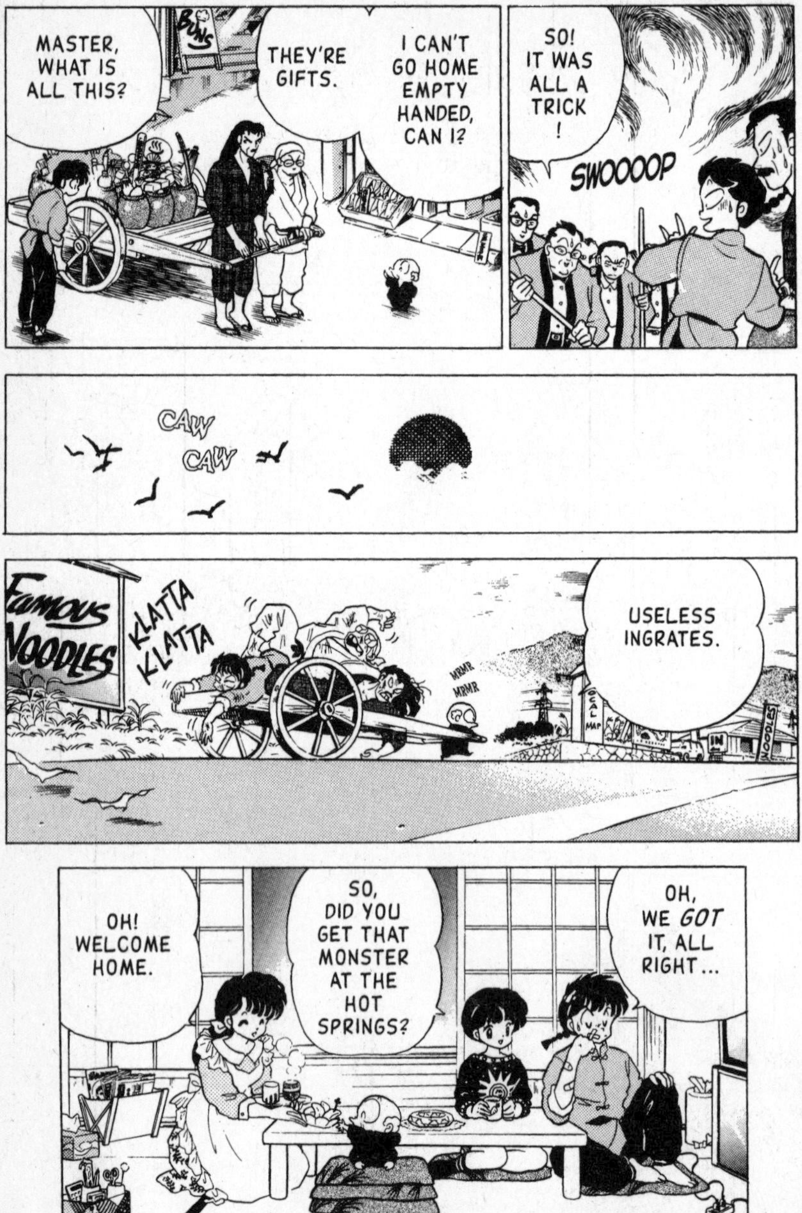
BUNS
MASTER, WHAT IS ALL THIS?
THEY'RE GIFTS.
I CAN'T GO HOME EMPTY HANDED, CAN I?
SO! IT WAS ALL A TRICK!
SWOOOOP
CAW
CAW
Famous Noodles
KLATTA KLATTA
MRMR MRMR
USELESS INGRATES.
NOODLES
OH! WELCOME HOME.
SO, DID YOU GET THAT MONSTER AT THE HOT SPRINGS?
OH, WE *GOT* IT, ALL RIGHT...

Part 10
PAPER DOLLS OF LOVE

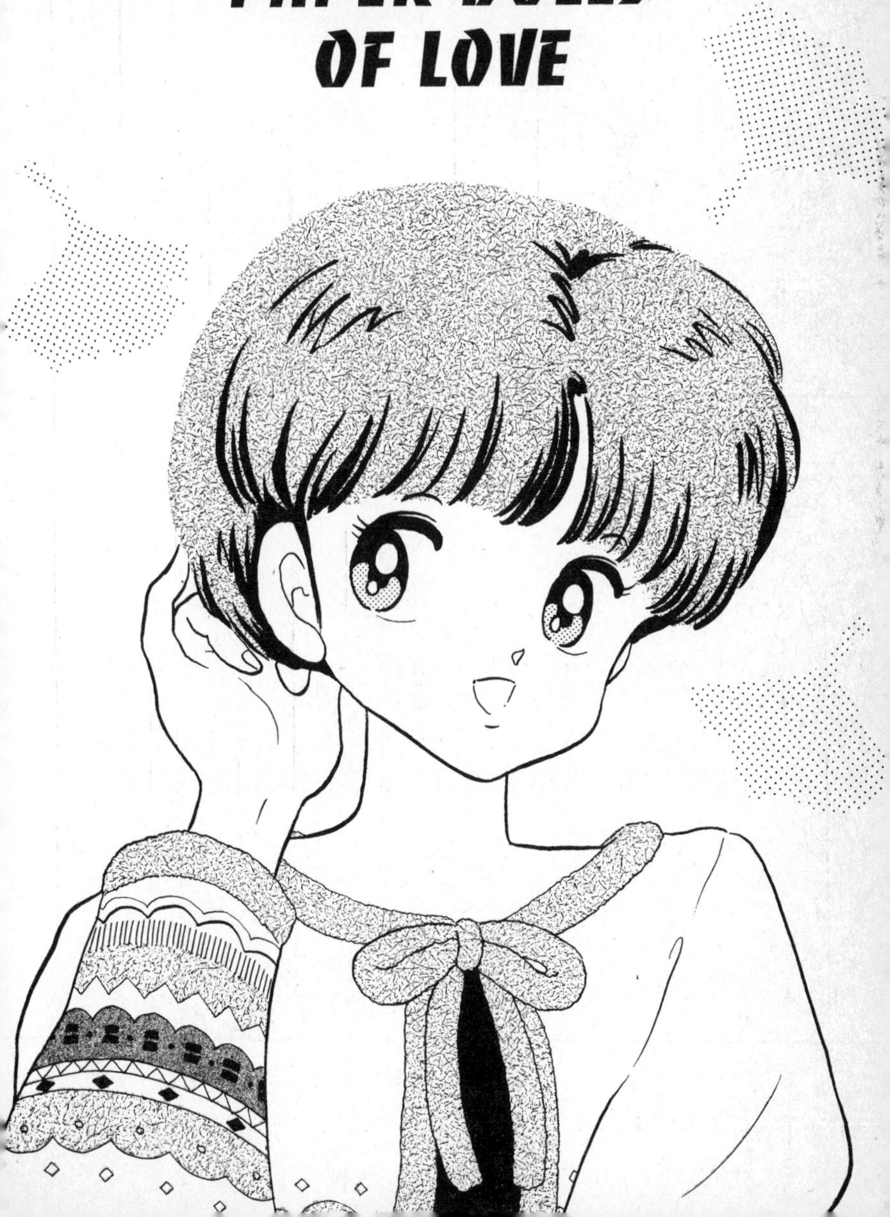

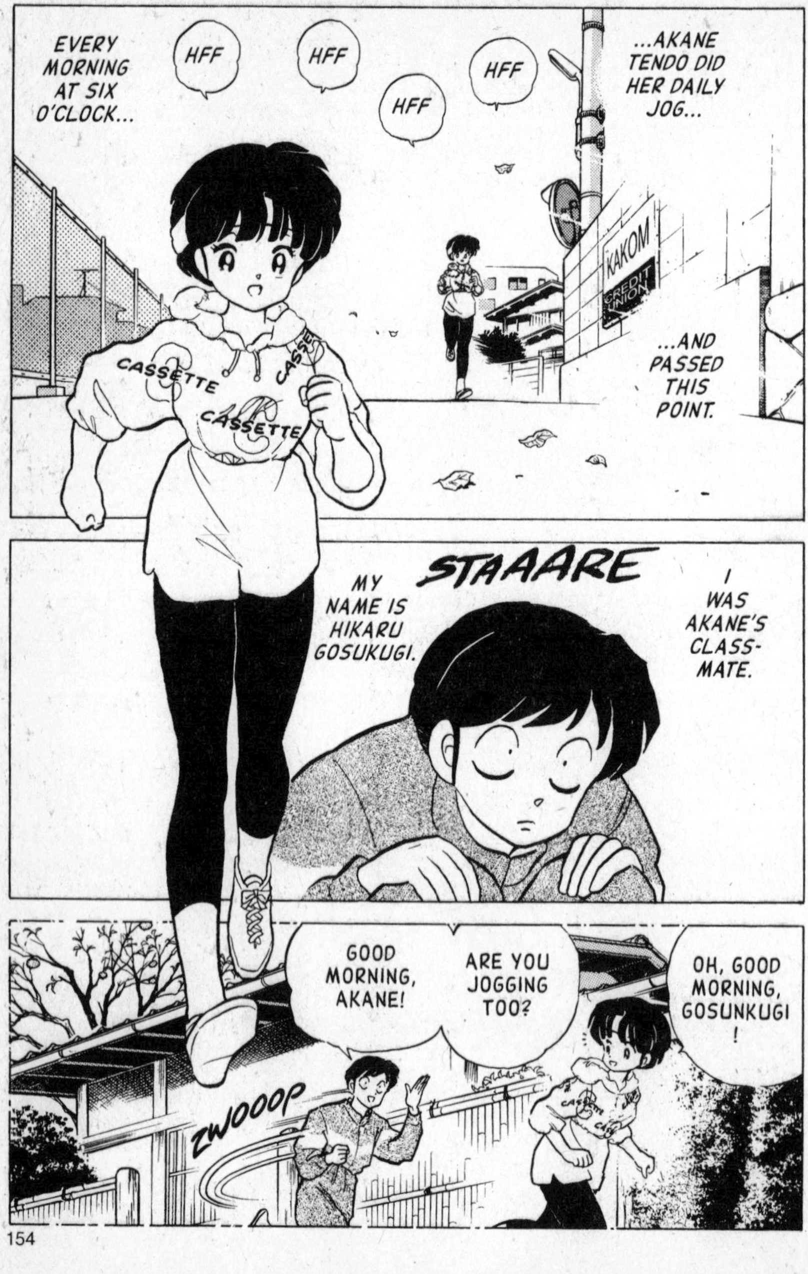
EVERY MORNING AT SIX O'CLOCK...
HFF
HFF
HFF
HFF
...AKANE TENDO DID HER DAILY JOG...
KAKOM
CREDIT UNION
...AND PASSED THIS POINT.
CASSETTE
CASSETTE
CASSETTE
MY NAME IS HIKARU GOSUKUGI.
STAAARE
I WAS AKANE'S CLASS-MATE.
GOOD MORNING, AKANE!
ARE YOU JOGGING TOO?
OH, GOOD MORNING, GOSUNKUGI!
ZWOOOP

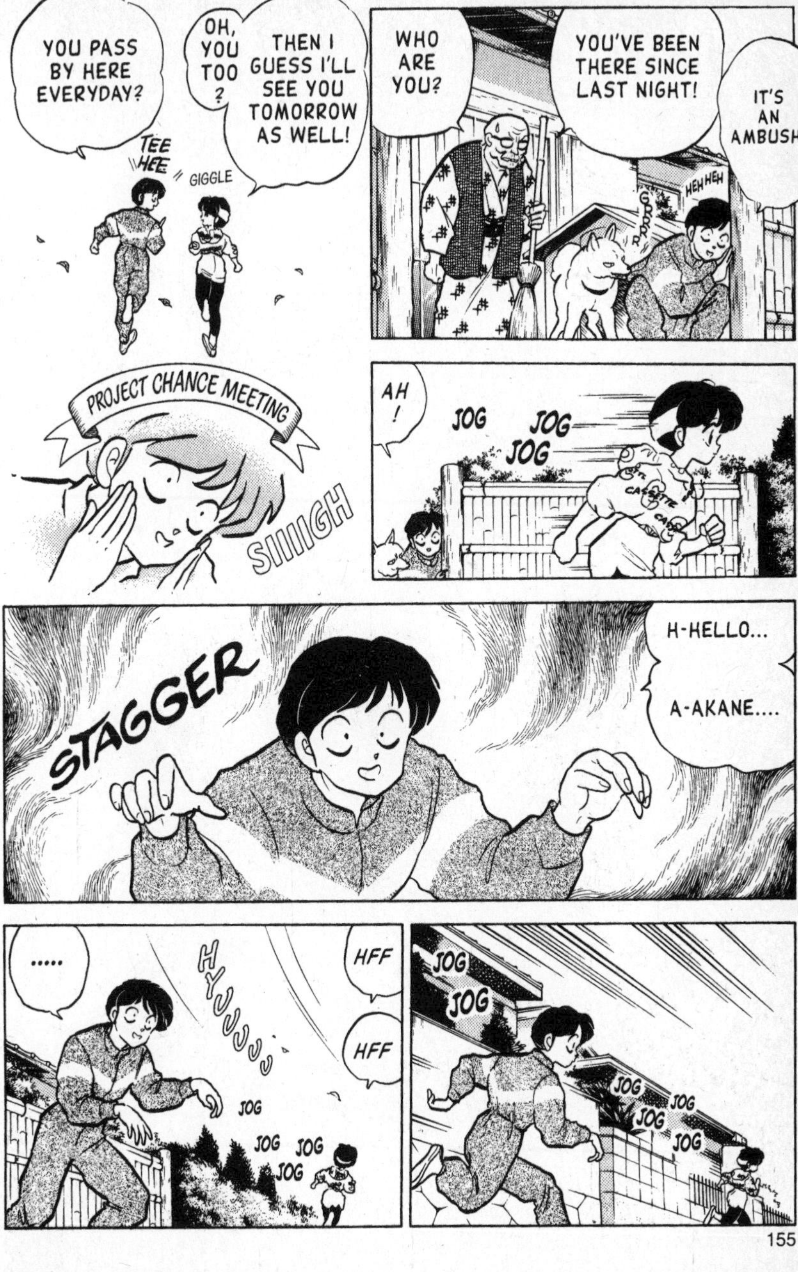
YOU PASS BY HERE EVERYDAY?
TEE HEE
OH, YOU TOO?
THEN I GUESS I'LL SEE YOU TOMORROW AS WELL!
GIGGLE
WHO ARE YOU?
YOU'VE BEEN THERE SINCE LAST NIGHT!
IT'S AN AMBUSH.
HEH HEH
GRRR
PROJECT CHANCE MEETING
SIIIIGH
AH!
JOG JOG JOG
CASSETTE
STAGGER
H-HELLO...
A-AKANE....
......
HYUUUUU
HFF
HFF
JOG JOG JOG JOG
JOG JOG
JOG JOG JOG JOG

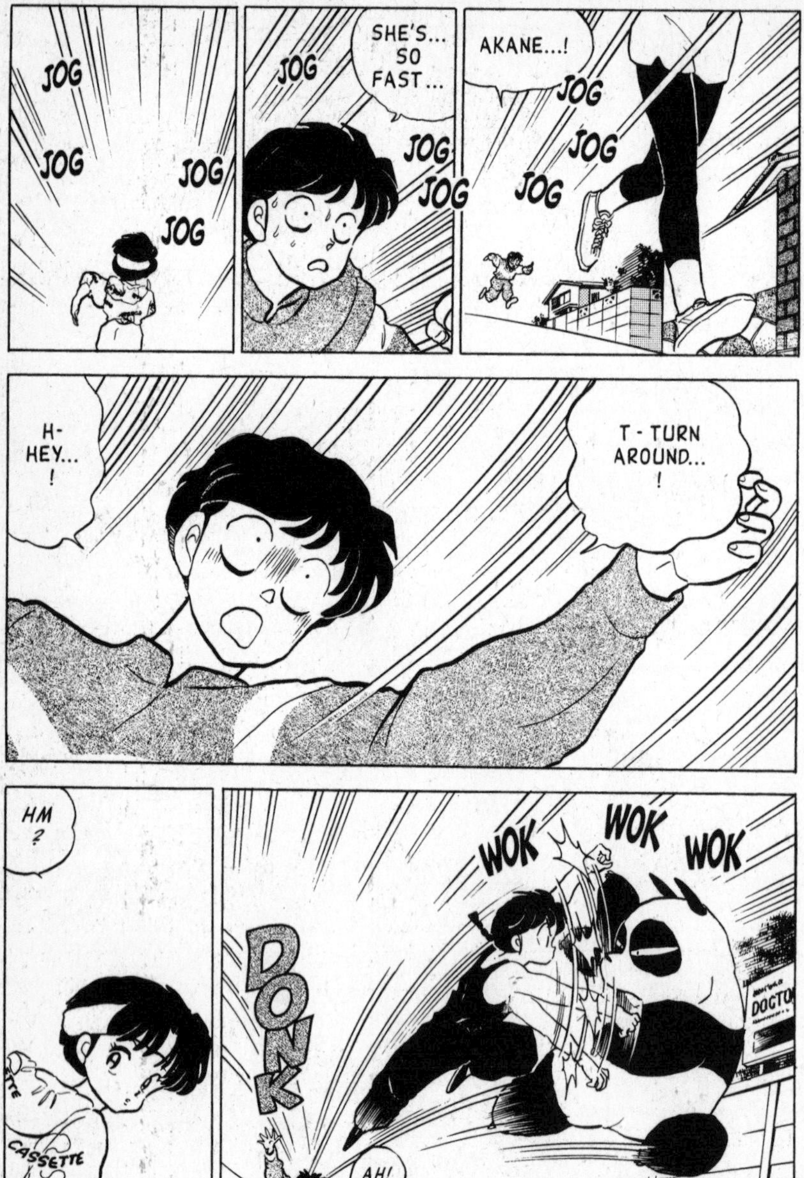
JOG
JOG
JOG
JOG
SHE'S... SO FAST...
JOG
JOG
JOG
AKANE...!
JOG
JOG
JOG
H-HEY...!
T-TURN AROUND...!
HM?
CASSETTE
WOK
WOK
WOK
DOCTOR
DONK
AH!
PLACE TRASH HERE

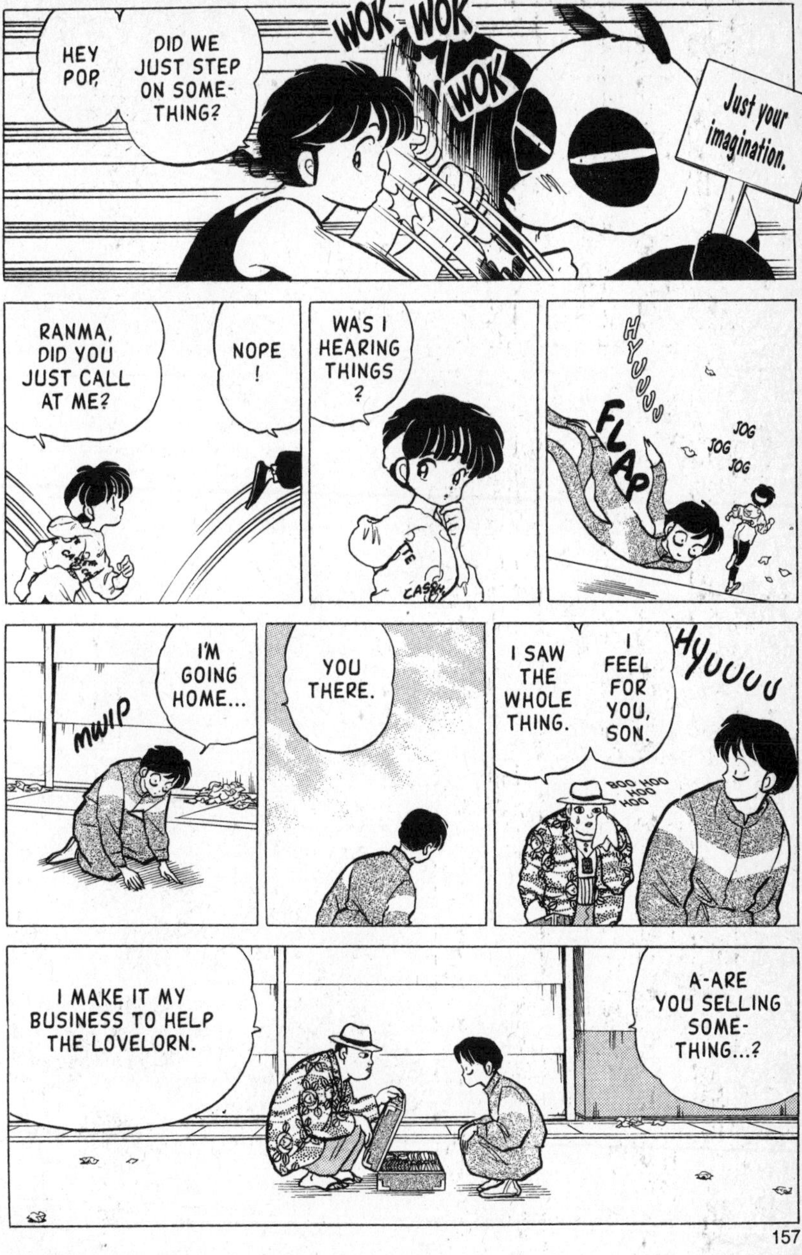
HEY POP,
DID WE JUST STEP ON SOME-THING?
WOK WOK
WOK
Just your imagination.
RANMA, DID YOU JUST CALL AT ME?
NOPE!
WAS I HEARING THINGS?
HYUUUU
FLAP
JOG JOG JOG
I'M GOING HOME...
MWIP
YOU THERE.
I SAW THE WHOLE THING.
I FEEL FOR YOU, SON.
HYUUUU
BOO HOO HOO HOO
I MAKE IT MY BUSINESS TO HELP THE LOVELORN.
A-ARE YOU SELLING SOME-THING...?

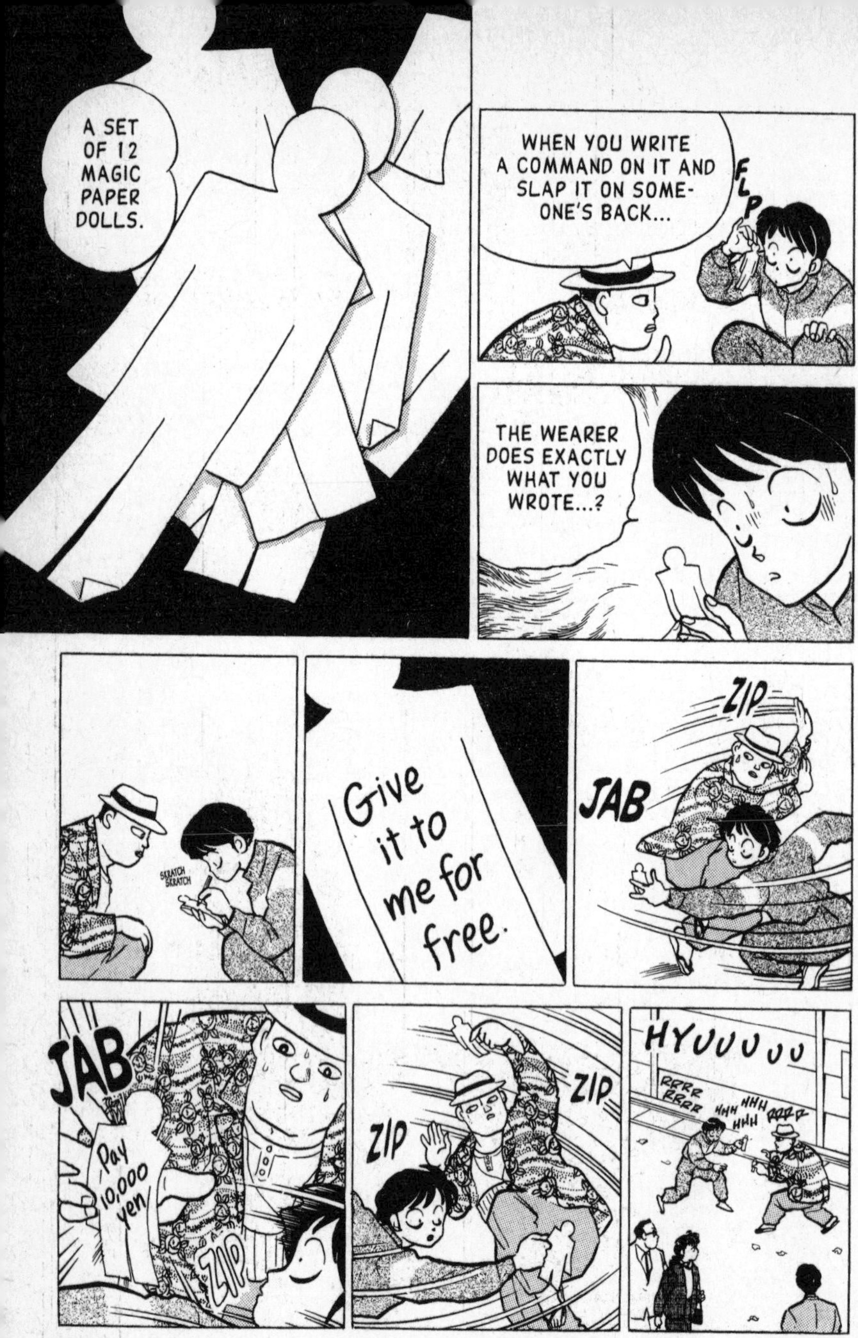
A SET OF 12 MAGIC PAPER DOLLS.
WHEN YOU WRITE A COMMAND ON IT AND SLAP IT ON SOME-ONE'S BACK...
FLP
THE WEARER DOES EXACTLY WHAT YOU WROTE...?
SKRATCH SKRATCH
Give it to me for free.
ZIP
JAB
JAB
Pay 10,000 yen
ZIP
ZIP
ZIP
HYUUUUUU
RRRR RRRR
HHH HHH HHH
RRRR

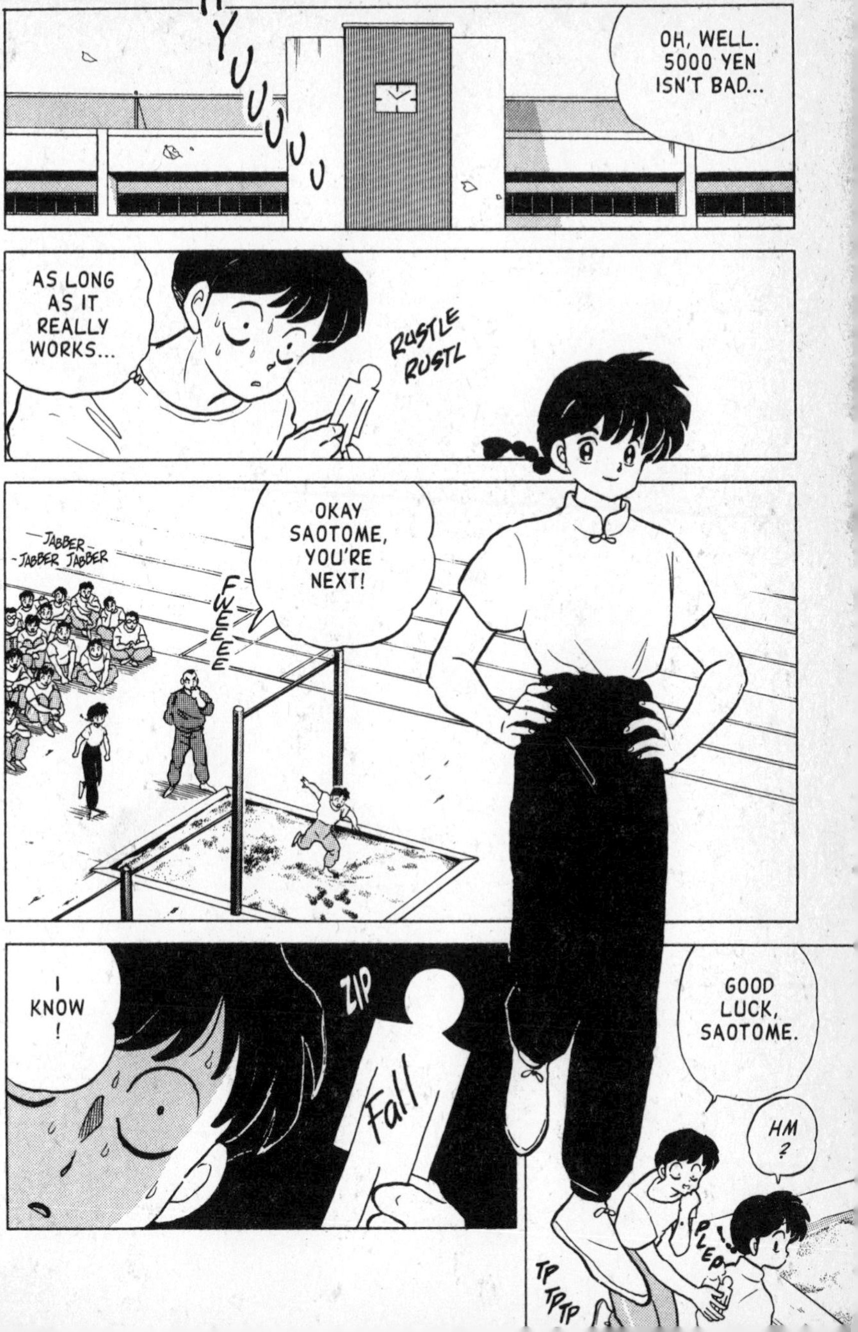
HYUUUUUU
OH, WELL. 5000 YEN ISN'T BAD...
AS LONG AS IT REALLY WORKS...
RUSTLE RUSTL
—JABBER— -JABBER JABBER
FWEEEE
OKAY SAOTOME, YOU'RE NEXT!
I KNOW!
ZIP
Fall
GOOD LUCK, SAOTOME.
HM?
PLEP
TP TP TP

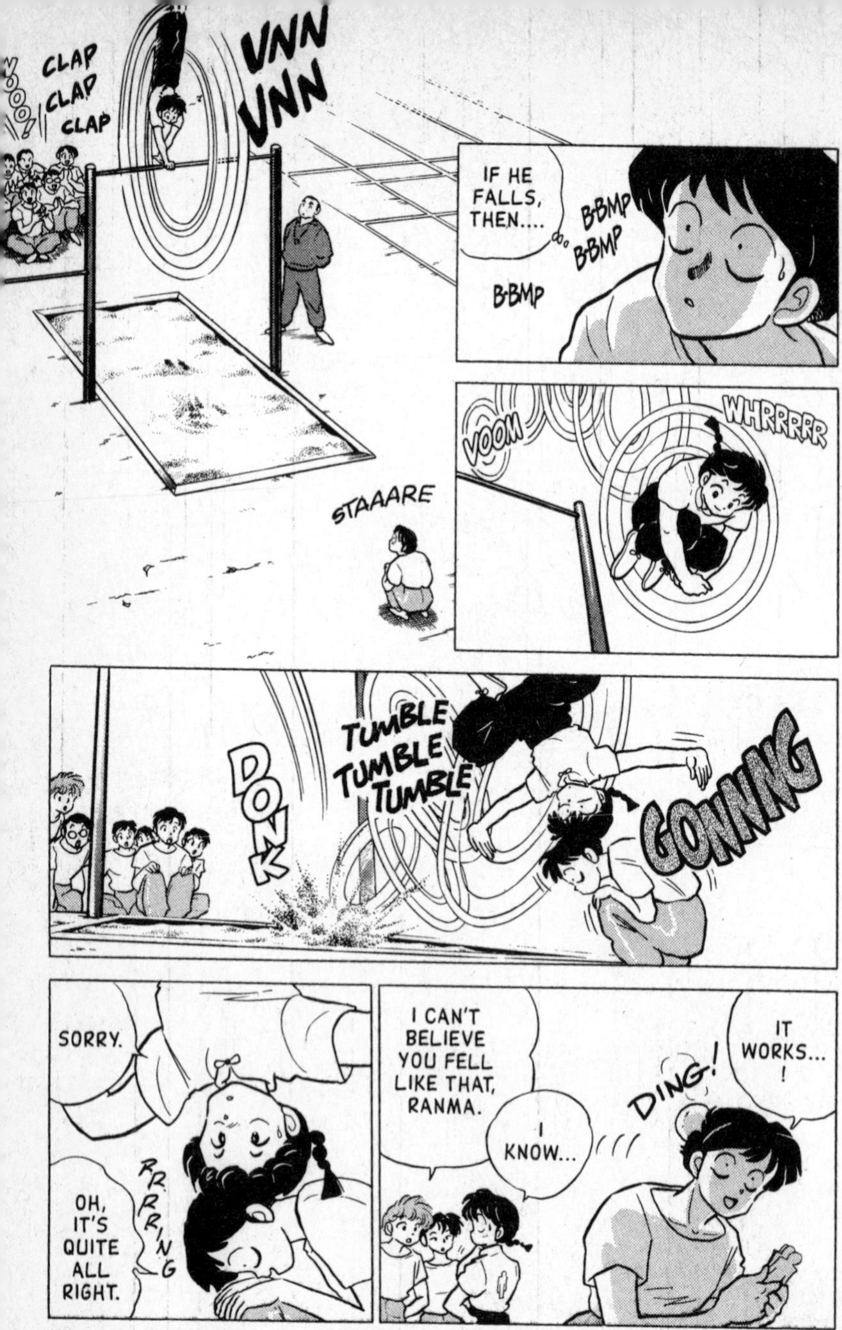
VOOO!
CLAP CLAP CLAP
UNN UNN
STAAARE
IF HE FALLS, THEN....
B-BMP B-BMP
B-BMP
VOOM
WHRRRRR
DONK
TUMBLE TUMBLE TUMBLE
GONNNG
SORRY.
OH, IT'S QUITE ALL RIGHT.
RRRRING
I CAN'T BELIEVE YOU FELL LIKE THAT, RANMA.
I KNOW...
DING!
IT WORKS... !

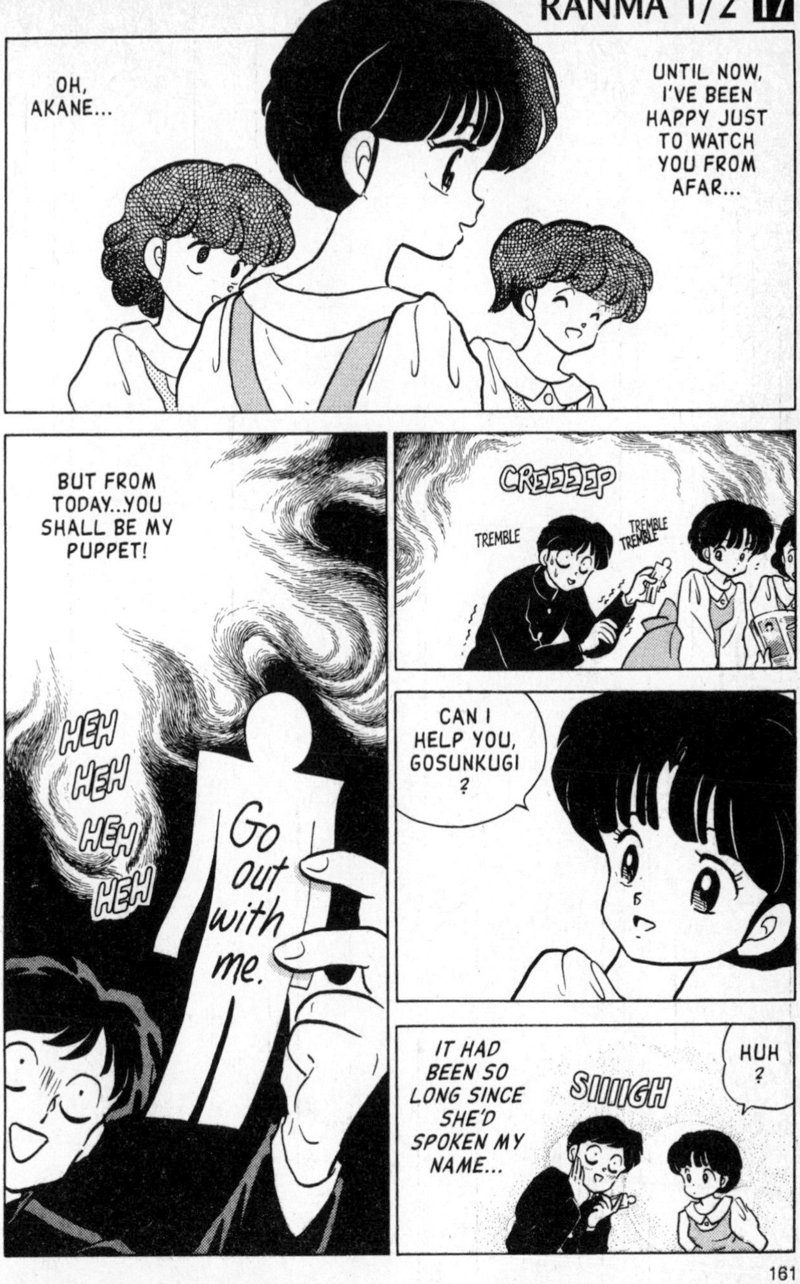
OH, AKANE...
UNTIL NOW, I'VE BEEN HAPPY JUST TO WATCH YOU FROM AFAR...
BUT FROM TODAY...YOU SHALL BE MY PUPPET!
HEH HEH HEH HEH
Go out with me.
CREEEEP
TREMBLE
TREMBLE TREMBLE
CAN I HELP YOU, GOSUNKUGI?
IT HAD BEEN SO LONG SINCE SHE'D SPOKEN MY NAME...
SIIIIGH
HUH?

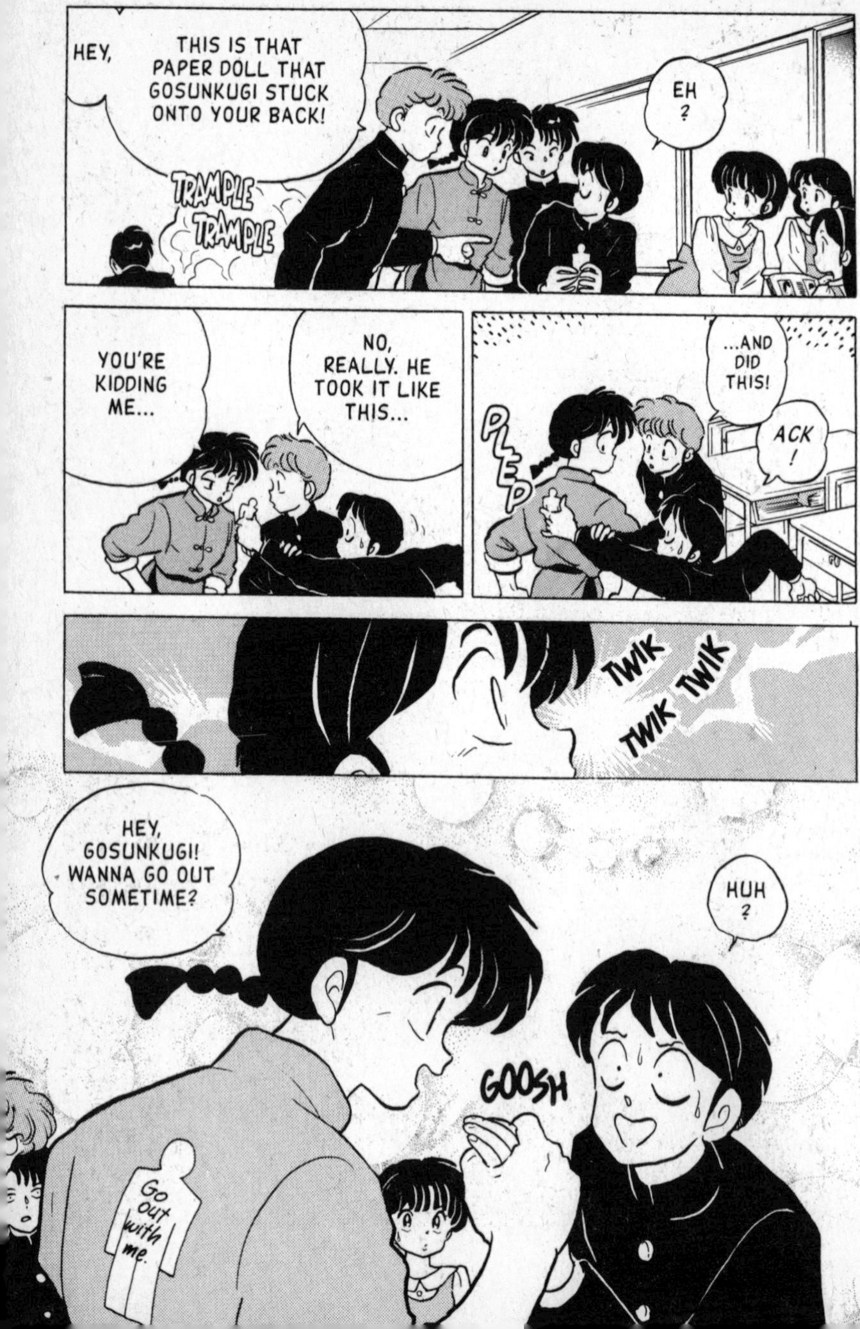
HEY,
THIS IS THAT PAPER DOLL THAT GOSUNKUGI STUCK ONTO YOUR BACK!
TRAMPLE TRAMPLE
EH?
YOU'RE KIDDING ME...
NO, REALLY. HE TOOK IT LIKE THIS...
PLEP
...AND DID THIS!
ACK!
TWIK TWIK TWIK
HEY, GOSUNKUGI! WANNA GO OUT SOMETIME?
HUH?
GOOSH
Go out with me.

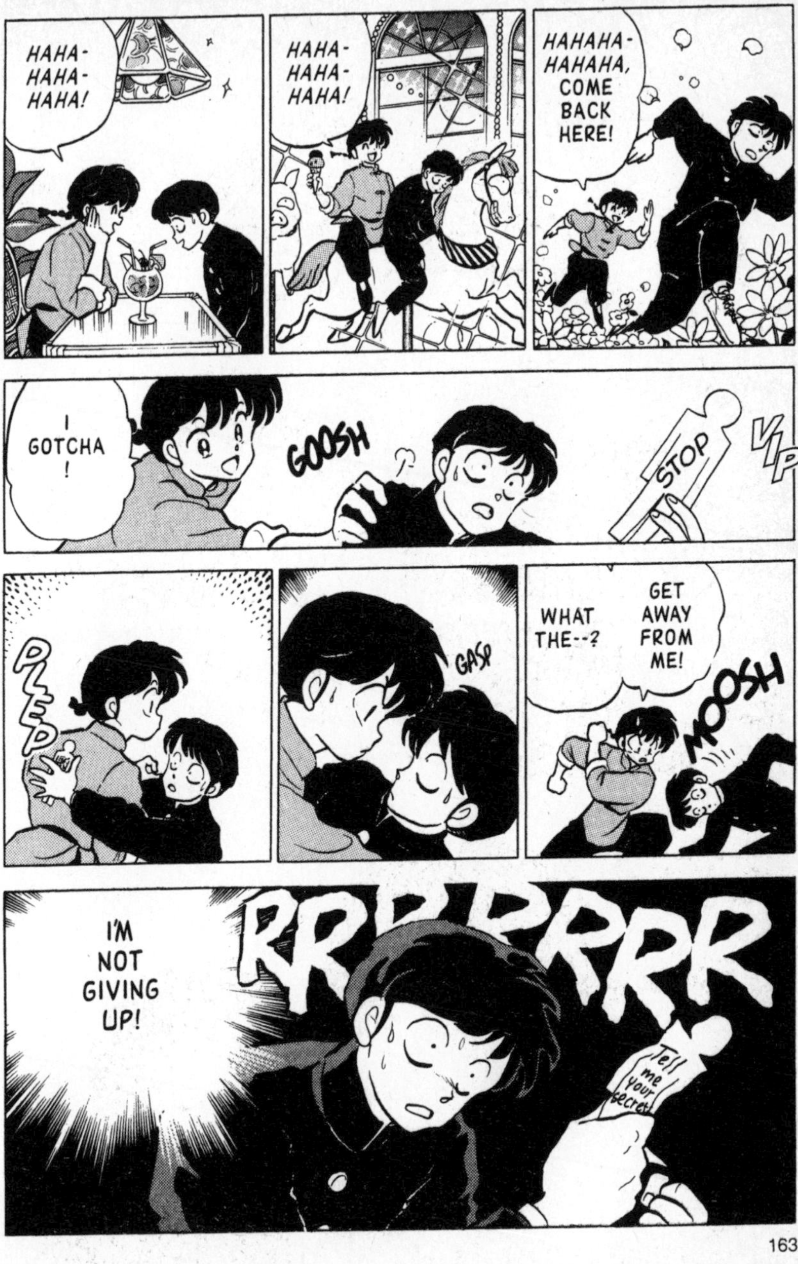
HAHA-HAHA-HAHA!
HAHA-HAHA-HAHA!
HAHAHA-HAHAHA, COME BACK HERE!
I GOTCHA!
GOOSH
STOP
VIP
PLEP
GASP
WHAT THE--?
GET AWAY FROM ME!
MOOSH
I'M NOT GIVING UP!
RRRRRRR
Tell me your secret

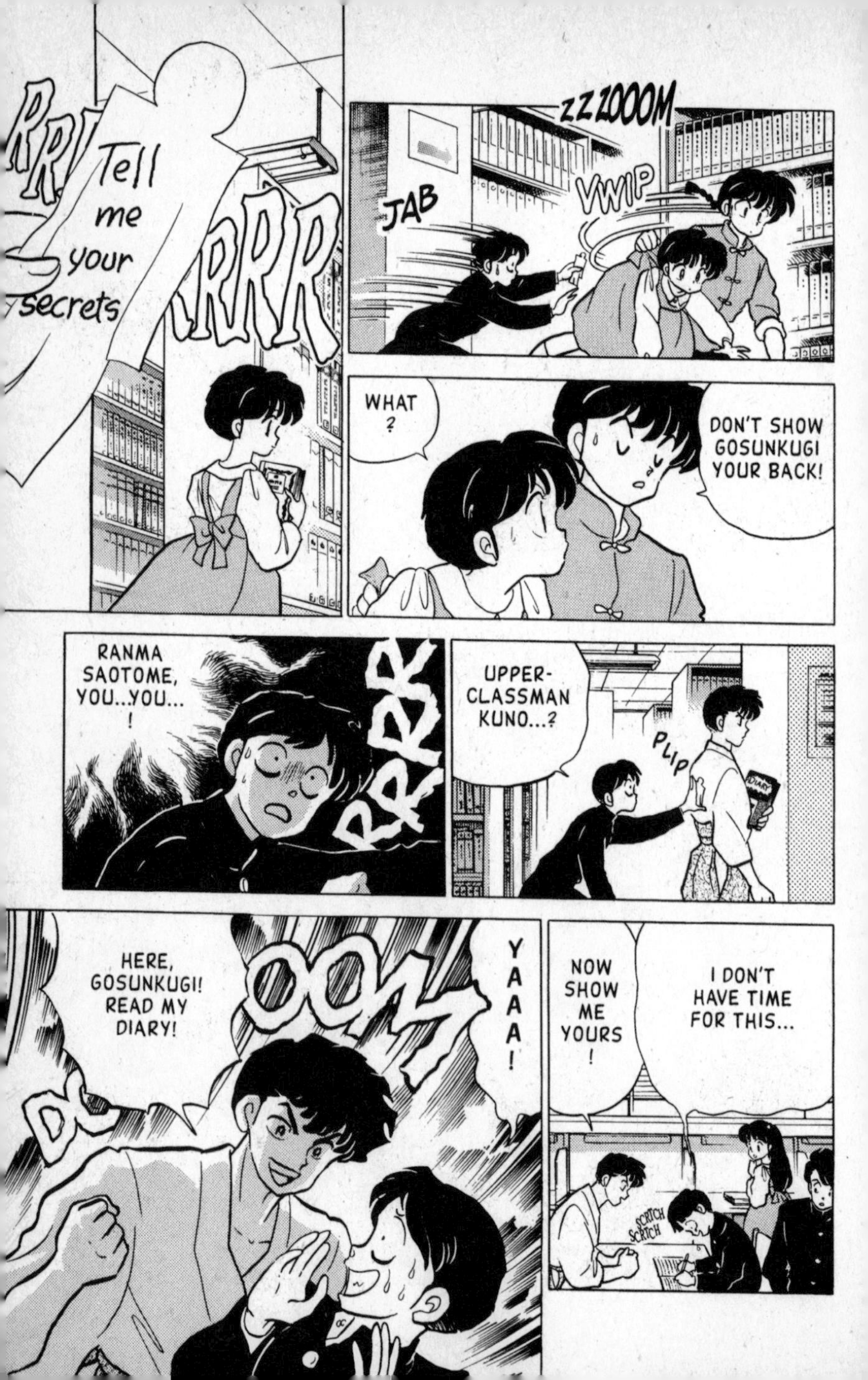
RRI
Tell me your secrets
RRRR
ZZZOOOM
JAB
VWIP
WHAT?
DON'T SHOW GOSUNKUGI YOUR BACK!
RANMA SAOTOME, YOU...YOU...!
RRRR
UPPER-CLASSMAN KUNO...?
PLIP
DIARY
HERE, GOSUNKUGI! READ MY DIARY!
YAAAA!
NOW SHOW ME YOURS!
I DON'T HAVE TIME FOR THIS...
SCRITCH SCRITCH

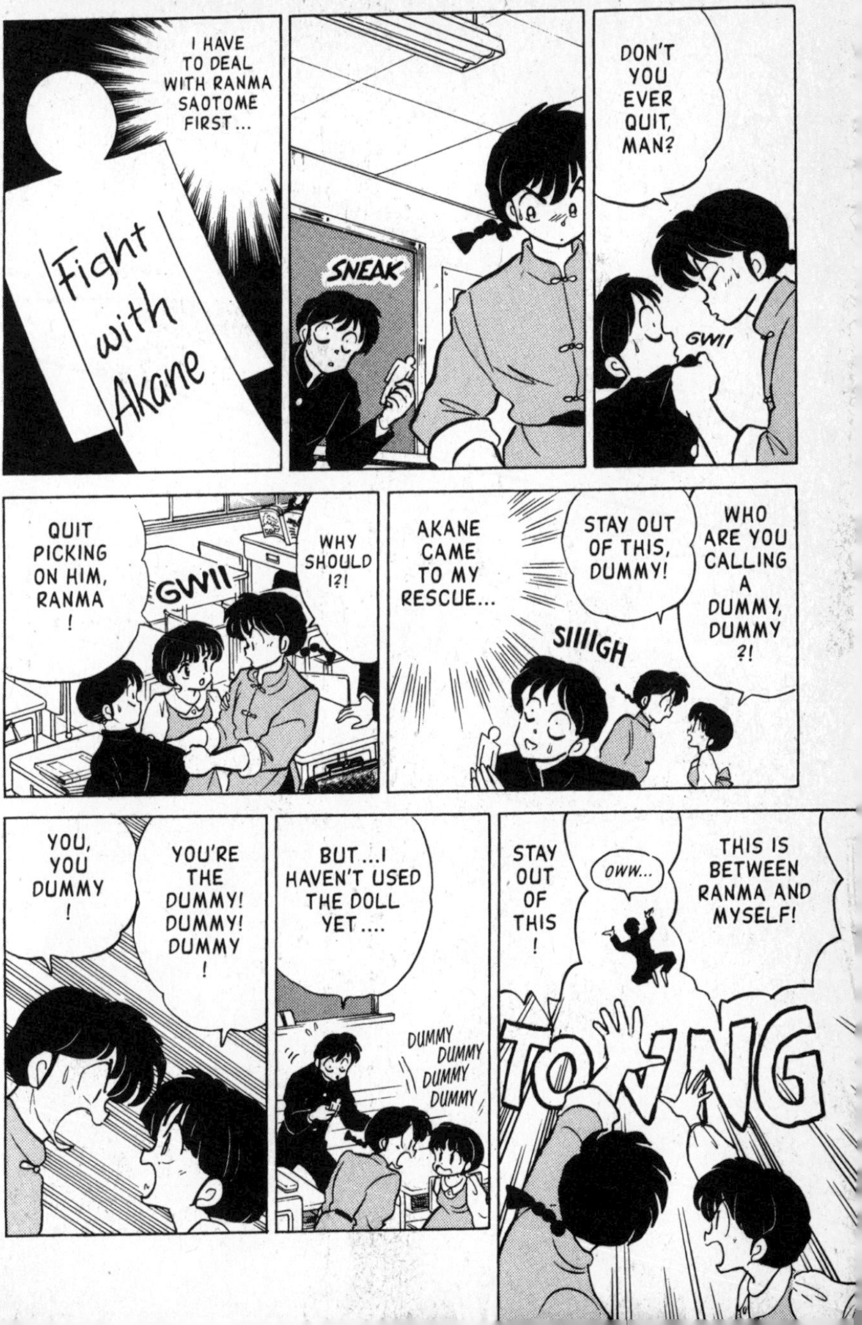
I HAVE TO DEAL WITH RANMA SAOTOME FIRST...
Fight with Akane
SNEAK
DON'T YOU EVER QUIT, MAN?
GWII
QUIT PICKING ON HIM, RANMA!
WHY SHOULD I?!
GWII
AKANE CAME TO MY RESCUE...
STAY OUT OF THIS, DUMMY!
WHO ARE YOU CALLING A DUMMY, DUMMY?!
SIIIGH
YOU, YOU DUMMY!
YOU'RE THE DUMMY! DUMMY! DUMMY!
BUT...I HAVEN'T USED THE DOLL YET....
DUMMY DUMMY DUMMY DUMMY
STAY OUT OF THIS!
OWW...
THIS IS BETWEEN RANMA AND MYSELF!
TO NG

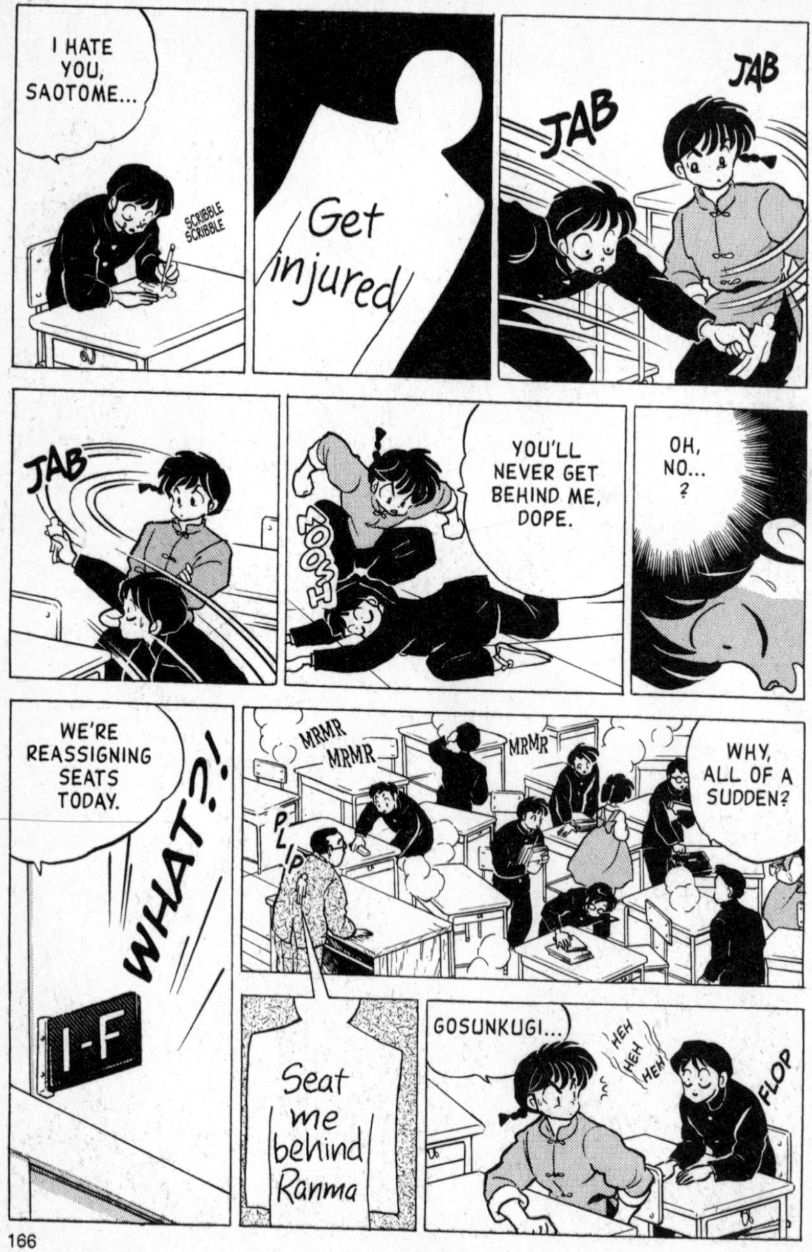
I HATE YOU, SAOTOME...
SCRIBBLE SCRIBBLE
Get injured
JAB
JAB
JAB
ZOOM
YOU'LL NEVER GET BEHIND ME, DOPE.
OH, NO...?
WE'RE REASSIGNING SEATS TODAY.
WHAT?!
I-F
MRMR
MRMR
MRMR
WHY, ALL OF A SUDDEN?
PLIP
Seat me behind Ranma
GOSUNKUGI...
HEH HEH HEH
FLOP

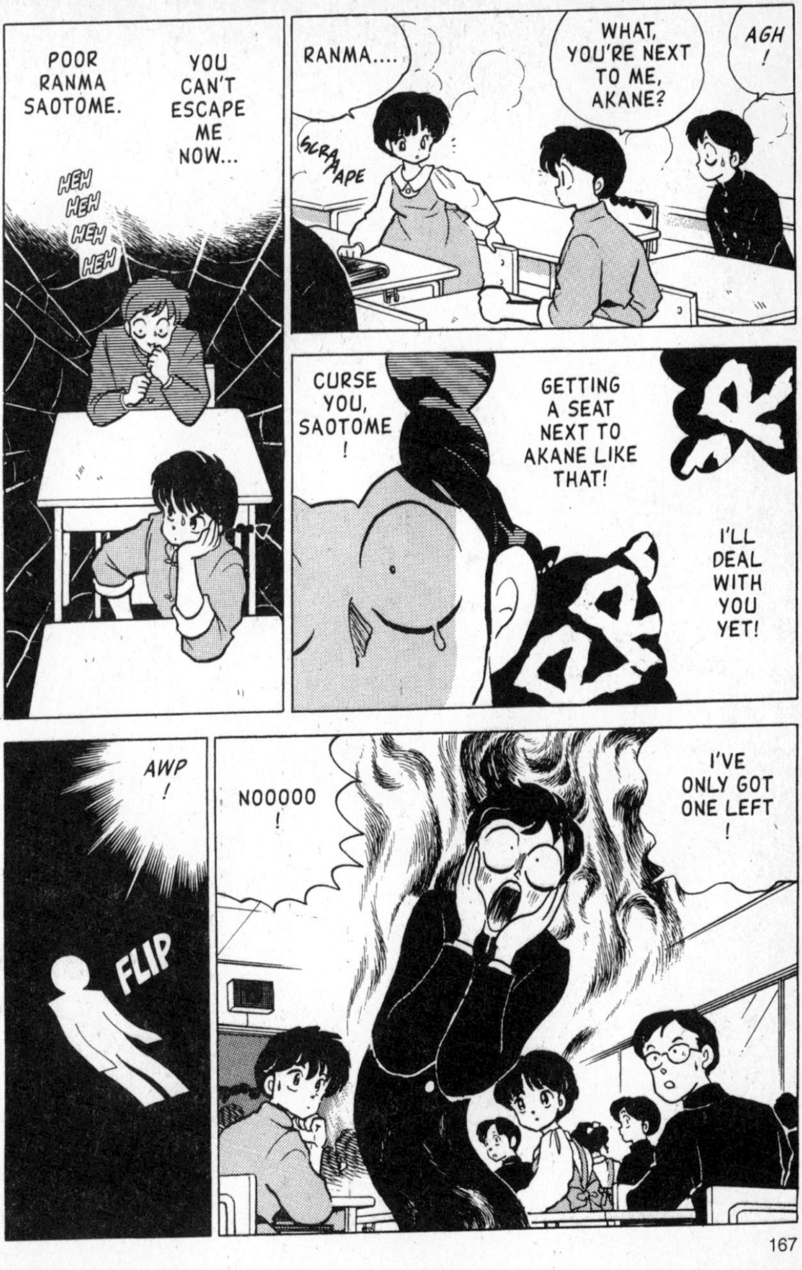
POOR RANMA SAOTOME.
YOU CAN'T ESCAPE ME NOW...
HEH HEH HEH HEH
RANMA....
SCRAAAPE
WHAT, YOU'RE NEXT TO ME, AKANE?
AGH!
CURSE YOU, SAOTOME!
GETTING A SEAT NEXT TO AKANE LIKE THAT!
I'LL DEAL WITH YOU YET!
AWP!
FLIP
NOOOOO!
I'VE ONLY GOT ONE LEFT!

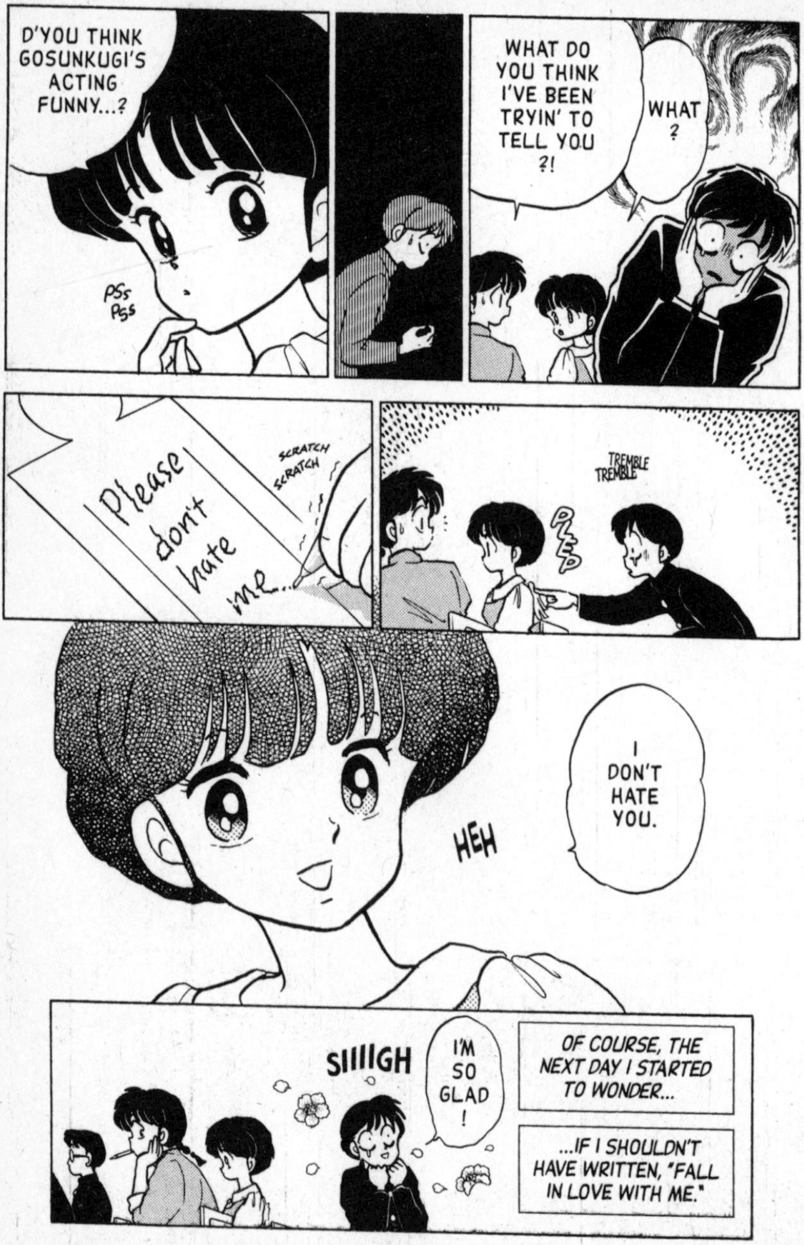
D'YOU THINK GOSUNKUGI'S ACTING FUNNY...?
PSS PSS
WHAT DO YOU THINK I'VE BEEN TRYIN' TO TELL YOU ?!
WHAT ?
Please don't hate me...
SCRATCH SCRATCH
TREMBLE TREMBLE
PLEP
I DON'T HATE YOU.
HEH
SIIIIGH
I'M SO GLAD !
OF COURSE, THE NEXT DAY I STARTED TO WONDER...
...IF I SHOULDN'T HAVE WRITTEN, "FALL IN LOVE WITH ME."

Part 11

THE PILL OF OBEDIENCE

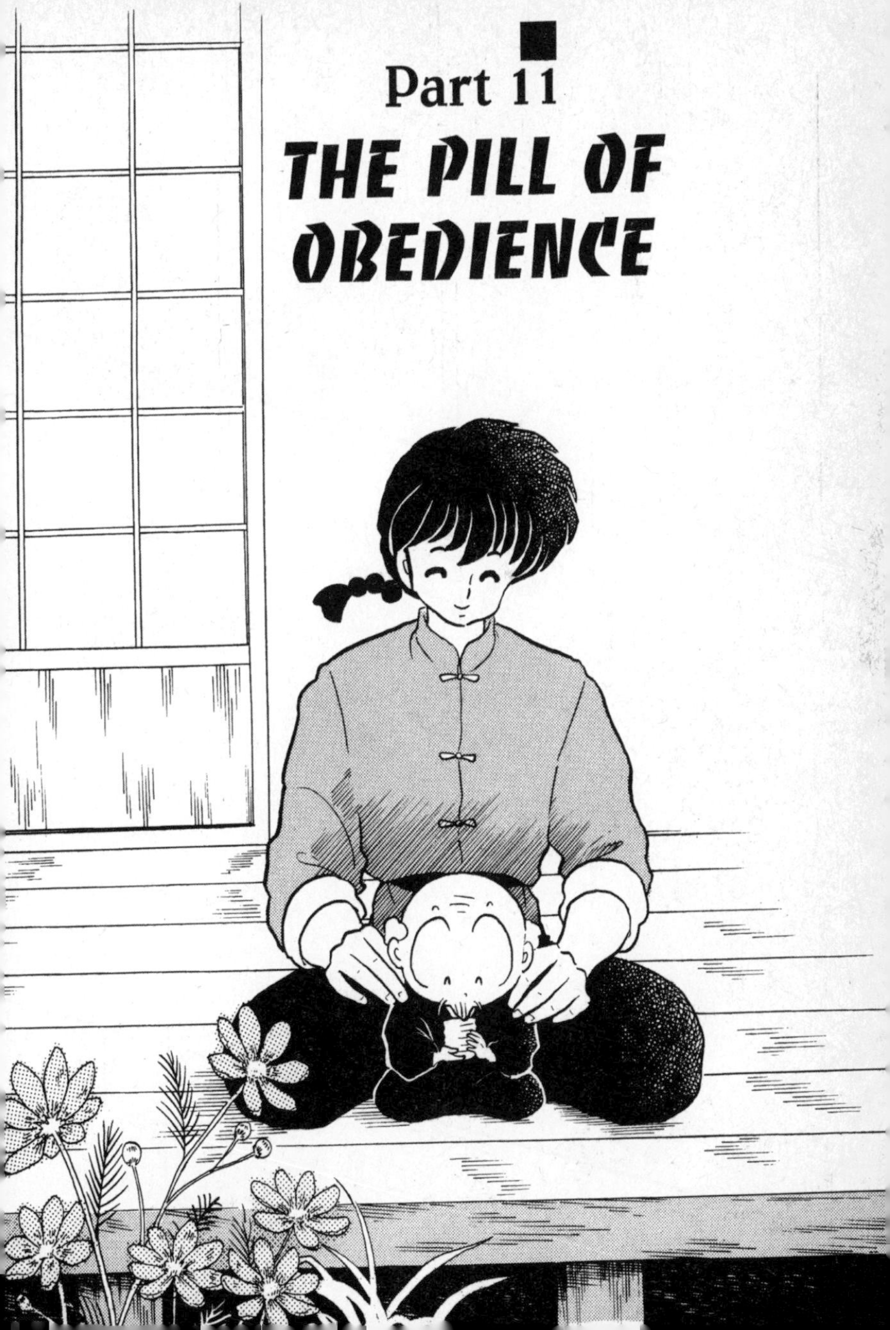

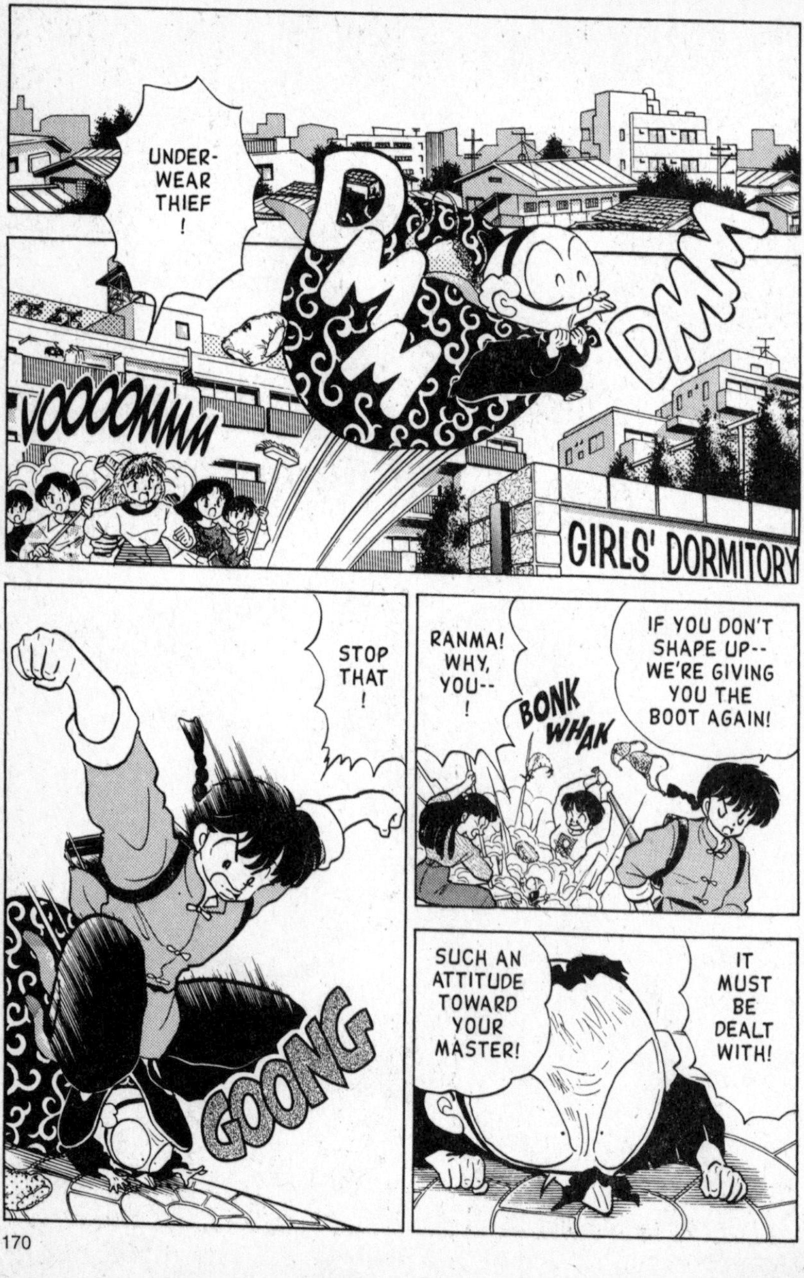
UNDER-WEAR THIEF !
DMM
DMM
VOOOOMMM
GIRLS' DORMITORY
STOP THAT !
GOONG
RANMA! WHY, YOU-- !
BONK
WHAK
IF YOU DON'T SHAPE UP-- WE'RE GIVING YOU THE BOOT AGAIN!
SUCH AN ATTITUDE TOWARD YOUR MASTER!
IT MUST BE DEALT WITH!

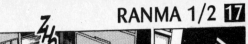

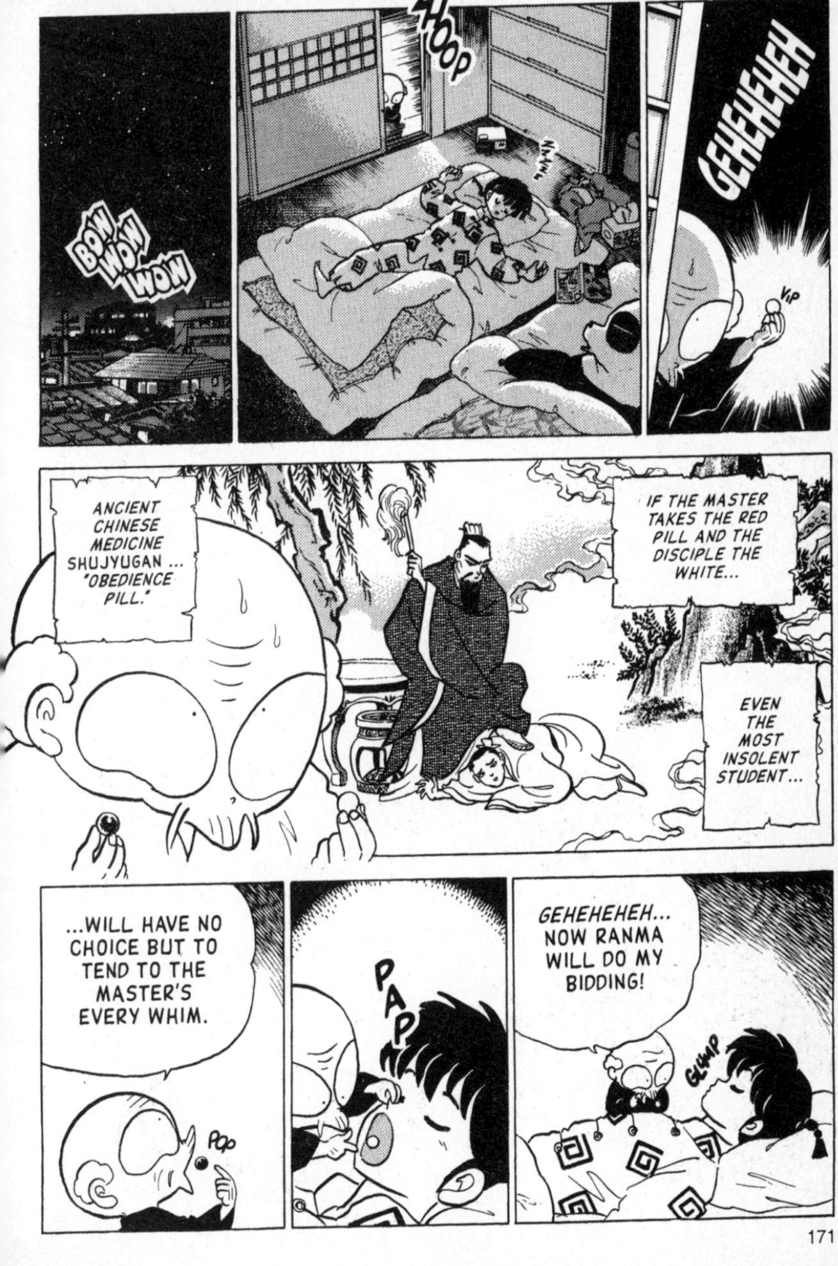
BOW WOW WOW
ZHOOP
GEHEHEH
VIP
ANCIENT CHINESE MEDICINE SHUJYUGAN ... "OBEDIENCE PILL."
IF THE MASTER TAKES THE RED PILL AND THE DISCIPLE THE WHITE...
EVEN THE MOST INSOLENT STUDENT...
...WILL HAVE NO CHOICE BUT TO TEND TO THE MASTER'S EVERY WHIM.
POP
PAP
GEHEHEHEH... NOW RANMA WILL DO MY BIDDING!
GLUMP

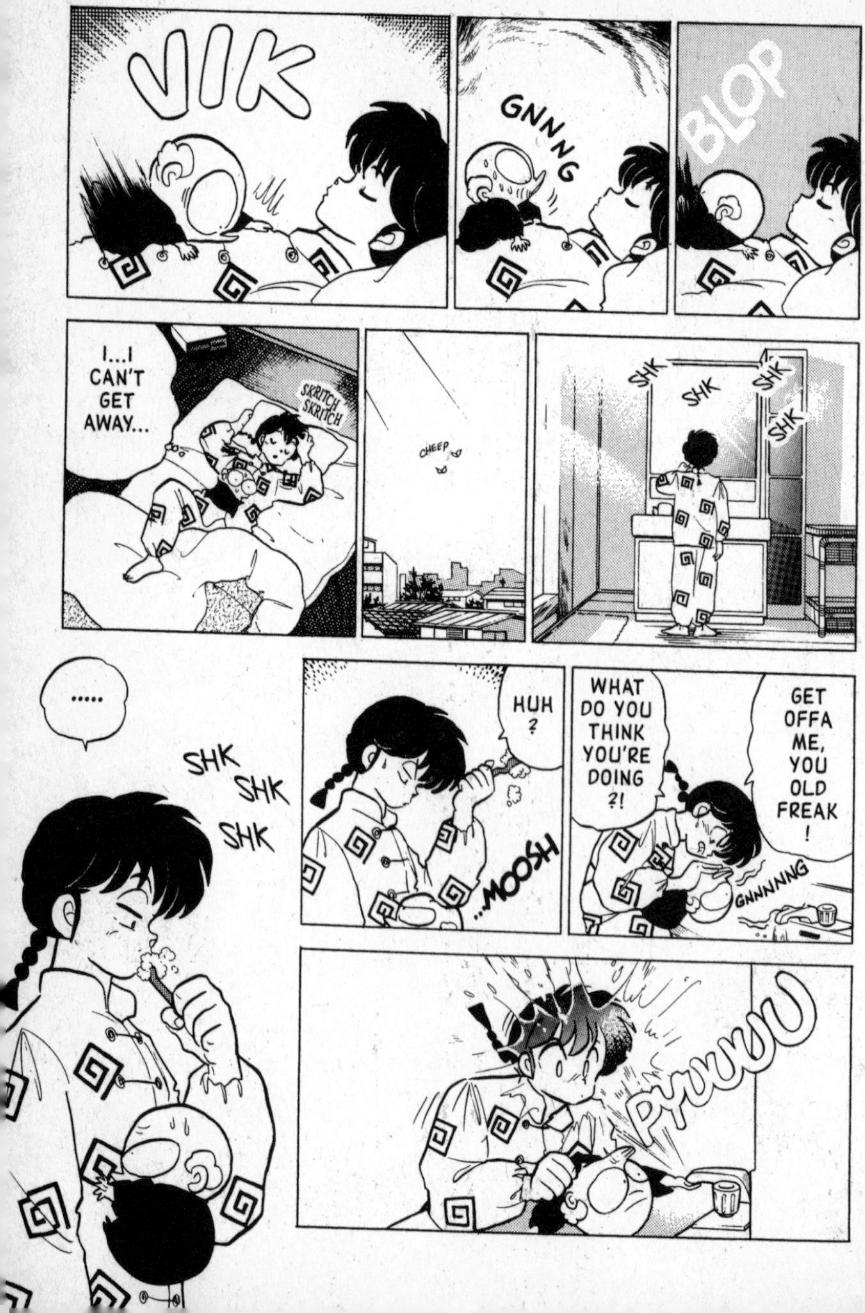
VIK
GNNNG
BLOP
I...I CAN'T GET AWAY...
SKRITCH SKRITCH
CHEEP
SHK
SHK
SHK
SHK
.....
SHK
SHK
SHK
HUH?
...MOOSH
WHAT DO YOU THINK YOU'RE DOING?!
GET OFFA ME, YOU OLD FREAK!
GNNNNNG
PFUUUU

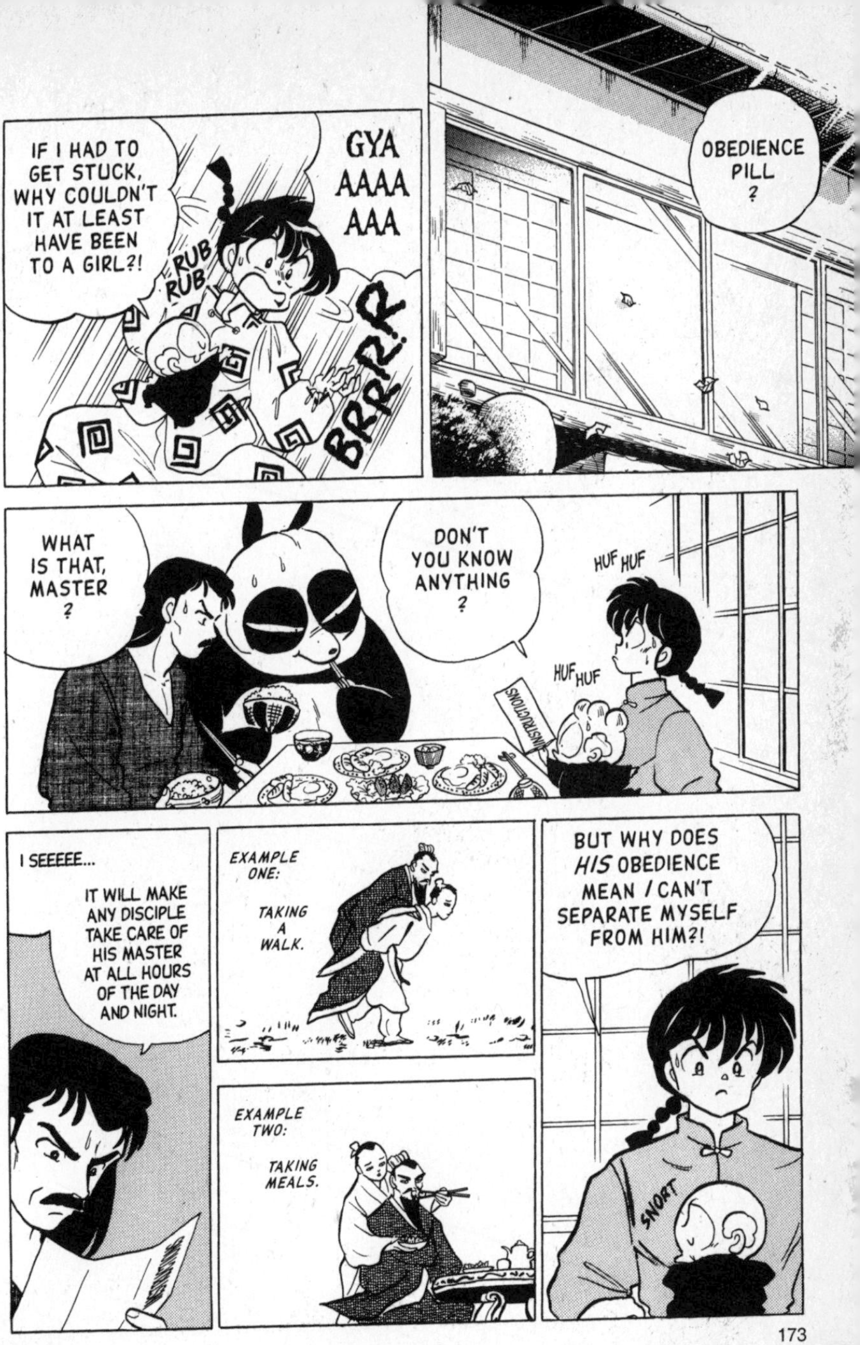
IF I HAD TO GET STUCK, WHY COULDN'T IT AT LEAST HAVE BEEN TO A GIRL?!
GYA AAAA AAA
RUB RUB
BRRRR
OBEDIENCE PILL?
WHAT IS THAT, MASTER?
DON'T YOU KNOW ANYTHING?
HUF HUF
HUF HUF
INSTRUCTIONS
I SEEEEE...
IT WILL MAKE ANY DISCIPLE TAKE CARE OF HIS MASTER AT ALL HOURS OF THE DAY AND NIGHT.
EXAMPLE ONE:
TAKING A WALK.
EXAMPLE TWO:
TAKING MEALS.
BUT WHY DOES HIS OBEDIENCE MEAN I CAN'T SEPARATE MYSELF FROM HIM?!
SNORT

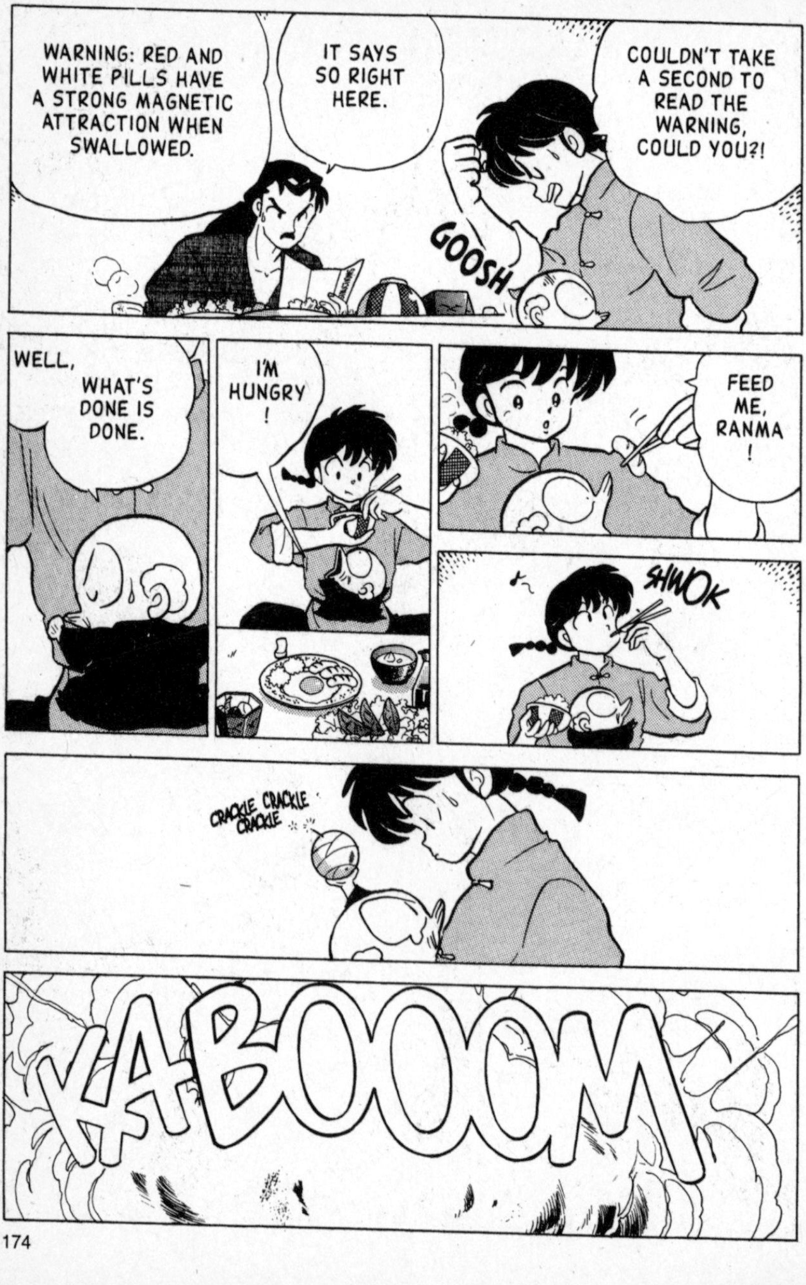
WARNING: RED AND WHITE PILLS HAVE A STRONG MAGNETIC ATTRACTION WHEN SWALLOWED.
IT SAYS SO RIGHT HERE.
COULDN'T TAKE A SECOND TO READ THE WARNING, COULD YOU?!
GOOSH
WELL, WHAT'S DONE IS DONE.
I'M HUNGRY!
FEED ME, RANMA!
SHWOK
CRACKLE CRACKLE CRACKLE
KABOOOM

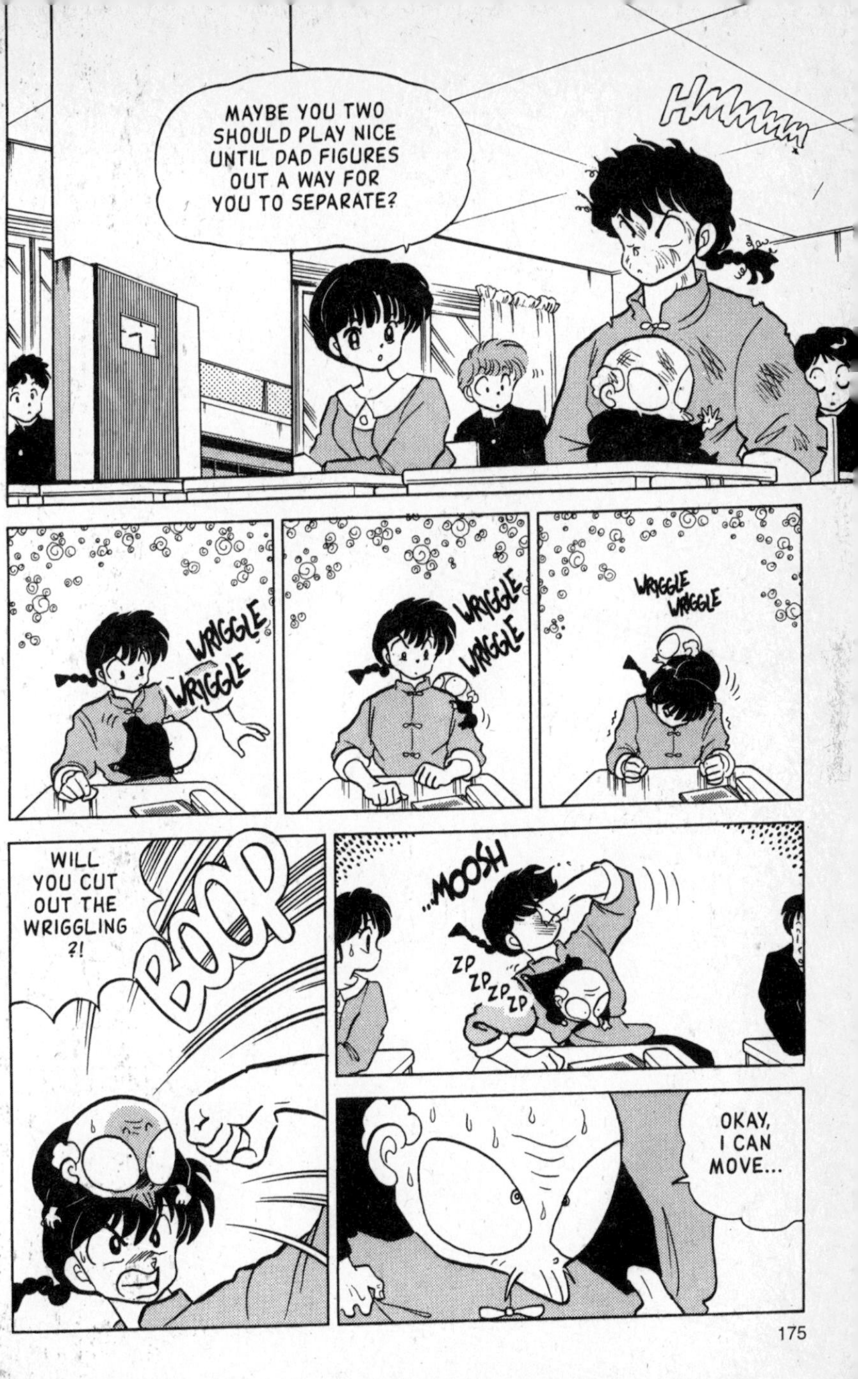
MAYBE YOU TWO SHOULD PLAY NICE UNTIL DAD FIGURES OUT A WAY FOR YOU TO SEPARATE?
HMMMMM
WRIGGLE
WRIGGLE
WRIGGLE
WRIGGLE
WRIGGLE
WRIGGLE
WILL YOU CUT OUT THE WRIGGLING ?!
BOOP
...MOOSH
ZP ZP ZP ZP
OKAY, I CAN MOVE...

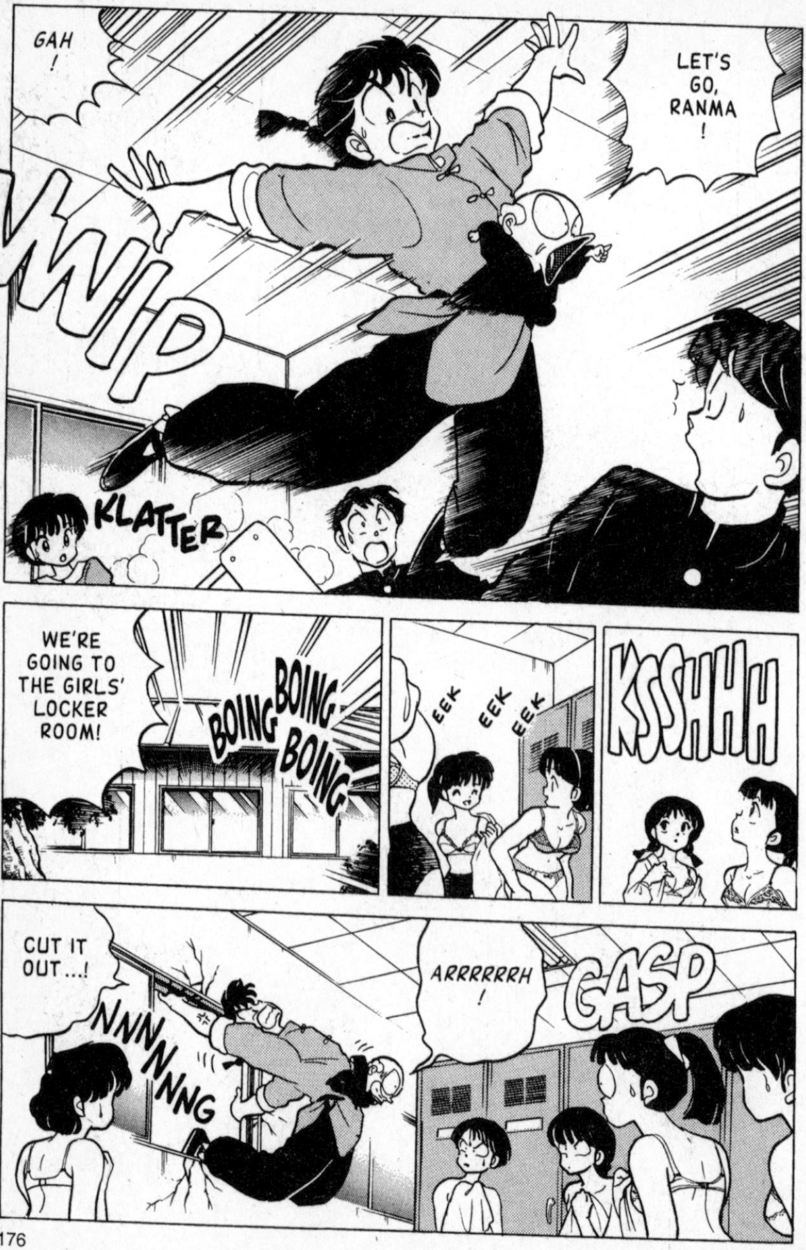

GAH !
LET'S GO, RANMA !
VWIP
KLATTER
WE'RE GOING TO THE GIRLS' LOCKER ROOM!
BOING BOING BOING
EEK EEK EEK
KSSHHH
CUT IT OUT...!
NNNNNNNG
ARRRRRRH !
GASP

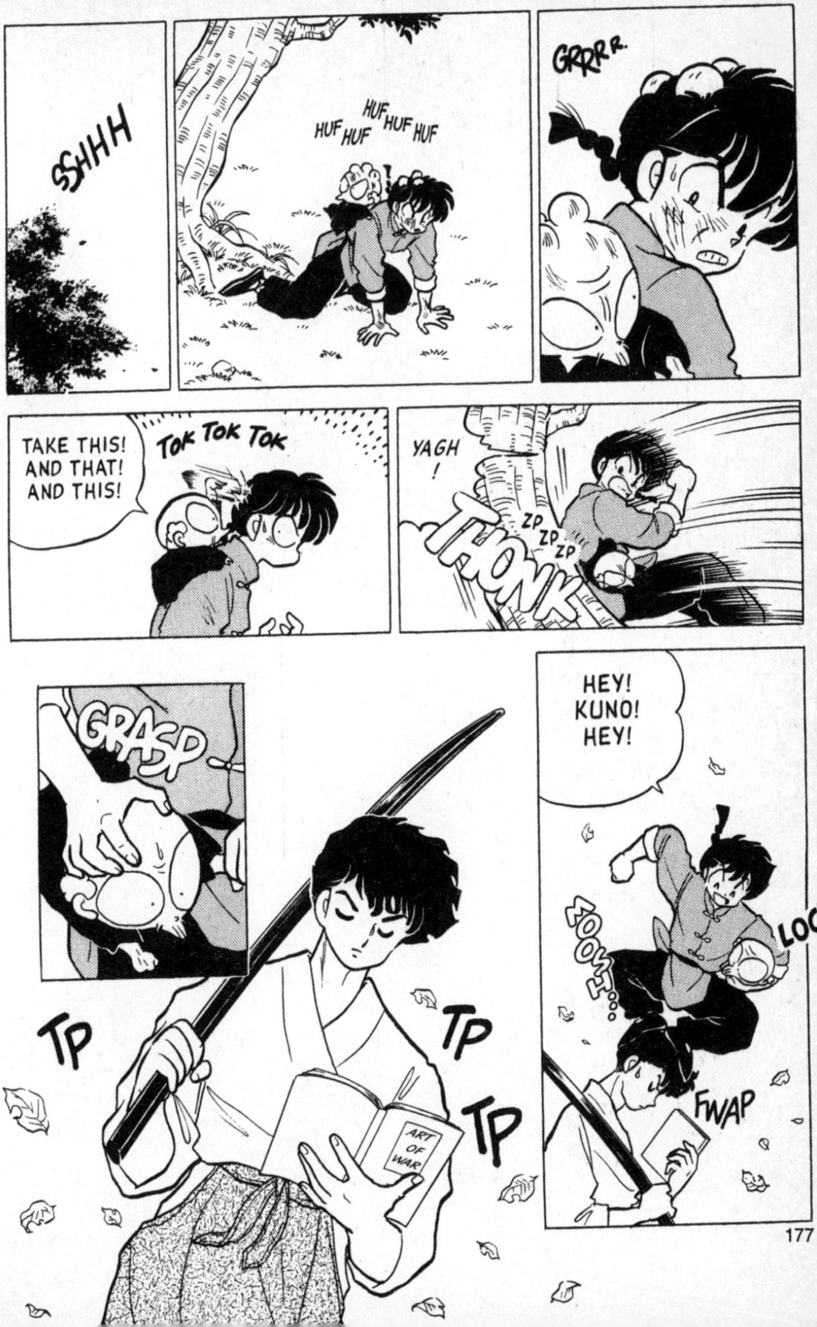
SSHHH
HUF HUF HUF HUF HUF
GRRRR.
TAKE THIS! AND THAT! AND THIS!
TOK TOK TOK
YAGH!
THONK
ZP ZP ZP
GRASP
TP
TP
TP
ART OF WAR
HEY! KUNO! HEY!
ZOOOM
LOCK
FWAP

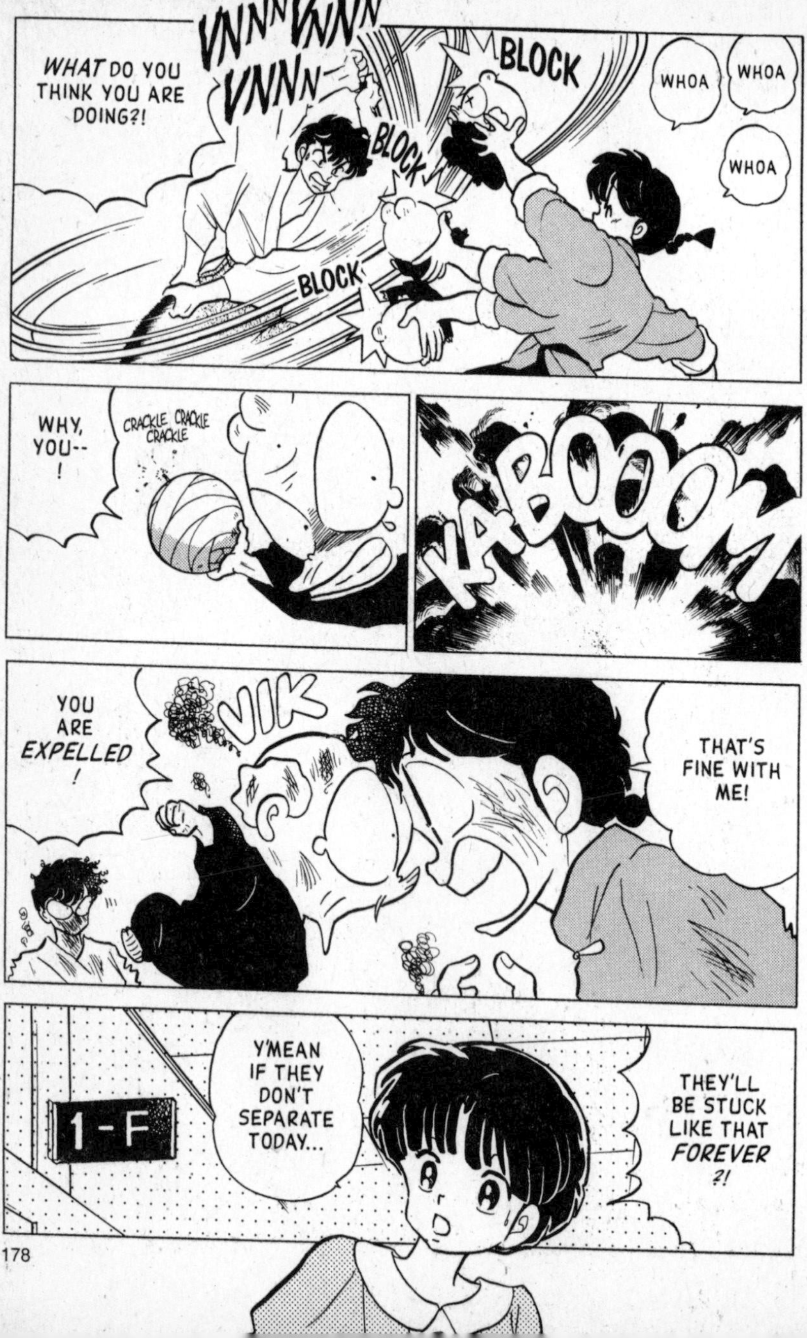
WHAT DO YOU THINK YOU ARE DOING?!
VNNNVNNN VNNN
BLOCK
BLOCK
BLOCK
WHOA
WHOA
WHOA
WHY, YOU-- !
CRACKLE CRACKLE CRACKLE
KABOOOM
YOU ARE EXPELLED !
VIK
THAT'S FINE WITH ME!
1-F
Y'MEAN IF THEY DON'T SEPARATE TODAY...
THEY'LL BE STUCK LIKE THAT FOREVER ?!

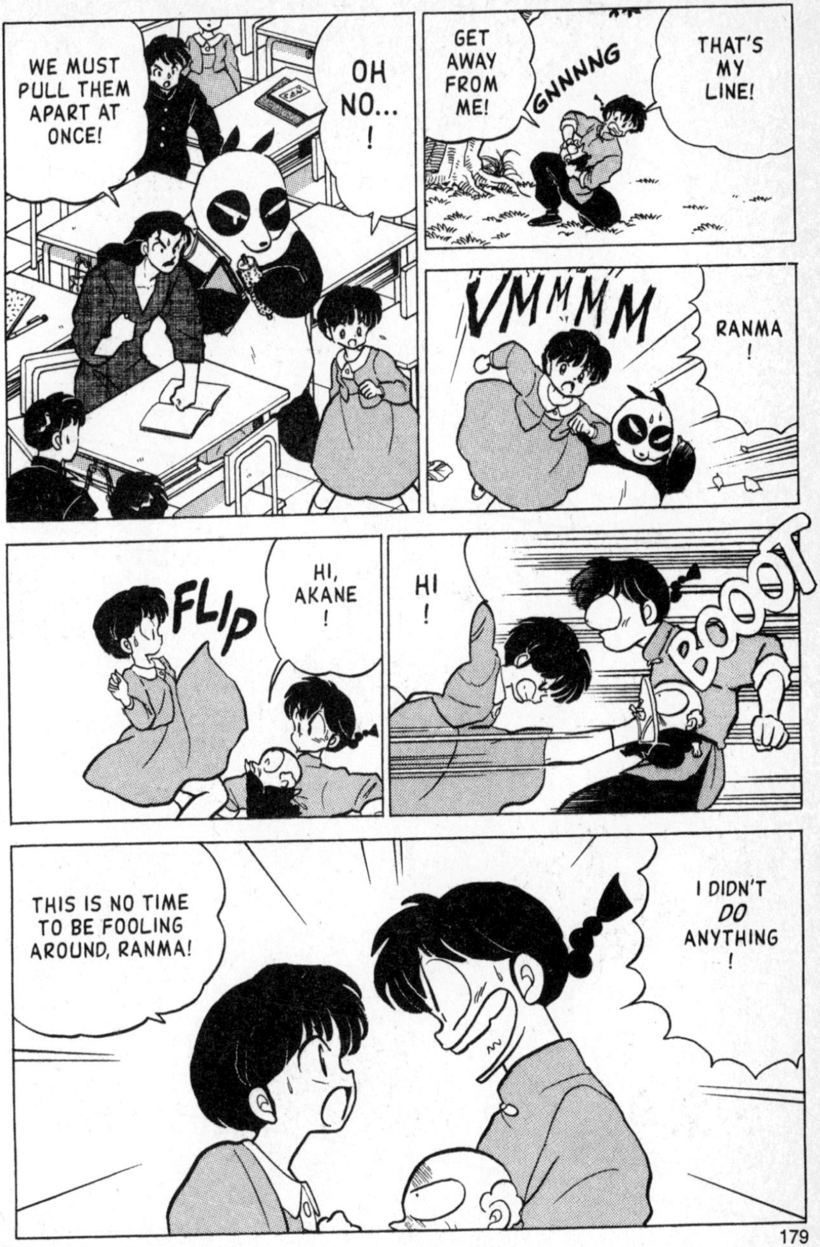
WE MUST PULL THEM APART AT ONCE!
OH NO... !
GET AWAY FROM ME!
GNNNNG
THAT'S MY LINE!
VMMMM
RANMA !
FLIP
HI, AKANE !
HI !
BOOOT
THIS IS NO TIME TO BE FOOLING AROUND, RANMA!
I DIDN'T *DO* ANYTHING !

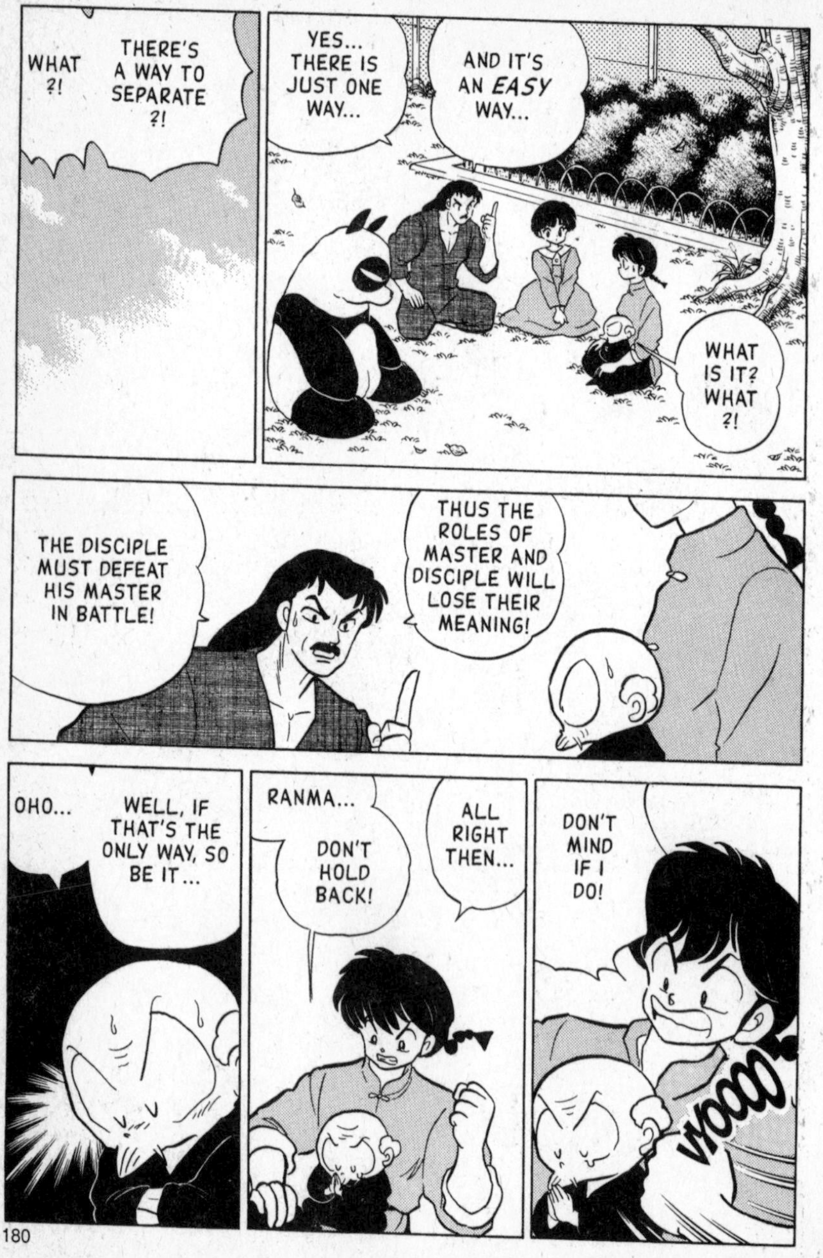
WHAT ?!
THERE'S A WAY TO SEPARATE ?!
YES... THERE IS JUST ONE WAY...
AND IT'S AN *EASY* WAY...
WHAT IS IT? WHAT ?!
THE DISCIPLE MUST DEFEAT HIS MASTER IN BATTLE!
THUS THE ROLES OF MASTER AND DISCIPLE WILL LOSE THEIR MEANING!
OHO...
WELL, IF THAT'S THE ONLY WAY, SO BE IT...
RANMA...
DON'T HOLD BACK!
ALL RIGHT THEN...
DON'T MIND IF I DO!
WOOOO

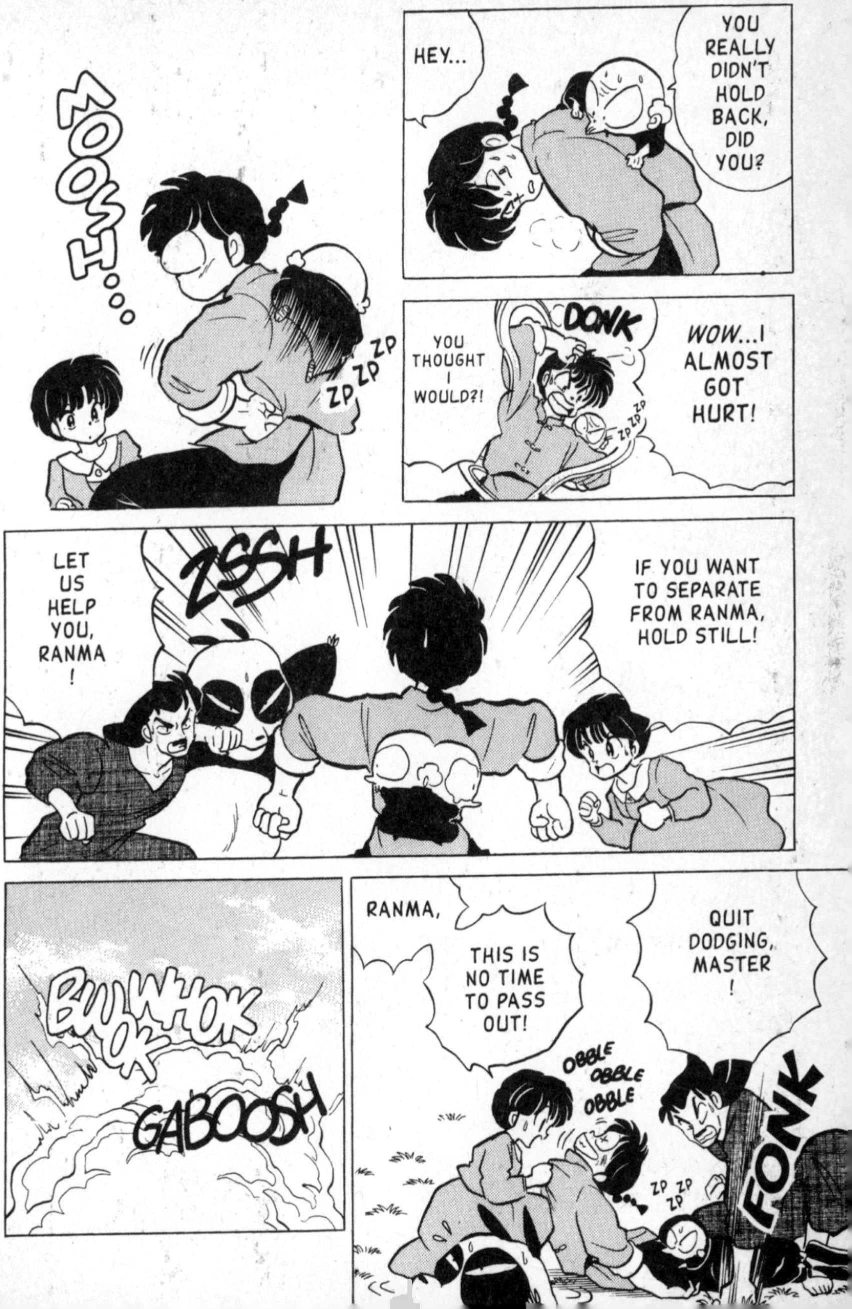
WOOSHooo
ZP ZP ZP
HEY...
YOU REALLY DIDN'T HOLD BACK, DID YOU?
YOU THOUGHT I WOULD?!
DONK
ZP ZP ZP
WOW...I ALMOST GOT HURT!
LET US HELP YOU, RANMA!
ZSSH
IF YOU WANT TO SEPARATE FROM RANMA, HOLD STILL!
BUWHOK
GABOOSH
RANMA,
THIS IS NO TIME TO PASS OUT!
QUIT DODGING, MASTER!
OBBLE OBBLE OBBLE
ZP ZP ZP
FONK

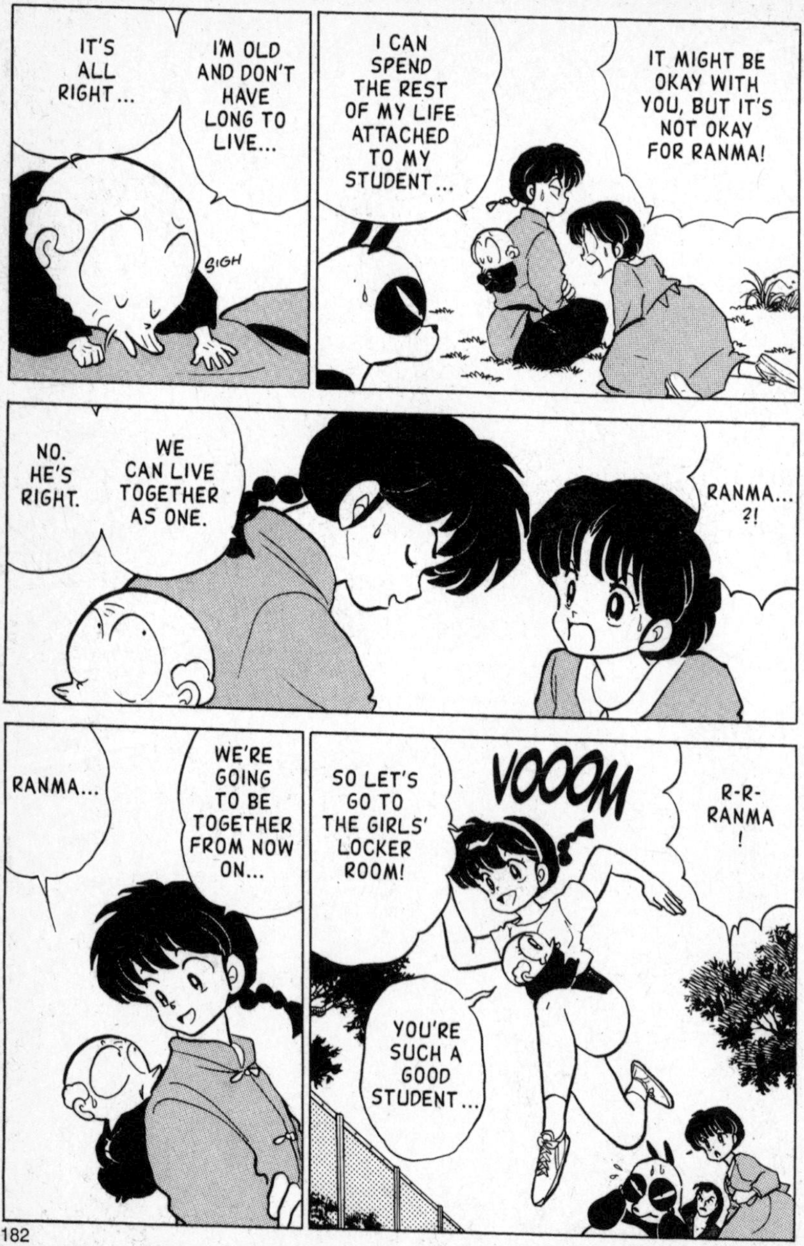
IT'S ALL RIGHT...
I'M OLD AND DON'T HAVE LONG TO LIVE...
SIGH
I CAN SPEND THE REST OF MY LIFE ATTACHED TO MY STUDENT...
IT MIGHT BE OKAY WITH YOU, BUT IT'S NOT OKAY FOR RANMA!
NO. HE'S RIGHT.
WE CAN LIVE TOGETHER AS ONE.
RANMA...?!
RANMA...
WE'RE GOING TO BE TOGETHER FROM NOW ON...
SO LET'S GO TO THE GIRLS' LOCKER ROOM!
VOOOM
R-R-RANMA!
YOU'RE SUCH A GOOD STUDENT...

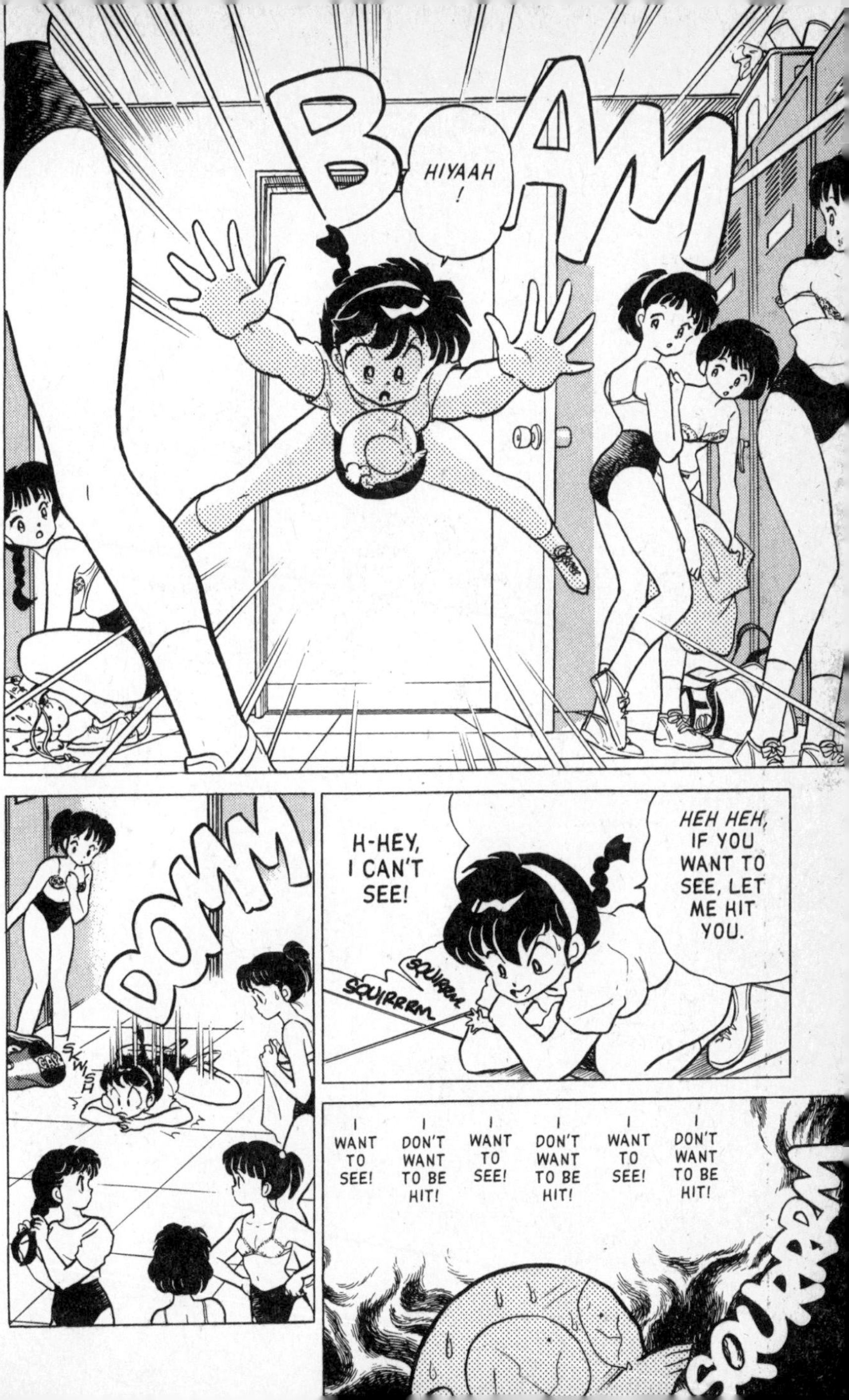
BAM
HIYAAH!
DOMM
SWISH
H-HEY, I CAN'T SEE!
HEH HEH, IF YOU WANT TO SEE, LET ME HIT YOU.
SQUIRRRM
SQUIRRRM
I WANT TO SEE!
I DON'T WANT TO BE HIT!
I WANT TO SEE!
I DON'T WANT TO BE HIT!
I WANT TO SEE!
I DON'T WANT TO BE HIT!
SQUIRRRM

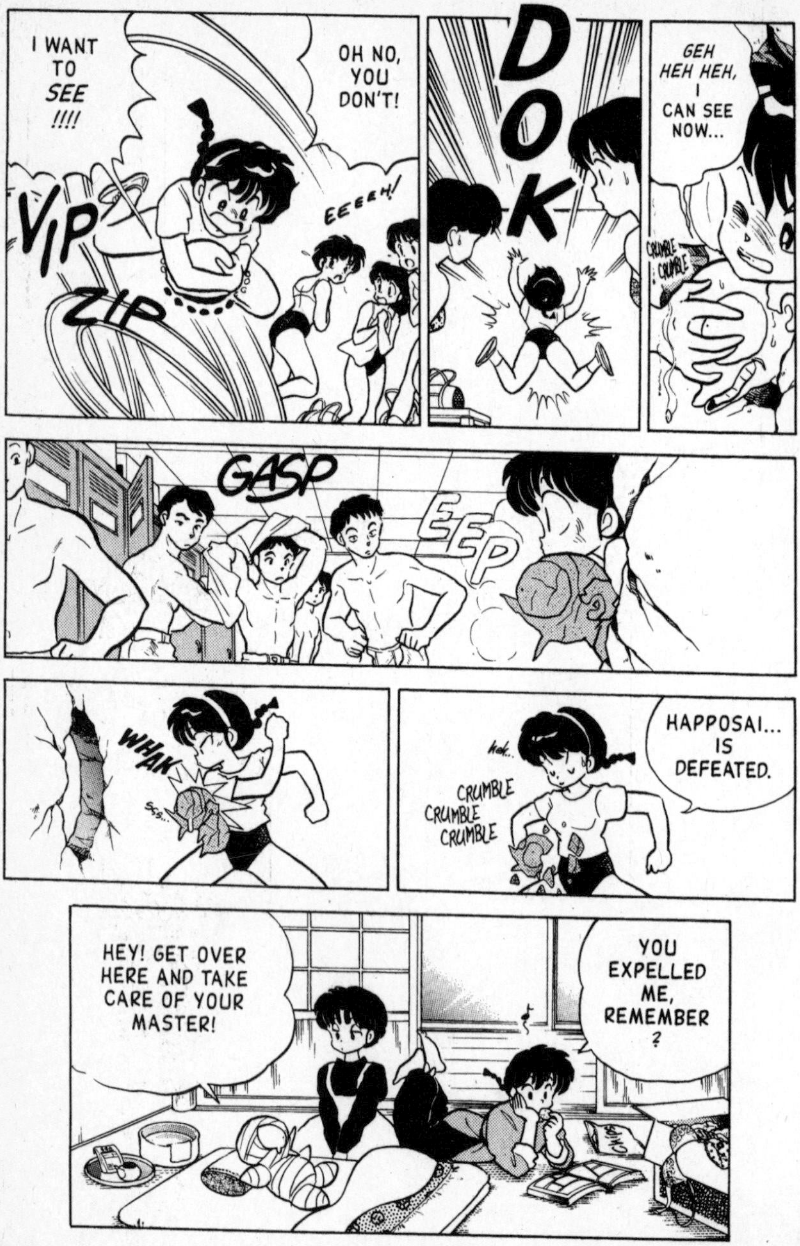
I WANT TO SEE !!!!
OH NO, YOU DON'T!
VIP
ZIP
EEEEH!
DOK
GEH HEH HEH, I CAN SEE NOW...
CRUMBLE CRUMBLE
GASP
EEP
WHAK
HAPPOSAI... IS DEFEATED.
CRUMBLE
CRUMBLE
CRUMBLE
HEY! GET OVER HERE AND TAKE CARE OF YOUR MASTER!
YOU EXPELLED ME, REMEMBER ?
CHIPS

About Rumiko Takahashi

Born in 1957 in Niigata, Japan, Rumiko Takahashi attended women's college in Tokyo, where she began studying comics with Kazuo Koike, author of CRYING FREEMAN. She later became an assistant to horror-manga artist Kazuo Umezu (OROCHI). In 1978, she won a prize in Shogakukan's annual "New Comic Artist Contest," and in that same year her boy-meets-alien comedy series URUSEI YATSURA began appearing in the weekly manga magazine SHÔNEN SUNDAY. This phenomenally successful series ran for nine years and sold over 22 million copies. Takahashi's later RANMA 1/2 series enjoyed even greater popularity.

Takahashi is considered by many to be one of the world's most popular manga artists. With the publication of Volume 34 of her RANMA 1/2 series in Japan, Takahashi's total sales passed one hundred million copies of her compiled works.

Takahashi's serial titles include URUSEI YATSURA, RANMA 1/2, ONE-POUND GOSPEL, MAISON IKKOKU and INUYASHA. Additionally, Takahashi has drawn many short stories which have been published in America under the title "Rumic Theater," and several installments of a saga known as her "Mermaid" series. Most of Takahashi's major stories have also been animated and are widely available in translation worldwide. INUYASHA is her most recent serial story, first published in SHÔNEN SUNDAY in 1996.

EDITOR'S RECOMMENDATIONS

If you enjoyed this volume of Ranma 1/2, then here is some more manga you might be interested in:

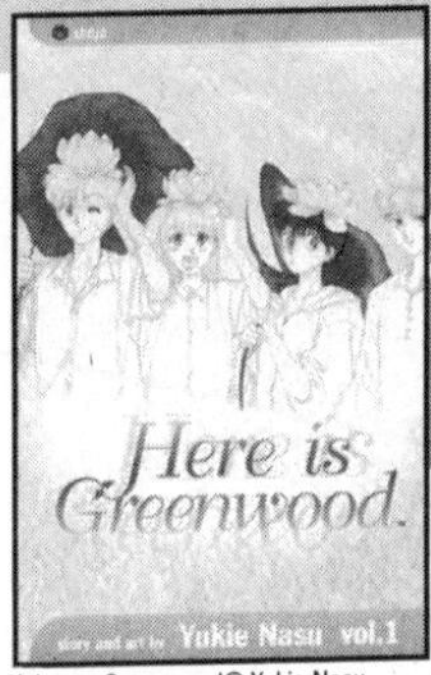
Here is Greenwood.
story and art by Yukie Nasu vol.1

Koko wa Greenwood© Yukie Nasu 1986/HAKUSENSHA, Inc.

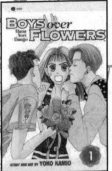

HERE IS GREENWOOD

Perhaps written for a slightly older audience than most of Rumiko Takahashi's work, Yukie Nasu's *Here is Greenwood* is exactly like *Ranma 1/2*, except for the martial arts (none), the wacky hijinks (almost none), and the occasional depiction of the adult relationships among its students. Okay, aside from the fact that they both have male high school students in them, they have nothing in common. But they're both cool!

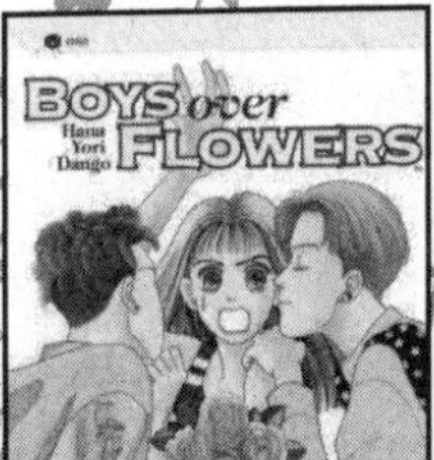
BOYS over FLOWERS
Hana Yori Dango
1
STORY AND ART BY YOKO KAMIO

HANA-YORI DANGO © 1992 by YOKO KAMIO/SHUEISHA Inc.

BOYS OVER FLOWERS (HANA YORI DANGO)

Another tale of high-school life in Japan, *Boys Over Flowers* (or "HanaDan" to most of its fans) is not without its serious side, but overall tends to fall into the "rabu-kome" or "love-comedy" genre.

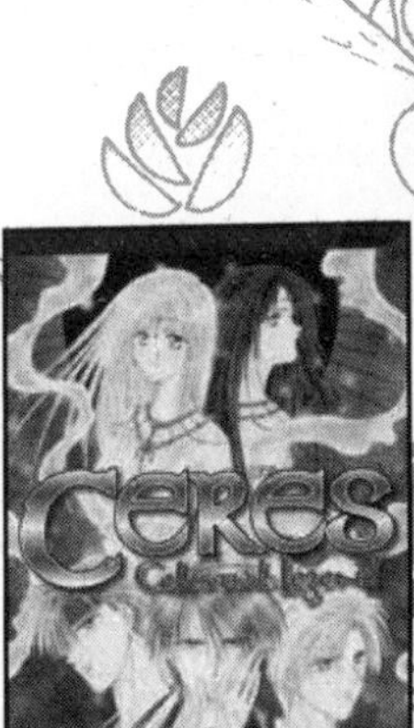
Ceres
YU WATASE
Vol. 1

CERES: CELESTIAL LEGEND © 1997 Yuu Watase/Shogakukan, Inc.

CERES CELESTIAL LEGEND

Aya Mikage is a trendy Tokyo teen with not much else on her mind but fashion, karaoke, and boys. But a terrible family secret involving an ancient family "curse" is about to make things a lot more difficult.

A Comedy That Redefines a Hot and Cold Relationship!

Due to an unfortunate accident, when martial artist Ranma gets splashed with cold water, he becomes a buxom young girl! Hot water reverses the effect, but when blamed for offenses both real and imagined, and pursued by lovesick suitors of both genders, what's a half-boy, half-girl to do?

From Rumiko Takahashi, creator of *Inuyasha* and *Maison Ikkoku*—complete your collection today!

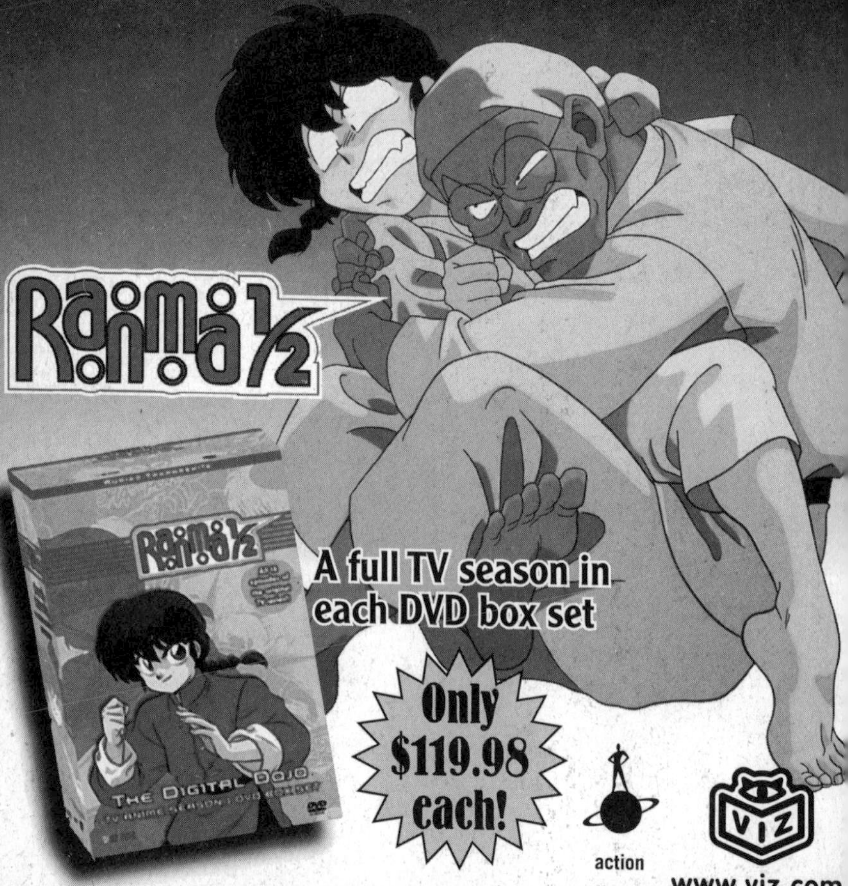
Ranma 1/2
Ranma 1/2
THE DIGITAL DOJO
A full TV season in each DVD box set
Only $119.98 each!

action

www.viz.com
store.viz.com